MW01195515

JFK

ALSO BY J. RANDY TARABORRELLI

Jackie: Public, Private, Secret

The Kennedy Heirs: John, Caroline, and the New Generation

*Jackie, Janet & Lee: The Secret Lives of Janet Auchincloss
and Her Daughters Jacqueline Kennedy Onassis and Lee Radziwill*

*After Camelot: A Personal History of the Kennedy Family,
1968 to the Present*

Jackie, Ethel, Joan: Women of Camelot

JFK

Public, Private, Secret

---★---

J. RANDY TARABORRELLI

ST. MARTIN'S PRESS
NEW YORK

First published in the United States by St. Martin's Press, an imprint of
St. Martin's Publishing Group

JFK. Copyright © 2025 by Rose Books, Inc. All rights reserved.
Printed in the United States of America. For information,
address St. Martin's Publishing Group, 120 Broadway, New York, NY 10271.

www.stmartins.com

The Library of Congress Cataloging-in-Publication Data is available
upon request.

ISBN 978-1-250-34638-4 (hardcover)

ISBN 978-1-250-34639-1 (ebook)

Our books may be purchased in bulk for promotional, educational,
or business use. Please contact your local bookseller or the
Macmillan Corporate and Premium Sales Department at 1-800-221-7945,
extension 5442, or by email at MacmillanSpecialMarkets@macmillan.com.

First Edition: 2025

10 9 8 7 6 5 4 3 2 1

This book is for anyone searching for and ready for second chances.
To step into the light of who we really are, we sometimes
need to confront the darkness in who we've been.
If only we're willing to see it and weep, after that dark night
The sun rises.

Sow a thought and you reap an action; sow an action and you reap a habit; sow a habit and you reap a character; sow a character and you reap a destiny.

—RALPH WALDO EMERSON

What makes biography so interesting is the struggle to answer that single question: "What's he like?"

—PRESIDENT JOHN FITZGERALD KENNEDY

CONTENTS

◇◇◇◇◇◇◇◇◇◇◇◇◇◇

Book I: Before the Presidency

PART VIII: THESE TIES THAT BIND

PART IX: THE LIFE WE CHOOSE

PART X: SCORCHED EARTH

PART XI: EVER MOVING FORWARD

Book II: The Presidency

PART II: COMMANDER IN CHIEF

PART III: ALL THAT GLITTERS

PART IV: HIS SEXUAL WAYWARDNESS

CHARACTER IS DESTINY

Three thousand years ago, the Greek philosopher Heraclitus wrote, "Character is destiny." In other words, our character, that inner quality of our true selves that not only drives and motivates us but mandates the way we treat others, is the thing that shapes our fate. We're all a mix of good and bad, imperfect people trying, hopefully, to do the right thing. In that respect, as we grow and as we change in character, so does our destiny.

As you will read in these pages, President John Fitzgerald Kennedy was evolving, his character in flux at the time of his death in 1963. Given as much, while writing this book it sometimes felt unfair to commit such a complex and many-sided person to a history that often showed him not at his best as he struggled to find his way. "If I had to live my life over again, I'd have a different father, a different wife, and a different religion," he was said to have told John Sharon, one of his foreign affairs advisers. When I read that quote at the start of writing this book, it sounded to me like a man unwilling to accept responsibility for his own life. However, as his story unfolded for me, I discovered a man who, at the end of his life, had made a decision to come face-to-face with and confront his demons. He'd begun to ask himself hard questions, the answers to which most certainly would've changed him, both as a president in his second term and, more importantly, as a man in his later years.

So, how are we to remember a man who died in the midst of such personal evolution, a work in progress, if you will? We've been grappling with this question ever since the assassination of President Kennedy on November 22, 1963. Do we revere him as the idealistic president who believed that the strength of our democracy lay in hope and activism, as demonstrated by the aspirational words of his inauguration speech on January 20, 1961: "Ask not what your country can do for you, ask what you can do for your country"? Or, do we denounce him as the husband we now know had been chronically unfaithful to his long-suffering wife? How do we square the public servant with the flawed individual?

My previous five books about the Kennedys weren't about JFK, its most famous standard bearer. For the most part, those books centered on the life and times of his wife, Jacqueline Kennedy. While I always touched on Jack's life in those books, many questions about him arose for me during the research and writing, particularly in my most recent biography, *Jackie: Public, Private, Secret,* in 2023. When I finished writing that book, I felt a strong impulse to try to figure out what had made her husband act the way he had toward her in those pages. I wanted to make some sense of this extraordinarily complex figure and consider him not as an icon but, rather, as just a man. That's why I've now added this work, *JFK: Public, Private, Secret,* to my atheneum of Kennedy studies.

The subtitle of the previous book and of this one, *Public, Private, Secret,* was actually inspired by Jackie herself a few weeks before her sixtieth birthday in 1989. She was having a conversation with her former lover and lifelong friend, the acclaimed architect John Carl Warnecke, also known as "Jack," who'd designed President Kennedy's memorial at Arlington National Cemetery. Warnecke told me that while she reflected back on her life years later, he asked her about her relationship with Aristotle Onassis. In her characteristically oblique way, she said, "Oh, Jack, you know me. I have three lives: public, private, and secret."

I think we can all relate to Jackie's aphorism. We all have the same three lives of which she spoke: the one lived publicly for the world, the one lived privately for our friends and family, and then, of course, the one lived secretly. That third one is known only to us. It's the one we keep from even our most loved ones as we grapple with whatever it is inside us that makes us who we are. The person who says he has no secrets is a person lying to himself and to the world.

This book has the same subtitle, *Public, Private, Secret,* because I consider it an extension of the one I wrote about Jackie. You might say this is JFK's side of the story. You should know, though, that this isn't a presidential biography in the conventional sense. Not every move in politics or in governance ever made by John Kennedy as a congressman, senator, and then president is presented and analyzed in these pages. Other books have undertaken that task—literally, more than a hundred have done just that over the last sixty years. I was also not interested in addressing in depth the many conspiracy theories relating to his assassination.

This book is about John Kennedy's life, not his death. It's an exploration of the pivotal moments and touchstones that can make a person who he is—the impact of a son's relentless desire to avoid remaking himself in his father's image, for instance, or of a son who goes on to become a father himself and how that can change him in unexpected ways. The story of a person's life is replete with such moments, each with its own richness, complexity, and depth, each a whole story to be told on its own. These fragments of time don't always link up in a linear way. That's why I've chosen to present some of them here without chronological order, as fragments of a larger picture that, once assembled, reveal the dark truth and the bright light of the man who came to be known simply as "JFK."

In writing this book, I reviewed almost thirty years of my own research in search of stories about John Kennedy and his family that weren't quite right for my other Kennedy histories, and there were many. I spent many hours listening to the haunting tape-recorded voices of people long gone from this world who once shared memories with me I never published and that I've now, at long last, memorialized in this book. Along with my trusted researcher, Cathy Griffin, who's been at my side on every book for the last thirty-five years, I also interviewed new people for my research. Some are in their nineties, such as Marilyn Monroe's publicist and intimate, Pat Newcomb. A few are even in their hundreds, like Joe Kennedy's personal secretary, Janet DesRosiers Fontaine. Also, the sons and daughters of pivotal people in JFK's life remember here for the first time their parents' fond association with him. Plus, I had access to several unpublished manuscripts of individuals who played key roles in his life, such as one written by his father, Joseph P. Kennedy. His book, if published, would've been called *Diplomatic Memoir.* Also invaluable to me were two unpublished transcripts of interviews Jackie's mother, Janet Auchincloss, gave in 1972 and 1973 intended for stories in a women's magazine. She and Jackie asked for both to be withdrawn because they felt they were too revealing. Indeed, they're quite telling. If they'd been published back then, a good many points of opaque history might've been clarified. I'm happy to bring Mrs.

Auchincloss's words to life now, almost sixty years later. Of course, the hundreds of oral histories and other historical documentation provided to me by the John F. Kennedy Presidential Library and Museum in Boston also proved, as with all my books about the Kennedys, to be invaluable.

In terms of Kennedy's presidency, which lasted only 1,036 days, I chose to focus primarily on consequential decisions he made against a background of family concerns, including historical moments such as his handling of the Bay of Pigs invasion and the Cuban Missile Crisis in 1962, and the Vietnam coup d'état in 1963. I wanted to tell these stories and others like them through the lens of his relationships with family, his and Jackie's—the Kennedys and the Auchinclosses. You'll learn as much about them here as you will about him because, like all of us, he didn't live in a vacuum. In order to better understand him, I think one has to also understand those close to him and how they dealt with the utterly extraordinary experience of watching such an imperfect loved one become the president of the United States.

As a politician, Jack always reminded people of American exceptionalism, a strong America that exercised global leadership while at the same time encouraged its people to be of service to their country. It's a paradox, then, that he wasn't always able to be of service to those he treasured, in particular, Jackie. In one book after another, the question of why she was never enough for him has been considered with a wide brushstroke: he was his father's son and his father was a cheater. But I believe that is too simple, too easy. On a deeper level, I knew there had to be more, and I did discover some larger truths. As you will read, Rose agreed to a long-term relationship between her husband and a woman in the Kennedys' employ. While that decision gave her the freedom to travel and live a life of her own, it also contributed to the shaping of Jack's own view of love and marriage and, specifically, of how much a wife should tolerate in it.

If the public knew of JFK's marital infidelities in the 1960s, would he have been elected? I reveal in this book for what I'm fairly certain is the first time that, shortly before he won his second term in the Senate in 1958, he learned that a woman he'd had an affair with had become pregnant. If that had become known at the time, would he still have been able to later campaign for the presidency? In addition to his infidelity, if his many illnesses and addictions had become known, one has to wonder if he could've been elected at all, and if so, how long he might've remained in the Oval Office.

Can we accept that a fundamentally decent person sometimes does bad things? Maybe a bigger question, at least where the presidency is concerned, is this: Does the character of which Heraclitus spoke matter? In 1965, Arthur Schlesinger addressed his good friend's character in his book *A Thousand Days: John F. Kennedy in the White House*. In it, he said that JFK defined character as "that combination of toughness of fiber and courage." Maybe politically that's true, but personally it's more than that, and Kennedy knew it, as you'll read in these pages.

I have one regret about this work. I'm sorry it's not the story of a more complete life. If it feels unfinished, that's because it *is* unfinished. John Kennedy was just forty-six years old and in the prime of his life when he was murdered. If he had lived another thirty years or more, like his wife did, he likely would've experienced the full evolution of character that had begun in 1963, the year of his death.

If we accept Heraclitus's proposition that the inner life, our character, influences the outer, we can also accept that whatever was stirring within Jack in his final months likely would've shaped his true destiny. He'd realized he'd made terrible decisions and, in the process, had hurt people he loved, his wife in particular. He was finally being honest with himself and, in doing so, was deeply regretful. "I haven't been the best husband," he told his sister-in-law Joan Kennedy as they grieved the death of his infant son Patrick, a loss he couldn't help but feel was divine retribution. "It's very painful," he admitted to her, "and by painful, I mean shameful." Perhaps, with the passage of more time, he would've figured out certain things about himself and worked to square things with those he loved. People are usually not in old age who they were in their careless youth. He was already on his way to being a better president. Who knows what JFK the elderly statesman might've been like?

My hope is that as you read this book, you'll have a fuller, more well-rounded impression of John Fitzgerald Kennedy, our nation's thirty-fifth president. Perhaps by the time you finish his story, you'll have opened your imagination of Jack in a new and different way and you'll wonder, as I often did while writing it, just what might have been.

J. Randy Taraborrelli
January 2025

PROLOGUE

THE SECRET PLACE

THURSDAY, JULY 3, 1952. HYANNIS PORT, MASSACHUSETTS.

While gazing out at an endless stretch of sea and sand, Jack Kennedy set himself down on a small bench and placed his crutches next to it. He hated those things. He was only thirty-five. What healthy, able-bodied man of his age, he often asked himself, had to use crutches to get around? One might've thought he'd be used to them by now, considering he'd been on and off them for years. However, hailing from an athletic family like his own, he could never accept being the only one hobbling about as if he were disabled. His bad back, however, made it impossible for him to get around when it flared up, which was more often than not, especially in the years since the war.

Jack had awakened early to go outside and fill his lungs with ocean air, his way of starting the day off with the kind of limitless peace he could only find in these parts. He'd been all over the world and nothing could compare to good ol' Cape Cod, his childhood stomping grounds. These serene few moments alone were the only ones he knew he could count on, given that the Big House—that's what the Kennedys always called the family's beachside homestead—would soon be filled to capacity. His many siblings as well as other relatives and friends were set to gather for the annual Fourth of July celebration. Soon would begin the daily ritual of holiday sports, meaning sailing and fishing out on the Sound, or tennis, softball, and football on the beach, all activities Jack had loved ever since he was a boy but that, these days, filled him with as much pain as joy.

Turning back to the house, Jack spotted a small woman walking briskly from the front entrance, down a graveled pathway, and out onto the blue-green lawn. She squinted as she gazed out at the sea, its shimmering clarity seeming to hurt her eyes. She then started to walk toward what appeared to be some sort of shed or utility structure, the kind in which one might store garden tools. After taking a single key from the pocket of her summery silk dress, she unlocked its door. Swiftly, she slipped inside and closed the door behind her. Jack smiled to himself. Strange, yes, but that was Mother, so it wasn't necessarily surprising, not if you knew Rose Kennedy.

About an hour passed.

Now, Jack sat at the large table in the kitchen of the Big House and, as he did every morning, perused the stack of newspapers carefully arranged for him by the help. Every day, he'd absorb anything he could find relating to American politics given that he was presently a congressman, elected a little over five years ago. He had bigger ambitions, though, than the House of Representatives. He had his eye on the Senate and then, after that? The presidency, of course. He wasn't shy about it, either. He knew that's where he was headed, and so did everyone else. If you found it hard to fathom, you were probably on the outside looking in, because everyone on the inside looking out knew exactly what he intended to do with his life.

Jack was competitive, taught by his father, Joseph P. Kennedy, that failure was not an option. However, unlike Joe, a man always motivated by naked ambition and a thirst for power, Jack was of genuinely good heart and purpose. He was idealistic, truly wanting to serve and make a difference. He could also be shrewd, as he'd already proven, a fearsome political adversary when necessary. Stumping for the Senate, as he was doing these days, was hard work, but he was up to the task. He was proud of the campaign he'd thus far waged and of the machinery his greatest benefactor—namely, his wealthy father—had put into place to get him to the finish line. Looking ahead, though, was always his way, and the White House definitely beckoned. But, as they say, first things first, and the election for that Senate seat was coming up in November.

With his political career on track, Jack was also attempting to carve out a personal life with a new love interest, a young woman named Jacqueline Bouvier, "Jackie" for short, of course. He'd been seeing her for about six months. She was twenty-two and a real beauty, a brunette with big, luminous eyes set far apart on a classic-looking face with its full mouth and dazzling smile. He had invited her to the compound for the Fourth of July celebration, her first time in Hyannis Port, to meet his mother; the rest of the family had already made her acquaintance.

In cold, hard political terms, Jackie was the perfect asset. Well-bred, -educated, and -traveled, she looked great on Jack's arm and was usually personable even if somewhat removed when in the company of strangers. "I'm actually not that fond of the public," she'd told him. He figured he could work with her, though. There was just something so fresh and beguiling about her; he knew people would take to her. He definitely needed a wife if he was going to be president, or so his father had warned him. It's just the way it was and, in fact, everyone in the family was a little surprised Jack was still single. The time had come; they all knew it.

While Jack was captivated by Jackie, he definitely wasn't in love with her. They hadn't even slept together yet, and success in the bedroom was a pre-qualifier for him in terms of how he'd feel about any woman. She was presently up in one of the guest rooms. She liked to sleep late, she'd told him, which was fine with him. She wanted his attention and required a lot of it. He wanted to impress her if he could, but, he had to admit, it was work.

As Jack became engrossed in a news item, a pretty young woman in a colorful print dress strode into the kitchen. This was Janet DesRosiers, secretary to Jack's father. Janet was, at twenty-nine, pretty with a pink-and-white complexion, flaxen hair, and dancing green eyes. She was smart and personable, efficient at her job of running not just Joe's businesses but his entire household. "Have you seen your mother?" she asked Jack. Without looking up from his paper, he said he'd spotted her out on the beach earlier but wasn't sure if she'd returned. When Janet supposed Rose might still be in what she called her "cottage," Jack glanced at his watch and agreed. Taking a final sip of coffee, he said they should probably check on her.

Wincing, Jack rose on his crutches and made his way from the kitchen, through the living room, and out the front door, with Janet following. If she were being honest, she was more than a little dazzled by this man. His angular face really drew a person in—that tanned, olive complexion, those sturdy cheekbones, the lively blue-green eyes, and all those great teeth. He was tall, about six feet, and very wiry at maybe 140 pounds. Truth be told, he looked as if he'd recently been ill, he was just that thin. In fact, he usually *was* sick with one thing or another, and not just this business with his back but all sorts of other maladies. It had been so ever since he was a boy.

The congressman stood on the porch and hugged himself against the unseasonably crisp breeze. With Janet still following, he then hobbled a few hundred feet down the graveled pathway. Finally, they came to that small structure, the one he'd seen his mother enter earlier. It was just four rickety plywood walls, a shingled roof, and no windows. He walked up to the door and knocked. "Mother?" There was no answer. He looked at Janet and knocked again. "Mother, are you in there?"

Then, the familiar, always trembling voice: "Yes, Jack, I'm in here."

"That girl I told you about," he said. "Jackie? She arrived late last night, Mother. She'll be down for breakfast."

"Won't you join us, Mrs. Kennedy," Janet asked, "and meet her?"

The door cracked open. Rose Kennedy peeked out. She screwed up her eyes and pursed her lips. "Breakfast isn't served until nine," she said before slamming the door closed.

———

"Rose's Cottage" is what they called it. Joe built it for his wife in 1950. Since that time, every day would find Rose Kennedy in there, usually in the mornings. She'd remain for an hour or two, sometimes even more. "How to describe it?" asked Janet DesRosiers in a 2024 interview, by then a still-energetic hundred years old with an excellent memory of her life with the Kennedys. "It was a small building," she continued. "No electricity. No plumbing. We had no idea what Rose kept in there. The door was always locked. I felt such sadness at the sight of this small, lonely woman walking across the sand in the morning to her little shed."

"That's where Mother makes moonshine," Jack joked to Jackie when she asked about it at breakfast. She'd seen the shed during an earlier stroll on the beach. Jack, Joe, and Janet along with Jack's younger brother Bobby and his wife, Ethel, were at the breakfast table, as were siblings Eunice, Jean, Pat, and Teddy.

"If I know Mother, she's in there counting my money," Joe quipped.

Jack tried to clarify things by explaining that this place was where his mother went in search of peace and tranquility. Jackie was surprised. The house was so enormous, she remarked, couldn't Rose find a room somewhere in it to be alone? Jack said no, it was always too noisy. She needed a quiet, private sanctuary, he explained, where she could commune with her maker, which is precisely why his father had the shed built for her. "She prays, says the rosary, that sort of thing," he explained. He added that his mother had attended a convent school in her youth, so maybe that explained things. What he didn't say was that Rose's Cottage was also where she went to put some distance between herself and her husband. Any time she didn't have to be around Joe was, as far as she was concerned, time well spent. With a wry smile at his father, Jack noted that even though they called it Rose's Cottage, it really wasn't much of a cottage at all, was it?

Jackie wondered why Joe hadn't put electricity and plumbing in the shed. "She didn't ask for it," he answered bluntly.

After a moment's thought, it suddenly became more clear to her. "It's about humility, isn't it?" Jackie whispered, almost to herself. She said Rose probably kept it humble on purpose. For her, opulence wasn't necessary in that space, and neither was the idea of privilege. All that mattered in that space was her relationship to her God. "It's her . . . secret place," Jackie concluded, wistfully.

Now Jackie couldn't help but spin a little fantasy. She imagined lit candles on tables with pictures of old saints on walls and stacks of ancient prayer books on shelves. "I'll bet it's just lovely in there," she said.

She was so whimsical and imaginative, Jack couldn't help but chuckle. He doubted it, though. "A chair, a card table, a Bible, and a rosary," he said. Knowing his mother, that was probably the extent of it. Janet then mentioned that Rose had asked for a battery-operated record player. She suspected she was using it to play language records so she could practice her French.

"*Oooh, French,*" Jackie cooed. She thought that was "just marvelous."

When Jackie said she wanted to see it for herself, Jack told her it was impossible. None of them had ever been inside Rose's Cottage. She was surprised. If it were her mother, she said, she wouldn't rest until she knew exactly what was going on in there.

"But we all have a secret life," Jack said, matter-of-factly, "and that's Mother's."

Eunice tried to change the subject by asking Jack a question about his work in Congress. He was about to answer when the back door opened and slammed shut. Moments later, Rose appeared. Instantly, each person bolted to their feet, all except for Jackie. When she realized the breach in protocol, she, too, stood but did so slowly and sheepishly.

Rose took her place next to her husband and his secretary. Looking alertly at the newcomer, she said, "Jackie, I presume?"

Jackie nodded and smiled as she noted the pearls on Rose's neck, the diamond pin at her shoulder, both such dressy choices for the early hour. Though sixty-two, Rose's face was barely lined or scored by the years. "She was like a little doll," Jackie said later. "Porcelain, fragile, and . . . breakable."

Rose made a quick assessment of her as well, this intruder sitting in her chair straight as a rod in her perfect little dress with her perfect little hairdo and her perfect little smile. "You do make a rather nice addition to the table, dear," Rose finally decided.

"Lovely morning, isn't it, Mrs. Kennedy?" Janet asked as everyone else chimed in with their good mornings to the matriarch. Rose nodded at her and smiled. She then told Janet it was chilly outside, so she should be sure to put on a sweater when she went for her morning walk. After a purposeful beat, she looked at Janet and added, "*With my husband.*" The table fell silent. Jackie's eyes darted from one person to the next until finally settling on Jack, but he quickly looked away.

Following a very tense breakfast, a full morning of activities commenced before everyone came together again for a barbecue lunch on the patio. Later that night, a veritable feast of a dinner was served, and then they all adjourned to the parlor to chat over coffee. After about an hour, Jackie noticed Jack get up, walk to a chest of drawers, open one, and take from it a flashlight. He went to a corner where his crutches were propped and took them both under his arms. He then made his way to the foyer and out of the house, softly closing the door behind him. It was pitch-black out there. Jackie wondered where he could possibly be going.

Moments later, Rose stood, walked to the same bureau, opened the same drawer, and took out a flashlight of her own. She put on her coat and walked out the door.

After about fifteen minutes, Jackie couldn't help herself. She had to see. She, too, got up and left the house. Once she was standing on the porch, she peered out into the darkness, searching the dusky shadows for her boyfriend and his mother. The air was hushed, the silence broken only by the sound of gently crashing waves. The air smelled like brine. The breeze was brisk, but Jackie didn't care as she continued to stare steadily into the night. When the door opened behind her, Janet DesRosiers appeared with a light coat. She told her to wear it, "or you'll catch your death of cold out here."

After Jackie put on the coat, she and Janet stood squinting out at the stark and lonely reaches of the shoreline. Finally, in the deep blackness, they spotted two luminous spheres in the sand. Straining to see more, they finally found them, Rose and Jack. They weren't speaking to each other. They were just standing in place like two sentinels keeping watch, both looking out at the shadowy sea, their lit flashlights at their sides. Jackie huddled further into her coat as she watched them in fascination, mother and son alone, together.

BOOK I

Before the Presidency

PART I

Ties That Bind

MATRIARCH

The little boy was in his bed, his mother sitting next to him as she read from one of his favorite books, *King Arthur and the Round Table*. "Then those two dragons, one of which was white, the other red, rose up," she read as he followed along with each word, "and came near one another and began a sword fight and cast forth fire with their breath."

"Sore fight," the six-year-old interrupted.

"No, Jack. *Sword* fight."

He shook his head no and pointed at the page. "It says right here," he insisted, "*sore* fight." His small, round face was very intense for a six-year-old, and his reading comprehension remarkable.

She looked down at the book. "That's a mistake," she said. "Think about it. It makes no sense."

"But it says . . ."

"Stop it," she told him, her tone suddenly sharp. "Listen quietly," she scolded him. "Don't interrupt."

Young Jack Kennedy studied his mother, Rose, for a moment. Then: "Can Dad read to me, now?"

She slammed the book closed. "As you wish," she said. She stood, walked to the doorway, turned out the light, and left the room, closing the door behind her.

Many years later, as Jack relayed this childhood story, he closed his eyes as he drew on the memory. "I could tell I'd hurt her," he said. "She was trying, I guess. At least she was trying."

Rose Kennedy did try to be a good mother but, more often than not, she missed the mark. Not a warm woman but, rather, a practical one, she compensated for her lack of maternal instinct by paying an inordinate amount of attention to the minutiae of parenting her nine children. For instance, she had a file of notecards for each child that included their birthday, shoe size, dates of doctor's visits, and vaccinations. On one of Jack's, she wrote of ailments such as "whooping cough, measles, chicken pox." She weighed him and his siblings weekly. If one of them lost a few pounds, she made sure the cook fed that child more food. She lectured them on posture, especially the girls, who she taught to stand in ways that made them appear thinner. She'd quiz them at the dinner table about American history and geography, with world maps she'd taped on walls all around them. Or, she'd read Bible passages to them or have them learn and memorize prayers. "She'd convinced herself that a good talking-to was good parenting," said Barbara Gibson, who was Rose's secretary in the 1970s. "But when it came to basic, maternal tenderness—a hug, a kiss, or even a comforting word, that was challenging for her. She told me she'd sometimes managed it with her firstborn, Joe Jr. However, she wished she hadn't allowed further sex with Joe Sr. because that caused her to have more children. She then had to figure out how to divide her time between all of them, which wasn't possible for her. Being maternal wasn't her way. It's not how she'd been raised by her mother, and not how she would, or could, raise her own children."

"Aunt Rose was brought up with a Victorian mindset," said her grandniece Kathleen "Kerry" McCarthy. "She was taught that showing emotion was weak, and she never wanted to be looked at as weak. She went through life with a sort of square-jawed countenance, a raw determination. However, she thought, and I really do believe this, that she was a good mother who was doing her best for her children."

As he grew into young adulthood, young Jack in particular took after Rose in many ways. His emotional detachment came from Rose. His inability to express emotions, especially feelings of love, came from her, too. His refusal to be beaten down by circumstances, even if that meant cultivating a secret life as a coping mechanism, was also passed down to him from her. Jack often felt the need to go off and seek solitude, too, like his mother, to sometimes figure out why things had gone so wrong in his life. Had it been God's plan all along, he would wonder, to make his getting along with loved ones so complicated because he was so flawed? Even his vocal pattern with that strong and distinctive Bostonian accent was all Rose. His father didn't speak that way at all; Joe sounded "blue-blooded," not Bostonian.

Rose had the same hairstyle her entire life, closely cropped on the sides, bouffant on top, salt-and-pepper as she aged, though she sometimes wore wigs. She had cobalt-blue eyes that always seemed somehow distant and sad. Her skin glowed because she was so meticulous about moisturizing, her bathroom shelves always stocked with expensive creams from Europe. She loved wearing makeup and was seldom seen without it. "If someone dropped in unexpectedly she'd be annoyed, but not because she didn't welcome company but because she hadn't put her makeup on yet," said her nephew Joey Gargan. "She'd disappear and then reappear fifteen minutes later, ready. Even her hands and arms would be coated with a thick makeup because, especially as she got older, she hated what she called 'those awful age marks.'"

Rose Elizabeth Fitzgerald was born on July 22, 1890, in Boston, the eldest of six children, to Mary Josephine "Josie" Fitzgerald (née Hannon) and John Francis "Honey Fitz" Fitzgerald, at the time a member of the Boston Common Council. She had five siblings: Mary, Thomas, John Jr., Eunice, and Frederick. Her father, John Francis Fitzgerald—after whom she'd name her second son—served as a U.S. congressman and was then elected to two terms as Boston's mayor.

In 1897, the Fitzgeralds moved to West Concord, Massachusetts, and then, six years later, relocated to the Ashmont Hill section of Dorchester, Massachusetts. After studying at the convent school Kasteel Bloemendal in Vaals, Netherlands, she graduated from Dorchester High School in 1906. She also attended the New England Conservatory in Boston, where she studied piano. She'd wanted to attend Wellesley but was forced by her father to go to the strict Academy of Sacred Heart (later Manhattan College of the Sacred Heart) in New York. Though the religious training would become the foundation of her life, she'd always regret her missed educational opportunities, calling it "something I'd feel sad about all my life."

When she was much older, Rose and her teenage grandniece Kerry McCarthy would go for long walks on the Cape Cod beach or a nearby golf course on many mornings, time together they'd both treasure. Rose would sometimes give her advice, such as, "You have a little bit of weight, honey, and you have to watch that because you've got such a pretty face."

Kerry recalled, "On these walks, Aunt Rose would speak of the frustration she felt being sent away, especially to the convent school [Sacred Heart]. She didn't want to study with nuns in far-off places. While she adored her father, when she'd speak of how she was lorded over by him, she'd squeeze my hand tightly. She felt she had the brainpower and drive to have had a very different kind of life."

While still in her teens, Rose met her future husband, Joseph Patrick Kennedy, when their families vacationed in Maine. He was the elder son of Mary Augusta Kennedy (née Hickey) and Patrick Joseph "P.J." Kennedy, a political rival of Honey Fitz's. Like Rose's parents, Joe's were also Irish immigrants. After dating him for about seven years, all much to the chagrin of her disapproving father, Rose married Joe on October 7, 1914; she was twenty-four and he, twenty-six. They then moved to Brookline, Massachusetts.

Over the next seventeen years, Rose would bear nine children: Joseph Jr. (Joe) in 1915; John (Jack), 1917; Rose (Rosemary or Rosie), 1918; Kathleen (Kick), 1920; Eunice, 1921; Patricia (Pat), 1924; Robert (Bobby), 1925; Jean, 1928; and Edward (Ted or Teddy), 1932. A small, fragile woman, she worked hard to regain her strength after each birth. It felt to her, though, as if she was always pregnant and always sick.

Missing from most accounts of Rose Kennedy's life is the despair she felt at having had so many children in such a short period of time. Even though the times called for women to have large families, especially Catholics not using birth control, Rose, with her strong wanderlust, had other objectives. From the time she was a young girl, she'd wanted to live abroad. She loved Europe, especially Paris and Rome, and fantasized about moving there. However, like a lot of young women of her time, she was taught to turn away from those kinds of dreams, not toward them. *Some* women of the early 1900s actually wanted more than to just marry and have children. Some of them wanted to live their own lives and maybe have jobs and make it in a man's world when women weren't ordinarily doing that. Those women usually ended up miserable because they were forced, just by the tide of the times, to submit to traditional thinking, their dreams be damned.

It was after the birth of her third child, Rosie, that Rose Kennedy began to feel profoundly unhappy, due not only to her being forced to live within the constraints of a preordained life but also to her discovery of Joe's rampant infidelity. Rose at first tried to curb his unfaithfulness. However, arguments with him about it were never productive. She was always left feeling unheard, unvalued, and unloved. When she was about seven months pregnant with her fourth child, Rose left Joe and returned to her parents' home, leaving her children with their nannies. She said she needed to think things over. But what, her father asked, was there to think about? She was married and, due to her faith, divorce wasn't an option. After three weeks, he told her it was time to pull herself together and go back to where she belonged.

By the beginning of the 1920s, Rose was stuck in a bad marriage. Over time, she developed the coping mechanism of self-isolation. She not only felt alone, she wanted to *be* alone, or at least by herself with her faith and the God she knew would never let her down. In the process, she wasn't always there for her children. "I'm afraid poor little sickly Jack was left on his own too much of the time," she later said. "The thought still bothers me a bit that he may have felt neglected when he was a little boy."

In fact, Jack took Rose's indifference harder than his siblings. Maybe that was because he was so chronically ill and needed his mother more than the others. Even when he was at his sickest, though, Rose was emotionally removed. For instance, when he nearly died of scarlet fever in February 1920 at the age of two, she never went to Boston City Hospital to visit him. When he was old enough to hear stories about this crisis, Jack couldn't understand it. He learned it had been Joe who'd appealed to Mayor Andrew Peters to have him admitted to a hospital that was already filled to capacity with children suffering from the near epidemic. It was Joe who sat with him every afternoon and into the night. It was Joe who worried about him so much that he went to church every day to pray for him, and he wasn't even that religious!

After 1929, when Joe started his affair with the famous actress Gloria Swanson, Rose took off for Europe seventeen times in seven years. Once, when she was getting ready for a three-week trip, six-year-old Jack protested, saying, "Gee, you're a great mother to go away and leave your children alone." That quote is found in just about every JFK biography. The reason it resonates so with historians is because it so purely reflects his true feelings at the time. Another quote about his mother attributed to Kennedy in almost every biography is: "She was never there when we really needed her. She never really held me and hugged me. Never. Never!"

A big issue between Jack and Rose was her faith. As he got older, he began to question many of the tenets of Catholicism to which Rose clung so fiercely. For instance, she went to Mass every morning and sometimes afternoons, too, which Jack thought was fanatical. When he'd confide in her about his life, she'd give him a reproving look and recite an applicable scripture. She even made it clear that she preferred Catholics to others, which Jack thought was wrong. Years later, her daughter-in-law Jackie would note,

"She'll say when you say someone's coming for dinner—'Is he a Catholic?' or 'Is she a Catholic?'—as if that will make them nicer." Jack was skeptical of Catholicism and often quoted a statement attributed to Abraham Lincoln when talking about its fallible nature: "The Savior of the whole world chose twelve disciples, and even one of that small number, selected by superhuman wisdom, turned out a traitor and a devil."

Whenever his mother would take out her rosary during a crisis, it would drive Jack mad. He looked at it as her way of distancing herself from whatever was going on. Dr. Adolph "Doc" Brown, a leading clinical psychologist and parenting expert, today sees it differently: "Saying the rosary is, for many people in many cultures, a form of love. In fact, for some, and I imagine this was the case with Mrs. Kennedy, it's truly the greatest form of love a mother can show. She's going to God for assistance and, in her mind, how much more can she do for her child?"

Today, when we think of Rose Kennedy, we think of a stoic woman of faith, someone strong, brave, and fearless in her religion no matter the tragedy. "God won't give us a cross that's heavier than we can bear," she was known to say. Privately, though, she was a very anxious person known to nervously twist her hands for no apparent reason. She seemed secretly on the edge of despair, and the fact that she had to work so hard to disguise it wore her down. Today, she might even be considered neurotic.

We also think of Rose as a traditional mother, content with her many children and the life she had that revolved around them. The truth, though, is that she got little joy out of being a mother. Her intuition told her she was entitled to some measure of happiness, and being foisted with a gaggle of children was never her dream. So, she was secretly frustrated by it all. Every now and then, she'd let her public image slip a little and would reveal something surprisingly truthful, as in this passage from her book *Times to Remember*:

> *Bringing up children isn't easy. Mothers get tired, or feel unwell, or become inundated in obligations and demands. Also, children can be uncooperative. Or worse: shirk, interrupt, show off, rebel. Break into arguments among themselves. Punch one another over the table and kick one another under the table.*

Jackie Kennedy could be particularly stinging in her remembrances of Rose Kennedy to Arthur Schlesinger for her oral history of 1964. "I always thought he [Joe] was the tiger mother," she said. "And Mrs. Kennedy, poor little thing, was running around, trying to keep up with this demon of energy, seeing if she had enough placemats in Palm Beach, or should she send the ones from Bronxville, or had she put the London ones in storage? Her little mind went to pieces, and . . . and she loves to say now how she sat around the table and talked to them about Plymouth Rock and molded their minds, but she was really just saying, '*Children! Don't disturb your father!*'"

Rose knew she had a role, though, and she had to fill it. Maybe if Joe had been a better husband, everything else might've followed suit. "He was everything to everyone," she said of Joe in the 1970s, after he was gone. "Everything to everyone, but me. He was also fearless," she added. "He'd see something and he'd go after it. I hoped some of that might rub off on me. It didn't."

As mothers often are for their sons, Rose was the template not only for how Jack would later view his own wife but also for how much he believed she should put up with in a marriage. Growing up, he was very aware of Rose's chronic unhappiness. He accepted it as a fact of her life, a fact of all their lives. Though he felt alone a lot of the time, he grew to understand that it was because Rose felt alone, too. His experience of his mother along with society's view of women of her time all but cemented his opinion that women weren't meant to be happy as much as they were meant to sacrifice, serve their husbands, and bear children. They weren't supposed to follow their dreams. They weren't even supposed to have dreams. They were just supposed to be like Rose.

In the holdings of the JFK Library and Museum, there's a revealing photograph of Rose Kennedy standing before a gilt mirror in the foyer of her Hyannis Port home wearing a waistcoat jacket with a mink collar and hat. Jackie took it from a vantage point from which she couldn't be seen as she watched the matriarch apply the final touches of makeup before leaving for church.

Jackie later recalled Rose pressing her thin mouth on a tissue to blot her lipstick, after which she stared intently at her reflection. "As I stood there, I wondered what she was thinking," Jackie later told her own mother. "I knew whatever her thoughts were, they were especially sad." She said Rose's eyes shone with tears but, as she continued to stare hard at her image, she took a deep breath and straightened her back. She would *not* cry. Noticing something stirring behind her, she whirled around and found her daughter-in-law. "Oh, hello, dear," she said, forcing a smile.

"Are you all right, Mrs. Kennedy?" Jackie asked as she approached. She reached out and lovingly patted the matriarch's hand.

"Of course I am, dear," Rose told her. "Why wouldn't I be?"

PATRIARCH

Few men in American history have been as confounding as John Kennedy's father, Joseph Patrick Kennedy. Born on September 6, 1888, in Boston, Joe was so smart, so focused, and so gifted with, at least in his youth, such uncanny political instinct, some people figured he'd one day be president. He certainly wanted it for himself. "But we're Catholic," Rose would remind him, "and what Catholic has ever been president?" To that, he would angrily counter, "*I am also American.*" Besides, Joe was barely Catholic; he rarely, if ever, went to church and certainly not to Confession. Patriotic bluster aside, he also knew the truth. The chances of America voting for a Roman Catholic president, practicing or not, in the first half of the twentieth century were slim to none. It might take another generation before people would be able to accept such a thing, meaning it would be his sons who'd have that advantage.

In marrying Rose Fitzgerald, Joseph found the ideal wife, at least for his purposes. She'd be silent about any grievances, she'd be devoted to the Kennedy name, and, at least as far as the public was concerned, she'd be fiercely loyal to him. He was quite taken with her at the beginning, sometimes sweeping her into his arms with such gusto her feet would leave the floor. Everyone thought they were the perfect couple. Privately, though, he'd complain that he found her a little dull. She was interested in fashion, gardening, and socializing, and he thought of her as a frivolous, fun kind of woman—not, at least as far as he could tell, a deeply introspective one. But, like a lot of men of his time, he didn't expect women to be smart. He actually didn't *want* women to be smart.

Rose, of course, had her own concerns about Joe. There was an aggression about him she found disconcerting. In those rare times she stood up for herself, his face would tighten as he threw both palms up to declare, "No, Mother. No need for rebuttal." (Yes, he called her "Mother.") She'd say, "But can I ask . . . ?" and he'd shout at her, "No!" as he walked away. It reminded her of her own father; she didn't like it when he shut her down, either.

Joe's grandniece Kerry McCarthy recalled, "Uncle Joe's way was absolute power. He was a man of assurance and conceit. 'Don't question me! I am the boss. Period.'"

There have been decades' worth of rumors about Joe Kennedy, one of the most famous being that he was a bootlegger. However, if one traces the bootlegging stories, there's not a lot of evidence to support them. From one book to the next, the source is always gangster Al Capone's piano tuner, who overheard some kind of conversation between Joe and Al about bootlegging, or it's mobster Sam Giancana's half brother, or his nephew, or his ex-wife, all claiming knowledge of Sam being in the liquor business with Joe. But Joe was the first chairman of the Securities and Exchange Commission, and then was appointed U.S. ambassador to the United Kingdom. He had to have been extensively vetted for those jobs and, most certainly, those investigations would've turned up bootlegging activity. More to the point, though, Joe Kennedy was just too careful to be a bootlegger. He was always worried about his reputation and that of his family, and even if he'd walk right up to the line of legality, which he did quite often, he'd seldom, if ever, cross it.

Joe did make a lot of money on alcohol, but that happened later, after Prohibition. In the fall of 1933, when it was clear Prohibition would be overturned, he used his contacts and his wealth to secure exclusive contracts with British distillers, such as Dewar's and Gordon's. These deals allowed him to import high-end Scotch whiskey and gin from the U.K., which is how he made his fortune in liquor, and maybe also where some of the bootlegging stories came from. When he sold his liquor franchise in the 1940s, he pulled in $8.2 million, more than $100 million in today's money.

Another popular rumor about Joe Kennedy was that he was an anti-Semite. "If being anti-Semitic means he believed there was something biologically wrong with Jews which made them inferior, that wasn't Uncle Joe's thinking," said his nephew Joey Gargan. "However, he definitely had some bigoted leanings, as evidenced by some of his writings and diary entries. Not to excuse it, but Washington was full of anti-Semites in the 1930s and '40s," said Gargan, "as was Hollywood. Uncle Joe was a product of his times. For instance, he belonged to many golf clubs that did not admit Jews.

That practice was common back then, though it was unquestionably wrong. People just didn't make as much of a deal of it as they should've. It was accepted behavior, unfortunately."

In the heat and passion of war, Joe did begin to blame everything on the Jews. He insisted that the media was controlled by Jews, show business was, too, and all of it was to everyone else's detriment. He also felt Jews pushed Great Britain and the United States into war to get revenge on Hitler. This was untrue and inexcusable. Paradoxically, Joe was also sympathetic to the Jews' persecution by Hitler. "No people should suffer at the hands of someone else simply because of religious beliefs, concerns, or anything else, for that matter," he said at the time. "That's a simple truth." Kennedy seemed to be all over the map on this important issue, though, which did him no good as a diplomat and, in the end, would be the catalyst for the end of his career.

Before setting his sights on politics, Joe made an impact on the Hollywood film industry with his own production company. He turned a fortune in that business, too, by smartly insisting on being paid in stock options as well as in salary. Then, because of his experience as chairman of the Securities and Exchange, he knew just how to manipulate the stock market to his advantage. He sold most of his holdings just before the 1929 crash and, by implementing a few other moves that were close to being illegal, he walked away on Black Tuesday richer than ever. Later, in the political world, Joe tried to act committed to American democracy, but that was pretty much an act. Mostly, he viewed politics as a ladder of social mobility and finance, not an instrument of social change. Still, his zest for it, and for the idea of seeing his sons hold powerful government positions, would become the focus of his life from the 1940s through the 1960s.

Though he had his particular character flaws, Joe Kennedy was a very good father. Often tough and unyielding, he had an undeniable paternal quality. It was he who most openly demonstrated love to his children and made them all feel they belonged. "No matter what," he'd tell them, "family is family." He was the parent they went to with their problems, not Rose. Always available for advice, solace, and whatever else they needed, he somehow managed to be equally attentive to each of them. Many of the letters he wrote to them, dozens of which can be found in the JFK Library and Museum, are astonishing. He didn't just write a blanket letter, copy it, and then distribute it, like Rose usually did. He'd write to each child individually. He knew exactly what he or she needed to hear, what the issues at hand were, and just how to address them.

Jack's good friend Kirk LeMoyne Billings, known as "Lem," whom Jack met at the elite prep school Choate in Wallingford, Connecticut, recalled, "Joe's decision from the beginning was that the girls would all go to Catholic schools, and that was mostly because of Rose. But he also felt strongly that the boys should have a wider knowledge of people aside from Catholics. He felt Catholic schools offered too narrow an education and that his sons should go to nonsectarian schools—and I mean strictly nonsectarian schools, such as Episcopalian schools. Choate and all the other schools they attended, which were nonsectarian. This was so important to Mr. Kennedy."

One word that best describes the way Joe Kennedy parented his children is "aspirational." He always made them believe something great was right around the corner. While he could be demeaning and even insulting if they let him down, he'd still find ways to cheer them on, make them want to do better, *be* better. It was in large part because he believed in them so much that they aspired to contribute something worthwhile to the world, whether as public servants or as humanitarians. That's how Joe raised the Kennedys. That's certainly how he raised the one who'd go on to become the thirty-fifth president of the United States.

A LIFE OF PRIVILEGE

A dreamer. That's one good way to think of a youthful and sickly John Fitzgerald Kennedy, all alone in his bedroom or in a hospital room, voraciously reading about some historical or fictional hero but certainly never imagining himself as one. How could he? He was always battling one sickness or another, starting at the age of two with that bout of scarlet fever and then, as he grew older, adrenal issues, allergies, arthritis, and other problems, like digestion aliments—"the Kennedy stomach," Jackie called it in 1964, "which obviously comes from nerves. His mother had it, Eunice had it, they all did."

Lem Billings recalled, "We used to joke that if I ever wrote his biography, I would call it *John F. Kennedy: A Medical History.*"

Seemingly never free from sickness, reading became Jack's salvation, his escape. While other youngsters were outside playing sports, he was intent on spending that time feeding his curiosity with his books. As Jackie Kennedy put it years later to the writer Theodore H. White, "You must think of this little boy, sick so much of the time, reading history, reading the Knights of the Roundtable, reading Marlborough. For Jack, history was full of heroes."

John Fitzgerald Kennedy was born on May 29, 1917, in Brookline, Massachusetts, the second of Rose and Joe's nine children after brother Joe. Siblings and close friends often called him "Johnny." To most others it was "Jack." While he was always a good-looking kid, even given those big ears of his, Jack was thin and wiry and his parents, especially his mother, would always be concerned about his weight. He never seemed to gain, no matter what or how much he ate. He was a happy youngster, though, fresh and full of vitality, less serious and intense than his older brother, Joe.

When Jack was about ten, his family moved from Boston to the Riverdale neighborhood of New York City. His sister Eunice once said their father decided to relocate because of "all the 'No Irish Need to Apply' work signs in Boston. Prejudice was strong against Irish Americans, and our father never wanted anything to influence us into believing we deserved less opportunity than any other American."

From the fifth to seventh grades, Jack attended the private Riverdale Country School for boys. For eighth grade, he was sent to the Canterbury School in New Milford, Connecticut. His education at Canterbury was interrupted after seven months, however, when an appendectomy forced him home to recover. A year later, in September 1931, he enrolled in the Choate School in Wallingford, Connecticut, two years behind Joe Jr. Jack was fourteen, Joe sixteen.

"You boys are all you will ever have in this world," Joe told his sons by the time Jack joined Joe Jr. at Choate. By this time, they had four sisters—Rosemary, Eunice, Kathleen, and Jean—and one younger brother, Bobby. Ted hadn't come along yet. While Joe loved his daughters, he believed they were limited by the roles assigned to women in contemporary society and felt they could never achieve anything close to his sons. While he didn't yet know what that might be for the boys, he figured it'd probably be in the political arena. "You should always be there for each other because that's how brothers are," he'd tell his sons. They'd feel the strength of his big hands as he gripped their shoulders. "I'm proud of you boys, no matter who wins," he'd say before setting them loose to wrestle in the backyard.

Brother Joe, who was born in 1915, always seemed to have it all. Everything he did was a cut above average, whether it was in the classroom or on the football field. As he grew up, he became even more vital and arresting, if not also somehow more socially awkward. Like the personable Jack, he, too, attracted people into his orbit but, unlike Jack, he was insecure around them. It was as if he recognized the pressure he was under to impress but, deep down, felt he wasn't up to it. Jack didn't have that problem. His way was always easier somehow. He also realized that the bar was set lower for him and it made him less afraid to fail. Free of paternal pressure, he had more latitude to figure out who he really was.

Though Jack was determined not to be a carbon copy of his brother at Choate, he didn't have to try that hard. He wasn't as good a student and, physically, was always more fragile. At seventeen, he was treated for colitis and again distracted from his studies. His father was understanding and patient even if sometimes offering a backhanded compliment. In one letter, he wrote:

After long experience in sizing up people, I definitely know you have the goods and you can go a long way. It is very difficult to make up fundamentals that you have neglected when you were very young, and that is why I am urging you to do the best you can. I am not expecting too much, and I will not be disappointed if you don't turn out to be a real genius. But I think you can be a really worthwhile citizen with good judgment and understanding.

In late 1937, Franklin Roosevelt appointed Jack's father as the U.S. ambassador to England. Because Joe had virtually no diplomatic experience, many people questioned the appointment. While he certainly had connections in Hollywood and obviously knew how to parlay them to help his mistress Gloria Swanson in her career, those contacts meant little politically. However, FDR didn't make a lot of mistakes; he usually knew what he was doing. Irish Americans comprised a large faction of the Democratic base, and Joe happened to be the most important, influential, and powerful Irish Catholic in the country. FDR knew it couldn't hurt having Joe represent him abroad.

In 1938, to fulfill the new job, Joe took his entire family to England with the exception of Joe Jr. and Jack, both now at Harvard. Eleven days after their arrival, Hitler's Nazi forces pushed their way into Austria. In what turned out to be a shortsighted assessment of the situation based on his discussions with Prime Minister Neville Chamberlain, Joe declared that Hitler's moves had "no long-range implications." This would be the first of many miscalculations for the new ambassador. In truth, of course, Hitler was determined to expand Germany by taking over the part of Czechoslovakia ripped from it by the Allies in 1919.

Adolf Hitler was cunning, evil, and utterly ruthless. By acting as if his only motivation was to see all Germans, including those living within the borders of other countries, united into one country, he was able to play on the world's trauma from the previous war. America's former European and British allies kept their heads safely buried in the sand, refusing to acknowledge what was happening—namely, a "strong man's" quest for world dominance. There was just no appetite at the time for another war, least of all on the part of Ambassador Kennedy, who insisted that the peace be kept at all costs. He, and others with whom he was aligned, didn't understand that a steady erosion of life and liberty was worth fighting against. Like a lot of people who disagreed with Joe Kennedy, his son Jack believed Hitler wasn't going to be stopped by just wishful thinking.

In the spring of 1939, Hitler moved to lay claim to all of Czechoslovakia. That same year, Jack Kennedy learned a lot more about the dangerous situation as he traveled through Europe preparing his Harvard senior honors thesis with his friend Torbert Macdonald. Torbert—who was known as both "Torb" and "Torby"—had a background very different from Jack's in that his family was strictly middle-class. Like Jack, Torb adored his own father, John "Jack" Macdonald. He was a hardworking plumber, gym teacher, and funeral director with his own business, Macdonald and Sons, though no son ever followed him into that line of work. Much later, when Torb became a senator, he and his family lived in Malden, a middle-class suburb, rather than Washington. Laurie Macdonald—Torb's daughter, who, like her siblings, always referred to JFK as "Uncle Jack"—recalled in 2024, "We were as blue-collar as blue-collar can get. But my father and Uncle Jack had an instant chemistry, different as they were, which turned into a sort of magical friendship. They loved each other madly, though they'd needle each other like crazy. In fact, my dad's nickname was 'the Needle' because he was such a master at it. Uncle Jack said my father was not only very funny but also one of the smartest men he'd ever known."

"My dad was, I guess you could say, Uncle Jack's other half in all things," said Torbert Jr., also in 2024. "He'd even sneak him food in the infirmary when he was sick to keep him strong. There was his friend Lem Billings, of course. But maybe, I don't know this for sure, but maybe Lem's affection for Jack was confused with sexuality, whereas my dad's was just brotherly. My father was always of robust health, and he had a postcard from Jack that said, 'Wish you were here. With your health and my wealth, we'd have a great time!' Theirs was a great love story. My dad never betrayed him. He took a lot to his grave."

By sophomore year at Harvard, Jack and Torb were roommates at Winthrop House, and they would remain so for the first part of junior and then all of senior year. As a freshman and sophomore, Jack played offensive end football and was a decent pass receiver. "When his brother Joe graduated and moved on, that's when Jack started to bloom at Harvard," Torbert once said. "He had great desire to play football, but his physical makeup was not that of an end who could block tackles, which, in those days, were the biggest defensive linemen the opponents ever had. His greatest success was in catching passes." Not always very well. While playing football at Harvard, Jack suffered a ruptured disk in his back, compounding a congenital defect that had already been troubling him. Eventually, he switched over to the Harvard University swim team, a smart move.

It was on a trip abroad with Torbert Macdonald that not only did Jack's deep interest in politics and world affairs take hold but he also saw what was really happening around him and felt an urgency to sound an alarm about it. "You'd have to be deaf, dumb, and blind not to see that the Germans were about to invade *everybody*," Torbert Sr. recalled. When the buddies returned to the States, Torb knew the trip had changed him, and he knew it had changed Jack, too.

On September 1, 1939, three days after Jack joined his parents and the rest of the family in London, Nazi Germany invaded Poland. Two days later, Prime Minister Chamberlain declared war on Germany and, indeed, World War II had begun. "The inevitable had happened," said Torbert Jr., "and my father saw in Jack Kennedy an almost immediate transition from a happy-go-lucky but thoughtful young man to someone deeply concerned about trying to understand world politics and, more specifically, how England had dropped the ball by being so late to understand that war was imminent."

Though war was declared, Ambassador Kennedy still believed there had to be some way toward a peaceful resolution with Hitler. Because he felt so sure that Britain and France would never survive against the German dictator, he continued to argue views that were becoming more isolationist in nature. But this didn't mean he was against the military or against defense. Quite the contrary, the very nature of isolationism is the belief that the military budget should be used to protect the United States, that destroyers and ammunition shouldn't be sent abroad but that the entire budget should be used to protect the Western Hemisphere. Today, of course, this philosophy might be thought of as "America first." When taken to an extreme, though, it is a philosophy used to justify the position that America should not protect its allies, which, of course, flies in the face of what America is all about.

Once back at Harvard in June 1940, Jack echoed his father's position with a letter to the *Harvard Crimson*, writing: "The failure to build up her armaments has not saved England from a war and may cost her one. Are we in America to let that lesson go unlearned?" He then expanded on that idea with his senior year's thesis, "Appeasement in Munich." That particular work would eventually be released as Jack's first book, *Why England Slept*. Its title was an allusion to Winston Churchill's 1938 tome, *While England Slept: A Survey of World Affairs, 1932–1938,* which had been about the growing influence of German power.

Jack's book deftly examined the many failures of the British government to prevent war, starting with its initial lack of response to the obvious threat posed by Hitler. Basically agreeing with his father's position, he framed it as a cautionary tale for the United States, arguing that it should take heed and *do better* than England in terms of preparation and forethought. "England made many mistakes; she is paying heavily for them now," he wrote. "In studying the reasons why England slept, let us try to profit by them and save ourselves her anguish."

Why England Slept revealed young Jack Kennedy as a serious student of history. Not only had it become more clear that he was a thoughtful and intelligent observer of international affairs, but his way of expressing those views, some of which were very complex, was vivid, colorful, and interesting. He was a fine writer, maybe no surprise considering how much he'd always loved to read.

Many historians consider the years after *Why England Slept* as that time when the patriarch shifted his opinion of his two eldest sons. Maybe it was Jack, not Joe, who was the more obvious statesman. Maybe it was Jack, not Joe, who was the more intellectually prepared for politics. Still, with Joe being the eldest, the father's bet would still be on him to be first. But the younger son had suddenly become a real factor in the father's calculation of how his sons might later be positioned politically—first Joe, then *definitely* Jack.

PART II

Prelude to Camelot

MERRYWOOD ROYALS

TWELVE YEARS LATER. MARCH 1952. MCLEAN, VIRGINIA.

It was a chilly winter evening when Jack Kennedy and his good friend Lem Billings tooled along in Jack's beat-up blue sedan from Washington, DC, to McLean to rendezvous with a young woman Jack had just begun dating. After meeting up, the three would then head to the home of Jack's brother Bobby for a St. Patrick's Day party hosted by him and his wife, Ethel. Jack's date was twenty-two-year-old Jacqueline Lee Bouvier, better known as just "Jackie," of course. Born on July 28, 1929, to Janet Norton Lee Bouvier, now Mrs. Hugh Auchincloss, and her first husband, Jack Vernou Bouvier III, known as "Black Jack," Jackie had one sister, Caroline Lee, or "Lee," born March 3, 1933.

Jack met Jackie almost a year earlier in May 1951 at a dinner party hosted by Martha Bartlett, wife of his friend Charlie. It had taken them this long to get together again because, after that first dinner, their lives went in different directions. Jackie was off to Europe with her sister for a vacation at the same time Jack went on a fact-finding mission to Israel and Southeast Asia with Bobby and Eunice. His seven-week trip was planned to buttress his knowledge of the regions for a possible Senate run, which was presently under consideration. Upon their return, Jack and Jackie reunited at a party at the Kennedys' Palm Beach estate in December 1951, again at the behest of the Bartletts.

It would be while in Palm Beach that Jackie first began to understand Congressman Kennedy's devotion to public service. She had recently seen him on *Meet the Press* discussing foreign policy. Now, up close, she was impressed. He was smart, witty, and, of course, handsome. Two months later, with Martha again playing matchmaker, Jackie met Jack again for a meal at the Bartletts' home. "He walked on air, the way he breezed through, making one person laugh, another think, another wonder," Jackie later recalled of him to her friend Joan Braden. "I watched and thought he has that thing people with money have, that lack of concern, I suppose. Then, I listened to what he had to say, and how he felt about people and the way he wanted to serve, I suppose, and the things he wanted to do with his life to make things better, and I thought, *My God, just look at him—those blue eyes, that hair, that face, and just the way he is . . . the way he thinks about the world and the way he talks about the world and the way he is in the world. He's just so . . . beautiful.*"

For his part, Jack thought Jackie was elegant and smart, "a cut above" is how he put it. He wanted Lem to weigh in, however. Jack valued Lem's opinion, which is why he had him accompany them to Bobby and Ethel's party.

Jack and Lem had been best friends since Choate. Though Lem was bookish, witty, and awkward, his friendship with Jack had been instantaneous, as if they'd always known each other. In Lem's eyes, Jack could do no wrong. If someone criticized him, Lem was the first to defend him. It didn't matter what was said, Lem would fight to the finish for his friend. Such unequivocal devotion allowed Jack to open up to Lem, knowing he'd never stand in judgment of him. Complicating things, however, was Lem's homosexuality. Most people felt he had feelings for Jack. The fact that he stayed at Choate an extra year just so he could graduate with Jack pretty much said it all. "To Lemmer," Jack signed his own graduation picture in 1935, he in suit and tie with carefully parted hair, "the gayest son I know—In memory of two tense years and in hopes of many more. Your old pal and supporter! Ken." With "gayest" here, of course, Jack was using a common vernacular for "happy." But, in fact, as they grew up, people did begin to think Lem was in love with his friend simply because of the correct speculation that Lem was homosexual. Maybe it was true back when they were fifteen. However, whatever romantic feelings Lem might have had in their youth gradually became less central to their bond.

"I remember this was the first time I'd even heard of Jackie Bouvier," Lem recalled. "Jack told me she was an attractive young girl engaged to somebody else." She was, in fact, set to marry a stockbroker at the time, John G. W. Husted. The wedding was set for June. "I had met many of his girls so, to me, this was just another one," Lem recalled. "It was interesting she was engaged, though, and from his description, I did feel she was awfully young for him." Lem also said he didn't get the impression Jackie was anyone particularly special.

As Jack pulled onto the driveway of Merrywood estate, an enormous and stately reproduction of an eighteenth-century Georgian mansion, he and Lem couldn't help but be immediately impressed by it. Merrywood was built in 1919 by Newbold Noyes, editor of the *Washington Star*. Hugh D. Auchincloss Jr. bought it in the 1930s with just a smidgeon of his vast fortune from Standard Oil. Auchincloss presently headed up a successful brokerage firm in Washington and, later, in New York: Auchincloss, Parker & Redpath.

The Auchinclosses' world was one of American aristocracy financed for generations by old WASP money, which meant, at least for Jackie and Lee, private boarding schools and first-class trips abroad, all expenses paid by their beloved Uncle Hughdie (as in Hugh D.). The Auchinclosses occupied two pages of the New York *Social Register,* forty-seven listings as compared to forty-two for the Rockefellers and eight for the Vanderbilts. Here at Merrywood, just as at Hugh's second estate, Hammersmith Farm in Newport, an army of maids and butlers was available to the family at all hours. It had been that way ever since the Bouvier girls became part of a blended family after their mother, Janet, married Hugh in the summer of 1942. There was Hugh Dudley III ("Yusha"), Hugh's son with first wife Maria "Maya" de Chrapovitsky; Nina ("Nini") and Thomas ("Tommy") from his second marriage to Nina Gore (who was also mother, through a previous marriage, to the novelist Gore Vidal); and Janet Jr. ("Ja-Je") and James ("Jamie"), born respectively in 1945 and 1947 to Janet and Hugh.

The Auchinclosses were Republican. *Very* Republican. "You never even dared mention the word 'Democrat' in my household," said Jackie's sister, Lee. "Uncle Hughdie mostly, but Mummy, too, was very conservative and didn't have time for liberals. Everything was about rules and regulations and behaving within certain guidelines, and also making as much money as possible and spending as little of it on taxes as you could get away with. I wouldn't say they hated Democrats and all their talk of civil rights, but then again, I might. They were political, well-read, and opinionated. They didn't live in a rich little bubble, though. None of us did. We were always surrounded by policymakers, but they were policymakers my mother and stepfather agreed with."

"Oh, Daddy loved public servants," confirmed Hugh and Janet's son, Jamie. "*Republican* public servants. Gore Vidal used to say Daddy was a 'senatorial groupie.' As a little boy, I'd watch these old, white-haired, fat men in their three-piece suits, dressed so inappropriately for Newport summer temperatures, all of them senators, come to Hammersmith Farm to drink my father's free alcohol and bake in the sun. Daddy would say, 'Presidents come and go, but popular senators remain almost 'til death do they part.'

"Where Mummy was concerned, she had convinced herself her side of the family was related to the Lees of Virginia," said Jamie. "As a result, she became an expert on the life and times of Robert E. Lee, general in chief of the Confederate armies. She was able to talk about him in such great detail, it was very convincing that she was, meaning we all were, related to him. As an adult, I once asked Jackie about it and she said, 'My God! How could you ever believe such a thing, Jamie? None of it is true! None of it!' But I grew up thinking it was."

A pair of uniformed butlers stood at attention at the Merrywood entrance in anticipation of the arriving guests. Once his old car came to a halting stop, the passenger door opened and out hobbled Jack Kennedy on crutches, wearing slippers with his ill-fitting suit, his socks drooping down past his ankles. He looked completely rumpled, his mop of reddish hair badly needing a cut and style. Quickly, he was ushered into the estate, Lem Billings following close behind.

As the two men walked into the foyer, they saw six-year-old Jamie, standing at the top of the red-carpeted steps. The youngster definitely looked entitled in his black velvet shorts, silk shirt with lace cuffs, and black patent-leather shoes with brass buckles. Jack glanced up at him with a smile. Jamie, even at that age, already had an opinion of the guest. As an Irish liberal Catholic Democrat, Jack was, in every way at least as Jamie understood it, a distinct outsider. "I stood at the top of the long staircase, glaring down at him as he entered the house," Jamie recalled, "and in my haughtiest voice, I said, 'Hello, *Kennedy.*' He looked up at me and retorted in exactly the same tone, 'Hello, *Auchincloss.*'"

"Madam is in the stables," lead butler Jack Owen said as he escorted the guests through a central hallway, across a high-ceilinged living room, and into an adjoining library. Immediately, a maid brought in a pitcher of ice water and poured two glasses before she rushed off. Jack and Lem took a look around at all of the eighteenth-century furnishings and oil paintings, including one of a stern-looking woman on a horse—Jackie's mom, as it would turn out, on her show jumper, Danseuse. Gore Vidal, who lived at Merrywood when his mother was married to Hugh, described the place as "a bit Henry Jamesian . . . deliberate quietude removed from twentieth-century tensions."

As they waited, the young men perused the many books on mahogany

shelves, each in alphabetical order not by author but, much more confus-
ingly, by title. Jack pulled one from the others and thumbed through it.
When he went to return it, he couldn't remember its place. "I'm screwed
now," he muttered to himself.

"I'll take that, young man," came a crisp voice from behind.

Jack turned around and standing behind him with her hand held out
was a woman who seemed so immediately imperious, he couldn't help but
just stare at her, book still in hand. "I *said,* I'll take that, young man," she
repeated as she snatched the volume. While scanning the shelves, she conceded that the alphabetical system was very confusing. It was her husband's
idea, she said, and, "don't ask me why." She found the place she was looking
for and pushed the book back in with the others. Then, turning to Jack, she
announced herself. "I'm Mrs. Auchincloss," she said. "Jacqueline's mother."
She pronounced it *Jack-leen.* Of course she did.

FUTURE IN-LAWS

With her salt-and-pepper hair styled short above a face best described not as pretty but as handsome, Janet Auchincloss reminded Jack Kennedy of some sort of a British royal. At forty-five, she was buttoned up in a gray tweed jacket and silk blouse but also wearing a whimsical, swinging kind of bright red skirt. Because her body was so toned and shapely, there was actually something quite sexy about her. Jack's impression of her was as a model of good breeding. He later said he immediately knew any daughter reared by a mother like this one had to be cultured with unmatched social refinement. He didn't know it at the time, but Janet could be as critical as she was upstanding. She'd raised Jackie and Lee with an iron fist, which, over the years, had provoked no small amount of resentment from both toward the woman they lovingly, and sometimes not so lovingly, called "Mummy." Now, as grown women, they were working to find ways to get along with her. She, too, was trying with them. It wasn't easy, though, as Jack would soon learn; there was definitely a lot of heavy baggage.

Stepping to his wife Janet's side in the library, his riding boots making a clicking sound against the hardwood floor, was her large-framed and gangly fifty-four-year-old husband, Hugh Auchincloss. Dressed in a shooting jacket, he, too, held himself with a bearing that could be described as regal. "He was like an old king on holiday" is how Jack later put it. Hugh mentioned that he'd just been targeting clay pigeons on the property's trapshooting range. While his charm and courtesy were obvious, when he shook Jack's hand his grip wasn't quite as firm as his wife's. Jack found that interesting. He sensed Hugh let Janet run things around there. However, while Hugh could be pushed pretty far, when he drew the line with Janet it was absolute.

"We've met before," Janet said. "Do you remember?" As Jack blushed, she said it was six years earlier, "at Captain McCauley's house. I sat next to you at dinner? Surely you remember."

"Oh, yes, of course," Jack said. "Dinner at the Captain's."

She studied him. "Do you lie like this often?" she asked. His face got even redder. Hugh, coming to Jack's rescue, reminded his wife that it was a politician who stood before them, "and it comes with the territory, right, son?"

It was true, though. Janet and Hugh had met Jack back in 1946, right after he was elected to Congress. He was living with his sister Eunice in Georgetown at the time; the siblings lived together for a couple years when Jack was a congressman. The Auchinclosses had been the guests of Edward McCauley, former head of naval intelligence in World War I, and his wife, Jean, at their Georgetown home. After being introduced to Jack by Charles Bartlett, Janet sat next to him at dinner. "I was very impressed by this young man," Mrs. Auchincloss recalled nearly twenty years later in her oral history for the Kennedy Library. "The thing I best remember about that night is that when we left, we were driving down the street and I saw this tall, straight, purposeful young man striding down the street. I said to Hugh, 'There's Jack Kennedy' or 'young Representative Kennedy. Shall we see if we can give him a lift?' He didn't seem to have any car and was just walking on into the night. So, we stopped and said, 'Can we take you anywhere?' And he said, 'Thank you very much. That would be very nice,' and hopped in our car. There was something about him, not bothering to ask anybody for a lift or bothering to call a taxi, but just finding him marching on, blocks from the McCauleys' house, that was very endearing. I can't describe it to you, but he had a sort of a Lindbergh [Charles A. Lindbergh] quality to me at that point. I certainly had, of course, no idea I would ever see him again."

Back in the library at Merrywood, Hugh stared at the crutches. "What the heck happened to you, son?" He really was a sight. Janet couldn't take her eyes off his dirty slippers. He certainly wasn't the same "straight, purposeful young man striding down the street" they'd met six years earlier.

In fact, recent years really had been challenging. Jack had been thinking of a career in journalism but wanted more sway than what he could have as a writer. His father was beginning to see it that way, too. Running for Congress happened quickly. So idealistic, eager to serve, and wanting to be someone who could facilitate change, he became difficult to resist as he campaigned for better health care, housing for veterans, organized labor to protect workers and their workplaces, and the right to strike and bargain. When he was elected to Congress in 1946, it seemed a fait accompli, at least as far as his friends and family were concerned. Assigned to the Committee on Education and Labor, he would serve in a freshman class with a politician whose political career would one day intersect with his own—Richard M. Nixon.

But then, in the summer of '47, and this is about a year after Jack first met the Auchinclosses at the McCauley dinner party, he and his sister Kick took a trip abroad. While in London, he ended up in the hospital diagnosed with Addison's disease, a failure of the adrenal glands that would afflict him for the rest of his life. He became so sick, he was even given last rites. Somehow, he pulled through. Then, in '51, while in Tokyo with Bobby and Eunice, he took ill again, this time his blood pressure plummeting dangerously low. When that happened, his body was unable to absorb the cortisone prescribed for his Addison's. One thing led to another and, soon, he was critical again. Somehow, he rebounded, but this time at what cost? Though just thirty-four, he walked as if he were ninety-four, his legs and back always in terrible pain, his body seeming to break down more and more each day. It seemed as if he woke up every morning with some new pain, whether joint or muscle or even digestion. Typical of him, though, he continued to troop forward, never letting anything stop him and never complaining about it, either. Of course, he didn't explain his medical history to his hosts. Instead, he blamed poor Lem. He said the two had played touch football a day earlier and that, unfortunately, Lem threw like a girl. As Lem frowned at him, Jack continued by saying that as he tried to catch one of Lem's "girl throws," he took a tumble, "and so here I am, crippled at the hands of my non-athletic friend."

"Are you in pain, young man?" Janet wondered. He said he wasn't. "Lying again!" she exclaimed. "My God," she added, "you're too young to be this old." When Jack asked for some aspirin, Janet dispatched a maid to fetch some. As they continued to wait for Jackie, the Auchinclosses chatted with Jack about his promising political career.

While pouring Scotch from a crystal decanter, Hugh noted that he was a Republican. Jack smiled and said that some of the best people he knew played on that side of the aisle.

Jack told the Auchinclosses he was done with Congress and not planning to run for another term. "I've been playing in the minor leagues too long," he told them. "Time for me to start playing in the majors." He said he was thinking about unseating the popular Henry Cabot Lodge in the Senate.

Hugh warned him that it wouldn't be easy. "People love that guy," he said. Jack had to agree. The Republican Lodge actually had some history with the Kennedys; he was the grandson of the Henry Cabot Lodge who'd once defeated Jack's grandfather Honey Fitz for a Senate seat.

"As we talked, we approved," Janet later said in previously unpublished remarks from 1973. "Jack was well-spoken, well-intentioned, and clearly wanting to do something worthwhile as a public servant. I didn't feel he was a frivolous person. He had a quality of noblesse. He was obviously learned and unafraid of being thought of as a blue stocking [slang for intellectual]. He said he had speaking engagements all over Massachusetts to make people aware of him. Hughdie and I thought—a young man who wants to serve, who cares about others, who wants to give back to his country? What could be so wrong with that? Of course, Jacqueline was engaged to someone else. We, therefore, had to tread lightly."

"Oh goody," came a voice from behind them. "I see you've met your toughest audience." They turned around and there she was, Jacqueline Bouvier, framed by the doorway as if in a portrait and looking gorgeous in it. She was wearing an elegant black cocktail dress embroidered with silver threading and accented by white pearls and matching earrings. The outfit was finished with a black fur coat. Her hair was a stylish brunette coif. Maybe she wasn't beautiful in the accepted sense, her polished teeth perhaps a tad misaligned, her eyes perhaps a tad too far apart. Still, her elegant comportment gave the impression of beauty. Without even making an effort, she seemed refined and aristocratic.

Jack couldn't have been more intrigued as she glided across the room, just like her mother had earlier. "My God," he whispered to Lem. "Will you just look at that!"

JACKIE

P leased to meet you," Jackie said as she strode toward Lem. "I'm Jacqueline," she added, pronouncing it *Jack-leen,* like her mother. As he
shook her hand, Lem noticed her diamond-and-emerald engagement ring.
She then walked over to Jack. "Mr. Kennedy, is it?" she asked with mock
seriousness.

He smiled. "Miss Bouvier, I presume," he said as he kissed her hand.
"Still engaged, I see," he added. "Happy?" he asked with a lopsided grin.

"Yes. Very much so," she answered.

"I'll just bet you are," he said with a wink.

As Janet shot Hugh a look of surprise, he smiled to himself.

After all of that, Jack, Lem, and Jackie got back into Jack's old blue sedan and took off for Bobby and Ethel's. Later that day, Janet walked outside
and, much to her horror, saw that Kennedy's car had left an unsightly oil
stain on the asphalt of their front entryway. Upset, she called Hugh outside
and the two then stood in front of the enormous black stain and couldn't
help it: they were furious about it.

That night at Bobby and Ethel's party, Jack and Jackie sequestered
themselves while she spoke to him about her work at the *Times-Herald* newspaper in Washington as the "Inquiring Photographer." She'd been writing
that column since October 1951. She told him she'd attended photography
classes and had studied female photographers she most admired, such as
Toni Frissell. She also said she wanted to be a successful writer and earn her
own living by maybe one day writing a book. She had a patrician manner
and spoke in a slow, polite manner, a bit stiff, but she was also smart and
funny, and Jack liked her right away.

Jackie was equally intrigued. Besides Jack's charisma and magnetism, there was another fascinating element to his appeal, something that might've seemed counter to making people comfortable: his indifference. He had absolutely no interest in impressing people. Maybe that wasn't surprising considering his pedigree. After all, he was the son of a man who'd given each of his children a million dollars for a rainy day, the equivalent of about ten million today. In a postwar America with everyone so uncertain about the future, Jack knew he'd be okay, at least financially. If that awareness made him a little cocky, it wasn't to an unappealing degree. In fact, what most people took away from first meeting him wasn't his arrogance but, rather, his keen curiosity. The total package, good looks and charisma, was irresistible. Men wanted to be him, women wanted to sleep with him, and it had always been just that way. "I can't help it," he once told Lem when trying to figure out his popularity at parties. "It can't be my good looks because I'm not much handsomer than anybody else," he said. "It must be my personality."

About an hour after the party began, everyone had a bit of a surprise. The hostess, Ethel Kennedy, had asked all guests to wear black. While that seemed an odd request given the occasion of St. Patrick's Day, it was Ethel's wish, so of course it was honored. Everyone showed up in black. But an hour into the proceedings, Ethel appeared at the top of her winding staircase to make her grand entrance in a surprising ensemble. "Here I am, everybody," she announced. "How's everybody doing?" she asked while descending the stairs in a bright green diaphanous skirt with a matching sweater and jade heels. She'd certainly found a way to stand out at her own party.

As Ethel floated down the stairs, Jackie looked at all the astonished faces around her and tried to stifle a giggle. Guest Jim Buckley, brother of magazine publisher William F. Buckley, recalled, "She turned to me and whispered, 'Interesting woman, this Ethel Kennedy.' I said, 'Once you get to know her, you'll like her. Does it upset you, the way she set this up?' She said, 'No. Not in the least. After all, it's her party and she can do whatever she likes. Personally,' she added, 'I'd never do anything like that, but how clever of her.' Then, a moment later, she said, 'It'll be refreshing to know someone who doesn't have any fashion sense.'"

Jack overheard Jackie's caustic remark and raised his eyebrows in surprise. As he looked over at her, Jackie gave him a sweet and innocent smile. He winked at her. How refreshing, indeed.

PERFECT ON PAPER

———

Soon after Ethel Kennedy's soiree, Jackie Bouvier broke off her engagement to John Husted. As it turned out, he wasn't earning as much money as her mother had thought, so that was the end of Mr. Husted.

"The secret to happily-ever-after," Janet Auchincloss had been preaching to Jackie and Lee ever since they were little girls, "is money and power." She always believed she was entitled to affluence and security. Rose Kennedy felt the same way. Many women of that time, in fact, felt similarly even if, like Rose, they didn't come right out and say it. While they dated and married with money and power in mind, to verbalize it would've been considered gauche, and certainly to explicitly pass it on to your daughters as a mandate, vulgar. They should learn by example, as Rose's daughters did. With the exception of Rosie, all of them would marry men who had the potential to make a lot of money and be very powerful. The Kennedy girls would go into their marriages with their own wealth, unlike Jackie and Lee, who had no money of their own. Jack Kennedy met both of Janet's standards, money *and* power. Her daughter could do a lot worse, and with John Husted she would have. Therefore, JFK had Mummy's approval, though she did have some reservations.

Janet knew her former husband, Jack Bouvier, and her father, Jim Lee, had strong feelings about Jack's father, Joe. Jackie's cousin John Davis explained: "In 1945, Jackie's grandfather, Jim Lee, confided in Joe that he was about to invest in the Merchandise Mart in Chicago. That was prime real estate. Joe acted quickly and bought it for himself, thereby double-crossing Jim. Earlier, when Joe was chairman of the Securities and Exchange Commission, his crackdown on the way certain stocks could be traded had decimated Jack Bouvier's portfolio. 'My father and ex-husband hate Jack's father,' Janet told Mrs. [Martha] Bartlett. 'So?' Mrs. Bartlett countered. 'What's that got to do with Jackie?' Janet couldn't disagree with that, I guess."

Joe Kennedy had been impressed with Jackie when he first met her in Palm Beach in December 1951. Once he realized she might be a factor in their lives, he took it upon himself to look into her background. "He'd heard she was an heiress, but when he checked it out he found it wasn't true," said his nephew Joey Gargan. "He also assumed she was mostly French, given her surname. In fact, he learned she was only about one-eighth French, no matter what her mother, who was mostly Irish, might claim. She had also said the Bouviers were descended from French aristocracy, which also wasn't true."

Joe Kennedy's secretary, Janet DesRosiers, recalled, "Joe used to say, 'It doesn't matter who you are. It matters who people think you are.' That was politics, after all. He decided to keep an eye on Jackie while also giving Jack the freedom to pursue her. After all, she was, by any measure, the perfect political wife on paper. We all saw that. She looked good on Jack's arm. That mattered."

At this same time, Jackie was given a promotion at the *Times-Herald*. Her "Inquiring Photographer" column would be known as the "Inquiring Camera Girl" and would carry her byline. While she was determined to continue working, she felt there was no reason she couldn't also date Jack. However, their budding romance would be complicated by his workload as he traveled about and laid the groundwork for his Senate campaign. "It was a very spasmodic courtship," she later said, "conducted mainly at long distance with a great clanking of coins in dozens of phone booths."

On April 6, after assembling a crackerjack team to help him get to the finish line, Jack officially announced his Senate run. His team included Dave Powers from Boston, a loyal friend who'd been in charge of his congressional campaign. There was also Larry O'Brien, an experienced politico from Springfield, and Kenny O'Donnell, Bobby's old college roommate, a fellow Irishman who had served in the Army Air Corps.

A big part of Kenny O'Donnell's job would be taming Jack's father, who was financing the whole operation but who everyone agreed had a damaged reputation and weak political instincts. Joe could be a bully, unreasonable, contentious, and prone to spreading conspiracy theories. On the plus side, he was a great media strategist, knew how to plant just the right stories at just the right times, and was able to secure the important endorsement of top newspapers, even if he had to pay for them. In a couple months' time, he'd write a check for half a million dollars to get the support of the conservative *Boston Post*. Jack would say his father had to "buy the newspaper" to get such great backing. Joe had plenty of money and would spend as much as he needed to in order to see his son win. "Kennedys must win" was his philosophy, always. There had to be a way around him, however, in building the kind of statewide campaign necessary for Jack to win. Kenny had the smarts to figure it out, and a big part of how he did that was to pass the buck on to someone who had real influence over the patriarch: his son Bobby.

Twenty-six-year-old RFK knew that to control his father he needed to act as if he was seeking his approval when, actually, he was strategizing ways around it. Jack too often vehemently disagreed with their father, which always caused havoc, and Teddy, of course, was too young to be a factor. Bobby had turned pacifying the old man into a fine art; he'd been doing it all his life. When his two older brothers were off finding themselves, he was home sparring with Joe. Now, he would be used to tame him. Bobby would end up being a titanic force on Jack's team, from this point forward . . . and all the way to the White House.

FROM THIS MOMENT ON

On May 17, 1952, Jackie was invited to the Dancing Class for the 1951–52 social season. This annual ball for upper-crust WASPS had been a big social event in Washington since before the war. When she asked Jack to be her date, he begged off, explaining he had a lot on his mind. He had a political event scheduled for the next day at the Hotel Sheraton in Worcester, Massachusetts. It was a "tea party," as they were called, which meant mostly women in attendance. The idea was to introduce him as a senatorial candidate, but also to recruit female volunteers. Playing off their well-known British ties, it was a clever way for the Kennedys to generate interest in their son. Rose, Eunice, and Pat were set to greet more than two thousand female voters, after which Jack would speak. He hadn't written his speech yet, he told Jackie, and was afraid he'd have to wing it. If so, he'd need his sleep and shouldn't be out late. Jackie understood but also felt he deserved a night off. When she promised to get him home early, he reluctantly agreed.

About thirty minutes after Jackie and Jack got to the Sulgrave Club on Dupont Circle for the ball, the Meyer Davis Orchestra began to play the Cole Porter song "From This Moment On." Jackie looked for Jack, who had already isolated and was standing by himself, seemingly staring off into space, oddly alone in a room full of people. He seemed detached and disinterested, and she wondered if she should've just let him stay home. She walked over to him, took him by the hand, and escorted him out to the dance floor. He could barely walk. How did she expect him to dance? But, true to form, he seemed determined to figure it out.

As he shuffled awkwardly across the floor with Jackie in his arms, Jack suddenly realized something: he was having a good time. She clung to him and buried her head in his shoulder. It felt good. She was soft and seemed to melt right into him. After a few moments, she drew away gently and looked up at him. That's when, to hear him talk about it later, he realized there was something special about her. The citrus scent of her perfume brought forth in him such an unexpected feeling of nostalgia, it took him back to a different time and place. He was reminded that it'd been almost ten years since he'd been so taken by any one woman.

Had it really been that long? It was hard to believe how much time had passed since he fell hard for the first time. Unfortunately, it hadn't ended well. For him, or for her.

PART III

First Love

Inga

A FATED MEETING

There's someone I want you to meet," Kick Kennedy told her brother Jack. "Come to F Street Club tomorrow. I'm having a little party. You'll love her. She's great." When he tried to beg off, she was persistent. "Jack, you simply must," she said. "You won't regret it. I promise."

Twenty-one-year-old Kathleen Kennedy, nicknamed "Kick," was the second-eldest daughter of Joseph and Rose Kennedy. She and Jack were so close and resembled each other so much, some people thought they were twins. They definitely had a special kind of chemistry. He felt no one understood him the way she did, and she felt the same about him.

Kick was a pixie-sized woman with an outsized personality, lots of auburn hair, and a great face with a wide smile and dancing blue eyes. She had a deep, throaty kind of voice and a laugh that could fill a room. She'd just started working for the local *Times-Herald* newspaper a month earlier and had already made a good many connections. She especially enjoyed networking at the paper given that she was such a social butterfly. People gravitated to her and loved being in her company because she had such unflagging energy, was always so lighthearted and fun, and could also be campy. For instance, on this night she was flashing a blue sapphire ring. When someone asked where she'd bought it, she purred, "Darling, I don't *buy* jewelry. I'm *given* jewelry." That was Kick. (Actually, her father had given it to her for her eighteenth birthday.)

The 1925 F Street Club was named for its address, private membership to it being a special Washington distinction. The classic Georgian brick mansion, blocks away from the White House, was built in 1849 for a U.S. Navy captain, and then became the home of a Washington socialite named

Laura Merriam Curtis. She lived there until she married in the early 1930s, then restored the place into a private club, furnishing it with her own exquisite paintings and antique furniture. She also staffed it with specially trained butlers and maids who dressed in traditional uniforms as if working in an English country manor. Today, the mansion is the official residence of the president of George Washington University.

Jack, who'd never been to F Street, was underdressed for the occasion in brown slacks and an open-collar white shirt. He must've realized it, too, as he walked up to the house and saw other men milling about in flawlessly cut, unerringly tailored suits. As he approached the front door, he was met by a butler, clipboard in hand. "Name, please," he intoned. He found Jack's on the list, nodded, and asked him to follow.

Walking at the butler's side, Jack was escorted down a long, ornately furnished hallway until they came to a proper sitting room where he saw that about twenty people had gathered, all dressed to the nines and sipping aperitifs. Spotting Kick, he walked over to her.

"*Darling,*" she exclaimed as she embraced him.

"What *is* this place?" Jack asked, gazing about.

She held him at arm's length. "My God. What are you wearing?"

Just then, a tall, fetching blonde approached. Jack quickly took her in head to toe. "Inga Arvad," Kick announced, "meet my brother, Jack. The one I told you about."

As they shook hands, Inga's face lit up with delight. She said Kick was right, he *was* handsome. Kick giggled and said, "Told you so."

As Inga stood before him, Jack was hit by her perfume—oranges, maybe roses, and . . . was that baby powder? Later, he would learn it was Chantilly Houbigant. He'd never forget it, either. Kick told them that she'd seated them together, "so do try to get along."

AN AWAKENING

She was born Inga Marie Arvad on October 6, 1913, in Copenhagen. Always gorgeous, at sixteen she was crowned Beauty Queen of Denmark and, at seventeen, competed for the title of Miss Europe. That same year, she eloped with an Egyptian diplomat. They divorced before she turned twenty. A year later, she married a film director twice her age, Paul Fejos. She made one movie with him before she realized that acting wasn't for her, and neither was Paul Fejos. Though still married to him, she left Fejos and embarked to Berlin to work as a reporter there before eventually finding her way to America, specifically Washington. Since July 1941, she'd been writing a column for the *Times-Herald* called "Did You Happen to See?" It was human-interest in nature, spotlighting notable people in Washington society and politics.

Dinner at the F Club was served in the formal dining room where six round tables were properly adorned with elaborate floral centerpieces and expensive fine china. Though Jack sat with many of Kick's other friends, nobody mattered to him as much as the woman he'd just met, Inga. He was taken by her as she talked about her work as a writer and her other interests. At twenty-eight and four years his senior, she was very much unlike other young women he'd known along the way.

"My mom had intellectual depth," said Inga Arvad's son Ron McCoy in 2024. "She spoke English, French, German, and Danish. She was a voracious reader, a great storyteller with a real interest in human psychology. She was also well-traveled: Asia, North Africa, and Europe. She was an idealist, like JFK. She always believed people were well-intentioned and could surprise you in wonderful ways. She was kind and loving and had an understanding heart. It's no wonder he was intrigued by her."

In later writings, Inga recalled the moment she'd first heard about Jack from Kick:

"He's coming to Washington, I'm going to give a party at the F Street Club, you will just love him!" "Who?" said I. Was it one of her many admirers. "WHO?" "Jack. He's in the Navy and is going to be stationed in Washington. Super, super." She had not exaggerated. He had charm that makes the birds come out of the trees . . . natural, engaging, ambitious, warm, and when he walked into a room you knew he was there, not pushing, not domineering but exuding animal magnetism.

Ron McCoy added, "Their girlish gaiety aside, Mom and Kick were powerful young women, both reporters at the *Times-Herald,* involved and invested in current events while trying to stay on top of changing times. Sure, they had fun, too; I have pictures of my mom posing in Kick's apartment in a naval officer's coat and jaunty officer's cap. It was just before the war and, like all Americans, they were worried about the future and how their lives were about to change. They had this sense that they should have fun while it was still possible because it might not last. That's how America was back then, though. Get it while you can because soon you won't be able to get it at all."

As they talked, Inga asked Jack, "What are you afraid of?" She leaned in and waited for the answer.

He tapped his teeth with his right index finger, a habit of his when he was trying to concentrate. Generally, he was anything but open. All of the Kennedys were that way. He once noted of his brother Joe, "I suppose I knew Joe as well as anyone. Yet, I sometimes wonder whether I ever knew him. He had always a slight detachment from things around him, a wall of reserve which few people ever succeeded in penetrating." So, how candid was Jack going to be with a woman he'd just met? Feeling oddly vulnerable, he took a deep breath and plunged in. "I'm afraid I'm not as good as my brother," he said. Inga nodded thoughtfully.

Jack then told Inga that on the day Joe was born, his maternal grandfather, Boston mayor John "Honey Fitz" Fitzgerald, announced to the press, "This child is the future president of the nation." Honey Fitz said it'd already been decided that the boy was going to Harvard, "where he'll play on the football and baseball teams and also take all scholastic honors." Years later, of course, Joe did go to Harvard and, while he was a student there, would sometimes echo his grandfather's prediction: "I'll be the first Catholic president."

When Inga asked Jack, "What about you? What do you want?" he couldn't help but smile.

"I want to be the second," he answered.

"You're serious?" she asked.

"Very," he said. He then told her a little about his more recent past.

Back in June 1940, Jack graduated cum laude from Harvard with a bachelor of arts in government. He then enrolled at Stanford Graduate School of Business, thinking he might want to be a reporter. However, he left after just a semester. He'd intended to enroll at Yale Law School but instead decided to join the military, which his brother had already done by enlisting for active duty in the Navy Air Corps.

Given his health problems, however, it wasn't much of a surprise that Jack failed the entrance physical. Still, he was determined to somehow enlist. "Well, there was some doubt about it at first," clarified Chuck Spalding, who met JFK in the summer of 1939, "because he opposed [America] entering the war. He still was distrustful of everything being said about saving the world for democracy. He used such phrases in a chiding and humorous way, never convinced by them. But events were sweeping at such a pace, opposition was pointless. The war was involving everybody and his nature responded pretty actively to the atmosphere."

Joseph Kennedy didn't want either of his eldest sons to serve. "I hate to think how much money I would give rather than sacrifice Joe and Jack in war," he'd said. Some people thought maybe that was the real reason behind his isolationism. Perhaps that's partially true, at least to the extent that most fathers didn't want to see their sons shipped off to war. It said a lot about Joe, though, that he worked behind the scenes to get Jack into the navy if only to satisfy his son's dream. He did it, however, in a way he thought might be safe. He contacted his former naval attaché at the American embassy in London, now head of the Office of Naval Intelligence (ONI) in Washington. The two men then made a few quick fixes to Jack's medical records, and that's how, in October 1941, Jack was able to enlist in the navy.

Jack was immediately assigned to an ONI desk job in Washington. While he may have looked like a soldier in his crisp blue uniform, he certainly didn't feel like one while spending long days organizing military reports and summarizing them for weekly ONI newsletters. It sure wasn't what he'd had in mind when he said he wanted to serve. However, the job did get him a bit closer to his goal, which was to see real action. While some young men of affluence might've used their stations in life to avoid being called up, JFK felt a strong duty to serve, just like his brother. He was so clear about it as he told her his story, Inga couldn't help but admire his patriotism.

"So, what are *you* afraid of?" Jack asked, returning Inga's question.

She didn't have to think long about it. "You," she said with a smile.

"Maybe it's a cliché," Inga's son Ron observed, "but for my mom, it was pretty much love at first sight. That's how she described it to me, anyway. She called it an 'awakening,' her chemistry with Jack Kennedy being so instantaneous. It was as if they'd known each other in some other life and were now picking up where they'd left off. It felt natural. It felt organic. Above all, she said, it felt real."

Jack, too, was quickly taken, not just emotionally but also physically. Inga had it all—great looks, great talk, and, as he would soon learn, great sex. Before long, he was spending all of his nights with her. He gave her a humorous nickname, "Inga Binga." She'd often sign correspondence using that pet name or, sometimes, just "Binga." In return, she called him "White House Man," in a nod to his goal. With the passing of a couple weeks, she joined Jack's friends and family in encouraging those political aspirations. She said he should first consider Congress, then the Senate, and not stop until he made it all the way to the presidency. She believed he could do it, too, and, in fact, she felt he *must* do it, or as she later wrote:

> *We all built him up, he was devoid of conceit, but maybe a tiny hope was gleaming. He was all of 24 and torn between a life of service to his country and teaching at some college. We planned half-heartedly and in some fun that someday he should be President. He laughed and said, "If I ever decide to run for office, you can be my manager."*

Calling his growing passion for politics "an unequaled highway to the White House," Inga took him seriously enough to agree to profile him in her column on November 27, 1941. It had been the idea of Cissy Patterson, publisher of the *Times-Herald*, after meeting Jack at a cocktail party. "You must get an interview for your column with young Kennedy," she told her. In that column, Inga then wrote:

If former Ambassador Joe Kennedy has a brilliant mind (not even his political enemies will deny the fact), charm galore, and a certain way of walking into the hearts of people . . . then son No. 2 has inherited more than his due. The 24 years of Jack's existence on our planet have proved that here is really a boy with a future. "Right now, I am in the Navy, that is most important, but I have many plans for the future," says Jack Kennedy. "Someday, when I have time, I am going to study law." Jack hates only one subject—himself. He is the best listener I have come across . . . Young Kennedy—don't call him that, he will resent it greatly . . .

SLEEPING WITH THE ENEMY?

Jack and Lem had just finished a game of touch football near the Washington Monument and were getting ready to join Inga and Kick for dinner when they heard that the Japanese had attacked Pearl Harbor. The next day, President Roosevelt referred to the Japanese assault as "a date which will live in infamy" and asked Congress to declare "a state of war between the United States and Japanese empire." Four days later, on December 11, Hitler declared that Nazi Germany would join Japan in its warfare against the United States. "I remind myself, I remind my students . . . how did we get into war in Europe?" Joe Kennedy's biographer David Nasaw, a professor of history, notes. "Hitler declared war on us after Pearl Harbor. And historians do not know to this day what Roosevelt would have done had Hitler not made his job easier and declared war on the United States, thereby getting us into a war in Europe."

It was in the midst of this troubling cultural backdrop that Inga began to be suspected of being, of all things, a Nazi spy! The accusation against her was made by an "informant" with an apparent axe to grind, a former roommate of hers and now a reporter at the *Times-Herald* named Page Huidekoper. Her proof? She'd *heard* that someone had seen a picture of Inga with Hitler taken during the Berlin Olympics in August 1936. The caption, or so Page understood, stated that Inga had worked for the German propaganda ministry. When Kick told Jack about it he, of course, didn't believe a word of it. After he confronted Inga, she assured him it was untrue. Page Huidekoper, she said, had a hidden agenda. She had a crush on Jack, Inga alleged, and was just trying to get her out of the way. From 1938 to 1940, Page had worked on Joseph Kennedy's staff in London. She would go on to become a noted reporter and activist who, as Page Wilson, handled public relations for the 1963 March on Washington, and then walked with Martin Luther King Jr. in the 1965 Selma March.

Inga explained that what actually happened was that, while in Berlin in October 1935, she managed to get an interview with Hitler for a Danish newspaper. With the Holocaust years just ahead (1941–1945), Inga's interview with Hitler was strictly from a human-interest standpoint. She asked, for instance, about his vegetarianism, why he'd never married, and how he'd become such a good speaker.

A year later, in 1936, Inga and some friends of hers joined Hitler, at his invitation, in his box at the Olympics. He also invited her to a private luncheon, and it was there that he presented her with a silver-framed, autographed picture of himself. She accepted it, but it made her nervous because it was starting to feel to her that maybe he was interested in her. After that luncheon, she said, someone with strong Nazi connections suddenly tried to recruit her as a spy. Inga immediately rejected the proposition, but she was very shaken by it. Then, a German foreign minister warned her that she needed to get out of the country right away. Being recruited was bad enough, he told her, but turning it down? That was even worse. Now very frightened, Inga took the first plane she could get out of Germany, headed to Denmark. After that, she eventually ended up in Washington. That was the whole story, she promised, nothing more. "Do you believe me?" she asked Jack. Of course he believed her.

Soon after Inga spoke to Jack about the allegations, Frank Waldrop, editor of the *Times-Herald,* was also made aware of them. On December 12, he took both Inga and Page to the FBI to explain themselves. The women were interviewed separately. Things got off to a good start for Inga when Page admitted she'd never actually *seen* the damning picture with Hitler, she'd just heard about it. But then things took a real turn when, in an effort to be fully transparent, Inga revealed that she had, indeed, sat with Hitler at the Olympics, that she'd interviewed him and had even dined with him. As the investigators furiously wrote their notes, she knew she was in big trouble. After all, this was now a time of high-alert paranoia. A person couldn't even know Hitler remotely without it being assumed they were in league with him in some way, especially a reporter working for an isolationist newspaper in Washington. Suddenly, the impression of Inga Arvad was of a femme fatale spy, a trope in the tradition of Mata Hari.

About two weeks later, Page Huidekoper produced the picture at the center of the controversy. However, Hitler wasn't even in it. It was just a publicity shot of Inga taken in 1939 during her short-lived career as an actress. Its caption, however, was provocative:

> *Meet Miss Inga Arvad, Danish Beauty, who so captivated Chancellor Adolf Hitler during a visit to Berlin that he made her Chief of Nazi Publicity in Denmark. Miss Arvad had a colorful career as a dancer, Movie Actress and newspaper woman before Herr Hitler honored her for her "perfect Nordic beauty."*

Inga insisted she'd never seen the picture before. She also admitted, however, that the caption was at least partially true. Hitler had, in fact, remarked that she was "the most perfect example of Nordic beauty" after her interview with him. Though still insistent that she'd never worked for Nazis, she was now definitely a person the FBI felt required a lot more investigation. Thus, on Christmas Eve 1941, Inga's case file went straight to the top, to director J. Edgar Hoover. Hoover said he wanted updates on it "not less frequently than weekly."

Though Jack was shaken by these recent surprising developments, he still believed in Inga. "We're going to fight this," he told her, though he didn't know exactly how. Despite the latest trouble, they had actually begun talking marriage. Even given how fast romances developed during these uncertain war times—couples often moved swiftly, feeling that tomorrow was in such question—this one had sure grown quickly. It had only been three months since Jack met Inga. Obviously, they couldn't move forward, though, until she divorced Paul Fejos, from whom she'd now been separated for about two years. Meanwhile, Jack's father had summoned Jack for a sit-down in Palm Beach. Therefore, the plan was for Jack to go to Florida after the Christmas holiday, while she would head to New York to ask Fejos for a divorce.

GOOD NEWS AND BAD NEWS

So, what's the story, Jack?" Joe wanted to know as he stared at the son standing before him. "Sit down," he commanded. Already tense, Jack said he preferred to stand. Joe's best friend, Arthur Houghton, was also present. He offered to leave, but Joe said no; he wanted him to stay. "I want you to hear this," he said. The three men were in the study of the Kennedys' mansion on North Ocean Boulevard, where the family always retreated for the winter months.

Arthur Houghton, a former entertainment manager, was about ten years Joe's senior. The two had met in 1917 and, in the 1930s, tried to start a production company. While that didn't work out, they became best friends. Arthur was married to vaudeville star Sallie Fisher; they had two grown children, Arthur (Andrew) and Mary. They lived in California, but Arthur often visited the Kennedys in Palm Beach or Hyannis Port. Later, in 1945, Arthur would hire Mary's best friend, eighteen-year-old Janine Burke, as his secretary. Janine, who is now in her nineties, wrote an unpublished memoir about her life with Houghton and the Kennedys called *Unlikely Alliances*. In her book, Janine remembered the story of the showdown between father and son over Inga Arvad, as per Arthur's telling of it to her.

Joe had heard about Inga and wanted an explanation. Jack knew there was no point in trying to hide anything from him. He was right about that. His father already knew everything there was to know, even about the FBI's investigation, since he and J. Edgar Hoover were good friends. Jack told him he was certain Inga wasn't a spy, that it was a ridiculous and specious story. "Conjecture presented as fact" is what he called it. That didn't matter, Joe told him, because "perception is reality. The truth is whatever it looks like." The bottom line, he said, was that Jack couldn't continue with Inga, that she was bad for his future and bad for the future of their family.

Jack disagreed, of course. "I want her in my life, Dad," he insisted. He wasn't going to end it with her.

Joe couldn't believe his son's imprudence. "Are you aware that she's been married twice before and is still with her second husband?" he asked.

Yes, Jack said, he knew it.

"But we're *Catholics,*" Joe reminded him, raising his voice. "Have you thought about your mother? Why, this'll send her to the nearest hospital. You know how she gets!"

The real reason for this meeting, Joe said, was because he had upsetting news. Inga's story, he told Jack, had reached the navy. ONI assistant director Howard Kingman was about to file papers to have Jack discharged. Getting cashiered, as it was called, would be a disaster for Jack. Not only would it be an indelible black mark on his name, it would lay waste to any dream he ever had of seeing action. He could forget about politics, too, Joe told him. Maybe he could do something about Kingman, Joe said, but not as long as Inga remained in the picture.

Joe stood up. Glaring down at Jack, he concluded, "I have good news and bad." He said the good news was that Jack was one of the smartest people he knew. He'd always felt that way, he reminded him. The bad news was that Jack had allowed things to get this far. As soon as he'd learned that Inga was divorced once, let alone twice, Joe said, he should've walked away from her. Most certainly, learning about the espionage allegations should've been the end of it. "But there's better news," Joe concluded. "You were born a Kennedy," he said, "so, of course, you'll do what's right."

"Thanks for the condescending words of wisdom," Jack said, barely under his breath. This kind of backtalk was very out of character. He wasn't known to mouth off to his father. Joe looked at him as if he'd lost his mind. Trying not to completely lose his temper, Joe lowered his voice to an angry whisper and warned Jack that he needed to learn his "goddamn place." Bending down and with his face inches from his son's, he told him what would happen next. Jack would break up with his "Nazi bitch," and he would do so with a smile on his face. He then turned and stormed from the room.

Now alone with Arthur Houghton, Jack was clearly angry, his face twisted into a scowl. He wasn't the type to back down, even with his own father. As if his political instincts were already fixed, he considered the reprimand to be a challenge.

"What're you going to do now, son?" Arthur asked him.

Jack looked at him with hard eyes. "Marry the Nazi bitch, Mr. Houghton," he said. "What do you think I'm going to do?"

JOE'S UNLIKELY ALLIANCE

While Jack was in Palm Beach conferring with his father, Inga was in New York meeting with Paul Fejos, as planned. She was truthful with him and told him she was in love with someone else, which, she later wrote, "made him insanely jealous," especially given that the "someone else" was a famous Kennedy twenty years his junior. She wrote that Fejos was "unable to keep a sneer from his tone of voice" when talking about Jack. He told her there was no way he would ever give her a divorce. She left, upset. She wasn't gone more than an hour, she later estimated, before Paul apparently figured out how to get in touch with Joe Kennedy. He called him in Palm Beach, introduced himself, and said he had a matter of extreme urgency to discuss relating to his son Jack.

It had been only a couple of days since Joe talked to Jack about Inga, and now the woman's ex-husband wanted to meet with him? How could he resist? On December 30, Joe told the family he had to leave for a day or two on business.

The next day, Joe flew to New York to meet with Paul Fejos. Fejos told him Inga had asked him for a divorce so that she could marry Jack and become a Kennedy. Joe assured him that this would never happen. "I'll take care of it," Joe told Fejos. After their brief meeting, Joe returned to Florida, not telling anyone why he'd left or where he'd been.

On January 1, Inga collected Jack at Union Station upon his return to Washington. She wrote that, reunited with him, she was "happy as a bird, without a care, a fear or trouble in the world—just in love." She wrote:

He is so big and strong and when you talk to him or see him you always have the impression that his big white teeth are ready to bite off a huge chunk of life. There is determination in his green Irish eyes. He has two backbones, his own and his father's. Somehow he has hit the bull's eye in every respect. "He can't fail," I have said to myself very often. I love him more than anything else or anybody in the world.

Clearly, Inga had fallen for this man and believed all was well in her world, despite the unsuccessful meeting she'd just had with her estranged husband. Her happiness wouldn't last long, however. By the end of the week, the FBI's round-the-clock surveillance of her was underway. She soon realized she was being followed, her mail confiscated, her bank account scrutinized, her phone tapped. They even broke into her apartment and rifled through her papers, taking pictures of anything they thought might lead to an espionage charge. "I felt the walls closing in," she recalled. "I had heard of innocent people spending years in jail, even going as far as the electric chair. Every time I heard the phone click, I was sure that it was the FBI, and every man who looked at me twice or followed me for a block, I was convinced must be an FBI agent." Then, on January 11, 1942, Paul Fejos sent her a troubling telegram:

There is one thing I want to tell you in connection with your Jack. Before you let yourself go into this thing any deeper, lock, stock and barrel, have you thought that maybe the boy's father or family might not like the idea?

What was *that* supposed to mean? It wouldn't take long for her to find out.

On Monday morning, January 12, the day after Paul Fejos's warning, Inga picked up the *Times-Herald* to search out her column. When she came across Walter Winchell's, she was shocked to read:

One of ex-Ambassador Kennedy's eligible sons is the target of a Washington gal columnist's affections. So much so—she's consulted her barrister about divorcing her explorer-groom . . . Pa Kennedy no like.

Alarmed, Inga immediately called Jack. After he raced over to her apartment, he telephoned the paper's editor and publisher, Frank Waldrop and Cissy Patterson, to demand a meeting. An hour later, he and Inga were sitting on one side of Patterson's desk, Frank Waldrop on a chair in the corner. "How could this happen?" Jack demanded as he slapped the newspaper onto Patterson's desk. She apologized and said she hadn't seen the item prior to publication, or she wouldn't have let it run. When Jack asked how many other papers syndicated Winchell's column, she told him about a thousand. At that, his eyes went dark, his face went red, and, raising his voice to a roar, he demanded that she "keep my goddamn name and the name of my goddamn family out of your newspaper."

Who tipped off Walter Winchell? Right away, Jack felt he knew. It had to have been Joe. He figured his father planted the item in hopes of sparking a controversy so big it would bring the problem of Inga to a head, which is exactly what it did. Jack didn't know about his father's meeting with Paul Fejos, not yet anyway, and that it had been the motivation behind the item. Now, he felt he'd made a big mistake in standing up to his father in Palm Beach. "Poking the bear is never a good idea," he later said. "You don't know how the bear will poke you back."

The next day, Joe called Jack to talk things over. Inga was in the room listening to her boyfriend's side of the conversation, which was with an attitude much more conciliatory than what Jack had shown in Palm Beach. In a diary entry, she wrote:

> He [Joe] starts out the conversation amiably and asks John about trivial matters, then he gets down to the item in the column. From years of habit, which John hasn't outgrown, he is scared of his father. "Of course," the old man says, "you are not going to marry her, are you?" John wants to explain but feels that it can't be done on the phone. He replies meekly, "Honestly, Dad, I don't know, she is a great girl."

A FATHER'S SCHEME

Things started moving quickly. The very day after Jack's telephone conversation with his father, he got a surprising telephone call: he was being transferred out of Washington to a desk job in Charleston, South Carolina.

What the hell?

Immediately, the young Kennedy flew to Boston, where the patriarch was at the time. When he told Joe there was no way he was going to South Carolina, the old man held up a silencing hand. "You should be thanking me," he told him. He explained that higher-ups in the military had read the Winchell column and, for them, it was the final straw. They'd decided to give Jack the boot. Luckily, someone called Joe to warn him about their plans. To protect Jack's future, Joe said, he arranged for the transfer. It was either that or be cashiered dishonorably and maybe even face a court-martial. The transfer was set to happen in ten days. Unfortunately, Joe added, due to wartime restrictions Jack wouldn't be able to leave a seventy-mile radius of the Charleston Naval Yard, meaning, though Joe didn't actually come out and say it, he wouldn't be able to fly to Washington to see Inga.

Of course, Jack knew exactly what was going on. His father had orchestrated a transfer for the sole purpose of putting distance between him and Inga. Jack was enraged by it. He flew back to Washington, went to his office, swept everything off his desk, and hurled a typewriter across the room, all the while cursing his father. "I don't run from a fight," Jack then told Inga, "even one with my old man." He then spent the nights of January 16, 17, and 18 with her in Washington, according to the FBI agent maintaining a vigil outside her apartment. He left on January 19, en route to Palm Beach.

Once in Florida, Jack ran into an old friend from his brief Stanford days named Henry James. Of Inga, he said, "I'm afraid she's dangerous. She has connections with fascists in Germany. But as to being a spy, it's hard to believe she's doing that, because she's not only beautiful, she's warm, she's affectionate, she's wonderful in bed. But you know, goddamn it, Henry," he concluded, "I found out that son of a bitch Hoover put a microphone under the mattress."

Henry James warned Jack there was more at stake than just his future with a woman he'd known for only a brief time. He could actually be sentenced to prison, James said, for consorting with the enemy. When James urged him to stay away from Inga, Jack just stared at him. It was one thing hearing this kind of thing from his disapproving father, quite another from a trusted friend. James's words made a real impression.

Meanwhile, Inga, completely unwilling to ever accept her boyfriend's pending transfer, was determined to make an impression of her own.

"DISTRUST IS A VERY FUNNY THING"

Father and son Kennedy were having breakfast in the kitchen when the doorbell rang and, soon after, a servant handed Joe a telegram. It was for Rose, who was at church. As Joe read it, he pounded his fist on the table. "It's from your goddamn spy!" he roared. "She sends Mother telegrams now? I thought we agreed, Jack?" Jack asked to see it, but Joe tore it into pieces and shoved them into his pocket as he bolted from the room, upset.

Later, after Joe cooled off, he and Jack talked about it. Trying to keep a level head now, Joe said it was obvious to him that Inga was trying to establish a rapport with Rose in order to make it more difficult for Jack to cut ties. As much as it pained him, Jack couldn't disagree. A line had definitely been crossed. What Inga had done combined with Henry James's earlier warning caused him to now feel he should probably end it. He was exhausted and worn down.

On January 24, Jack arrived for duty in Charleston, South Carolina. A couple days later, Inga showed up unannounced. Immediately, Jack's defenses melted. The two went to a dive bar, spent the night drinking and dancing, and then went back to his place for sex. The next night, the same thing—the bar and then home for sex. Inga noticed, however, that Jack seemed withdrawn and less talkative and wasn't sure what to make of it. When she got back to Washington, Kick leveled with her. Jack had told her he was thinking about ending it with Inga because of the telegram. Inga knew Joe had to be behind it all. Upset, she shot off an angry letter to Jack:

*Distrust is a very funny thing, isn't it? A peculiar feeling at the realization
that the person I love most in the world is afraid of me. Not of me directly but
of the actions I might take some day. I know who prompted you to believe or
rather disbelieve in me, but still, I dislike it. However, I am not going to try and
make you change . . . because big Joe has a stronger hand than I. I can kick and
scream, and it will not bring me any further. A very passive part in a tragic-
comic play, that is the one I have . . .*

When Jack got the letter almost a week later, it sounded to him like
Inga was becoming unhinged. He was concerned. When he first met her,
she was so self-reliant and confident. Now, she seemed weak and clingy,
and after such a short time together? It was starting to feel to him like she
might become a real responsibility, and he wasn't sure he was up for it. He
called her. Even if they were to break up, he told her, she'd have to know
she'd still be okay. They'd both survive. In fact, he'd already survived a
hell of a lot more in his short life, he said. Despite his words, she was very
weepy. Moved, he suggested she fly to Charleston so they could talk about
it further, which she did on Friday, February 6.

Aware of the ongoing surveillance, Jack had Inga check into the Fort
Sumter Hotel using the alias "Barbara White." Years later he'd tell George
Smathers of this time: "I actually don't know how it happened, but I was
in so goddamn deep and couldn't make up my mind about her. I'd never
been in love, so what did I know? I was confused about a lot of things, but
not about the way I felt for this girl, just about how I should handle it, or
whether I should even try to handle it, at all."

Even with the alias, the FBI was well aware of the couple's location.
A listening device planted by the agency recorded the two of them in their
most intimate moments. The subsequent report stated: "It's worth noting
the amount of times Kennedy had sexual intercourse with Mrs. Fejos."

THE BIRD STOPS SINGING

In the middle of February 1942, a letter from Jack's influential friend Lem Billings turned out to be the catalyst for a final decision about Inga. Lem felt Jack was being foolish and shortsighted for continuing with her. There were far more important things going on in the world, he wrote, such as, obviously, the war. If Jack truly wanted to serve in the military, why then was he allowing his life to be hijacked by a woman he'd known for just a few months? Even Lem, with eyesight so poor he'd been rejected for service until Joe Kennedy pulled some strings for him, was about to leave for Africa with an ambulance corps. He'd be seeing real combat, whereas Jack would be stuck in his, as Lem put it, "boring, lousy, stinking desk job in Charleston."

Jack decided that maybe Lem was right. He called his father and told him he'd made the tough decision to end it with Inga, but felt he owed it to her to do it in person. Because of the travel restrictions, he needed assistance to get to Washington. Happy about the news, Joe made a few calls and obtained the necessary permission.

On Saturday, February 28, Jack arrived in Washington. The next morning, Lem showed up at Inga's front door. Jack explained that he'd wanted to see his pal before he left for Africa. Inga was suspicious, however, especially when, after the two went for a long walk, Lem took off without saying goodbye. Later, he'd say he'd only come to be with his friend because "Jack was very afraid he'd change his mind and felt he might need backup just in case."

"Sit down," Jack told Inga once they were alone. "There's something I need to tell you." Ironically, of all the conversations the FBI recorded, this one, when Jack told Inga it was over, wasn't one of them. The agency's wire-tapping mechanism malfunctioned, giving the couple accidental privacy.

"I couldn't fight it," Inga said many years later. "I wanted to beg him, but I caught myself. I thought, *Wait. What am I doing? Stop it, Inga. Don't you dare beg. Don't you dare.*"

It was over, but not really. There would be many more letters and phone calls over the next few weeks. It was difficult to just end it cold, as is often the case when love is still in the early stages of passion. Plus, Jack wasn't a quitter. If he really wanted something, he'd fight hard for it. Ending it with Inga was something he knew he needed to do, but not something he wanted to do, and Inga knew it. In March, she wrote to Jack:

> *It is funny, we are so well matched. Only because I have done some foolish things, must I say to myself, No. At last, I realize that it is true: We pay for everything in life.*

At the end of that same month, Jack suffered a crippling attack of back spasms. In his weakened state, he called Inga and begged to see her. Completely folding, he now said that everything that happened had been his father's fault. None of it would've occurred, he told her, had Joe not planted the Walter Winchell item. He called it "a stone-cold move," and, in fact, would feel this way for many years to come. Now, he wanted to forget everything and start over again, this time without his father's undue influence. Inga knew better. It was time to get off this merry-go-round, and she wrote:

> *A human breast to me has always been a little like a cage, where a bird sits behind. Some birds sing cheerfully, some mourn, others are envious and nasty. Mine always sang. It did especially for a few months this winter. In fact, it sang so loudly that I refused to listen to that other little sensible creature called reason. It took the FBI, the US Navy, nasty gossip, envy, hatred and big Joe, before the bird stopped singing.*
>
> *In the beginning, I was just stunned, darling. Then . . . I slowly woke up.*

HOW LOVE ENDS

―――――――

I don't know who I am anymore," Inga told Kick over lunch in a French restaurant. She said she felt as if she'd lost her entire identity now that she'd lost Jack. When she looked in the mirror, a stranger stared back at her. It had been a little more than three months since Jack ended it. She appeared drawn and tired, her beauty somehow faded from recent weeks of big emotion and great sorrow.

"I'm sorry I ever introduced you two," Kick told her.

"I guess I just never knew for sure how love ends," was Inga's response. Kick was surprised, especially since Inga had been married twice before.

In July, Inga resigned from the *Times-Herald,* her once-promising career as a journalist ruined by everything that had happened. Kick took over her column and, about ten years later, Jack's future wife, Jackie Bouvier, would also write for the same newspaper.

In August, J. Edgar Hoover and the FBI sought to drop the investigation into Inga Arvad, having found no tangible evidence against her. However, FDR personally directed the agency to continue looking into the matter. It was thought that bad blood between him and Joe Kennedy was behind the president's decision to keep pressing against Inga. No wrongdoing would ever be discovered, though, not a thing. She would never be indicted, never brought to court, never convicted of anything. For Inga, it was all a life-ruining experience for no reason. She would try to stay positive, though, if only for the man she still loved. Again, her words to him:

I can't wait to see you on top of the world. That is a very good reason why war should stop, so that it may give you a chance to show the world and yourself that here is a man of the future. Should I die before you reach the top step of the golden ladder, then Jack, dear—if there is life after death, as you believe in—be I in heaven or hell, that's the moment I shall stretch a hand out and try to keep you balancing on that—the most precarious of all steps.

PART IV

Miss Bouvier

GETTING TO KNOW YOU

When the Kennedys congregated in Hyannis Port for their annual Fourth of July celebration, making it even more special was Jack Kennedy's decision to bring his new girlfriend, Jackie Bouvier. His family had certainly never known anyone quite like her. Whereas Eunice, Jean, and Pat walked around in shorts and T-shirts with sneakers, Jackie favored flowing skirts and strappy sandals. She was meticulous with her careful coif and perfect makeup. She preferred smoking and reading fashion magazines to playing touch football. In decades' worth of books and articles about the Kennedys, there've been reams of analysis about how different she was from the others. It can all be boiled down to one simple fact: she knew who she was, she liked who she was, and she wasn't going to be anyone else, even for them.

The accommodations at the Big House during that time were, as usual, casual yet elegant. In Jackie's large room facing the bay, she found blue stationery, envelopes, and postcards with pens, pencils, and even stamps, all arranged on a small desk. There was also a breakfast menu on the bedside table in case she wanted to dine in her room. This was actually a big concession on Rose's part. She usually insisted breakfast be served in the kitchen, but . . . anything for Jack's special friend, who she called "Miss Bouvier." There was also a fireplace behind a pleated paper fan. A small note was attached to it, the writing neat: "Not for summer use. Thank you. The Kennedys." A bowl of fresh flowers was placed at the center of a window ledge. Outside Jackie's room, the hallway was lined with framed photographs of Kennedy and Fitzgerald relatives, most of them long departed. In the middle of the display was a portrait of Rose and Joe, both with gravely staring eyes.

There were sixteen for dinner on Jackie's first night, and that included Bobby and Ethel; Eunice and her fiancé, Sargent Shriver; Pat, Jean, Teddy, and their cousins, Joey, Ann, and Mary Jo Gargan, who were practically being raised by Rose and Joe. Their mother, Agnes, was Rose's sister. Joe's good friend Morton Downey and Downey's son, Morton Jr.—nineteen at the time and later a controversial talk show host—were also present. In a 1999 interview, Downey Jr. recalled, "It was what you'd expect of the Kennedys—boisterous, talking over themselves, current events, history. You had to keep up but, as I recall it, Jackie held her own."

"As we ate, an odd little woman ran about inspecting lampshades," recalled Joey Gargan in 1997. "Later, when Jackie asked me about her, I explained that Aunt Rose always asked the help to be sure to check all the expensive silk shades and make sure light bulbs weren't burning brown spots into them. 'Oh my gosh,' Jackie said. 'My mother does the same thing.'"

Jackie found Rose reserved. "Aunt Rose wanted you to be immediately charming, fascinating, and delightful," said her grandniece Kerry McCarthy. "She had those expectations. If you were an entertaining person, she would be interested in you. If you were dull, she wouldn't be. Jack was the same way. If you were too slow, or maybe not that fascinating, he'd move on to the next person very quickly. Jackie wasn't one to prove herself, though. She wanted you to be charmed by her, of course, but she wasn't going to work for it."

Jackie didn't mind Rose, though. In fact, she found her intriguing. When the subject turned to fashion, Rose told her that whenever she couldn't decide on a gown, she'd hire a photographer to take pictures of her in all the different choices. She'd then make her final decision based on how well the outfits were photographed. Jackie thought that was brilliant. She said she admired that Rose was "her own person in a family where that has to be difficult because, to be honest, they all look alike and all act alike."

Jackie also couldn't help but notice that Rose's relationship to Joe was very different than her mother's to Hugh. Jackie later wrote that Joe "has so overpowered Mrs. Kennedy he doesn't even speak to her when she's around and her only solace now is her religion. I don't think Jack's mother is too bright," she concluded, "and she would rather say a rosary than read a book." Jackie said that when Rose would tell Joe, "I'll pray for you," it sounded like a judgment against him, not an act of kindness toward him.

For her part, Jackie had enjoyed Joe when she met him earlier, and during this visit they became even closer. She appreciated his humor. For instance, before dessert was served, a maid brought out finger bowls. According to protocol, once the treat was finished guests were supposed to dip and rinse their fingers before leaving the table. Joe winked at Jackie, put the bowl to his mouth, and gulped the contents as if it were a shot of whiskey. Rose frowned her disapproval while Joe and Jackie shared their secret giggle. Jackie said later that she was familiar with finger bowls because her mother insisted upon them, "even at breakfast and lunch."

Morton Downey Jr. had one more story about Jackie's stay. On the last night, Jack asked him if he could borrow his car, a 1950 Plymouth, so that he could take Jackie for a drive. "Me and Joey Gargan decide to follow them to see where Jack is taking her," Downey recalled. "He gets to the bottom of a hill and stops. Joey and I park a little distance away, get out, crouch down, and sneak over to their car. I tell Joey, 'When I say *one, two, three,* I'll swing open the car door and we'll surprise them.' So, we do that—*one, two, three*—and I fling open the door.

"There's Jackie, lying on her back on the front seat, her head jammed up against the driver's door, her dress way above her hips, one leg slung over the seat. When she sees me, she lets out a scream. Jack, who's kneeling on the floor next to her, hits his head hard on the steering wheel as he jumps up. He looks at me and there's this awkward moment before he says, 'Um . . . we lost the cigarette lighter down here, somewhere.' I laugh and say, 'Yeah, sure, Jack. The cigarette lighter.' Right."

THE JOB DESCRIPTION

After the holiday, the Republican National Convention convened in Chicago. Its delegates nominated General Dwight D. Eisenhower for president and Senator Richard Nixon of California for vice president. What a stunning climb to the top this was for Nixon, who'd started in Congress the same time as Jack and had just gotten into the Senate in 1950. A couple weeks later, Democrats nominated Illinois governor Adlai Stevenson for president and Senator John Sparkman of Alabama for VP.

For the rest of 1952, Jack would continue to canvass the state while stumping for his own senatorial campaign against Henry Cabot Lodge, as well as for Stevenson's presidential run. Joe had already come to believe his son had what it took to be a persuasive politician, but watching him in action these days was still a revelation. The energy Jack created and the way people reacted to it was exciting. "Time to turn on the ol' BP," he'd say before an event, meaning "big personality." Joe noted, "My son's an actor, the way he turns himself on. Who does that? Movie stars. That's who do that."

Because he was so busy, Jack wouldn't see Jackie for two months. He felt a little bad about it, especially after having had sex with her in Hyannis Port, but it had been the equivalent of a one-night stand for him. It didn't mean much compared to what he'd had with Inga so many years earlier. She had been spectacular and, in a very real sense, he still wasn't over her. He talked about her all the time and said he regretted the way it ended. None of the women he'd been with in the last ten years meant as much to him. He still blamed his father for ruining what he feared was his only chance at ever being happy. The two men never discussed it, though. It was as if they knew better; it would only lead to a fight, and what was the point? Joe didn't want to hear it. If he hadn't stepped in and ended it with Inga, he told his own intimates, there was no way Jack would be in the position he was in today, and if he couldn't see that, "the hell with him." Joe wasn't going to apologize for anything he'd done back then to protect his son, his future, and the Kennedy name. "If he finds someone who's not a Nazi spy," he liked to tell people, "maybe I'll approve of her. Until then, he needs to shut up about it because it's in the past and what's done is done."

For her part, Jackie was just as uninspired by Jack as he was by her. She told Lee that being with him was "okay but sort of . . . blah." In today's world, their dynamic would likely be chalked up to a lack of chemistry, especially where Jack was concerned. When he was with Jackie, it was fine. When he wasn't, that was fine, too. His days were so full, it sometimes felt there was barely a moment to breathe. Mostly, he was just on autopilot, moving from one scheduled moment to the next, all the while keeping an incredibly tight schedule.

In October 1952, on a flight from Miami to Palm Beach, the subject of Jackie came up in discussion between Jack, Joe, and Senator George Smathers. As Jack sat in his seat with his head tilted back, tired to the bone and not wanting to engage, Joe asked George his opinion about Jackie. "I think Jack can do better," he answered, turning to his friend. "Don't get me wrong. I like the girl just fine," George said, "but I don't see you marrying her. You're obviously lukewarm on her." He also sensed Jackie was too independent to be a politician's wife. "You need a woman who'll just shut up, stand there, and smile," he said.

Joe couldn't disagree. "That *is* the job description," he concluded.

Jackie or no Jackie, Joe felt Jack needed a wife. He was never going to get into the White House without one. The last time a president didn't have a First Lady was James Buchanan in the 1800s, before the Civil War. Joe said Jack needed to start thinking seriously about moving forward with Jackie or someone else.

While Joe thought maybe an Irish Catholic girl would do, George wasn't so sure. Jack's Catholicism was already controversial enough, he said, what if his wife was of another faith? Protestant, maybe? Would that, George wondered, work better in a general election? "I don't know," Joe decided, "but if not Jackie Bouvier, who?" George didn't have an answer. "I actually don't care who," Joe concluded, "as long as she didn't go to Hitler's funeral." Jack shot his father a look. George later said he had no idea what Joe was talking about since he hadn't yet been briefed on the saga of Inga Arvad.

Jack reclined in his chair, opened his newspaper, and laid it over his face.

"BARELY PLAUSIBLE"

O n election night, November 4, 1952, Joe Kennedy's apartment on Beacon Street in Boston was filled with family and friends. Janet Des-Rosiers recalled, "By 1:00 A.M., the results were still unknown. That night, I slept in a small room off the living room next to a telephone. It was my responsibility to answer it should Henry Cabot Lodge decide to concede. At 6:30 A.M. he did just that. With great pleasure, I woke up Jack and his father with the good news that he'd just won his Senate seat. Cheers of joy filled the air!"

Though the Dwight Eisenhower–Richard Nixon ticket had carried the country by seven million votes, and Republicans also had both chambers, JFK had overcome the general Republican sweep with his own seventy-thousand-vote plurality against Lodge. He was now Senator John F. Kennedy and his victory real. It was just the beginning, too. His father was already sporting a blue tie with a silver inscription: "Kennedy for President."

A couple of days later, Jack finally called Jackie. By this time, it'd been five months since she'd heard from him and she'd pretty much given up on him. She was hurt. It was as if he'd gotten what he wanted from her, then ditched her. Still, she had to admit she was happy to hear from him and did want to congratulate him on his victory. She didn't see the point in just writing him off or, as she later put it, "he wasn't necessarily someone a woman could simply just forget. There was a thing about him which, I don't know, rather lingered . . ." Therefore, she invited him to join her and her stepbrother Yusha for dinner at Merrywood. The three got together that night, and the next night, as well. However, Jack felt pressured, or so he told Lem: "I think she wants more from me than what I can give." The next day, he and Jackie had an awkward phone call. The tone felt final, like a breakup. By the time she hung up, she was angry. "I feel like I got slapped in the face with a wet fish," she told her mother.

Jackie hadn't deluded herself into thinking she and Jack were in the midst of some sort of great love affair. Still, she felt he could've been a little nicer to her. She couldn't understand how a man with such passion for politics could be so utterly dispassionate about his personal life or, more to the point, about her. Was he so emotionally hollow? If only he could be more outgoing and fun, like his father. Instead, he seemed withholding and cold, like his mother.

Shortly after that phone conversation, Jack left for a European trip with Torbert Macdonald. Working at a newspaper, it didn't take long for Jackie to figure out he'd gone overseas without even saying goodbye. He'd be gone for three weeks, she learned, returning on December 17. She decided it must be over and she wasn't going to beg for more attention. Janet agreed and urged her to forget all about Jack Kennedy. He's "barely plausible," she said, "and not worth the oil stain he leaves in our driveway." But then something happened to change her mind.

One evening, Hugh came home from a business trip to New York with surprising news. His Wall Street contacts had done a little research into the Kennedys' wealth and learned the family was worth $200 million (about $2 billion in today's money). He'd also heard that Jack alone had a $2 million trust fund (more than $40 million in today's money). In five years' time, *Fortune* would publish its first list of the richest people in the country. It would place Joe Kennedy in the $100 to $200 million group, which is equivalent to about $2.5 billion to $3.6 billion in today's money.

Janet knew the Kennedys were wealthy, but *this* wealthy? That changed everything.

In the past, Jackie would often ask her mother, "Why do you care so much about how we spend our money?"

Janet would shoot back, "*Our* money? You mean *my* money." True, it was hers now, but only by marriage to Hugh Auchincloss.

How well Janet remembered what it was like after divorcing Jack Bouvier, when she found herself pounding away on a small adding machine in her sewing room, trying to figure out which bills to pay so she could still have money left for Jackie's braces. She was even forced to take a job as a model at a Macy's department store in Manhattan.

Janet wore her present wealth proudly because she felt she deserved it after a hard-knocks life. In her heart, though, she knew the truth: she hadn't earned affluence, she'd married into it. That's what she also wanted for her daughter—marriage to a wealthy man. She felt it was the only way Jackie would ever be secure, since she was unlikely to inherit money from her own father given his financial unpredictability. While Hugh was certainly rich, most of his estate would go to his biological children from previous marriages with little, if any, left for Jackie and Lee. This was a reality that had been worrying Janet ever since she and her daughters moved into the Auchincloss manse, back when Jackie was thirteen and Lee, nine.

Given this latest revelation about the Kennedys' prosperity, Janet had a change of heart about Jack. Now, she wasn't so sure Jackie should end it with him. She told her they both needed to "wake up and smell the coffee." It was very possible Jack Kennedy was the answer to their problems.

At the end of December, Jack asked Jackie to be at his side for a very important event, his swearing in as a senator during the opening session of the Eighty-Third Congress in Washington on January 3, 1953. This was such a momentous occasion, Jackie couldn't help but be flattered and she was excited to be included. That evening, after keeping him waiting an appropriate amount of time, she glided down the staircase in a full-length blue fox coat with a fur hood.

"Wow," he exclaimed, his eyes popping.

"Too much?" she asked.

"Not at all," he told her with a grin. "In fact, they should swear *you* in."

Two weeks later, Jack asked her to accompany him to the first of President Eisenhower's two inaugural balls on January 20, another big deal. Jack now apparently wanted her at his side at major events, and Jackie was excited, as was her mother. Prior to that event, he was hosting a cocktail party at his home, to which Jackie and Lee, along with Lee's fiancé, Michael Canfield, were also invited.

Watching his friend move forward with Jackie seemed to put Lem on guard. Was he being territorial? Or was he just looking out for his friend? He would often talk about the way Jack lost himself with Inga ten years earlier, and had even taken credit for giving Jack clarity that helped him end it with her. A lot of people in Jack's life felt that Lem wouldn't be happy with any girl who stepped into Jack's world, and he may have even spoken to Jackie herself with an eye to making trouble. He later claimed he only wanted to give her "a little perspective." At the risk of being what he later described as "an awfully disloyal friend," he filled her in on what she might

be up against in dating Jack. "You're going to have to be very understanding at the beginning because he has never really settled down with one girl
before," he told her. She said she'd figured as much. "A man of thirty-five
is very difficult to live with," Lem continued, and Jackie agreed. Years later,
she'd bring it up to Lem and tell him, "I realized all that you said, and I took
it as a challenge."

At that same cocktail party, Michael Canfield brought something else
up to Jackie that worried her. "You know you've got yourself a war hero
there," he told her. "So, what has he told you about it?"

Her answer: "Nothing."

While he was always asking her questions about herself and her family,
he rarely was forthcoming about his own life. He was always evasive—
about everything.

Blair Fuller, later the editor emeritus of the *Paris Review* but who, in the
1950s, consulted with Michael Canfield at Hamish Hamilton Publishers,
recalled, "Michael was very intuitive about people, and he felt Kennedy
was very controlling in making sure people only had information about
him he wanted them to have, nothing more. I'm not sure we realized it at
the time, but today we understand this behavior to be a form of narcissism.
While we traditionally think of the narcissist as the person who can't stop
talking about himself, conversely it can also be the person who controls
what's known about him, and that was definitely Kennedy's way.

"Michael told Jackie it was a bad sign that Jack wouldn't talk about his
life. 'But I know better than to push him,' Jackie said. She said his mother
had raised Jack to believe it was a sin of pride to go on and on about himself.
Michael didn't buy it. PT-109 wasn't a secret, after all. Jack often alluded to it
in his campaign speeches. 'Does this mean he doesn't love me?' Jackie asked
him. Michael said maybe a better question was: 'Should *you* love *him*?' She
didn't know what to say to that. 'He's just such an odd duck,' she told him,
to which Michael said, 'No, Jackie, *you're* the odd duck.' When she looked at
him with those doe eyes of hers, he said, 'You work at a goddamn newspaper, don't you? Look it up. It was on the front page of the *New York Times*,
for Christ's sake. Where've you been?' Now, she was embarrassed. 'You're
right,' she said. 'I guess I am the odd duck.'"

Two days later, Jackie called her brother-in-law. "My God, Michael,"
she exclaimed. "All of that really happened? He's an American hero!"

Michael chuckled and said, "Yes, Jackie, all that really happened and,
yes, he *is* an American hero.'"

PART V

Destiny

HERO

====

The story of every great man of history has that one seminal moment that defines who he is not only for himself but for the world. Certainly, the saga of John Fitzgerald Kennedy has more than just a single occurrence to distinguish it. However, one that most certainly stands out is his heroism on the PT-109 in the deep Pacific in 1943. What happened then was a rite of passage for young Jack in that it was the moment a sickly, studious youngster was transformed into a soldier, a man of great distinction and honor, just like many of those characters he'd been so fascinated by in fantasy and history books . . . indeed, a hero.

By the spring of '43, Joe Kennedy couldn't understand why Jack was still so despondent and melancholy after Inga. Certainly, he'd never before spent a single second bereft over any woman, let alone one he'd known for only a few months. He viewed it as a weakness and he didn't like it. "Don't you dare get weak on me," Joe kept telling Jack. "Vulnerability is a liability." Jack couldn't help it. It was as if he was going through some sort of withdrawal, and he was simply unable to snap out of it. He was just sad, every day sad.

Joe wanted Jack to get on with things and decided that one way to ensure it was to get him away from the tedious desk job in Charleston, which he'd arranged just to get Jack away from Inga. Because he knew Jack still wanted to see active duty, he appealed to the head of the Office of Naval Intelligence to allow a private Boston doctor to vouch for his good health. Joe had lied to get Jack the miserable desk job, and now he was lying to get him away from it. With the doctor's note in hand, Joe petitioned the PT lieutenant to enroll Jack in the Motor Torpedo Boat Squadron Training Center in Melville, Rhode Island. Eventually, Jack would be assigned a PT boat—patrol torpedo boat. While Joe was certainly controlling things as always, he was also protecting his son, because the PT-109 on which Jack was assigned was set to patrol a relatively safe zone in the Panama Canal. Joe never intended for Jack to see real action, just for him to get out of Charleston.

This time, Jack was aware of what his father was doing behind his back. He was also sick of being manipulated. He felt he had to assert himself, and the time was now. Therefore, while preparing for the Panama mission, he took it upon himself to contact a family friend who was chairman of the Naval Affairs Committee. Jack asked if there was some way he could get into real combat. That friend helped facilitate his transfer, which eventually led to Jack commanding the PT-109 in the Solomon Islands.

In the push-and-pull of their father-son relationship, Joe had given a little but, this time, Jack had taken a lot more. Of course, Joe was unhappy about it. For his boy to end up in the middle of combat was never what he wanted. However, what was done was done and, for once, Jack had scored a big point over him. Joe actually had a begrudging respect for the way he'd maneuvered things. It showed something in him he hadn't seen much of since Inga, something he knew he'd need in politics. "He's got gumption," Joe said. "You can't go wrong with gumption." Joe told Arthur Houghton that Jack was probably in some "disgusting little hole-in-the-wall bar getting drunk off his ass while celebrating getting one over on the old bastard—me."

So, now, Lieutenant John F. Kennedy and his crew of twelve were headed for the South Pacific, right in the middle of what Jack hoped and prayed was some pretty good action. He wrote to Lem, with typical humor:

I'm rather glad to be on my way, although I understand that this South Pacific is not a place where you lie on a white beach with a cool breeze, while those native girls who aren't out hunting for your daily supply of bananas are busy popping grapes in your mouth. It would seem to consist of heat and rain and dysentery + cold beans, all of which won't of course bother anyone with a good stomach. If it's as bad as they say it is, I imagine I'll be voting Republican in '44.

Before he even reached his assigned PT base in the Solomon Islands, Jack acquitted himself nicely in a fierce air strike by the Japanese. Describing a terrifying battle scene with a soldier from the other side, Jack again wrote to Lem:

> We returned the fire with everything we had—the water boiled around him—but everyone was too surprised to shoot straight. Finally an old soldier standing next to me—picked up his rifle—fired once—and blew the top of his head off. He threw up his arms—plunged forward—and sank—and we hauled our ass out of there. That was the start of a very interesting month—and it brought home very strongly how long it is going to take to finish this war.

TRUE MEASURE OF THE MAN

The primary mission of Skipper Jack Kennedy's torpedo boat in the Pacific, along with a squad of similar cruisers, was to block Japanese ships from delivering supplies to their soldiers. But then on August 2, a disaster occurred, one that would turn out to be of historical proportions. At about 2:30 A.M. while PT-109 was on its mission, a much larger Japanese destroyer called *Amagiri* came right for it at a dangerously high speed and without running lights. Though Jack tried to evade it, the war ship rammed into his boat, splitting it in half and instantly killing two men in a cataclysmic fireball. To avoid surrender, Jack's crew jumped ship. In the ensuing melee, Jack was thrown hard, once again injuring the back that had given him so much trouble since college.

One of Jack's crew, chief engineer Patrick "Pappy" McMahon, suffered burns on 70 percent of his body, including his face and hands. In foggy, pitch-black darkness, Jack somehow found him struggling in the water. "Go on, Skipper," Pappy whispered. "You go on. I've had it." Undaunted, Jack dragged him and another crew member to the other survivors, who were also trying to stay afloat. All of the men then clung to PT-109's bow section, which would drift along for many long hours. Jack had always said he wanted to see action. He was certainly seeing it now, and it was terrifying.

By about 1:30 in the afternoon, it was clear the only way the soldiers would ever survive would be to swim for the land they could see out in the distance. Therefore, for the next several hours, they did their best, with those unable to swim hanging on to the boat's smoking timbers for dear life. "It can be done," Jack kept insisting to his exhausted and freezing crew. "It can be done!" Incredibly, especially considering his own injuries, Jack towed Pappy the entire way with a strap from his life jacket *clenched between his teeth.* How this was even possible still boggles the mind all these years later. Finally, the men came to a small strip of land called Plum Pudding Island. Once finally there, Jack could only lie on the sand, panting and gasping for air. As soon as he stood up, he vomited seawater. "I just kept thinking, is this thing true?" he later told his cousin Ann Gargan. "What I kept coming to was that it really was true and it was real, and that I had to survive it no matter what, and had to make sure my men did, too."

Since Plum Pudding Island was only a hundred yards in diameter with no food or water, the men had to somehow move on from it. Therefore, over the next two days, they swam another five miles, Jack again dragging McMahon by the teeth, finally ending up on Olasana Island. By this time, PT-109's abandoned wreckage had been noticed by a reconnaissance plane and its crew presumed lost. There was even a memorial service at the squadron's operating base. It would be six more days before they were finally spotted by two native islanders. Those locals went for help, delivering a message that Jack had carved onto, of all things, a coconut shell. Finally, on August 8, the crew of the PT-109 was rescued.

A man who'd pull to safety a wounded soldier by a belt in his teeth isn't thinking about the fame that might result from such heroism, or even about one day telling the incredible story to others. Such courage and bravery is rare and it demonstrated that Jack Kennedy was a true hero. In a very real sense, it's not just what happened later in the 1960s in Washington that shows us who John Fitzgerald Kennedy was as a man. His true measure was first in evidence in 1943 in the Pacific Ocean.

Joe Kennedy kept his wife in the dark about their son's missing-in-action status; he decided to wait until he could confirm Jack's fate. When Rose accidentally received a phone call telling her Jack had been found, she was shocked. "My God! I didn't even know he was missing," she exclaimed. At her later suggestion, the coconut with Jack's carved message on it would be cast in a paperweight and sit on his desk in the Oval Office. It's now on display at the John F. Kennedy Library and Museum in Boston. Later, Jack wrote to his father from overseas:

Fortunately, they misjudged the durability of a Kennedy.

He also wrote to Lem, downplaying the events, not surprisingly:

We have been having a difficult time for the past two months—lost our boat a month ago when a Jap cut us in two + lost some of our boys. We had a bad time—a week on a Jap island—but finally got picked up—and have got another boat. It really makes me wonder if most success is merely a great deal of fortuitous accidents.

Though Jack's PT-109 injuries were significant, he was still anxious to return to duty. After a short recovery, he was back in the South Pacific in September 1943 as the commander of another PT boat, PT 59. "He'd certainly earned the right by navy custom to return to the States," Torbert Macdonald recalled, "but, typical of him, he chose to stay and to fight, but now with a ship boasting far heavier weapons and armament."

Jack would eventually be awarded the Navy and Marine Corps Medal for leadership and courage and the Purple Heart for his injuries. Even given all he'd been through, someone remained on his mind, especially since he'd come so close to death, and he still couldn't shake her.

Inga. Of course.

WHAT WE GET THROUGH

Coming so close to death made Jack Kennedy more aware than ever of the unpredictability and brevity of life. Perhaps he shouldn't give up on being with the only woman he'd ever really loved. Typing in block letters, he wrote a long letter to Inga Arvad after PT-109 in which he revealed some of his deepest thoughts:

> The war is a dirty business. I don't know what it all adds up to, nothing I guess, but you said that you figured I'd write about my experiences. I wouldn't go near a book like that. This thing is so stupid, that while it has a sickening fascination for some of us, myself included, I want to leave it far behind when I go. Inga Binga, I'll be glad to see you again. I'm tired now. I used to have the feeling that no matter what happened I'd get through. It's a funny thing that as long as you have that feeling you seem to get through. I've lost that feeling lately but as a matter of fact I don't feel badly about it. If anything happens to me I have this knowledge that if I had lived to be a hundred I could only have improved the quantity of my life, not the quality. This sounds gloomy as hell. I'll cut it. You are the only person I'm saying it to. As a matter of fact knowing you has been the brightest point in an already bright twenty-six years.

By the end of 1944, Jack couldn't bear it any longer; he needed to see her. Inga was now living in Los Angeles and working at MGM. Having finally obtained her divorce from Paul Fejos, she was engaged to an air force medic. Much to Jack's disappointment, when he knocked on her door, it was the fiancé who answered. Jack was polite but disappointed as the three of them chatted in her parlor. Eventually, he got up and left, feeling sad and dejected.

The next day, Inga called Jack and said she wanted to see him again, but only for a story she wanted to write about his PT-109 adventure. Apparently, she was now writing columns for syndication. Reluctantly, he agreed. That story appeared in the *Boston Globe* on January 11, 1944, with the headline "Tells Story of PT Epic: Kennedy Lauds Men, Disdains Hero Stuff." In it, Jack was quoted as saying:

> *None of that hero stuff about me. The real heroes are not the men who return, but those who stay out there, like plenty of them do—two of my men included.*

Jack hadn't flown all the way to California just to be interviewed by Inga for some newspaper. He wanted to be with her and was heartsick about barely having even seen her. They agreed, as always, to stay in touch.

Two years later, in the summer of 1946, Jack called Inga again. She was still working in Hollywood and, by this time, her engagement had been called off. Jack flew to California to visit. The two met for lunch at the Brown Derby on Wilshire Boulevard in Beverly Hills. This time, they couldn't resist each other. They spent several nights together, not hiding it either, but out in public. Joe Kennedy tried to tone down his concern in a letter to Arthur Houghton, who lived in California, dated July 30, 1946:

> *I saw in Jack Lait's column that my congressman son was paying attention to Inga Arvad, Hitler's Nordic. Well, I suppose youth must be served. We haven't heard anything from him. Do you know when he is coming back?*

By this time, Inga was a different woman, disillusioned not only by the loss of her Washington career but also by her track record with men. At thirty-four, she was jaded, worn down, and suffering from physical maladies such as rheumatoid arthritis and gout. She'd just begun dating an actor named Tim McCoy, more than twenty-five years older than Jack. Though not in love with him, she was thinking about leaving California and going to New York with him for a much-needed fresh start. She also wanted children before it was too late.

Now at a crossroads in life, Inga asked Jack if he thought he could give her what Tim could give her. Could he promise her a family? Jack knew the answer right away. Of course not. His father would never allow it. Her heart sank when he said no. She was distraught and Jack could see it. It was as if all he could ever offer her was sadness. He tried to lift her spirits. "I now know we get through one hundred percent of the days we think we'll never get through," he told her. He said he never thought he'd survive PT-109, and he did. "You'd be amazed at what we can get through," he told her. He said he knew she'd be fine, that they would both somehow be fine, but, no, he could not marry her.

They'd see each other one more time, in New York four months later, in November. Old habits dying hard, they spent that night together, too. Three months later on Valentine's Day 1947, Inga married Tim McCoy. It was Kick who told Jack about it; she didn't want him to read about it in the papers. Virtually every news account mentioned Inga's connection to Adolf Hitler, who had killed himself two years earlier. Jack was very sorry to hear about Inga's marriage, or as he wrote to Lem:

> *As you have probably heard, Inga Binga got married—and not to me. She married some guy she had known for years who loved her but whom she didn't love. Anyway, she's gone and that leaves the situation rather blank.*

Many people would later come to believe that Inga's son Ron McCoy was the product of that one night she spent with Jack Kennedy in New York. The math makes sense. She married Tim McCoy after learning she was pregnant. She didn't tell him she'd been with Jack three months earlier. Ron was born in August 1947, seven months after Inga wed Tim and nine months after her night with Jack. But Ron McCoy, who grew up to be blond like Inga and Tim, today is certain there's no biological connection to Kennedy. Inga later gave birth to another son, Terry.

One more postscript to the story of Jack and Inga: Tim McCoy's middle name? John Fitzgerald.*

---

* See "Inga Arvad Postscript" in Source Notes.

PART VI

Mr. and Mrs. Kennedy

SOMETHING LIKE THAT

W̶ith the passing of seven years, it was now January 1953. Jack Kennedy's world was quite different from what it had been when he kissed Inga Arvad goodbye for the last time.

November 1946 was the last time Jack ever saw Inga. It was also the same month he met Janet and Hugh Auchincloss at Captain McCauley's house in Georgetown, sitting next to Janet at dinner and then, that same night, given a lift home by the Auchinclosses. Now, he was a United States senator, thirty-six years old, and still in the midst of a patchy romance with Janet's daughter Jackie Bouvier, which Jackie called a "spasmodic courtship." That status was about to change, however. The young senator needed assistance with an important matter, and he realized that Jackie was the only woman who could help.

Jack wanted to look into the issue of American support of France in Indochina, specifically Vietnam, where the French were battling against Communist fighters backed by China. Because he needed help with research, he turned to one of the smartest, most well-read people he knew and one who also spoke French—Jackie. "He had all of these history books, most of them in French," Lem Billings recalled, "and asked me, 'Who the hell can we get to take this information, translate it, and make it understandable so I can speak on the Senate floor about it?' He basically required a comprehensive report about the history of the French in Indochina. Who? Jackie."

Joey Gargan elaborated, "Jack was beginning to make a name for himself in foreign affairs. He asked Jackie to translate from French to English all of these books and papers and then distill them into a cogent report. It wasn't for public consumption but rather for his use in the Senate in opposing

America's support of France's war against Communist insurgents in Vietnam. I told him, 'You're out of your mind. You can't ask a girl to do that. You want her to be an overnight expert on Indochina? If that doesn't send her running for the hills, nothing will.' We thought she'd say no. But, goddamn it if she didn't say yes."

When Jackie agreed to do it, it made Jack realize how truly unique she was because he actually didn't know any other person who could've tackled the project for him. Making it even more an effort for her, Jackie was actually bored to death by geopolitical subject matter, and he knew it. Her taking it on anyway showed him something about her he really admired.

At the end of January 1953, Janet and Hugh Auchincloss left for a two-month trip to Beirut and Rome, and then to Lebanon to visit Yusha, who was now working for an oil company there. Jackie took advantage of their absence to work in solitude at Merrywood on what would end up being an in-depth, eighty-four-page report, some typed, most handwritten. Jack had placed his trust in her, and she wasn't going to let him down. "I'd stay up all these hot nights, translating these books, and . . . I couldn't tell what was important and what was not," she later recalled. "I mean, all these—they were all in French on Indochina . . . Adm. D'Argenlieu and Ho Chi Minh, and the Ammonites and the Mennonites. I think I translated about ten books."

Jackie's report was both cohesive and articulate, ending with her editorial opinions about the dangers of a war in Vietnam and what each side had to lose as the French and Viet Minh fought for power. "What's the point," she opined, "of a fight with neither side winning?" She concluded that the Vietnamese "want a new way of life—no foreign domination, no corrupt mandarinate. It is to them that we must give the reins." The complexities of the situation didn't escape her as she made a case for France granting Vietnam its independence. She not only showed a fine grasp of the most minute details of the history of both regions, she also pointed out the danger of leaping to conclusions about the future. It was fine work and the senator was impressed with it, and with her. "She's not just another dumb girl, that's for sure," he said.

Even given his admiration, Jack still wasn't head-over-heels in love. Maybe it just wasn't his way, a frustrated Jackie thought. Or . . . maybe it just wasn't going to happen. After she gave him the report, he thanked her and told her how much he appreciated it. "You've made me very happy," he said. Then, he walked out of the house and into the woods to read it alone. While she longed to join him, somehow she knew better.

APRIL 1953. HYANNIS PORT, MASSACHUSETTS.

"I don't know what he's waiting for. Bells and whistles?" Joe asked Arthur Houghton, who was visiting from Los Angeles. The two men were sitting with Hyannis Port general practitioner Dr. Robert D. Watt and his wife, Madeline. Robert had recently befriended Joe, introduced to him by Ethel Kennedy, and in time would become the family's doctor. It was early afternoon and the three men, bundled up in thick sweaters, had just finished lunch and were sipping aperitifs while playing cards on the porch. "I think the Bouvier girl is good for him," Joe said. "I don't understand the problem. Is he still in love with Hitler's girl? After all this time? That makes no sense."

In a 1994 interview, Dr. Watt recalled, "Mrs. Kennedy came out of the house with Joe's secretary, Janet DesRosiers. 'What are you discussing?' she asked. Joe answered, 'Mother, we're trying to figure out why Jack won't move forward with the Bouvier girl.' Mrs. Kennedy walked to the edge of the porch and stared out at the ocean. 'Maybe there's no love there,' she said, turning to Joe. 'Have you thought of that?' Joe gave her a curious look. 'If it's not there, fine,' Rose decided. 'Obviously he can still marry her, but let's not expect him to be over the moon about it.'"

The silence that followed Rose's statement was heavy with meaning. After all, she had been in a loveless marriage for many years. Would it be too much of a stretch to imagine she wanted more for her son?

In May, a friend of Jackie's named Aileen Bowdoin called to tell her she was going to England for the coronation of Queen Elizabeth. She thought it might be fun if Jackie tagged along. However, Jackie wasn't so sure she wanted to go. "Why are you sitting around here waiting for him to make a move?" Janet asked, referring to Jack. As she recalled in her oral history for the JFK Library, she said, "If you're so much in love with Jack Kennedy you don't want to leave him, I should think he'd be more likely to find out how he felt about you if you were seeing exciting people and doing exciting things, instead of sitting here waiting for the telephone to ring." She suggested Jackie could also write about the coronation for the *Times-Herald* while she was in England. Jackie thought her mother might be right—not about her being "in love" with Jack, because that was definitely overstating her feelings, but, at the very least, she could write about the coronation. Therefore, yes, she decided to go. She and Aileen left for Europe on May 22.

The next day, Janet and Hugh attended Eunice Kennedy's wedding to Sargent Shriver at St. Patrick's Cathedral. The fact that Jack had invited them did bode well, Janet figured, for Jackie's future with the family. At the reception at the Waldorf, she couldn't help herself. Janet went up to Jack and said, "You should know that Jacqueline really didn't want to go to England. She hated leaving you." He smiled at her but didn't know how to respond.

While in England, Jackie received three transatlantic phone calls from Jack, maybe proving the adage about absence making the heart grow fonder. Then, one afternoon, she got a telegram:

Articles Excellent—But You Are Missed. Jack.

Those few words were certainly more of a proclamation of interest from Jack than Jackie had ever gotten before, so maybe Mummy had the right idea. Janet recalled, "Jack called me up from, I think, Cape Cod, the day she was flying back from England. He asked if I knew what flight she was on and what airline. I did. He said, 'Is she landing in Washington or New York?' I said, 'She's landing in New York and then flying down to Washington.' He said, 'I think that plane stops in Boston. I'm going to meet her there.' It was the first time I felt that this was really a serious romance."

When Jackie got off the plane, she found Jack standing there waiting. After he embraced her, they went off to a corner and chatted for a few moments. He kissed her on the cheek and she smiled at him. Maybe he even asked her to marry him. That's how the family history has it, anyway. Only the two of them ever really knew for sure. However, it doesn't seem as if there was ever that romantic moment when Jack fell to one knee and asked for Jackie's hand in marriage. "I don't know how he ever got himself to do it," said Lem Billings. "He wouldn't like to say all those things that are important if you want a girl to marry you. He'd just rather have it happen without talking about it. Probably, that's the way it happened."

When asked years later if what actually happened was maybe just a quick conversation in an airport, which then somehow led to the idea of marriage, Jackie smiled in that enigmatic way of hers and answered, "Well, something like that."

"DO. YOU. LOVE. HIM?"

It was bright and early when Jack Kennedy and Lem Billings pulled up to the grand entrance of the Auchinclosses' Hammersmith Farm estate in Jack's beat-up old car. Jack exited the vehicle while Lem stayed behind to wait.

Twenty minutes later, Janet and Hugh met Jack in the Great Room, where they were soon joined by Jackie. While Jack's exact words have been lost, he suggested to Jackie's mother and stepfather that he and Jackie had decided to wed. According to Janet's later account, she was surprised and turned to Jackie and asked, "Is this true, Jacqueline?" Jackie took a nervous hit off her cigarette, glanced at Jack, and then back at her mother. "Yes, Mummy, it is," was her answer. Janet and Hugh shared a secretive look, after which Hugh suddenly got to his feet and, slapping Jack on the shoulder, exclaimed, "Congratulations, son." Janet embraced her daughter and then Jack. "Welcome to the family," she told him.

Years later, in 1972, Janet would recall in an unpublished interview that she asked Jackie precisely when it was that Jack had proposed. Though Jackie was vague, she suggested that Jack had proposed when he met her at the airport.

"Do you love him?" Janet asked.

"It's not that simple," Jackie answered.

"It is, Jacqueline," Janet insisted, her temper rising. "*Do. You. Love. Him?*" she repeated, this time punctuating each word.

"I *enjoy* him," was Jackie's response.

Jackie's vague answer was nonetheless acceptable to her mother. Janet always valued practicality over emotion, and that's how she'd raised her daughter. Janet had been deeply in love with Jackie's father, Jack Bouvier, and that had not turned out well.

A bigger problem for Janet was that her secretary, Kay Donovan, had told her some stories about Joe Kennedy's wandering eye, and she was now worried about his son's possible fidelity in marriage. Just as worrisome was Jackie's revelation of the conversation she'd had with Lem Billings before the Eisenhower inaugural ball, the one about lowering her expectations of Jack in terms of his ability to be faithful. Janet saw that as a problem. But Jackie herself found it hard to believe Jack would ever cheat on her. "Don't be stupid," Janet warned her. "You're being blind to the fact that a man will hurt you just to make himself feel better."

While she had concerns about Jack's fidelity, Janet still couldn't help but be impressed by his sense of duty. She felt it spoke well of him. He was rich but, at the same time, he wanted to give back. Since she and Hugh were both patriotic, JFK was very appealing, particularly when he started talking policy. The Auchinclosses didn't agree with him on a lot of issues, but the fact that he had strong views, that he was now a senator, and that he was becoming a figure to be reckoned with in American politics counted for something. "I love this country so much," he told them, and they believed him.

After the engagement was announced in the papers, Janet and Jackie felt the time had come to call Rose Kennedy and start planning the wedding. They decided to invite her to Hammersmith Farm for a weekend.

While the Auchinclosses had had at least a vague conversation with Jack about the pending nuptials, Rose hadn't been so lucky. Barbara Gibson, Rose's secretary in the 1970s, recalled, "She once told me there was never a conversation with Jack about the engagement. She'd heard about it from Joe. When I asked Eunice, she laughed and said, 'Oh, yes, Father's marriage. He announced it over dinner.' The only conversation Rose had with her son was when she told him, 'When you marry someone, that's it. You're with that person for life.' When Jack said she made it sound like 'prison,' Rose said, 'Good, because it is. Marriage isn't for the faint of heart, believe you me.'"

Early on Sunday, June 21, Rose and Jack drove toward the gates of the shingled Hammersmith mansion in their polished white chauffeured limousine. As they approached, they gazed out their windows at the rolling green hills upon which the Auchinclosses had built an assortment of barns, stables, and guesthouses with names like the Castle, the Windmill, and the Carriage House. Hugh was born there in 1897 and later, in 1942, inherited it upon the death of his mother, Emma. The property spanned at least a hundred acres. The Kennedy compound in Hyannis Port? All of six acres.

Rose tried to act unimpressed. "They have *cattle*?" she asked as she stared at a herd of Black Angus grazing out in the distance. "How can they stand the smell?"

Jack smiled tolerantly. "Mother, now be nice."

The steer were actually just decorative. Hugh liked looking out the windows at the cows. Therefore, every spring when he and Janet opened the house for the season, he purchased twenty of them. When they closed up the place in the fall, he returned them.

The car carrying mother and son pulled up to the long graveled drive and came to a stop under the wide porte cochere. There, a team of maids and butlers stood at attention. "We have no bags," Rose told them. Then to her chauffeur, she said, "Be back here at six, and not a minute later."

Janet decided she and Jackie would take the Kennedys to lunch at Bailey's Beach Club, one of the most exclusive private clubs in the country. After greetings all around, they piled into Janet's Ford Thunderbird, the two matriarchs in the front seat and Jack and Jackie in the back, and were on their way. Much to his mother's chagrin, Jack hadn't dressed for the occasion. He was in a worn T-shirt, shorts, and slippers with white socks as he slumped in the back seat. Jackie later jokingly remarked, "It was, I'm sure, one of his favorite days."

At Bailey's, the conversation was stiff and difficult. Jackie tried to keep things moving by bringing up subjects she hoped the mothers might have in common, while Jack just sat looking bored while staring out at the ocean. Annoyed, Jackie kept kicking him under the table. "What?" he'd respond. "*What?*"

"From what Mummy told me years later, it wasn't an easy day," said Jamie Auchincloss. "The first thing she realized was that Rose was the wrong person to talk to about the wedding. 'That would be Joe's decision,' was her response to everything Mummy suggested. Mummy realized Rose was powerless, unable to make a single decision without deferring to a husband who wasn't present. Mummy was very much *not* like Rose. I couldn't imagine Daddy lording over her. I think Mummy was perplexed as to how any woman could ever allow such a thing."

Janet's friend Marion "Oatsie" Charles recalled in 1998, "At the end of the trying day, Mrs. Auchincloss had her secretary prepare bedrooms for the Kennedys to spend the night. She'd even had her put heavy plywood under one of the beds since Jackie warned her about Jack's back. However, Mrs. Kennedy had made prior arrangements with her friends the Robert Youngs at the former John R. Drexel estate called Fairholme at Ochre Point." At 6 P.M., as if on cue, the Kennedys' white limousine appeared. Rose got in and waited for Jack. He shrugged, kissed Jackie on the cheek, and joined his mother. Moments later, they were gone."

Though Janet was, as Oatsie Charles put it, "absolutely fit to be tied," she still gave Rose the benefit of the doubt. Her heart actually went out to her, she later told Oatsie, especially as she watched her constantly playing with and adjusting her collar out of nervousness. She was ill at ease and distracted the entire time they were together. Janet said she would catch her staring into space as if she didn't have a thought in her head. She later told Oatsie, "I think this woman's been suffering for years because she doesn't realize she deserves better."

On Sunday, July 12, three weeks later, Joe Kennedy showed up at Hammersmith. "It was as if a bit of storm descended upon our peaceful haven," Jamie Auchincloss recalled. "I was only six but you don't forget Joseph P. Kennedy walking into your great room and sucking up all the oxygen. Things got off to a rocky start when he wanted Mummy and Daddy to call him 'the ambassador,' whereas he'd call them by their first names."

When Janet said she wanted the wedding to be small in an intimate Newport chapel, Joe couldn't help but chuckle. The haggling that then occurred about details has been lost, but in the end all parties agreed it would be a big ceremony held in Newport's St. Mary's Church. Though Joe suggested the reception be in Hyannis Port, he conceded that it could be at Hammersmith, and he'd even pay for it.

CRAZIER THAN A CORKSCREW

At the end of the month, the Kennedys returned the favor and hosted the Auchinclosses at their home in Hyannis Port. Their guests were Janet and Hugh, Jackie and Lee and Lee's husband, Michael Canfield. Lee and Michael had just married back in April, much to Janet's chagrin. She just didn't think it would last. "Oh, you haven't met Lee's first husband?" she asked someone who wanted to meet Michael after the ceremony. Now, they were all trying to put forth a united front while visiting Jackie's future in-laws. They quickly learned, though, that the Kennedys were a very different kind of family.

"Hammersmith was a serene place where we spoke in hushed tones while watching the tide roll in and the sun set while we sipped on our lovely cocktails," Jackie's sister, Lee, said. "Why, we wouldn't raise our voices if our hair was on fire! But the Kennedys' home was one filled with people always coming and going, all of them excited as they argued and bickered about their liberal politics or played their silly little sports games. It wasn't what one might call restful."

Lee recalled a moment when she was standing at the front door and chatting with Michael when, all of a sudden, twenty-one-year-old Ted Kennedy raced into the house. As he dashed past her, he handed her his coat as if she were a maid, "or, worse," Lee said, "a woman!" Lee, who was twenty, gave her husband a look and dropped the garment onto the floor.

Joe Kennedy later walked up to Janet and said, "Well, just look at you, all dolled up."

Janet was insulted by his patronizing attitude. "Ambassador, I am a grown woman," she said as she brushed by him. "I do not get dolled up."

An hour after arriving, the guests sat in the large kitchen and watched with dismay as the Kennedy women bickered over what foods to serve for lunch, how they should be served and where, the kitchen or dining room? Meanwhile, Jack, Bobby, Teddy, and other relatives not known to the guests kept going into the kitchen demanding to know when the meal would be ready so they could all go sailing. Later, when Lee was told the Hyannis Port house was called the Big House, she quipped, "Mad house is more like it."

At dinner that night, Jackie insisted on having some say over her wedding trousseau. She said she wanted something simple, sleek, and elegant. However, Janet and Joe were in agreement that the design should be much more dramatic. Janet suggested a designer she'd worked with in the past, the African American Ann Lowe. Ann had designed Janet's wedding trousseau when she married Hugh in 1942. She'd previously commissioned her to design Jackie's gown for her marriage to John Husted, which, of course, never took place. She'd also designed Janet's and Lee's dresses for Lee's wedding to Michael. Joe approved of commissioning a Black seamstress and felt her hiring might even help Jack politically. Ann would also, it was decided, design the gowns for Jackie's female attendants.

Later, when Jackie saw Ann's sketches, she was unhappy about them. Fifty yards of ivory silk taffeta and tulle wasn't at all what she had in mind. Janet and Joe, however, were both bowled over and so insistent Jackie felt she had no choice but to give in. The gown cost $500, the equivalent of about $6,000 in today's money; Hugh bought it for his stepdaughter as a wedding gift.

In the days that followed, Jackie couldn't help but complain to Jack about her mother's authority over the wedding. Though he was certainly getting a sampling of the often strained dynamic between the two women, he wasn't as angry about it as Jackie hoped. "Are you kidding?" he asked her. "I'd give anything to have a mother like yours." Indeed, he and his future mother-in-law had already forged an understanding. It happened at Bailey's Beach when the Kennedys came to Newport. When Jack said something critical about Rose to Janet, Janet quickly came to her defense. "Clearly, you don't understand mothers," she told him. "The worry," she said, "never goes away." All she'd ever done from the day Jackie was born, she said, was worry about her. She said she'd long ago accepted Jackie's opinion of her as overbearing and critical, but she said she would never stop worrying about her, "not until I'm dead and in the ground six feet under, and even then." Janet's candor had a real impact on Jack. What must it be like, he wondered, to have a mother so invested in her child's welfare? Had Rose ever really worried about him? When he said as much to Janet, again she defended Rose. What he felt may be true, she told him, "but since she's your mother, don't you ever say it again."

Though she'd established a rapport with him, that didn't mean Janet was always going to agree with Jack. About a week later when he announced plans to go to Eden Roc in Cap d'Antibes, the south of France, for a vacation, Janet asked, "You and Jackie? So close to the wedding?" No, Jack told her; he was going with his friend Torbert Macdonald. He explained the purpose of the trip was to confer with French officials about Vietnam. Janet didn't believe him. To her, it sounded like an extravagant vacation without her daughter. In fact, a lot of what she'd seen so far pointed to a real disaster in the making.

"This is not normal," she told her daughter.

While Jackie couldn't disagree, she'd already made her peace with it. "We no longer have a normal life," she told her mother. "We have this one."

Betty Beale, society columnist at the *Washington Evening Star* at the time, recalled in a 1999 interview, "When Jackie told me Jack was going to Eden Roc without her, I thought, *My goodness, what's this about?* I said, 'Jackie, are you okay with this?' and she said, 'Betty, he goes every year the same time with Torb. What am I to do? Stop him?' I said, 'Yes, my dear! That's exactly what you should do. Stop him because he's up to no good.'"

Jackie then confided in Betty that it felt to her as if Jack had been pulling away ever since the engagement was announced. True to his character, while they had been dating, he was interested in her on some days, less interested on others. She said she saw in him what she often noticed in his father toward his mother: indifference. Betty recalled, "This told me Jack wasn't really in love with her, and that she was naive to it, the poor dear. When she said, 'He treats me the way his father treats his mother,' I said, 'But, Jackie, have you seen their marriage, the two of them together? They're miserable. That should be a warning to you.'"

An incident at the Big House during the Auchinclosses' recent visit went a long way toward explaining the marital dynamic between Jack's parents.

One night, everyone gathered in the parlor to watch television. Joe, having had so much to drink he actually smelled of whiskey, grabbed a young woman from the household staff. "Come over here and sit on my lap," he told her. Everyone watched, including Rose. Embarrassed, the employee pulled away. Joe tugged her back. "I said, *sit here*," he demanded, patting his leg.

"Mr. Kennedy, please stop," she pleaded.

"Why not give me a little smooch?" he asked, holding the woman's arm tightly.

Rose walked over, snatched the employee's arm away from Joe, and said, "She's quite clear, Joe. She does not wish to sit on your lap. Now, leave her be."

Joe gave his wife a crippling stare. "Watch your tone with me, Mother," he said.

Hearing that, Rose lost all courage and scurried from the room like a scared bunny. There was then silence. Hugh finally broke it. "You people are crazier than a corkscrew, aren't you?" he asked with a chuckle.

In no mood, Joe got up and left the room, followed by the female employee. The remaining Kennedys, including Jack, continued talking as if nothing unusual had occurred. Janet Auchincloss couldn't get over it. "If he would do that in front of his wife," she later noted, "what is he doing behind her back?"

A couple weeks after the visit to Hyannis, Janet received a proposed wedding guest list from his secretary, Janet DesRosiers. On it, at the very bottom, was the name "Gloria Swanson." Though Janet had heard the rumors about Joe Kennedy and the famous film star, she didn't know if they were true. Apparently, she now figured, they must be, thus her addition to the list. With a bold black pen, in sympathy with Rose, Janet scratched out Gloria's name.

PRE-WEDDING TRYST?

AUGUST 1953. CANNES, FRANCE.

She was one of the sexiest women he'd ever seen. As he stared into her ice-blue eyes, Jack Kennedy couldn't help but wonder what it might be like to be with her. She was Swedish and only twenty-one, definitely young, but he didn't see that as a problem. Fair and blond, she was very different from the dark brunette he was supposed to marry in about a month. However, she was very much like the woman with whom she shared Scandinavian heritage, the one who'd captured his heart so long ago: Inga, of course.

This woman and a friend were also on vacation in Cannes. They'd been hitchhiking when they were picked up by a man named Gavin Sterling, a travel agent. Once they were in his car, he invited the women to dinner at Le Chateau, a romantic restaurant in Haut-de-Cagnes. While they were on their way, Gavin spotted someone, slowed down, and hollered out the open car window: "Hey, Jack! What the hell are you doing here?" Apparently, Jack had done business with Gavin's travel agency in the past.

Jack was dressed casually in tan slacks and a short-sleeved shirt, his hair tousled in the JFK tradition. He gave the surprising explanation that an "Italian contessa" was chasing him on a Vespa, "and I'm trying to avoid her. Oh!" he exclaimed as he quickened his pace. "Here she comes now." After Gavin suggested, "Meet us for dinner at Le Chateau," Jack glanced at the women in the back seat and said, "Okay. I'll see what I can do." He then dashed off.

An hour later, Gavin and his two female friends arrived at the restaurant. When they walked in, they found Jack sitting in a booth waiting for them, now wearing a light gray cotton suit and white shirt. He bolted to his feet and extended his hand to the blonde. "Jack Kennedy," he said.

"Gunilla von Post," she announced. "This is Anne Marie," she then added, gesturing to her friend. The three then slid into the booth, Jack next to Gunilla, Gavin next to Anne Marie.

It didn't take long before Gavin and Anne Marie seemed to recede into the background, at least as far as Jack was concerned, his connection with Gunilla was that strong. Over a candlelit seafood meal, he leaned in close as they spoke. She talked about her life in Sweden and her recent travels to Scotland. Jack teased her about her hitchhiking. He took her hand as she went on and on, but he was barely listening, mostly just fascinated. She was definitely his type—young, blond, Nordic, and very . . . Inga. She was sexy but perhaps not as intelligent as Inga. She had no worldview, not that he could tell, anyway. Somehow, their birthdays came up; Gunilla's was on July 10, the same day as Eunice's. It was all just flirty and fun.

Barely a month earlier, Jack had been on the Senate floor delivering his argument against the $400 million in foreign aid that had been earmarked to fight the North Vietnamese. Much of what he reported was drawn directly from Jackie's hard work. In the end, his proposal to amend the act responsible for such aid would be defeated. However, he would not abandon the fight against the government's support of the war in Vietnam. Shortly after his speech, he was hospitalized for what was described as "recurring malarial chills and fever." Or, as he put it, "more of the same goddamn same." Then, on August 5, with Congress adjourned and Jack still shaky and weak, he and Torbert set sail. Torb was now on his own for a couple of days, having his own adventure with someone else somewhere else, leaving Jack to his own devices with Gunilla.

Jackie had been a big help to Jack, and he appreciated it. But now she was thousands of miles away and he was on vacation. Anything that happened while he was on this holiday had, in his mind anyway, nothing to do with her. Yet, when he got to France, he sent her a telegram, albeit not a very romantic one:

Get a hold of Ed Berube. He knows a fellow that's going to make our wedding cake.

While Jack was in France, Jackie did as she was told and tracked down a man named Ed Berube, who'd been the head of the 1952 Senate campaign in Fall River, Massachusetts. Berube later recalled, "I was home one morning and I got a phone call from Newport. 'Mr. Berube? This is Jackie Bouvier.' It didn't ring a bell. I'd never met her. She said, 'I'm Senator Kennedy's fiancée. He's in Europe, and I got a cablegram from him to get ahold of you. You might be able to help with our wedding cake? Do you have a baker? Could you come down this afternoon?' I said, 'Yes, fine.' I got ahold of the baker, Babe Plourde, and we went down there, and she was in shorts, you know, just the typical, excited girl about to be married. She was deeply in love. You could tell by looking at her. She asked us about our families. 'Are you married, Ed?' I said yes and she said, 'Have you any children?' I told her I had three boys. 'Oh,' she said, 'that's wonderful. Jack wants ten children.' I said, 'Well, he certainly can afford them. You're marrying quite a guy.' And, today, all these years later, I remember exactly what she said next, and every time I remember it, I get goose pimples. She said, 'Yes, I'm the luckiest girl in the world.'"

———————

After Jack's dinner that first night in Cannes with Gunilla and her friends, the foursome went to a popular nightclub. A band was playing, so Jack took Gunilla's hand and walked her to the dance floor. As he took her into his arms, she would later recall, he winced in pain. She suggested they stop but he insisted on continuing, saying he wanted to feel her in his arms. He was a good dancer; she was surprised and delighted.

Hours passed before the foursome found themselves at Eden Roc at Cap d'Antibes. Gavin and Anne Marie went off, leaving Jack and Gunilla sitting on the edge of a cliff gazing out at the Mediterranean. It was a romantic moment and Jack couldn't help himself. He kissed her. "I have to tell you something," he then whispered in her ear. "I'm getting married next month."

She stood up abruptly. "Well, that's it, then," she decided.

Gunilla would later claim Jack told her, "I fell in love with you tonight. If I'd met you one month ago, I would've canceled the whole thing."

While that may have been her memory, it certainly doesn't sound like Jack Kennedy, this man who rarely if ever expressed emotion for any woman after Inga. Besides that, would he really have defied his father and canceled the wedding to Jackie? That doesn't seem likely, either.

He drove Gunilla home. Standing at her front door, he asked if he could come up for a nightcap. She said no. He pushed a little but wasn't able to change her mind. She kissed him, turned on her heel, went inside, and closed the door.

On August 27, Jack returned home and got back to the real world. He'd been a single man on a final vacation before getting hitched and, being generous, maybe it could be argued that anything he did—or might've done—could be chalked up to the last vestiges of bachelorhood. But the flirtation with Gunilla does underscore that what he had with Jackie wasn't completely fulfilling. The question remained: If not for his and his father's political aspirations, would he even be planning to marry Miss Bouvier?

Making things all the more complicated, upon Jack's return he sent a letter to his mother-in-law asking her to add, of all people, Inga Arvad to the wedding's guest list; that letter remains among the holdings of the JFK Library.

While Jack hadn't seen Inga in six years, apparently he was still in touch with her. Maybe it shows the bond he still had with her that he wanted her at his wedding, but it also shows a foolish lapse in judgment. Certainly not much good would come from Inga's presence.

Because Janet didn't recognize the name, she called Joe Kennedy to ask for clarification. He explained that Inga had once been a friend of Jack's, but also said she shouldn't be added to the list. Janet found it curious. When she told Jackie about it, of course the bride-to-be wanted to know more. True to his nature, Jack wasn't forthcoming about it. He simply said that Inga was someone from his past. If his father didn't want her at the wedding, he told her, that was fine with him. He definitely didn't want to turn it into a big deal. Jackie let it go. For now, Inga would have to remain another of Jack's many secrets.

SEPTEMBER NUPTIALS

The day had finally arrived when John Fitzgerald Kennedy was to take Jacqueline Lee Bouvier as his wife at St. Mary's Church in Newport. He certainly looked the part in his black suit and vest with striped pants while standing at the altar alongside his best man, Bobby. Among the ushers were Jack's brother Teddy, his brother-in-law Sargent Shriver, cousin Joe Gargan, brother-in-law Michael Canfield, pal Paul "Red" Fay from the navy, Torbert Macdonald from Harvard, and Lem Billings from Choate. Senator George Smathers also stood alongside him, as did his good friends Chuck Spalding and Charlie Bartlett, the man responsible for introducing him to Jackie.

Typical of Jack, he had scrapes on his rugged face, the result of having fallen into a briar patch a day earlier while playing touch football. Betty Beale, reporting for the *Washington Evening Star,* recalled, "I remember Jackie being walked down the aisle by the stately Hugh Auchincloss, and then meeting Jack at the altar. She looked at the scratches on his cheeks and rolled her eyes as if to say, 'Figures.' But then, as Jack stared at her, his lovely bride, my God, how his face lit with pleasure. It was a sight to see and I thought, *Okay, well, maybe I'm wrong about him,* because in that particular moment, I felt I was seeing real love."

Jackie's half brother Jamie Auchincloss is the only surviving member of the wedding party. He recalled, "I was dressed in black velvet shorts, a silk shirt with a lace chapeau and lace at my wrists. I also had white cotton socks and black patent shoes with brass buckles. I looked like something out of *Gone with the Wind.* When couples got up to dance, they often left champagne in their glasses to which I helped myself. I got quite drunk and made a real scene as I spun my six-year-old self about like a whirling dervish to get attention."

"I'm so happy you're a Kennedy now," Joe told Jackie as guests swirled all around them on the dance floor. "You'll make a great wife for Jack," he said. "It's a good calculation."

Jackie gave him a look. "*A good calculation?*" Rather than give it much thought, she gave him a vague smile and kissed him on the cheek.

A week later, Rose Kennedy wrote to Janet Auchincloss:

Joe and I want to thank you again for Jackie. She was so beautiful to look upon. So charming to meet, that she again captured our hearts. I am sure she and you know by now how deeply we all love her—and with what affection we shall always cherish her.

"Looking back, there's no way my family knew what we were getting into," Jamie Auchincloss observed. "Jack was thirty-six and worldly. Jackie was twenty-four and even though she'd been abroad, had been very sheltered by Mummy and Daddy. The ambassador had gotten what he wanted. Mummy, too. I suppose Jackie, as well. However, even as a young boy, I wondered how it was all going to turn out. Jack Kennedy was such a wild card in our lives, anything was possible."

For now, though, Jack was happy with his new bride and ready to go on their honeymoon. "I love your daughter beyond measure," he told Janet. "I hope you know that." She smiled and said yes, she did know it.

Someone important was missing from the wedding, though. Jack knew that if he'd been there he most certainly would've been his best man. It was actually difficult to believe he was gone, or as he told his cousin Joey Gargan on that special day, "Time has taken the most important person from my life, and I don't think time can ever replace him."

It had been almost ten years. Still, it felt like just yesterday.

PART VII

Joe

FALLEN BROTHER

Twenty-seven-year-old Jack Kennedy, his face thin and drawn and his body weak and aged in the year since the PT-109 tragedy, slowly made his way along the beach in front of his parents' home on the Cape. It hadn't been an easy summer. He was still suffering from spinal problems that were the result of injuries he'd sustained in the Pacific. His persistent limp attested to the ongoing struggle. Still, the childhood memory of good times spent on this stretch of sand and sea somehow always felt healing to him, like good medicine.

Reading, drawing, coloring, and listening to the radio were the usual summer activities for young Jack, but only on stormy Cape days. Every free sunny moment he ever had was spent outside roughhousing on the beach with his brother Joe. If he fell and scratched his knee, Joe would spit on his own finger and rub it on the wound. Like magic, it seemed like it was then healed. As brothers, they had so many secret places known only to them, sometimes Jack would forget the location of one but Joe would always remember it: a crevice between two rocks, a corner behind a broken wooden fence, a small space under a dock into which no grown-up could ever fit. Right now, as he walked along, Jack could still call to mind each and every one of them.

While the memories would always remain, this was the day everything changed. A couple hours earlier, two grim-faced military personnel appeared at the front door of the Big House. Jack's father was napping, as he always did after lunch and before golfing. His mother was reading the Sunday paper in her rocking chair in the sun-room. Eunice, twenty-three; Bobby, nineteen; and Teddy, twelve, had gathered on the porch to play records. Cousin Joey Gargan, fourteen, was also present. He had a bad feeling, he'd recall many years later, as he watched a black sedan drive up carrying the two visitors, one with a clerical collar.

"I began to perspire," Joey recalled. "I had a sixth sense this was not good. I went down to speak to them. Very solemnly, they said, 'We'd like to see Ambassador Kennedy.' Again, my heart got shaky as I anticipated the worst. I said to myself, no, I'm not going to do that. I said, 'Why don't you wait here on the porch and I'll get Mrs. Kennedy.' I went in and spoke quietly to Aunt Rose. 'There are two naval officers on the front porch and they'd like to see Uncle Joe,' I said. 'I think it would be a good idea if you spoke to them first.'" In fact, as it would happen, only one was actually a naval officer, the other was a priest, Father Francis O'Leary, a rotund navy chaplain who'd just returned to Boston from duty on the Pacific.

Though the men asked Rose to be seated, she refused and told them that whatever they had to say to her they could say as she stood. In a low, solemn voice, the priest then told her that her son Joe had been killed in action. He explained that the PB4Y-1 Liberator he'd been piloting exploded during a top-secret combat mission. "Did you find him?" Rose whispered. The priest shook his head, no.

As the visitors whispered to Rose, her children saw her wilt as if she was about to faint. Ted later recalled, "While she received the men in the sun-room, we on the porch could hear a couple words: 'missing,' 'lost.' All of us just froze."

Stunned, Rose backed away from the visitors and retreated into the house to tell Joe the news. Once she was with him in the bedroom, as she later remembered, she could barely get the words out. Her mind was a jumble, she was in such shock.

"Uncle Joe then came down," Joey Gargan recalled, "and walked into the entranceway of the sun-room. He just stood there, didn't come into the room, just stood in the doorway and burst into tears. 'Children,' he said, 'we've just been notified by the navy department that your brother Joe has been lost. He died flying a volunteer mission.' He was sobbing as he told us this. 'I want you now to be particularly good to your mother,' he said. He then turned around, walked slowly into the house, back up to his bedroom, and locked the door behind him. We all broke down, very upset, consoling each other, holding each other."

Jack would remember thinking, *How could this be?* After all, this was Joe they were talking about. *Perfect Joe. Invincible Joe.* He was just twenty-nine. As Jack tried to process it, a troubling memory came to mind.

Earlier, in September 1943, there was a dinner in Hyannis Port to celebrate the patriarch's fifty-fifth birthday. This was right after Jack's heroism on PT-109. In a few days' time, Joe Jr. would be off to England to fight in the war. Perhaps he expected some sort of acknowledgment of his pending service at the dinner, especially since he was wearing his navy whites. Halfway through the evening, a judge raised a glass for a birthday toast to the ambassador, expressing his "insufficient appreciation," and calling him "the father of our hero, Lieutenant John F. Kennedy, of the United States Navy." Ignoring Joe Jr., the judge honored the brother who wasn't even present. Joe Jr. was crushed.

Jack knew that part of the story was true; his father had told him about it. Later that same evening, according to witnesses, when Joe Jr. returned to his ship docked just outside Hyannis, he was seen sitting with clenched hands on the edge of his bunk. "I'll show 'em," he swore. "*By God, I'll show 'em.*" Was this also true? Jack didn't know for sure, but he hoped not. Joe had definitely acted strangely after Jack's PT-109 heroics made all the papers. He became evasive, hard to reach. His father had even chastised him about it in a letter:

We were considerably upset that during those few days after the news of Jack's rescue we had no word from you. I thought that you would very likely call up to see whether we had had any news as to how Jack was.

Joe had flown more than thirty-five missions and was eligible to return home with honors. In fact, on June 12, he wrote to his father:

It looks like I am going to be on my way home in ten days.

Rose was elated. "He's coming home," she kept exclaiming to relatives on the telephone. "*He's coming home!*" But, then, Joe volunteered for one more high-risk assignment, the odds of which he admitted were fifty-fifty. "Joe never asked for odds better than that," Jack later said.

Did Joe feel Jack had one up on him because of his PT-109 valor? Did he now feel the need to even the score? Was that why he had undertaken one more mission? Even Joe Sr. had been worried about the decision, writing to his namesake:

I can quite understand how you feel about staying there, but don't force your luck too much.

His sibling rivalry with Joe Jr. was always difficult for Jack to reconcile. When he was at Choate, his father sent him to a psychologist from Columbia, Dr. Prescott Lecky, to talk about it. The idea behind the therapy was to determine whether there might be some psychological issue underpinning Jack's many physical ailments. Imagine it: This was the 1930s, and the Kennedy patriarch was so progressive that he'd send his son to a psychologist. Therapy was rarely a consideration at this time and frowned upon by most people, especially in Catholic circles, except in the most dire of circumstances. Certainly, Rose wouldn't have approved, which is why Joe didn't tell her about it. A priest, yes, but not a psychologist.

In the doctor's report, he wrote that Jack was "a very able boy, but definitely in a trap psychologically, a good deal of his trouble due to comparison with an older brother." Apparently, Jack had told the doctor, "I am the boy that doesn't get things done. If my brother were not so efficient, it would be easier for me to be efficient. He does it so much better than I do." The doctor theorized that in order to discourage comparisons to Joe, "Jack withdraws from the race." Jack had told him he was comfortable with his reputation for "thoughtlessness, sloppiness and inefficiency," because at least he knew how he fit into the equation with his brother. He had to agree, though, or so he told the doctor, that if he didn't change, "I might never amount to anything." Apparently, therapy did little to help him feel more confident in relation to Joe, though. As soon as he got to Harvard, the first thing Jack did was write a note to the dorm master: "Dr. Wild, I want you to know I'm not bright like my brother Joe."

As Jack walked the beach that afternoon, he got it. He understood. If the tables had been turned, if Joe had become the American hero, he probably would've wanted to even things out, too.

Upon returning to the house, Jack saw his siblings crying. His father's head was in his hands, a shot glass on the table before him. His mother stared tight-faced at a corner as she fingered her rosary. "Joe wouldn't want us sitting here crying," Jack told them. "He would want us to go sailing. Joey," he said, turning to his cousin, "go with Teddy to get the sails to the

Wianno Senior." That was the family's twenty-six-foot sloop with a gaff rig, the sailboat also known as the *Victura* (Latin for "about to conquer").

Jack's father sat bold upright, catching his breath in surprise. "Are you joking?" he asked. For a moment, Jack had to wonder about it, himself. He was suddenly so bone-tired, he wasn't sure he could do anything more than just collapse into a chair.

"No, Joe," Rose said, pulling herself up. "He's right," she added as she steeled herself. "We need to be just as brave as Joe was." She then turned to Jack and said, "I'll go get our jackets."

SHADOWBOXING WITH GHOSTS

Within just weeks of Joe Kennedy Jr.'s death, the family was dealt another terrible blow. Kick had fallen in love with William Cavendish, the Marquess of Hartington. He was the eldest son of the Duke of Devonshire and a Protestant, known as "Billy." They planned to marry. Upset by the relationship because of his religion, Rose refused to give her approval. After Kick married Billy in England on May 6, 1944, Rose became so distraught she actually had to check herself into a hospital. She wrote in her diary:

What a blow to the family prestige. We should think of a way to extricate her.

By this time, Joe was tired of Rose's judgmental nature, especially where Kick was concerned. Or, as he wrote to Arthur Houghton on May 27, 1944:

Of course, we've had a little excitement over Kathleen's marriage, but I'm sure that whatever Kathleen does or will do for the rest of her life is just right by me.

Four months later, tragedy struck once again; Billy was shot dead on the front lines in Belgium. "What a terrible shame," Rose now wrote. "One can't know what God has in store."

Now newly widowed, Kick clung close to Jack as always, knowing he would be there for her. How their lives had changed in just a few short years from their halcyon days in Washington, back when everything was so carefree and fun, back when she introduced him to Inga.

"Uncle Joe spent much of his time reading condolence letters, walking the beach alone, not wanting to talk, not wanting to remember—*especially* not wanting to remember," said Joey Gargan. "Unlike Aunt Rose, he didn't have his religion to rely on. 'Because she has her God,' Uncle Joe said to me, 'I think maybe her heart is a little less broken than mine.'"

A couple months later, Joe was still no better. The Broadway producer Mike Todd, who'd go on to marry Elizabeth Taylor in 1957, contacted him to ask him to invest in a new production of *Hamlet* starring English Shakespearean actor Maurice Evans. But Joe still wasn't ready to do anything, or as he wrote to Arthur on September 11, 1944:

> *I'm considering a proposition with Mike Todd but not too seriously. I think I probably have to interest myself in something because all of my plans for my own future were all tied up with young Joe, and that has gone smash.*

It took months for him to return to the world. On October 23, he wrote to his friend Lord Beaverbrook, who he knew as "Max":

> *For a fellow who didn't want this war to touch your country or mine, I have had a rather bad dose. Joe dead, Billy Hartington dead, my son Jack in the Naval hospital. I have had brought home to me very personally what I saw for all the mothers and fathers of the world.*

Joe had no choice but to reconcile that while one prized son was gone the other was still with him, and it was on that remaining son that his hopes and dreams must hang. Still, he couldn't help but sometimes think of Jack as being in Joe's shadow. Maybe it was just force of habit. It made Jack feel less favored, though. One day he heard his father refer to Joe Jr. as having been "the heart of this family." After that, Jack told Lem, "I'm shadowboxing in a match which the shadow is always going to win."

Joseph Kennedy knew he had to steel himself for the future and begin to focus on Jack, the son who could carry on for him. With the passing of the years, a mythology would be created that it was at this time, after his eldest son's death, that he coaxed Jack into politics. But Joe had begun thinking of Jack's potential in politics back when he was still at Choate.

During the Christmas holidays of 1944, he sat down with Jack to discuss his future. If Jack really wanted to make a difference in the world, Joe told him, he should definitely go into politics. Jack agreed; he was more than ready. Besides, these days when his dad talked about the future, Jack started to see something in his old man he hadn't seen since before his brother was killed: Kennedy spirit.

PART VIII

These Ties
That Bind

JOE'S SURPRISING CONFESSION

We have just had the most perfect four days imaginable at your house. How can the rest of our lives help but be a tragic anticlimax?

Those had been the words of the new Mrs. John Kennedy in a note to actress Marion Davies after she and Jack spent part of their honeymoon at the Beverly Hills estate Davies once shared with her late partner, the tycoon William Randolph Hearst. Unfortunately, Jackie's sentiment was more prophetic than she could've imagined at the time she committed those words to paper. Within just a year, she and Jack would face their first major crucible.

In the summer of 1954, Jackie noticed that Jack seemed to be suffering more and more physically. Of course, she'd gotten used to watching him cope with chronic pain. Lately, though, it seemed to be taking over. She also thought he looked skeletal. When she asked him to weigh himself, she was shocked to find he came in at just 140 pounds. She knew his clothes had been hanging off him. He told her he hadn't been that thin since his brother Joe's death. He could barely make it onto the floor of the Senate, even with his crutches. Some wondered how he ever got through the day. "It's no way for a man to live," said Bobby.

In August, the Kennedys went to New York to meet with one of the best orthopedic specialists in the country. X-rays taken at that time showed that Jack's fifth lumbar vertebra had collapsed. The physician believed it was the result of steroid use prescribed over the years for his Addison's. (Later that interpretation of these X-rays would be disputed.) This doctor and others suggested a complex surgery known as a double spinal fusion. It involved breaking bones in Jack's back and resetting and fusing them. He was told the chances for a successful outcome were slim. He might not even survive it or, as he later said, "This is the one that kills you or cures you."

Jack, at just thirty-seven, was determined to not live in pain or on crutches for the rest of his life. He decided he could deal with the uncertainty of the operation. He was used to uncertainty. His entire life had been nothing if not uncertain. So, yes, he wanted the risky operation and just hoped Jackie could understand. Of course she did. She went with him to the Cape to talk to his parents about it. "I have to go under the knife," Jack told his father. "I have no choice, Dad. I can't live like this."

When Joe wanted to know the chances of success, Jack leveled with him that they weren't great. Rose Kennedy remembered, "He told his father that even if the risks were fifty-fifty, he would rather be dead than spend the rest of his life hobbling on crutches and paralyzed by pain. Joe told him, 'Think about this carefully. In my experience, second thoughts are best.'" When Jack said his mind was made up, Joe just nodded, rose, and walked out of the room.

That night, while everyone was asleep, the patriarch paced the house, his mind racing. He went to the library, sat down, and let out a loud cry, "like a wounded animal," Jackie later remembered. In bed at the time, she looked over at Jack, who was sound asleep next to her. She got out of bed and walked softly down the stairs. Searching the house room by room, she eventually found Joe in the library. She walked over to him and wrapped her arms around him. "What's wrong, Grandpa?"

It was then that Joe confided in her his greatest fear. Everything Jack was going through, indeed, all he'd been through up until this point in his life, was the fault of the father.

"But how can that be?" Jackie asked.

"I wished him pain," Joe said, his eyes filling with the tears he'd been trying to withhold.

According to what Jackie later remembered to family members, Joe said he once feared Jack enjoyed such a privileged lifestyle he'd find it impossible to relate to the less fortunate. "I wanted him to become a better man," he explained, "and, when we decided on politics, a better public servant." He said he realized there was something distant and removed about his son, and he couldn't put his finger on it. Like many others in Jack's life, Joe recognized Jack's apparent lack of empathy. He concluded that if Jack were to face some serious challenges, perhaps it would deepen his compassion for others. He could barely choke the words out again: "I wished him pain." He said it had just been a fleeting thought, but that he'd had it several times, this hope that his son might suffer, "but nothing like this," he promised Jackie, "nothing at all like this."

Jackie didn't know what to say. She'd never heard of a father wishing hardship on his son. However, she could see how much pain Joe was in as he gave her his confession. She sat with him, tried to comfort him, console him. "We will never speak of this again, Grandpa," she told him. In fact, it would be eighteen years, 1972, before she would tell anyone in her family this troubling story.

The operation was set for October 21, 1954, at the New York Hospital for Special Surgery. Jackie spent the night before the surgery with Jack in his room. The next morning, she held his hand as he was wheeled down the corridor to the operating room. When they stopped before the elevator, she kissed him on the lips. When the doors closed, she said, "That was the first time I ever really prayed."

The operation took three hours. When Jack was finally brought back to his room, doctors were somewhat hopeful and told the family the surgery had been a success. Three days later, however, things took a turn for the worse. Jack slipped into a coma. Doctors summoned the family to tell them he wasn't expected to live. Joe called his friend Cardinal Francis Spellman, Archbishop of New York, and asked him to perform last rites. He'd lost track of how many times the sacrament had been performed on his son. Everyone was bereft, especially Jackie, who'd been married a little more than a year and might soon become a widow. Slowly, though, Jack rallied, as he always did.

For weeks, Jack would lay with a draining, open, eight-inch wound on his back. "I was sitting in bed with a lot of acute discomfort," he recalled. "I didn't read much because it was so goddamned uncomfortable, and then I was being woken up every half hour to do this test on my blood."

Kenny O'Donnell recalled, "It felt to me as if he'd given up, as if he'd finally met his match. He was disinterested in politics for the first time since running for Congress. He couldn't think straight; who cared about politics?"

It's a shame, considering the hell he went through, that years later in 1964 the wisdom of this surgery would have to be called into question by his wife. "He didn't even need the operation," Jackie said. "It was that he'd had a bad back since college, and then the war, and he'd had a disc operation he never needed [this was the 1954 surgery], so all those muscles had gotten weak, had gone into spasm, and that was what was giving him pain, the muscles." She called the operation "just criminal."

Dr. Nassir Ghaemi, an MD, MPH, professor of psychiatry at Tufts University, and lecturer in psychiatry at Harvard Medical School, was the first psychiatrist and one of the few physicians to ever access JFK's complete medical records. After he reviewed them, he agreed with Jackie. In 2024, he said, "Kennedy's back pain was not due to a war injury; his spinal X-rays did *not* show major bony abnormalities. He did have the harmful evidence of a prior, probably unnecessary, spinal fusion [meaning, again, the 1954 surgery]. Most of his back pain, though, was likely just due to serious muscle spasms, nothing more."

Just before Christmas 1954, Jack was well enough to be released from the New York hospital and return to Palm Beach. While it was hoped the Florida sunshine would aid in his recuperation, by February 1955 he was no better. That month, he went back to New York for yet another surgery. Then, he went back to Palm Beach again for more recuperation. Barbara Gibson recalled, "Rose later told me it had been that second surgery that really did him in. Every morning he'd sit up in bed with a dazed expression as Jackie forced him to eat breakfast. 'Do you feel any better today, Jack?' she'd ask. He'd just stare at her, unable to speak or move, his entire body aching. His medication was so strong, he was delirious. When anyone sat on his bed, he'd scream out in pain."

Changing her husband's bandages every few hours became Jackie's job, which she took on with great bravery. As she administered to him, it was as if she had real nursing experience. "It was an open wound that seemed to be infected most of the time," recalled Lem Billings, who stayed with his friend for three weeks, "and now and then a piece of bone would come out of this wound. We'd find pieces of bone in his dressings, little bone fragments, four weeks after the operation. It was constantly draining. His pain was excruciating. We almost lost him. I don't mean just lost him by dying—we almost lost him as a person, quite frankly."

PROFILES IN COURAGE

While recovering in Palm Beach, Jack Kennedy used his long hours of suffering to mull over an idea for a project that might take his mind off his recovery. He wanted to write a series of articles about noteworthy senators who, by their own acts of courage, rose to meet their moments in history and then faced great controversy as a result. John Adams, the second U.S. president, had been Jack's muse for his bold 1800 decision to break with his Federalist Party and pursue diplomacy over war with France during the Quasi-War. He tasked his young aide, twenty-four-year-old Ted Sorensen, with the job of finding more stories about such men.

In years to come, Ted Sorensen would become Jack's special counsel, adviser, and primary speechwriter. Few would ever be as loyal to him as Sorensen was. He took this particular task as seriously as any other he'd ever tackle and came back to Jack with many examples of courageous senators, such as Massachusetts's Daniel Webster, who championed the Compromise of 1850; Edmund G. Ross from Kansas, who voted for Andrew Johnson's acquittal in his impeachment trial; and Texas's Sam Houston, who spoke out against the Kansas-Nebraska Act of 1854.

Ten years earlier, after his brother's death, Jack had compiled a book of tributes called *We Remember Joe*. Sorensen now suggested they whittle down the list of subjects he'd compiled to eight and then write a book of vignettes about them, instead of just an article. Joe loved the idea and thought it might even help better position Jack politically. Though he didn't tip his hand at the time, he actually anticipated pulling whatever strings necessary to have his son be awarded a Pulitzer Prize. It was a lofty goal, but the senior Kennedy was confident that he could pull it off. What was the point of writing a book if you're not going to get a Pulitzer for it?

The challenge Jack faced was that he had so many ideas and had done so much research, he couldn't distill the material into easily read chapters. "Read by scholars, yes," Ted Sorensen later said. "Read by politicians, yes. But read by the person at home? No. For that, he needed help."

"Joe asked me to find other writers, people who could come in and take what Jack wrote and fine-tune it," recalled his secretary, Janet DesRosiers. "It wasn't to deceive people. It was just to get the job done. I typed up research papers which Joe had paid to be written by others, and these papers eventually became chapters in the book."

"Jack was still sick," said Joey Gargan. "There was no way on God's green earth he could write a whole book. He outlined things, talked to others about what he wanted, supervised things, but sitting there and writing a book while he was in that kind of pain? That was asking a lot of any man."

In the end, Ted Sorensen wrote most of what would become *Profiles in Courage*. It wasn't unusual then, and isn't today, for a public person to have a ghostwriter. Chuck Spalding noted, "That's the way Churchill's books were written, by dictation and organization and a group of people putting it together, and then finally he puts his stamp on it. He [Jack] must have said, 'Well, that's the way for me to handle it.' *Profiles* was all organized around material which he originally conceived of." Sorensen would later elaborate that while Jack wrote the first and last chapters, he himself had written most of the rest. It was then Jackie's idea to show the finished manuscript to Michael Canfield, Lee's husband, in the hope that he'd show it to his father, Cass Canfield, president of the Harper & Row publishing company. That turned out to be a good idea. *Profiles in Courage* was published in January 1956 and soon became a bestseller.

> *In whatever arena of life one may meet the challenge of courage, whatever may be the sacrifices he faces if he follows his conscience—the loss of his friends, his fortune, his contentment, even the esteem of his fellow men—each man must decide for himself the course he will follow. The stories of past courage can define that ingredient—they can teach, they can offer hope, they can provide inspiration. But they cannot supply courage itself. For this each man must look into his own soul.*

Two years later, in December 1957, there would be a huge controversy about *Profiles in Courage*.

After it became a national bestseller, Joe went for that Pulitzer, as planned. He appealed to his friend Arthur Krock at the *New York Times* to convince enough people on the board to vote for *Profiles,* and sure enough it was awarded the prize. This was an achievement that took everyone's breath away. Joe proved once again that he'd stop at nothing to make his and his son's dreams come true. "It was for Joe as much as for Jack," Janet DesRosiers said. "Let's be honest."

Trouble started when newspaper columnist Drew Pearson asserted to Mike Wallace of ABC News that JFK had been awarded a top prize for a book he hadn't actually written. Pearson said the lie "indicates the kind of public relations setup he's had." Naturally, the report infuriated Jack, who now felt his integrity was being impugned. Of course, he really *hadn't* written *all* of it—and maybe, to hear Ted Sorensen later tell it, not even most of it. "I think Ted Sorensen got this rumor started, if you want to know the truth," Lem Billings bitterly stated in his JFK oral history. "I heard Jack bawl Sorensen out because he knew Sorensen had leaked that story," said Lem. "This is the one thing Sorensen did wrong in his career with Jack, giving himself more credit than he deserved. It was a mean, mean thing [for Sorensen] to do."

Feeling backed against a wall, Jack did what politicians usually do when they're in the wrong: he doubled down. He instructed his attorney Clark Clifford to threaten a $50 million lawsuit against the ABC network unless it retracted its statement. Despite Mike Wallace's ire, because he really did believe Pearson was telling the truth, ABC issued a fulsome retraction and apology.

BAD BLOOD

In March 1955, Jackie announced she was pregnant with their first child. A few months later, the Kennedys moved into a large estate called Hickory Hill not far from Merrywood in Virginia. An enormous and stately Georgian mansion on six lush acres, it was many, *many* times bigger than the small Georgetown home they'd been living in at this time. They paid $125,000 for it, about $1.5 million in today's money.

By the time Jack returned to the Senate in the summer, he was still weak but trying his best to project an image of restored health and vitality. "He'd walk all around the Senate looking wonderful and tan in his gray suit," Jackie said, "and then he'd come home and go in a hospital bed."

He'd been through such a terrible ordeal, many people thought it had changed him. "Something important happened to him when he had that illness," said his friend Joseph Alsop, "because he came out of it a very much more serious fellow than he was prior to it. He had gone through the valley of the shadow of death and had displayed immense courage."

Somehow, Jack had survived, maybe not physically stronger but definitely with renewed determination to live life to the fullest. If only the man thought to have written *Profiles in Courage* had the courage to resist temptation. Apparently, he didn't. After all this time and all he'd endured—and maybe *because* of all he'd endured—the Scandinavian beauty Gunilla von Post was still on his mind. She had previously rebuffed him but, somehow, that rejection made him want her even more, especially with the passing of time. He figured he might be able to persuade her to change her mind and do what she hadn't wanted to do the first time they met, which was to sleep with him. Therefore, when he was finally well enough to travel, he wrote to her to suggest that they meet up again in the summer. In his head, of course, none of this had anything to do with Jackie.

"He said he'd be visiting Indochina and Formosa when the Senate adjourned in July, but first he was coming to Europe," Gunilla recalled. "Obsessed with the Riviera, he wanted me to suggest an Italian beach where we could relax and watch the surf roll in for a couple of weeks." No, she said. She wanted him to meet her folks and suggested he come to Sweden. He agreed and later wrote that he'd arranged to be in Sweden on July 10, again traveling with his partner in crime, Torbert Macdonald.

Three months into her pregnancy, Jackie suffered a miscarriage. Afterward, she fell into a depression. She'd really wanted the baby, as did Jack. Soon after the miscarriage, she began having bouts of extreme fear, dizziness, her breath going shallow, her hands going numb. She would throw up. Today, we think of this phenomenon as a panic attack, or an anxiety episode. Back in 1955, though, no such formal diagnosis existed. Janet used to say her daughter just needed to calm down, get more sleep, or maybe go out and get some fresh air. It wouldn't be until 1980 that the idea of panic attacks, or panic disorders, was officially recognized and understood by the medical community. Jackie began experiencing these episodes as early as 1955, and would continue to do so for her entire marriage to Jack Kennedy. It's worth noting that they decreased significantly by the mid-1960s, after he was gone.

Because losing the baby had been such a bitter disappointment, Jack's response to it was mystifying to Jackie. While he tried to be sympathetic and attentive, Jackie intuited that it didn't come naturally for him. He seemed unable to communicate such feelings of comfort to her. Worse, he said that given all they'd been through of late, they should take separate vacations. He said Jackie could go to visit her sister in England while he and Torbert Macdonald would go "somewhere else," meaning Sweden. Naturally, Jackie was unhappy about it. It was precisely *because* of all they'd been through, she argued, that they should be together, not apart. He was insistent. For her, it was maddening and confusing. She felt it obvious that he was planning to meet another woman abroad. What other explanation could there be?

In May, Jackie called her father, Jack Bouvier, to ask about his summer plans. Her cousin John Davis recalled, "Bouvier said he was going to the south of France at the end of August. Jackie decided to take her husband up on his suggestion, go to England to be with Lee and then go to France to be with her father. Therefore, at the beginning of July, she sailed alone to Europe."

"It's over," Jackie told Lee when she got to her and Michael's flat. She said her marriage had been a big mistake. He definitely wasn't the man she'd thought he was, and she said there was "too much bad blood between us." She said she believed he was cheating on her, so "I'm never going back."

Lee was astonished. "Are you sure?" she asked. How else could the idea of separate vacations be explained, Jackie responded. Even if true, Lee felt Jackie was overreacting. "After all, Daddy did it to Mummy the entire time we were growing up," she said, "and it all worked out just fine."

Jackie looked at her with astonishment. "*For whom?*" she asked in disbelief.

JACK'S "MISTAKE"

O n August 7, Gunilla von Post booked two rooms for Jack Kennedy and Torbert Macdonald at the Skanegarden Hotel in Bastad in southwestern Sweden. The next day, she received a telegram from Jack, which he'd sent from the USS *United States*:

A Bientot—Jack

French for "See you soon."

Jack had been married to Jackie for almost two years. He'd been sick for most of that time and so she, as his primary caregiver, had been the only woman in his life since the day they wed. That was about to change.

On August 11, the best friends arrived in Sweden, Jack on crutches. Two years had passed since he'd last seen Gunilla in Cannes. At that time, he told her he was engaged, after which she made the decision not to sleep with him. Apparently, Gunilla now felt differently. Jack asked Torb to handle their bags while he took her to his room.

Some of Gunilla's descriptions of her time with Jack that week—"We were wonderfully sensual. There were times when just the stillness of being together was thrilling enough."—sound a great deal more like some sort of starry-eyed, fictional version of JFK than a realistic one. Much of what she'd recall in a series of 1997 interviews, and then in a book she wrote called *Love, Jack,* sounds unlikely given what we now know of his remote personality of the 1950s. It does, however, maybe sound like the JFK of the 1940s, the more romantic version of him back in the days when he was with Inga Arvad. Maybe, in this case, the devil isn't in the details, though. There are enough witnesses to Jack and Gunilla's public outings, including close friends and relatives she identified by name, to confirm that they were definitely together. While they were the only two who could testify to their private encounters, is it realistic to think Jack would've been with such a beautiful woman for a week and not have sex with her?

"It was Torby, and Torby alone, who slipped some clues about Jack's unhappy marriage," Gunilla recalled, "although during his entire visit, Jack never mentioned it." Gunilla said Torb told her, "Just watching the way Jack is with you, I don't know—it's funny. He's never that way with his wife. He's written you all those letters, but I don't think he's even sent her a card!"

It's untrue that Jack never sent Jackie a card. Back when they were dating in April 1953, he'd sent her a postcard from Palm Beach, simply writing, "Wish you were here." Jackie would later say it had been his only written expression of affection during their courtship. He did send her a telegram when she was in England covering the queen. It pales in comparison to the many letters that had flown back and forth between him and Inga.

"He was away from his father, the pressures of Washington, the competitive traditions of his family," Gunilla wrote. Apparently, not for long. In the middle of the week, Jack got a telephone call from Joe, who'd tracked him down. He was upset, having had no inkling of his son's plans to go to Sweden. What was he thinking, Joe asked, cheating on Jackie in such a public way in front of witnesses? Joe told him he'd heard Jackie would soon be at a flat in Antibes with Lee and Michael. Instead, he said he was arranging for them to be moved to the Kennedy family's villa at Cap d'Antibes for the rest of August. He'd meet them there, he said, and tell them Jack would also be joining them. He also arranged for Jackie's father, Jack Bouvier, who was already vacationing in the vicinity, to join them. Though the next stop of his and Torb's trip was to be Italy, Jack begrudgingly agreed to his father's plan. He was angry about it, though. Joe had interfered with Inga many years ago, and was now apparently doing the same thing with Gunilla. He told Torbert he wished his father would just keep his nose out of his personal life. He still resented Joe for forcing him to end his relationship with Inga, even after all these years.

Jack's last night with Gunilla was spent at the mansion of her friend Gustav Hageman, outside Gstaad, in southwestern Switzerland. She hoped he'd extend his trip and was disappointed that he couldn't.

"Is that the way you live your life?" she asked. "Doing what your father wants you to do?"

He lied and said, "No, of course not."

The next morning, Gunilla drove Jack and Torb to the airport in

Gstaad. After a kiss, Jack announced, "It's time, Gunilla." Then, he turned away from her and walked with Torb to the plane.

Torb later told a mutual friend that, on the plane en route to France, Jack was filled with remorse. "This was a shitty thing to do to Jackie," he said. "I don't know what's wrong with me." Torb suggested Jack blame any bad decision-making on the many drugs he'd been taking for his pain. Jack vowed to make it up to Jackie, somehow. "I'm just glad she'll never know about Gunilla," he said. "This was a mistake."

"I knew that John Kennedy and I were still very unfinished." That's what Gunilla von Post would later recall thinking after he left her side that day. However, she was very wrong. He would never return to her.

THE ONLY TWO CHOICES

Back in October 1953, a month after she married Jack Kennedy, Jackie Bouvier penned a poem about him and what she viewed as his, to use her term, "emotional wanderlust." From the time they met, she'd felt as if he was searching for something else, something better. He was never consistent with her. Jackie later gave the poem to Rose Kennedy for safekeeping. Not recognizing the subtext, Rose just viewed it as lovely prose. Indeed, typical of Jackie's whimsy, she'd framed Jack in romantic terms.

> *All the things he was going to be . . .*
> *He would build empires*
> *And he would have sons*
> *Others would fall where the current runs*
> *He would find love*
> *He would never find peace*
> *For he must go seeking*
> *The Golden Fleece.*
> *All the things he was going to be*
> *All the things in the wind and sea.*

Jackie always suspected Jack wasn't completely hers. She just hoped that one day that would change. But, almost two years after their wedding, he was more distant than ever. While she wasn't sure there was someone else, she certainly suspected it. She found it hard to believe, though. Would he really do that to her? After everything they'd been through? After the way she'd cared for him at his lowest moments? Was he capable of such betrayal?

The same week Jack was with Gunilla, Jackie was with Lee and Michael in Cap d'Antibes. They were joined there by Lee's English friends Peter Alistair Ward and Claire Baring. "One morning [on August 15], we learned we were being moved to Vista Bella in Cap d'Antibes," Claire Baring once recalled. "It was all very cloak-and-dagger. No one knew what was going on other than that it was arranged by the ambassador. We packed up and moved, like obedient schoolchildren."

"The villa was magnificent, richly furnished with rare antiques by its owners, the Heinz 57 family," said Janet DesRosiers. "It was huge and sat high above the Mediterranean, surrounded by layers of terraced gardens, marble statues gracing every turn, and a back-breaking walk to the sea for a swim. Entering the villa involved climbing a flight of stairs and crossing an iron bridge over railroad tracks. Fabulous, really. What a life this was!"

A day after the contingent relocated, Jack and Torb showed up. That same day, the group was joined at the villa by Joe and Rose Kennedy, Janet DesRosiers, Arthur Houghton, Janine Burke, and a host of high society friends, such as the politician and playwright William Douglas-Home and his wife, Rachel, and the Italian industrialist Gianni Agnelli and his wife, Marella.

With the arrival of so many people, Jackie became frustrated. Why, she wondered, did everything have to always end up a big Kennedy shindig? All she wanted to do was to see her father, who was expected to arrive soon. Once Black Jack showed up, Jackie was better. But then, he told her he'd talked things over with Joe and Arthur and they agreed to send her to a Parisian spa in the Hotel Lutetia so she could clear her head of any thoughts of infidelity or, worse, divorce. Janine Burke made an appointment for a five-day stay beginning on August 29. Jackie was unhappy about it but wasn't able to fight it, not that she tried very hard.

Before leaving the villa, Jackie and Jack shared an embrace. After he whispered something in her ear and kissed her on the forehead, she turned and walked away, her expression steely. She was joined by Janine, and they walked swiftly in lock step through the outdoor patio.

"Is there anything else I can do for you, Mrs. Kennedy?" Janine asked before they parted ways.

Without stopping, Jackie answered, "No, thank you. I think everyone here has done quite enough."

As they walked through the pool area, they saw Rose lying on a chaise lounge reading. While sunbathers were gathered here and there, Rose had taken her lounge and moved it as far away from the others as she could. As she walked over to her, Jackie noticed Rose's large sunglasses and big floppy hat, which shielded her from the sun. More interesting, though, was the fact that she was reading, of all books, the controversial at the time *Lady Chatterley's Lover*. Maybe that's why she'd separated herself.

As Jackie walked over to her, Rose noticed she was dressed in traveling clothes. She sat up and asked, "Going somewhere, dear?" Jackie said she was being sent to "some spa, somewhere." Rose took off her sunglasses. "I certainly hope we're not paying for that, dear," she said, peering at her. Jackie told her she had no idea who was footing the bill. Studying her, Rose must've sensed her discontentment. "You know, dear," she said, "sometimes in this life we women have to take what we get. Or walk away. Those are the only two choices we have. Take what we get. Or walk away." Rose then put her sunglasses back on and laid back down. Jackie stood before her for a moment and, as she later remembered it, couldn't help but stare at her while wondering about the choices the Kennedy matriarch might've made in her own marriage.

PART IX

The Life We Choose

FAMILY TRADITION

―――――――

SEVEN YEARS EARLIER. OCTOBER 1948. HYANNIS PORT, MASSACHUSETTS.

A young woman stood on the wraparound porch of the Kennedys' Hyannis Port house looking thoughtful as she watched Joe Kennedy and his congressman son, Jack, walk the beach. It was a gorgeous day with a seasonal nip in the air. Enfolding herself with her arms, she braced against the cool breeze coming in from the port. An attractive brunette with piercing green eyes, twenty-four-year-old Janet DesRosiers had, in the last month, practically become a Kennedy family member.

It was as if Janet was always around, always with Joe, not just at his estates in Hyannis Port and Palm Beach but even at his apartments in Boston and New York and his villa in France. As such, she was the subject of great curiosity. In fact, not only was she Joe's secretary, tending to his many complex business affairs, she was also the woman responsible for his emotional and physical needs. She was his companion, his lover . . . his mistress. She had also become a good friend to Rose Kennedy, who called her "Miss Dee" because she didn't think the servants would be able to pronounce her French last name. (Her last name is pronounced Day Rose-e-ay.)

As the Kennedy matriarch approached, Janet turned to her and said she was thinking they should start packing up the house for the season. Rose agreed. "The weather is changing, Miss Dee," she said. "Let's make a list as to what we need to leave behind and what we'll take to Palm Beach this season." Janet agreed. She always . . . agreed.

This is Janet's story:

It was around the time Jack was elected to his second term in Congress in 1948 that his parents came to a private, unconventional agreement about their marriage. It's often been said Rose had only submitted to Joe nine times, and that each time resulted in conception. If that's true, by 1948, sixteen years had passed since the youngest, Teddy, was born. From all available evidence, Joe never stopped having women in his bed during that time, though it wouldn't appear Rose was one of them. By the time he was sixty, "the thrill of the chase," as he called it, had waned. Now he wanted more stability and also more than just sex. He wanted common emotional ground with someone other than what little rapport he shared with his wife. He wanted intimacy, and a catalyst for this need was the shocking death of a beloved daughter.

Widowed when Billy Hartington was killed in 1945, Kick Kennedy had fallen for a married earl named Peter Wentworth-Fitzwilliam. Once again, Rose was dismayed because he was Protestant. As she had when Kick was with Billy Hartington, Rose threatened to oust her from the family if she continued with the relationship. "If you break one law, you break them all," she said, referencing James from the Bible. By this time, Rose had assumed the mantle of defender of the faith while apparently forgetting that she was also a mother. Kick could never win with her and went through the same emotional angst with her that she'd gone through with Billy. Everyone else in the family was torn. Kick had always been such an outsized presence and so beloved by her siblings—Jack, in particular—they all just wanted her to be happy. They'd grown weary of their mother's religious obstinance.

Then, in May 1948, another disaster struck: Kick and Peter were both killed in a plane crash in Europe. Jack, of course, was devastated, as was everyone else. Two of the most important people in his life were now gone as if in an instant. It was heartbreaking.

While the deaths of Joe and Kick had impacted the family, even in her grief Rose still wanted what she'd always wanted: her independence. She loved her family in her own way but would still rather travel than stay home, especially as everyone got older. She still wanted a marriage, though, or had at least reconciled herself to the fact that she couldn't leave it because of her religion. But by the time she was fifty-eight, she wanted it on her own terms. This meant spending less time with Joe. Not only did she not want to be intimate with him, she also didn't want to have to entertain deep conversations about their lost children. She had given him nine heirs, including sons to carry on his name and satisfy his political aspirations. He, in turn, had financed her life, and continued to do so. At this new crossroads, she told him to find someone else to satisfy his emotional and physical needs, and then she gave him carte blanche to do just that.

Joe selected Janet DesRosiers out of forty interviews he conducted personally at the Ritz-Carlton in Boston for what was advertised as a secretarial job. From a small town in Massachusetts, Janet worked for a law firm in Worcester before clerking for the Massachusetts Superior Court. She was capable, smart, and intuitive. With her glowing complexion and terrific figure, she looked as if she could've been a model. Months later, Joe would tell her she'd had the job from the moment he'd laid eyes on her. She was impressed with him, too. Today, more than seventy-five years later, her first impression of Joe Kennedy remains vivid. "Though Joe was sixty, he was vital and tall at six feet, about 190 pounds, and straight as an arrow, not at all stooped with age," Janet DesRosiers recalled. "His round glasses gave him a professorial look. When he walked into a room, he filled it up. His smile was on, the joviality was there. I could tell he enjoyed a joke and a laugh. Of course, I thought I was being hired as his secretary. Certainly, nothing more ever would've crossed my mind."

On Labor Day 1948, about two weeks after he hired her, Joe introduced Janet to Rose.

"What does she offer us?" Rose asked Joe when they were alone.

"Freedom," he answered.

"Is she Catholic?" Rose asked.

"Yes," he answered.

"Very good," concluded Rose. "Just do not disrespect me," she said. "That's all I ask."

According to what Joe later told Janet, that was the extent of his conversation with his wife about the young woman who'd spend the better part of the next ten years as a third party in their marriage.

Labor Day was also when Joe introduced Janet to Arthur Houghton. Arthur knew exactly what his best friend meant when he said he wanted a new secretary. Looking at Janet, however, so wide-eyed and innocent, he wasn't sure she was right for the job.

"She doesn't look like that kind of girl," he told Joe.

"Give her time," was Joe's response.

While they were speaking, Jack walked into the room with a white towel wrapped around him, having just showered. "Sorry. Didn't know we had guests," he said with a smile.

"Yes, *I* have a guest," Joe said, already staking out his territory. Jack winked at Arthur and left the room.

Janet would be in charge of the entire domestic staff, meaning the butler, cook, and other kitchen helpers as well as upstairs and downstairs maids, laundresses, chauffeurs, gardeners, and anyone employed at the property. Joe moved her into a small, furnished apartment in the Cape neighborhood. She'd report to work at the Big House at nine sharp and leave at five. He also rented a two-bedroom house for her in West Palm Beach, about ten minutes from the Kennedy estate there. Soon after her hiring, he began calling her late at night to talk. "I would just get home and the phone would ring. It would be him," she recalled. "He said he was lonely. He needed someone to talk to. I thought, *What about his wife?* But I could soon tell she wasn't that person for him."

While he was obviously tough-tempered, as she got to know him Janet found a paradoxical fragility in Joe. Whenever he talked about his deceased children, for instance, tears streamed down his face. He often spoke of his love for all his family. "All I want is for them to be okay," he'd say. "Everything I ever do I do for my children. There's not one minute when I am not thinking of them, planning for them, wanting for them."

In December 1948, three months after she was hired, Janet, who was a virgin, was finally seduced by Joe. They first made love in her rented Palm Beach house, which Joe had already begun calling "our home." Janet said, "He was powerful, charming, a man's man and very kind. From that day on, he clung to me with a possessiveness that was sometimes smothering. He had everything he needed in his kingdom except for somebody who belonged to him solely. I soon became that person.

"We started traveling to New York together and staying at his Park Avenue place. Or, his home in the South of France. Sometimes, Rose was with us, sometimes not. When she was in town, we would watch television together while I massaged Joe's scalp and neck, the three of us content in our strange, little world. I saw a side of him no one ever saw, or maybe knew even existed. He was so special. I remember many nights eating chocolate cake and giggling in the kitchen late at night after lovemaking. The servants understood and accepted it. If it was approved by Rose, a devout Catholic who went to Mass every day and sometimes twice, why wouldn't it be okay with the cook?"

For Janet, the arrangement allowed her an exciting, thrilling lifestyle. She didn't feel used; she felt valued. "He was wonderful to me," she said. "I was young. I was dumb. When he refurbished his yacht, the *Marlin,* which Rose was never fond of, we spent many summer days in the main cabin making love. If I'm honest, I was swept away by the power, the money, the glamour, all of which was so intoxicating."

For Rose, her acceptance of Janet had been an empowering decision, or at least that's how she looked at it. She thought of Janet as an asset, not an intrusion. After all, Janet took a lot of pressure off her by giving her the freedom to be occupied with her faith, charities, and travels. One of Joe's most distinguished biographers, David Nasaw, who wrote *The Patriarch,* estimates that she and Joe spent "three hundred or so days a year apart." At family dinners, Janet recalled, "Joe was at the head of the table, Jack on his right, Bobby and Teddy on his left, and I was buried somewhere in the middle between the girls. With Rose gone, I never sat opposite Joe as if I was replacing the mother. I always sat with the daughters, as if I was one of them."

When Janet was first hired, Rose's advice to her where Joe was concerned was, "Always be a supplicant, dear. That's what's best." It was the same advice she gave her daughters regarding the men in their lives. Even though she resented the fact that she long ago was forced to sublimate her desires to the whims of a domineering father and then spouse, Rose was still a woman of her time. She didn't hope for much different for Eunice, Pat, or Jean. "You have to know when to keep your mouth shut," she used to tell them. In contrast, imagine Janet Auchincloss ever telling Jackie and Lee to submit to or be subordinate to a man. To the contrary, Janet, always so forward thinking, would sometimes say, "I refuse to raise weak daughters," and she meant it. She even began to influence Janet DesRosiers in that respect. She and DesRosiers became close while planning the wedding of Jack and Jackie in 1953. Janet Auchincloss suspected something was going on between the young woman and the Kennedy patriarch, but she wasn't certain and didn't push for details.

On the big day, Joe decided he wanted Janet DesRosiers at the Hammersmith reception in case any problems arose she'd need to handle. However, he didn't make arrangements for her travel. Instead, he told her to drive herself to Newport in her Cadillac, which had been a gift from him. It was to be a three-hour drive. He also told her that he and Rose had made arrangements to spend the night somewhere else in Newport, so after the reception she should drive back to Hyannis, which was another three hours. While she agreed to the plan, she was unhappy about it.

"By this time, I was having serious reservations," Janet DesRosiers recalled. "I was wondering if maybe I was making a mistake with my life. I started feeling anxious, especially when Joe was so unkind about a wedding I'd spent so many hours planning with Mrs. Auchincloss. I felt it was unfair."

After the reception, Janet DesRosiers mentioned to Janet Auchincloss that she would be returning to Hyannis in the middle of the night. Janet was surprised that she'd agreed to such a thing.

"But, Mrs. Auchincloss, you don't understand," Janet DesRosiers told her. "Mr. Kennedy is up here," she said as she raised her left hand, palm down, "and we're all down here," she concluded, holding her right hand at a lower level.

Janet Auchincloss took the young woman's right hand into her own. "No," she said, as she raised it to a height equal to her left. "We're all up here," she said. "He's no better than any of us."

Janet Auchincloss then said something that would really stick with Miss DesRosiers. "You have to start living the life of the woman you want to be," she told her. Miss DesRosiers flinched. It was as if this matriarch had read her mind and somehow knew she was beginning to ache for more than what she presently had as Joe's companion. It would take a number of years, though, for her to finally make a decision where Joe was concerned, but Jackie's mother had definitely planted the seed.

While the arrangement Joe Kennedy had with Janet DesRosiers was advantageous for him and for Rose, one wonders how it affected their children. "I can't say what was going on in the family," Janet admitted in 2024. "I only knew what was going on for me. Looking back now, I wonder."

Though Janet didn't realize it at the time, Jack Kennedy never approved, and neither did his siblings. Of course, Jack knew his father had affairs; everyone knew it. This was different, though. This woman was practically living with the family, in the house with his mother.

"What's with you and Janet?" Jack asked his father while the two were in Arthur Houghton's company in early 1950.

"She's a wonderful woman," was Joe's answer.

Jack looked at him with narrowed eyes. "Half your age, and Mother's okay with this?" Joe glared at him and said it was between him and Rose. "I guess as long as you're happy," Jack said, "that's what matters, right, Dad?" Joe didn't respond. "I couldn't have Inga, yet you do this?" he asked, this time definitely, as Joe might've put it, poking the bear. Luckily for him, Joe ignored the remark.

Even though Jack knew his mother had not only approved of Janet but was complicit in the arrangement, it was a bridge too far for him. It actually made him lose a little respect for her. She was his mother, though, and the bond between them, tenuous as it was at times, remained. But when it came to his father, that was a different story: he hated him for the arrangement, and it wouldn't be the first time he felt that way.

PROTECTING THE LIE

It was another dreamy Cape Cod summer. The Kennedys had just moved into their Hyannis Port home and Joe wanted to show it off to his lover, the famous actress Gloria Swanson. Claiming that Rose wanted to meet her, he invited Gloria to join them for an August weekend. After the stunning Miss Swanson showed up on August 10, Rose acted as if it were the most natural thing in the world to chat with her husband's mistress while they sat on her veranda and enjoyed the ocean view. It was also the first time Gloria, who, at thirty, was on her third of six husbands, saw Joe as a family man. She couldn't help but note his pride as he introduced her to his brood of young sons and daughters.

One Sunday, Joe decided to take Gloria out sailing on Nantucket Sound in his yacht, the *Rose Elizabeth*, so named for his wife. As he and Gloria set sail, they didn't know they had a stowaway: young Jack. Once out on the Sound, Joe trimmed the sails and anchored the boat. It was a beautiful day as he and Gloria then stretched out on the deck.

Peeking out from his hiding spot, Jack saw something he'd never forget: Joe and Gloria, both clothed but doing something sexual. We don't know exactly what it was, but Jack was so stunned, he panicked and jumped overboard. Joe, hearing the splash, peered over the side of the boat and, much to his surprise, found his son in the water. Jack was actually a good swimmer but, still, Joe was alarmed. "Jack!" he hollered out in surprise as he took off his pants, shucked his glasses, and jumped in after him.

Joe quickly grabbed Jack and, with one arm, swam back to the boat. After Gloria dropped the rope ladder, she and Joe helped the boy up and then wrapped him in towels. Jack had no explanation, at least not one he wanted to offer in front of Joe's lover. Joe pulled him aside and gave him a whispered lecture, instructing him as to what to say to his mother once they returned to shore. "You just fell, Jack, that's it. For no good reason, you fell," he said, and that's exactly what Jack later said happened.

Years later, Jack would confide in close friends that it had been his mother who told him to sneak aboard that yacht. He came to believe she wanted him to see what his father was up to behind everyone's back. It was her way, at least this was Jack's theory, of poisoning him against his father. Once he realized what was happening, he explained, he jumped into the water because it was the only thing his young mind could think of to make Joe stop. He wished he could forget the incident, but try as he might to do so there remained in his head the striking image of his father having sex with Gloria Swanson. "I hated him for that," Jack said.

As instructed, young Kennedy never told his mother about what happened that sunny day on a yacht christened in her honor, not that she would've been the least bit surprised. Not only had he been put into the position of protecting his father's lie, his mother had made him a part of it.

He was twelve.

PART X

Scorched Earth

MOMENT OF TRUTH

It was January 1956 and Jack and Jackie Kennedy's marriage was in tatters since their separate vacations. While Jackie's sister, Lee, was in the States from England for the holidays, she ran into George Smathers's wife, Rosemary, at a New Year's Eve party. Lee's friend from London, Terrance Landow, recalled, "Lee told me that as the two women chatted, Rosemary said she'd heard Jack had been with some other woman when he was in Sweden. She regretted saying it right away, said she'd misspoke, and hoped Lee would forget all about it. However, that was wishful thinking." Lee felt she had no choice but to tell Jackie.

Shocked, Jackie immediately called the Smathers's home to talk to Rosemary. Rosemary told her all she had was secondhand information, but that Torbert Macdonald had said something about a woman named Gunilla. That's all she knew.

While Jackie certainly suspected Jack might've been with someone else, she didn't want to believe it. When she confronted him, he denied knowing anyone named Gunilla. Backed into a corner, he did what his political instincts usually had him do when challenged: he doubled down. According to one person with knowledge of the conversation, he became defensive and tried to turn the tables.

"What kind of marriage do we have if you can't trust me?" he asked.

But she refused to let him manipulate her. "Just admit it!" she challenged him. "I hate liars and you know this, Jack! *You know this!*"

A story circulated within the family about what happened; it may be apocryphal, but it sounds true. Jackie was said to have pulled back and struck Jack so hard, she heard his neck crack as his head whipped to one side. Then, with the back of the same hand, she went to slap him again. This time, he grabbed her wrist hard and said, "Don't you dare!" He then held it tightly until she relented. It sounds true because that's the way Janet Auchincloss would sometimes slap her daughters—the palm of one hand then, in swift and terrible succession, the back of the same hand.

"How could you do this to me?" Jackie tearfully asked him. "I would never do this to you. Never."

There was only one person Jackie could confide in about Gunilla—her mother. While she knew it would likely open a Pandora's box with Janet, she needed to talk to somebody. She didn't trust friends to keep what had happened confidential, and Lee was headed back to England.

Janet was upset. How, she asked her daughter, did she intend to proceed? If it were up to her, she'd go straight to the courthouse and file divorce papers. Jackie felt that would only escalate the situation because Jack would fight it tooth and nail.

"*But this does not happen to me,*" Jackie insisted.

Her mother wholeheartedly agreed. "If that son of a bitch thinks we're going to put up with this," Janet said, according to a later account, "he's wrong. This ends now."

Did Jackie want her to talk to him? No, Jackie said, she'd handle it herself.

In the end, while Jack never actually admitted to an affair with Gunilla, he did at least make an effort to be more solicitous toward his wife. When Jackie announced she was pregnant at the beginning of March, her mother was perplexed. She had been so disturbed about this other woman, and now she was pregnant again? Jackie claimed she didn't know how it happened. "We all know how it happened," Janet told her. Jackie said she was now going to move past her anger and just focus on the upcoming baby. Perhaps, she said, it might help put her marriage on the right track.

While fatherhood was now in the offing for Jack, that didn't mean he was going to stop compartmentalizing his life. In April 1956, he negotiated with a travel agency in Cannes to lease a yacht for the third week of August. He intended to take a Mediterranean cruise around Capri and Elba with the same cast of characters—George Smathers, Torb Macdonald, along with his brother Teddy. They were set to leave on August 18, right after the upcoming Democratic Convention.

In May 1956, Jean Kennedy married Stephen Smith in New York. Because Jack was busy making convention plans, he was unable to attend most of the after-parties. At one such event, Ethel went up to Jackie and, being an instigator, said, "How nice that you're letting Jack take a cruise after the convention. Personally, I would never let Bobby go anywhere while I'm pregnant, but bully for you."

Jackie, of course, didn't know anything about any of it. Lying, she said she felt he deserved time off. She then let it sit for three months, waiting for Jack to tell her about it. Finally, in July, a few weeks before the start of the convention, he revealed his plans, which he described as having *just* been arranged as a surprise gift to Teddy for graduating from Harvard.

Jackie's due date was in September. It made no sense to her that Jack would go abroad so close to it. He said the timing was perfect because he'd be back in time for the baby. Jackie Kennedy would have had to be a complete fool to not be suspicious. And Jackie Kennedy was no one's fool.

JACK'S DEFINING MOMENT

In early August 1956, Joe Kennedy was on holiday in the South of France, as usual for this time of year. "I'm worried about Jack," he told Arthur Houghton. "He's got a hard head these days. Doesn't listen to me like he used to." When Arthur noted that Jack had often been headstrong, Joe said, "Not when it matters most. Now, he wants to be vice president, which is a fool's errand." Joe felt it could be "his first big loss in politics."

There had been a growing movement in the Democratic Party to nominate Jack Kennedy for VP on the Democratic ticket with Adlai Stevenson II, governor of Illinois and grandson of Adlai Stevenson I, twenty-third VP of the United States. However, Joe felt that Republican incumbent Ike Eisenhower was invincible. He'd had a strong first term. Even a heart attack in 1955 hadn't weakened him. Joe felt there was no way Adlai would beat Eisenhower, and a lot of people agreed. Worse, Joe feared that as Adlai's running mate, Jack would be blamed for his defeat because of his Catholicism.

Now thirty-nine, Jack had begun to rely less on Joe's instincts and more on his own. The father's view of things, while at least heard by the son, wasn't going to be determinative. Jack had been calculating his next political move for some time, the goal, of course, being the White House. Unlike his father, he'd begun to think that the role of VP to Stevenson made some sense. By the time of the Democratic Convention at Chicago's International Amphitheater on August 13, he was ready to do whatever it took to get that nomination.

On Thursday of the convention, Adlai Stevenson made a surprising announcement. In trying to create more excitement for the ticket, he de-

cided to throw open the convention and let the delegates choose his running mate. He wanted the party to make the decision, not just one man. The
front runner was Senator Estes Kefauver of Tennessee. For the next twenty-
four hours, he and the other contenders, including JFK, would scramble for
that nomination. They'd have just one day to campaign among the delegates
before voting. "Call Dad and tell him I'm going for it," Jack told Bobby.

Joe was in France with Rose, Janet DesRosiers, Arthur Houghton, Janine Burke, and other friends. He was irritable and sleep-deprived, suffering
at the time from an enlarged prostate.

Janine Burke wrote in her journal:

> *When the phone rang and it was Bobby, we all held our breaths not knowing
> what to expect. Mr. Kennedy shouted at Bobby on the phone that he and Jack
> were "idiots"—his exact word. Then—"Hello? Hello?" Either the line went
> dead or Bobby hung up. "Get him back," Joe shouted. "Get that little prick
> back!" Arthur dialed the number but it was impossible, phone connections
> being what they were back then. Or, maybe Bobby didn't pick up. "That kid
> thinks he's bulletproof," he said of Jack. "But he's not." He said his lack of
> solid legislative achievement thus far would be a big detriment to him.*

What Joe thought about what Jack and Bobby were doing didn't matter.
"The train had left the station and Jack picked Governor Abraham Ribicoff
of Connecticut to place his name in nomination," recalled Senator George
Smathers. "Then, he called me in the middle of the night and said, 'Old pal,'
which was always when he wanted to get something from you, it was always
old pal—'have you heard that Stevenson has opened the convention up on
the vice president?' No, I hadn't heard that. 'Old pal, I want you to do me a
favor. I want you to nominate me.' 'Oh, my God, Jack,' I said. 'You've got no
business having me nominate you. In the first place, I'm a deep Southerner.'
However, he was adamant about me giving the seconding speech. I asked
what he wanted me to say. 'Just talk about the war and PT-109 and shit like
that,' he said. 'You'll have twenty minutes. Don't worry,' he said, revved up,
'nothing can go wrong. Tomorrow's my day, Senator! It's my goddamn day!'
I said, 'Sure, Jack,' hung up, chuckled to myself, and thought, *I'll do whatever
I can for the old pal.* Of course I would."

Jack would spend the next morning campaigning hard with delegates
to win their vote. Some were for him, some against him, no surprise
there. Some cited his Catholicism as a negative. Indeed, the prevailing

sentiment remained that a Catholic could never be president. But what about VP?

———

It was the last day of the convention. "Texas proudly casts its fifty-six votes for the fighting sailor who wears the scars of battle," Senate Majority Leader Lyndon Johnson shouted out when his state's delegation was recognized. "And the next vice president of the United States, Senator Kennedy of Massachusetts!" The placard-waving crowd of about ten thousand delegates, alternates, and onlookers cheered loudly as sheer pandemonium broke out. Sam Rayburn, Speaker of the House and chairman of the convention, banged his gavel repeatedly for order, but the cheering wouldn't subside.

In the first ballot count, JFK came in close behind Estes Kefauver in delegate votes. He drew even more support with the second ballot, and it seemed as if victory was assured with only thirty-nine votes shy. But then, things shifted and the tide turned. With one state after another going to Kefauver, it looked like Jack was going to fail. Even though things had turned against him, his determination to avoid looking like a loser gave way to what would be viewed as a real defining moment in his political career.

After Jack found his pregnant wife, insistent on being there despite doctors' orders, he and Jackie pushed their way through the bustling crowd. He bolted up to the stage and asked Sam Rayburn for permission to speak. After waiting for the crowd's cheers to die down, Jack celebrated Stevenson's decision to allow delegates to choose his running mate. He then made a noble statement: "I hope you'll make it unanimous. I move we suspend the rules and nominate Estes Kefauver by acclamation."

The applause was thunderous. If ever the cliché "snatching victory from the jaws of defeat" rang true, it was on this night. Jack had taken a loss and converted it into a win by showcasing his political savvy, his sportsmanship, and even his diplomacy. It was a truly great moment, one that would make a huge impression on a nation as the young, well-spoken, and handsome senator accepted defeat with graciousness. "He firmly set himself up as a politician of great consequence," noted Chuck Spalding. "Because so many millions had seen it unfold on this new television medium, a reality about Jack was established that couldn't be denied and which would only grow with time. Overnight, he became a major political figure. It definitely set him up for the presidency in the minds of a lot of people."

Time would also prove that Kennedy had managed to avoid being blamed for Adlai Stevenson's eventual loss to Eisenhower, which had been his father's biggest fear.

Despite this success, Jack was still crushed with a real sense of regret. "I saw him almost immediately after and, of course, he talked of nothing else but the convention," said Lem Billings. "It was a tremendous shock that this high office had touched him as closely as it did. He was disappointed as hell. That was his first reaction. It took a little time for common sense to take over and tell him this would've been the most harmful thing that could've happened to his career."

"I'd never been to an Irish wake, but this was sure close," said George Smathers. "Me, Bobby, and Jack sat in a hotel room for about an hour, and all Jack could talk about was what he should've done and should've said. He felt things might've turned out differently if it had been his brother in contention. All these years later, competition with Joe was still there. 'Joe was so goddamn funny. Did you know that?' he asked me. 'He had this incredible way with people, could charm anyone, even the biggest son of a bitch. He would've done so well at this thing,' he said, 'Pretty sure Dad thinks the same.'"

SALT SPRAY ON HIS LIPS

Now that the excitement was over, it was time for the Kennedys to confront their troubled marriage. The day after the Democratic Convention, Jack and Jackie, along with George Smathers and Ted Kennedy, boarded a plane at Chicago's O'Hare Airport destined for New York's Idlewood Airport. From there, Jack was scheduled to take a flight to Los Angeles and then, two days later, on to Italy. Jackie was booked on a separate flight to Newport.

On the way to the airport, Jack was still in a dark mood and Jackie was just as silent, the air thick between them. She still couldn't understand how he could go on a cruise so close to her due date. They'd been fighting about it ever since he told her about it, and he was sick of it. He was going, he told her, and that was the end of it. He needed the time away and didn't understand why she didn't want him to have it. He was so obstinate about it, she had no choice but to accept it. She decided that while he was gone, she would stay with her mother and stepfather at Hammersmith Farm in Newport.

Torbert Macdonald's wife, Phyllis, had also been pregnant and due any day, but she'd taken no issue with Torb's vacation plans. Though she'd previously suffered two miscarriages, she just hoped he'd at least visit after the new baby was born. He was at the convention in Chicago, working the floor for Jack, when she gave birth by cesarean section to a daughter. He waited until the proceedings were over before flying to see her and their baby in the hospital. Staying a short time, he then left for a flight to New York, where he'd rally with Jack, George, and Teddy.

Once Jackie and Jack arrived in New York, she got off their plane and, with Jack holding her hand, walked out to the other aircraft scheduled to fly her to Newport. Janet was standing on the tarmac waiting. When Jack tried to talk to her, his mother-in-law exclaimed, "No! Not one word," and walked away from him. Moments later, he tried to kiss Jackie goodbye, but she turned her head so that his lips brushed her hair. She'd once told her mother that when Jack kissed her she could sometimes taste "the salt spray on his lips," referring to the waters of Cape Cod. She'd always loved it, she said. It certainly seemed as if those days were over.

Or were they?

Seconds after Jackie walked up the steps and into the cabin of the plane, she came rushing back down to the tarmac. Janet, alarmed, remained in the plane's doorway. "Jacqueline, no," she exclaimed. "Don't!"

Jack turned and quickly walked back toward his wife. As soon as he was at her side, she kissed him fully on the lips. Surprised, he returned the kiss. He then stood watching as she walked back up the steps to join her mother. The two then entered the aircraft, and the door was closed.

TEMPTED

═══

A woman was standing in front of a Wurlitzer jukebox in a Santa Monica bar called the Sip and Surf, known as just "the Sip" to locals, and there he was, Senator Jack Kennedy. She tried not to stare. He was sitting on a stool, his back leaning up against the bar. Styled in an ersatz Tahitian motif with sand on the floor, stuffed fish mounted on the walls, and nets swooping down from the ceiling, the Sip was a real dive. Maybe two dozen people could squeeze into it at one time. What in the world, the woman wondered, was *he* doing here?

Anyone who knew Jack Kennedy knew he loved frequenting these kinds of joints, the seedier the better, going all the way back to his days with Inga. He'd always meet the most interesting people in such places, "real life Americans," as he called them. The women, in particular, were usually a real slice of life—wild life, that is. One thing was certain: Jackie would never be caught dead in the Sip, which somehow made it all the more attractive to him.

The woman standing before the jukebox was a real fan of Jack's. She'd been riveted while watching the Democratic Convention on television just a few nights earlier and had hoped he'd snare the vice president nomination. She was disappointed when he didn't, and now, just two days later, here he was, in this of all places, sucking on a cigar and nursing a cocktail. What were the chances? She would later write:

> *When I saw him sitting there, I couldn't believe my eyes. I thought, My God. I have to meet him. This will probably be the only chance I'll ever have to meet this man. I prayed silently, let him just talk to me.*

As his glance caught hers, she offered a furtive look. Out of the corner of her eye, she then saw him stand and start toward her. Again, from her writings:

I was so weak, I thought I would faint, as he finally just stood there before me smiling that incomparable smile of his.

"What are you gonna play?" he asked her.

As she took in his cologne—English Lavender, maybe?—she tried to stay calm. "I was thinking Elvis Presley, but what would you like to hear?" she asked.

He said he wanted to hear something "so I can concentrate on you."

Good line, she thought. *Corny, but not bad.* "I'm Joan," she said, extending her hand. "Joan Lundberg."

He took it. "John," he said. "John Kennedy." She smiled at him and told him she knew who he was. When he said she could call him "Jack," she said, no, she liked "Kennedy" better. She would call him "Kennedy."

Jack said he was sitting with his friend, Ted Sorensen, his sister Pat, and her husband, the actor Peter Lawford. "I had to know you," he said, "so I thought I'd say hello." Joan studied his handsome face and, as she later recalled, thought to herself, *I know where this is going. I'm just not sure how we'll get there.*

"My life has been a howling scandal" is how Joan Lucille Lundberg, born on December 29, 1932, later described her story in her unpublished memoir. "I've steered a reckless course through life," she wrote. It was true, even as far back as 1956, when she first met Senator Kennedy. She was twenty-three at the time and married to a used car salesman, Albert Uribe, thirty years her senior. "It was a shaky marriage," she wrote, "on again, off again. At the moment, off." She and her two toddlers, Lee Ann and Brent, were just getting by, living in a Pacific Palisades mobile home with a man named Norm Bishop. She described him as "a violent, unpredictable part time boxer, part time State Beach lifeguard, one of a crowd of beach-bums of which Peter Lawford was an emeritus member." Joan was a stewardess on Frontier Airlines, the Los Angeles–to–Las Vegas route, and also worked part-time as a cocktail waitress.

Joan Lundberg hailed from a humble background in Racine, Wisconsin; her father was a milkman. "She may have been from the other side of the tracks, but my mother was also an incredible, naturally beautiful woman," said her son Zachary Hitchcock, born later, in 1963. She was a tall and shapely brunette with a generous smile and striking green eyes. "Perfect body, perfect looks" is how Zachary summed her up. "She put Sophia Loren and Marilyn Monroe to shame. More than that, she had great vitality and energy." Joan's younger sister, Linda Lydon, added, "She sounded like Anne Baxter with that same raspy voice. I was always in her shadow. She was sort of fabulous."

As Norm Bishop, the man with whom she lived, sat at the bar talking to the bar's owner, Pat Dorian, Joan and Jack continued their flirtation. When they talked a bit about the convention, he said he was disappointed by its outcome. She told him she thought he did well and loved his speech; he just shrugged. "My God. You're a serious one, aren't you?" she observed. She told him he needed to loosen up, saying, "Life's not that bad, Kennedy." When he asked where she lived, she told him it was in a "trailer court close by," not hesitating at all and obviously not trying to impress.

"What the hell's a trailer court?" he asked.

She laughed and answered, "You don't want to know."

After about fifteen minutes, Jack said goodbye and returned to his friends. Joan went back to Norm Bishop, who'd been jealously glaring at her. Shortly after, Jack and his party walked out of the bar. When he didn't even turn around to glance at her, she was disappointed. She later wrote:

Well, what could I expect? His wife is one of the great beauties of the world. He meets thousands of girls every week. Why should he take so much notice of me?

He did take notice, though. Half an hour later, Joan and Norm were on their way out when Pat Dorian called her to the phone. Her brother, Lee, was on the line, he said. She picked it up. "What're you doing in town, and why am I just finding out you're here?" she asked the caller, whom she thought was her brother.

"How *ah ya*?" came back the voice with its broad Bostonian accent. It was Jack.

With her date eyeing her, Joan pretended to be talking to her brother. Meanwhile, Jack told her he was leaving town tomorrow for Italy but would return in two weeks. There was going to be a big party at the Lawfords', he said, and he would love it if she'd be his guest. Of course, she agreed. She wasn't going to turn down that kind of offer. She hung up wondering what was going to happen next, and she had a pretty good feeling she knew.

JACK'S STRANGE DETACHMENT

I'm so sorry, Jack," his secretary, Evelyn Lincoln, said, "but Jackie lost the baby."

Jack, George, Torb, and Teddy had been gone for five days, first to California and, from there, to Italy, where they boarded the luxury yacht Jack had leased. Because maritime law required the ship to have a radio telephone, Evelyn—who'd volunteered for Jack in 1952 and became official with him in '53—knew how to reach him. She told him she didn't have much information, only that Jackie had become ill at Hammersmith and was rushed to Newport Hospital, where the baby had died.

It's been written in numerous books over the last sixty years that Jack and his party were joined by a group of women before leaving Nice. Betty Beale, the reporter from the *Washington Evening Star,* once recalled, "I had friends who rented the same yacht a few years later. They were catered to by the same cook and skipper, who told them that when Jack was aboard he had women with him and, yes, there were orgies."

In a 1997 interview, George Smathers refused to specifically address that allegation but did say, "Nobody gets it right. What people don't know is that Jack was sick as a dog. He suffered from an *E. coli* urinary tract infection and severe diarrhea from the moment the yacht left the dock. He was sick in bed from that first day at sea and could barely raise his head. Then, we were bombarded with telegrams from his mother-in-law wondering when we'd be back. Jack said, 'Christ, almighty! She's not going to be easy, that one.' After Evelyn's call about Jackie, he was very distraught. I believe he thought the baby would save his marriage, and now he didn't know what to think," concluded Smathers. "He told me, 'If I go back [to the States], what am I gonna do? Just sit there, be sick, and wring my hands?' I said, 'Your wife needs you, Jack. We gotta get you back, no matter what.'"

On Sunday, August 26, the yacht docked in Genoa. It was from there that Bobby was able to talk to Jack, now three days since the baby's death. The day before that call, Bobby had accompanied Janet Auchincloss to St. Columba's Cemetery for the burial. Jackie had wanted to name the girl Arabella, which is how she and the rest of the family would always refer to her. However, since she wasn't baptized, the stone's engraving would simply say: "Daughter. August 23, 1956." Janet cried softly as the coffin was lowered into the ground, which took Bobby by surprise. He'd always thought of her as being just as stoic as his own mother. Should he hold her? Comfort her? Not knowing what to do, he just stood at her side, which Janet later said had been very reassuring. She'd always remember his quiet kindness to her.

Once he was able to speak to Jack, Bobby immediately arranged a call between him and Jackie's doctor. The physician explained that after Jackie hemorrhaged, he was forced to deliver the baby by cesarean section and she was then born dead. He assured Jack he'd done everything possible. Bobby then told Jack that the *Washington Post* was running with the headline "Sen. Kennedy on Mediterranean Trip Unaware His Wife Has Lost Baby." Jack told him they shouldn't worry about press they couldn't control. Bobby told his brother he needed to return home. "But the baby is lost," Jack said, "and what's done is done. I don't think there's any reason for me to return." After George took the phone, Bobby told him to get Jack back to the States.

Certainly, if Joe Kennedy had made the call he would've insisted his son return. However, Joe was also missing in action. His prostate had started acting up to the point where he needed surgery, and he didn't trust French doctors with it. Therefore, he left his friends and wife at the villa in France and, accompanied by Janet DesRosiers, flew to the States for medical care in Boston. After Janet checked him into New England Baptist Hospital, he pleaded with her to stay with him. "I happened to have strep throat," she recalled, "and by completely exaggerating my symptoms, I was somehow able to get a room right next to his. He was so scared, he simply could not be alone. He was just too frightened."

Joe, who was sixty-seven, would eventually end up having his prostate removed; the press reported it as "a kidney operation." Upset about what it might mean for his virility, he swore Janet to secrecy. She was never to tell Rose or anyone else about it and it seems Rose never knew.

After hanging up with Jack, Bobby then had the task of telling Jackie, still in the hospital, that her daughter was gone. Naturally, she was upset and crying. "She's already buried?" she asked in disbelief. When she asked about Jack's whereabouts, Bobby said he was still on a yacht somewhere off the coast of Genoa. Lying, he said he couldn't be reached.

That same night on the yacht, Jack talked things over with Torb, George, and Teddy. He said he felt guilty about having left Jackie alone and was now afraid to face her. They didn't know how to react. Jack was no coward. This was the PT-109 hero, after all, and he'd faced adversaries a lot more intimidating than his wife. However, he seemed oddly disengaged from everything going on. "Who knows how much time any of us have left?" he asked his friends.

George Smathers felt he had to be in shock. "Stop it, Jack," he told him. "If you ever want to be president, we need to get you back to your wife. Otherwise, every woman in America will vote for a rock before they vote for you."

PERSONA NON GRATA

Five days had passed since the death of Arabella before her father, Jack Kennedy, finally returned to the United States. Yusha met him at the Newport airport and drove him straight to the hospital to see his wife. Jackie's stepsister, Nini, from Hugh's second marriage, happened to be in the room when he arrived.

"How are you feeling?" Jack asked Jackie after a quick peck on the forehead. He seemed anxious.

"Fine, Jack," was her flat response.

Nini later reported that the couple was "polite," but with not much to say to each other. Jackie was smoking in bed, her lip trembling. No mention was made of Jack having been absent. After a few moments, he got up to leave. "I'll see you soon," he told her. Nini recalled, "I saw her heart sink."

The Auchinclosses were so unhappy with Jack, Janet didn't even want him to sleep in the main house at Hammersmith. Trying to keep the peace, Hugh asked Janet's personal secretary, Adora Rule, to take Jack's bags to the servants' quarters over the garage, certainly an unlikely place for a United States senator. On their way, they crossed paths with Janet, dressed in black mourning clothes like everyone else in the household.

"I liked you so much, Jack," she said, her voice cracking with emotion. "I welcomed you into our family, and you do this? After everything else?"

He took a breath and said, "Mummy, can we talk?"

She looked at him with hard eyes. "No!" she said as she walked away.

Later that same day, Jack found Hugh sitting in the Deck Room staring at a chess board, lost in thought as he played a solo game. "I would love to learn to play," Jack told him. When Hugh nodded, he sat down. Hugh then spent about an hour teaching his stepson-in-law the game. The older man had made quite a few mistakes in his own marriages before Janet, so he didn't feel he had the right to judge Jack. But Jack could see the deep disappointment on his face. Since Hugh was usually the most even-tempered one around there, Jack knew for sure he was now persona non grata in the family.

Even a disappointed Bobby didn't want anything to do with Jack. His other siblings were also unavailable to him. His father was in the hospital and not in communication with anyone, so at least Jack didn't have to worry about a lecture from him. Rose thought his behavior had been reprehensible. She'd borne nine children. If she'd ever given birth to a dead baby and Joe hadn't been there for her, she wasn't sure how she would've reacted. She couldn't believe she had a son that heartless and didn't want to speak to him when he called.

True to his nature, Jack felt he needed to justify his actions, even though nobody wanted to hear his defense. Determined to state his case to someone, he called his brother-in-law Michael Canfield, who was married to Jackie's sister, Lee. He'd always had a friendly relationship with Michael, who lived in England with his wife.

Jack explained that he'd not returned to Jackie's side because he believed there was nothing he could do for her. He felt she needed to be with family. "And you're not family?" Michael asked him. Giving it to him straight, Michael said Jack had handled everything wrong and that everyone had a right to be angry with him. If he needed to talk, Michael said, he'd always be available to him. However, he also said he didn't want to hear any more feeble excuses for bad behavior. "You need to change your attitude about this," he told him, "or you'll never make things right with your wife, and definitely not with our mother-in-law."

In the days that followed, Jackie fell into a deep depression compounded by postpartum. She was simply unable to make sense of Jack's strange behavior. She'd always felt something was missing in his nature, and now she knew what it was: empathy. He didn't have any. No matter the circumstances, he was always very detached, a trait that had vexed her ever since she'd known him and that now made her very angry. She now also better understood Joe Kennedy's earlier confession to her that he'd wanted his son to suffer so that he might learn empathy.

Making things worse, Jackie blamed herself for the baby's death and felt she shouldn't have gone to the Democratic Convention. She was also sorry she'd smoked during the pregnancy, though it wasn't understood at that time to be as dangerous as it is now. Moreover, she was embarrassed. Everyone knew how Jack had neglected her; it was in all the papers. She felt flayed open for the world to see. Obviously, she couldn't discuss it with anyone outside the walls of Hammersmith, the burden of secrecy further contributing to her anxiety. It was more than just the pain and anger of losing the baby. It was everything. She was miserable. "You can't imagine what it does to a person," she would say years later when remembering this dark time, "carrying a burden like this all by yourself."

There was plenty of blame to go around, though. When Jackie wept at the breakfast table and said, "How could I have been so stupid?" her mother reached out and took her hand.

"You're not stupid," she told her. "You just put your trust in the wrong person." She told Jackie that after everything she had gone through with Jackie's father, she never should've allowed her daughter to marry Jack Kennedy. She was completely to blame, she said, not Jackie.

Jack was scheduled to go to Los Angeles for meetings in mid-September and stay at Pat and Peter's for a few days. Feeling the sting of banishment, he decided to leave early and get as far away from Newport as soon as possible. When he saw Jackie crying in the kitchen, that was it for him. He looked at her and, to hear him tell it later, the only thing he could think of was, *Look what I've done to her.* How much happier would she be, he wondered, if she'd never even met him? He had wondered the same thing about Inga when she seemed to be going over the deep end for him. "I'm not good for these women," he told his brother Teddy. "I'm poison to them, in fact."

As he was packing, his mother-in-law confronted him, the very last thing he needed. "She wanted to know what had been going on out there on the Mediterranean," said Adora Rule. "Jack said nothing happened, he'd been sick the whole time. Mrs. A. didn't believe him. She was sure he'd been with other women. Nothing else made sense. How else could any of it be explained?"

"Let me tell you something," Janet told Jack, according to the family history. "If you think you'll do to my daughter what your father did to your mother, you have another thought coming."

Jack looked at Janet blankly. "I love Jackie," he said.

"Well, you certainly have a funny way of showing it," she shot back.

"Can we talk about this?" he pleaded.

Janet said no, that her agreeing to talk about it would suggest there was a discussion to be had, and there wasn't.

There was more to this argument; they were alone for a half hour. However, all these years later, we don't know the details. We do know, however, that Janet ended it by saying, "I'd appreciate it if you don't show your face around here again."

Jack needed time to think. Obviously, it had been a terrible decision to abandon his wife. He knew that now, but what he didn't know was why he'd done it. He simply wasn't able to connect with his own actions. In fact, he later confided in George Smathers, it was as if he was observing himself from outside his body. He couldn't recognize or make sense of his own thoughts and emotions. He'd have to leave for Los Angeles earlier than planned, that was all he knew for sure, tomorrow in fact. He needed to get away from all of . . . this.

Late that evening, Janet and Hugh watched as their son-in-law left the main house and walked toward the shoreline. His head hung low and his hands were pushed into his pockets as he followed a narrow path out to the pier. Alone and friendless, he walked into the thick fog.

OUT THERE SOMEWHERE

By the time he got to Santa Monica in early September 1956, Jack Kennedy was emotionally adrift and brutally alone. "The best way to describe him," said Peter Lawford in 1981, "is discombobulated. He wasn't himself. He was anxious, nervous. We knew Jackie had lost the baby, but we'd been told it was a miscarriage. He looked terrible, sort of gray."

After Jack rendezvoused with Ted Sorensen at the Lawfords' estate, the first thing he did was swipe a hundred dollar bill off Peter's dresser. Then, he and Ted took off in the new green Thunderbird sports car Peter had given Pat for her birthday. Jack was so distracted as he tooled down Pacific Coast Highway, he ran a red light and smashed into the back of someone else's car. Both vehicles were totaled. Luckily, no one was hurt. Jack and Ted had to hitch a ride back to Peter's.

Once Jack was at Peter's, he went up to his bedroom on the second floor and began trying to track down Jackie. She was nowhere to be found, or maybe she didn't want to be found. He called Janet, who immediately hung up on him. He spoke to Hugh, to Yusha, to Nini, but no one would help him find his wife. While placing these calls, Jack forgot he'd started a bath in the bathroom adjoining Peter's bedroom to Pat's. "I was sitting downstairs with Pat," Peter recalled. "I looked up and saw this curious patch on the ceiling. It started to spread. *Jesus,* I thought, *what the bloody hell is happening up there?* I raced upstairs to find John sitting on my bed deep in conversation. Then, I looked in the bathroom. My God. What a flood. It had already completely ruined the ceiling. I ran into the bedroom and screamed, 'What is wrong with you?' He looked at me, horrified. 'I'm not myself,' he said."

That night, the Lawfords hosted a party and, as planned weeks earlier, Joan Lundberg showed up. She later remembered feeling insecure and out of her element, though she certainly looked stylish in an outfit from Jax in Beverly Hills, a boutique favored by Marilyn Monroe. She couldn't help but wonder how she, a woman who lived in a trailer park, had found her way to such an opulent seaside mansion and surrounded by glamorous, affluent people. Pat Kennedy Lawford walked up to her and, with a surprised face, said, "We look like sisters. Who are you?" They really did resemble each other.

Joan wandered about until she found Jack. He certainly didn't remember inviting her. For a moment, he wasn't even sure who she was. She'd made all of the arrangements with Peter Lawford's new manager, a man named Milt Ebbins. Jack didn't know who Ebbins was, either. It didn't matter. He kissed her on the cheek and spent the rest of the evening at her side. She would later write:

> *He treated everyone as if he cared about them. He lit up the room. People came over just to be near him, his energy magnetic. I thought, well of course, that's the politician in him. But I soon realized that, no, that's just who he is. People loved being around him. His big grin. The way he slapped them on the back, the way he treated them. How could you not love this man? Power, charm, money, drive and masculinity.*

Jack immediately felt a connection to Joan. He'd certainly never known anyone who lived in a trailer park, so that was new. He wasn't an elitist, though. He had friends who were broke, friends who were rich. He just knew from the start that Joan was fun, lively, and sexy. He was also taken by her candor and optimism. She drank a lot, too; he noticed her downing three cocktails in rapid succession. She was a spitfire. A friend of Peter's named Sid Kaiser came up to him and drunkenly said that he'd heard that Jack didn't actually write *Profiles in Courage*. In his defense, Jack undersold the work, saying, "Any high school dropout could've written that book. *Of course* I wrote it."

Joan was less polite. She went up to Kaiser and, inches from his face, unloaded on him: "This man is a goddamn senator of the goddamn United States. How dare you?" Jack was taken aback but loved it; he chuckled as he led her away.

At about midnight, Jack drove Joan up Pacific Coast Highway to a nondescript 1930s motor court called the Sunset Motel, a dozen cheaply furnished cabins overlooking the ocean. Spending money extravagantly was never his strong suit. "What makes you think I'm that kind of girl?" Joan said as they sat in the parking lot. He was a little dumbfounded. Then, she smiled and said, "Oh, who am I kidding? I am *exactly* that kind of girl." He got out of the car and started walking quickly toward the motel. She stayed seated, waiting for him to open her door. He looked over his shoulder, raced back, and, mumbling an apology, opened it for her. They then walked into the lobby and checked in as "Mr. and Mrs. Robert Thompson."

The sex that night was "wild," claimed Joan. Sex being a great lure for him, Jack was quickly hooked. The next morning over breakfast, he unburdened himself. He must've felt comfortable with her because, although he'd always had trouble being open, now, with Joan, for some reason, it all just poured out from Jack—his fears, his insecurities, his problems. It was as if she was so removed from his circle, he could share anything with her and know it would never touch his "real" life. He was also in a very vulnerable place given that so many of his loved ones didn't want anything to do with him. It felt good being with someone who didn't know him well enough to stand in judgment of him, like starting off with a clean slate. It actually reminded him of that night at the F Club when he met the only other woman to whom he instantly opened up. Inga.

According to what Joan later recalled, Jack admitted that he and Jackie were the product of "an arranged marriage" and, as such marriages go, he said it was "fine. Not great, but okay." Years later, Joan recalled to one of her relatives, "He told me he could determine a woman's intelligence by looking at her eyebrow structure, the way her eyes were spaced. Jackie's eyes were set wide apart, he said, and that was something that had attracted him to her. Still, he had a nagging sense that something was missing. Jackie recognized his idealism, however, and the fact that he wanted to make people's lives better. 'She knows someone has to do something about the problems Americans face, especially with Russia and the Cold War,' he told me. 'And I'm pretty sure she believes I'm that someone.'"

As honest as he was, Jack still didn't tell Joan the whole truth. He said Jackie had suffered a miscarriage, not a stillbirth. He did allow that the entire family, both sides, had turned against him because he hadn't shown compassion after the loss of the baby. He admitted that he could've handled it better, but noted that "we Kennedys aren't the best at expressing emotion." Joan told him, "I'll bet that's the great excuse of your life." She was able to see right through him. He smiled; she had him there. He seemed sad and confused, she later recalled, especially when he confessed to her that it always felt as if he were grasping for a good life, but that it somehow eluded him and was out of reach or, as he put it, "out there somewhere." She was moved. "I know you want to serve your country, Kennedy," she told him, "but you also have to serve yourself. You need to work on being happy."

She recalled, "I told him I was also no saint. I'd done things people thought were horrible, one bad decision after another. But I also believed people could change, that there was always tomorrow. I tried to give him hope." Joan asked him if, after all this time had passed since his wedding, he'd grown to love his wife.

He hesitated. "I don't know that I love anything," was his answer. That can't be true, she said. After a moment, he added, "I love politics. I don't know how to love anything else."

She'd never known anyone so disaffected. She again told him to lighten up, soon to be a constant refrain in their relationship. He had made it big, she reminded him. He had money, he was famous, the youngest senator in the country. He had a great life, she told him. "Lots of people have it a lot worse," she said. "Don't let the moment pass," she told him, "because it ends faster than we think."

Jack and Joan spent the next day together. One of the things that fascinated him most about her was her pending divorce. Divorced women intrigued him. There was just something about divorce that made a woman somehow more exciting to some men, especially Catholic men like Jack. Divorce was forbidden, yet the divorcée had done it, anyway. What other forbidden things might she do? Jack said it made Joan seem like some sort of "outlaw." He also had to wonder about a woman who didn't put up with a worthless husband. What kind of superhuman courage must it require to leave a marriage and actually take a chance on life, or as he put it, "walk out on faith, not knowing what's next?" Indeed, he was intrigued by strong women.

Later that day, when Jack told his sister Pat that he was bringing Joan to her home for dinner, he didn't get the welcome he'd hoped for. Pat was torn. Her husband, Peter, was a driven philanderer and she had learned to live with it, like her mother before her. She grew up in a house where her father was an incorrigible philanderer, but this didn't mean she approved. She was pleasant enough to Joan, but no more than that. When Pat and Joan went off to a corner to chat, Jack didn't know what they were saying to each other but he was uneasy. When he left with Joan, Pat gave him a disapproving look. She didn't even say goodbye.

"TRAILER PARK JOAN"

———————

Jack Kennedy had no sooner walked into the foyer of Hammersmith Farm upon his return to Newport when Jackie hit him with a question he wasn't expecting: *"Who's Trailer Park Joan?"* He looked at her with surprise. As he collected his thoughts, she clarified things: "The divorcée! Your sister told me all about her!"

Pat!

This time, unlike the situation with Gunilla, Jack didn't even bother to lie, at least not completely. He explained that Joan was someone he'd met in Los Angeles who'd lent him an ear when he desperately needed to talk to someone. We don't know much more about what obviously had to have been a heated conversation. Joan is vague in her unpublished memoir when writing about how much Jack told Jackie, only that . . .

. . . he told her pretty much everything.

After the rendezvous with Gunilla von Post and then his abandonment following Arabella's death, Jackie was finally done with Jack. "I'm not enough for him," she told her mother as she tearfully explained the latest Joan situation.

"*You* are enough," Janet responded angrily. "*He's* not enough."

The next night, Jackie, Janet, and Hugh went to a dinner party at the 1925 F Street Club, the very same private club at which Jack had met Inga back in 1941. Jackie was seated next to Bill Merriam, nephew of the club's founder, Laura Merriam Curtis. Trying to make conversation, he asked Jackie, "How do you like being married to a senator?"

She was in no mood. "It was the biggest goddamn mistake of my life," she snapped.

He was taken aback, but she didn't care. Later, as she and her mother and stepfather left F Club, Bill went up to Hugh and apologized. "You have nothing to be sorry about," Hugh told him. "It's a rather delicate family matter we need to somehow resolve." He added, "We don't always make the right choices in marriage. I made two terrible choices before I finally snared Mrs. Auchincloss. She made a dreadful choice before she snared me. Jackie will make a better choice next time."

A couple days later, Jackie told Jack her mind was made up and she definitely wanted a divorce. He looked at her blankly as if he couldn't connect the dots. He then retreated to his dingy room over the garage and stayed there for a few hours alone. Thinking. As usual. Finally, he departed Newport for their Georgetown home, certain his marriage was all but over.

Jackie was so angry that she apparently decided secrecy was no longer required. The first thing she did was call the one woman she knew would spread the news far and wide: her sister-in-law Ethel. Ever the Kennedy loyalist, Ethel quickly reported everything to Joe Kennedy, who was still recovering from his surgery in his New York apartment. Since he hadn't talked to Jack about this crisis in his marriage, he was completely surprised to learn from his daughter-in-law that things had gotten so ugly, so quickly. He called his son that night in Georgetown. While it was a private conversation, we can certainly imagine how it went.

THE ILLUSION OF CHOICE

A few days after Joe's discussion with Jack, Jack received a telephone call from an attorney with the New York firm of Milbank, Tweed and Holt. The firm's principal, Jeremiah Milbank, was a friend of Janet's father, James T. Lee. He explained to Joe that he'd been retained to represent Jackie in a divorce. What the attorney didn't reveal was that, at Hugh's behest, he'd already met with Jackie at Hammersmith. During that meeting, Jackie said she knew nothing about Jack's finances. Hugh told her she was "on the horns of a dilemma," and that the only solution was for her to become a lot smarter about her husband's assets. The attorney warned them both that trying to divorce a Kennedy wouldn't be easy. "They have all the money in the world to fight it," he told them. Meanwhile, he said he'd sit down with Joe Kennedy and see where he stood on the matter.

Joe declined to meet with the attorney. He told him there was no need because Jack would never grant Jackie a divorce. In fact, he said he'd meet with her personally to settle it. He arranged a luncheon with his daughter-in-law at Le Pavilion, the famous French restaurant in the Ritz Tower Hotel in New York.

Joe was still not well. Jackie could tell something was wrong as soon as she laid eyes on him. Of course, he didn't tell her about the prostatectomy, instead explaining he'd had the flu. Their conversation took an interesting turn when he tried to defend Jack's callous behavior after Arabella by equating it to the experience of soldiers returning home from the war. They were often, he said, jaded and disaffected and, thus, desensitized to tragedy. "We don't know the terrible things they saw over there," he told her.

Today, Torbert Macdonald's daughter, Laurie Macdonald, doesn't completely discount the patriarch's theory. "Many men of the World War II generation couldn't really feel for the problems of women in childbirth," said Ms. Macdonald. "They went to war innocent boys and came home damaged men. They generally viewed the pain of childbirth as less radical than the terrible things they'd seen in battle. When it was time, they'd literally just drop their wives off at the hospital and go about their business. It's not an excuse, it's just a fact."

Joe said Jackie needed to stay married to Jack in order to benefit from his strong political aspirations, maybe even the presidency. "You won't be bored," he told her. "I can promise you that." Jackie said she wasn't the least bit interested in politics. Rather, she wanted to focus on art and literature. She also wanted to sell Hickory Hill because it was too big and lonely and its newly decorated nursery just reminded her of Arabella. "Done," Joe said. It would later be sold to Bobby and Ethel; Ethel would live there for fifty years.

Joe told Jackie that if she agreed to stay in the marriage he could give her the freedom to do whatever she liked. When she asked for how long, he told her there were no term limits in marriage, at least according to the Catholic Church. What he was doing was sweetening the pot. He would offer her $100,000 upon the birth of her and Jack's first child. She could spend it, he said, but he preferred she invest it. All that being said, if she really did want out of the marriage, he'd figure out a way for her to get her divorce. He wouldn't approve of it, he said, but he'd do it for her.

Joe's was a surprising proposition and Jackie said she needed to think about it. "I think you'll do as I say," he told her, "and you'll accept this generous gift with gratitude." She left the luncheon feeling anxious. She still suspected that there was no way he was ever going to allow a divorce; there'd never been one in the family and the first wasn't going to be Jack's. Joe wanted to give her the illusion of choice because he was confident he had her pegged . . . that she would definitely go for the money.

What followed were days of discussion between Jackie, her mother, and her stepfather as to how to proceed. Joe might have been surprised to learn that Janet wanted her daughter to turn down the money and just divorce Jack. Janet was fed up with her son-in-law and his lax moral code. "He's one part truth," she said, "and two parts lies." She now also felt if Jackie stayed with him it showed weakness, but she also understood why she might be tempted to remain in her marriage. After all, she'd stayed with Jackie's father for many years. "Weakness isn't something you're born with," she often said, "you learn it. I learned it from my mother, and she learned it from hers. But I'll be damned if Jackie learns it from me." Janet was also concerned because something about Jackie's current demeanor reminded her of someone else: Rose Kennedy. Jackie's eyes were dead, like Rose's. Jackie was nervous and skittish, like Rose. Jackie was powerless, like Rose. Janet wanted her out of the marriage as soon as possible before she was completely ruined. Like Rose.

Hugh disagreed. He felt Jackie should accept Joe's offer. She had no money of her own and his proposal would provide her with a nice nest egg. Hugh figured that fighting the Kennedys would be a losing battle, and who knew how much Jackie would end up with, anyway? Much to her mother's chagrin, Jackie agreed with her stepfather. The Auchincloss attorney from Milbank, Tweed and Holt then called Joe Kennedy and asked him to draw up the necessary papers.

There was a bit of back and forth over how long Jackie was obligated to stay in the marriage. Even though Joe had said "forever," the attorney felt there should be some specific time limit. Joe responded that forever meant forever. Joe agreed to make the money tax-free by adding to the total whatever taxes would be due on it. Within a week, Jackie signed the deal. At his behest, she then had lunch with Joe at the same French restaurant so that he could express his delight. "I feel as if I'm now seeing the real you for the first time," he said. She wasn't sure if that was a compliment, or not.

We don't know if Jackie ever told Jack about the arrangement, but even if she didn't he had to have known. It seems unlikely his father wouldn't have told him.

Many years later, in 1973, when Rose was writing her memoir, *Times to Remember,* she exaggerated things and told her secretary, Barbara Gibson, "You know, Joe paid Jackie a million dollars to stay in that marriage." A million dollars in 1960 would be worth $10 million in today's money, and there's no way Joe would've offered Jackie that much; $100,000 in 1960 is worth a million in today's money, which was the actual offer. Rose asked Barbara if she thought the deal should be included in the book. She was worried it might place Jackie in a bad light.

Barbara recalled, "I typed it up just as Mrs. Kennedy explained it, Jackie and Joe in the French restaurant, all of it. I then brought the pages back to her as we were walking on the beach. After she read them, she tore the pages in half and let the wind carry them out to sea. 'In traveling the world,' she told me, 'I've come to realize that people need to believe my son's marriage was some sort of Camelot. I don't think I can be the one to disabuse them of that notion.'"

RULES OF ENGAGEMENT

Jacqueline Kennedy Onassis once privately said, "No one knows what goes on in a marriage but the two people in it." What a simple, inarguable, and elegant statement from someone who would most certainly know. One surprising consequence of her husband's relationship with Joan Lundberg was that it forced Jackie to come to terms with the notion of infidelity. While it was obviously hurtful to her, she now knew she'd never change her husband. She felt she had no choice but to accept him for who he was, especially given the deal she'd just made with his father. Therefore, she established a permission structure. "Show me some respect," she told him, "and don't you dare rub it in my face." It was very much like what Rose had told Joe when they hired Janet DesRosiers. "Do not disrespect me," she had said.

In the nine months between January and September 1956, it would seem Jackie had gone from *This does not happen to me*—which is what she'd told her mother after Gunilla—to *This does happen to me, but only because I allow it,* which is how she now felt after Joan. Many years later, when looking back on the wisdom of this arrangement, Jackie told John Carl Warnecke, the architect who'd one day design John Kennedy's memorial gravesite at Arlington, "He didn't have to lie to me about this Joan woman. I was already lying to myself." Warnecke recalled, "She told me things changed for her when Jack became involved with Joan Hitchcock [her later, married name], but that it wasn't a subject she wanted to get into. It was very painful, that much I knew."

Ironically, the set of circumstances now put into place in Jack's marriage were similar to the arrangement his parents had with Miss DesRosiers. It wasn't just by his design, either—as Joe's wasn't only by his own design. Jackie was complicit in it, too, just as Rose had been.

It wouldn't be until 1973, ten years after JFK's death, that Janet Auchincloss revealed a conversation she had with Jackie about her marital rules of engagement. According to unpublished remarks, Janet said, "Jacqueline and I were talking about Jack one day and she told me, 'I had to choose. Either it was marriage to an honest man or marriage to a great one.' Jack Kennedy had many admirable qualities, fidelity not among them. Jacqueline decided, 'No more lies.' She told me, 'Once I figured out the game and was able to set the rules, it was quite liberating.' I didn't necessarily agree, but I knew she had grown to love him very much and I also knew it wasn't something she wished to defend."

A PARTING OF THE WAYS

While Jack and Jackie had Joan as a third in their marriage at the same time Joe and Rose had Janet in theirs, by September 1956 it appeared that the latter arrangement was about to end. It was a mutual decision Kennedy Sr. and DesRosiers came to in May before the annual holiday in France. By this time, Janet had been with Joe for eight years. He was now sixty-eight; she was thirty-two. She was, by now, truly considered family. "My mother was terribly fond of her," said Kerry McCarthy, daughter of Joe's sister, Loretta. "She knew how much Janet cared for Uncle Joe, and if you loved her brother she loved you back. Of course, she didn't know about the affair until many years later. Her one comment when she found out was, 'I just hope Joe was good to her. She deserved him to be good to her.'"

Because of Joe's prostate condition, he and Janet had stopped being intimate. It really hadn't been a physical attraction that had bound them in recent times, anyway, as much as it was history. She had been there for him, always. To say it was reciprocal would be overstating things, however. For years, Janet had no life other than Joe's, and that status quo was no longer acceptable to her. Also, as he got older, Joe became more possessive. "I accepted an invitation from my sister to attend a party in a neighboring town," she recalled. "On arriving back home I found him with tears streaming down his face. He wanted to know how I could have done this to him—didn't I know how much he loved me? How could I leave him for a whole night? Even an innocent party with family members had become more than he could bear. There was such a loneliness in his heart, it terrified me. I didn't want to be that responsible for anyone's well-being. It was too much.

"Four years earlier, in 1952, while we were in the South of France, he said he wanted to leave Rose and marry me," she continued. "I knew he'd just been swept away by some fleeting romantic moment, and that it wasn't true. I was no longer the naive, young girl who'd first fallen for him. I knew how complicated his life was and that he and Rose would never divorce. Besides, I didn't want to be married to a man forty years older. I wanted children. We had so much fun over the years and I treasured every moment, but I knew it was time to go."

One day, as Joe read his morning paper in the parlor, Janet approached him. "Can we talk?" she asked.

He looked at her over his glasses. "Always," he said with a smile.

"I think our time together is over," Janet told him.

He nodded at her with resignation, as if expecting it. "What'll you do now?" he asked.

"I don't know," she said. "I just know I need to make a new life for myself."

He said he understood and that it was what she deserved. "But, my God!" he concluded, now with tears. "How I will miss you, my dear Janet."

When Janet told Rose the news, the matriarch became undone. She was very sorry to hear it. "You've been such a blessing in my life," she told her. Since it appeared that Janet wouldn't be going to France with her and Joe, she wrote her a farewell note, dated May 19, 1956:

> My dear Janet, I do not want you to go away without telling you how deeply all of us Kennedys have appreciated your thoughtfulness, your willing cooperation under all circumstances, your light and cheerful disposition, besides many other sterling qualities of mind and heart which you have displayed to us so often during the last five [sic] years. Have a long, happy holiday, dear Janet, and be assured always of our affection and our deep gratitude. Sincerely, Rose Kennedy.

"After Joe hosted a lovely going-away party for me at La Pavilion in New York," Janet recalled, "I was on my own for the first time in many years. But not for long, as it would happen."

If, as they say, some things are meant to be, it would seem that Janet DesRosier's association with the Kennedys was one of them. After leaving Joe, she ended up working for a company that sold airplanes. "We were selling propeller Corvair 240s," she recalled, "and I heard that Jack Kennedy wanted to lease a plane, so I called his office and asked if he'd like a demo flight. He took the flight and liked it. The next thing I knew, Joe was calling me. 'Hell, Janet,' he said. 'Jack's not going to just rent the plane. I'm buying it for him, outright. Get it ready.' He paid $385,000 for it. [About $4 million in today's money.] Jack named it the *Caroline*. He then asked me if I'd like to be his onboard secretary and hostess. My job was to keep things operational—the food, laundry, handling anything having to do with his comfort and that of his guests. It was hard work; we'd sometimes hit six or seven cities in a day, but I loved it."

On one flight in particular, instead of preparing a meal for Jack in the galley as she usually did, Janet surprised him with a gourmet offering she'd ordered from La Caravelle in New York: chicken in champagne sauce with pureed mushrooms.

"I'm so happy you're back with us," he told her as he wolfed it down.

"It's like I never left," she said.

As he ate, the senator took a napkin, scribbled something on it, and handed it to her. It said:

Don't you think maybe it's time you were attracted to me?

Janet wrote on the paper and, with a smile, handed it back to him:

No!

PART XI

Ever Moving Forward

STUCK IN MYSELF

───

I hate this," Jackie whispered to her mother. The two women were seated at a long table in Pat Nixon's dining room in her Spring Valley, DC, home, Pat being the wife of Vice President Richard Nixon. There were eight ladies in all, four on each side.

"Just be quiet and roll," Janet whispered.

A long roll of gauze-thin muslin, four inches wide, ran down the middle of the table. Each woman rolled her section tightly and then moved it down the table until it got to the end in a perfect roll.

"How mindless," Jackie complained again under her breath.

"Fine," Janet hissed back. "It's not brain surgery. We agree. Now, just roll."

Once the reel of muslin was at the end of the table, Pat Nixon cut it and tied it off with a piece of twine. She then started a new roll back in the other direction, each woman rolling her section tightly. When it got there completely rolled, someone else cut it off and would then begin a new stretch headed back toward Pat. On and on this process went, for about an hour, every Tuesday night. That's when the so-called Ladies of the Senate Club would meet at Pat Nixon's for "bandage rolling." It was a volunteer effort for the Red Cross, something women often did during the war to feel useful. Now, they did it because it was custom. Mrs. Nixon, a champion of the Red Cross, always dressed in a white nurse's uniform for these nights. "She does bring a lot of enthusiasm to it," Janet said. "I'll give her that much."

As Jackie and Janet rolled bandages, Jack Kennedy was campaigning on the road. He told Jackie it was best for her to stay home. "He thought it wasn't serious to travel with your wife," she later said in her 1964 oral history. It's true that, back then, when men brought their wives on business trips, their colleagues often assumed they weren't serious about their jobs. It was fine with Jackie, though. She didn't want to be with Jack, anyway.

It was the onset of 1957, and as expected, Eisenhower and Nixon, having beaten Stevenson and Kefauver, were now president and vice president. Despite the loss for the Democratic Party, Jack was excited about the new year of politics and approached it with a sense of purpose. The kind of machinery needed for a presidential campaign didn't just happen overnight. It would take hard work and, in Jack's case with his many medical problems, great resolve. Laying the foundation for what would basically be a four-year marathon to the White House started right after the convention. Though it had thrusted him into the national spotlight, making more people aware of him, he knew the calculus to future primary victories was more complex than just being popular and giving speeches. While retail politics mattered, Jack needed to also figure out what the party leaders wanted in a candidate. He needed to know all the governors who controlled the delegates. To that end, he and Ted Sorensen jumped in, doing the necessary legwork to meet all of them. Larry O'Brien went to work, too, helping to build a future JFK 1960 campaign from the ground up.

That same year, Jack joined the Senate's Select Committee on Improper Activities in Labor and Management, also known as the McClellan Committee—or, even more famously, the Senate Rackets Committee—of which Bobby was chief counsel. While the purpose was to weed out racketeering in labor-management relations, it served as an investigation tool into Mob activity in all venues. The hearings became very popular on radio and television as the Kennedy brothers interrogated controversial figures such as Jimmy Hoffa of the Teamsters union.

To the outside world, Senator and Mrs. Kennedy appeared settled and happy after moving into a new home in Georgetown. Privately, though, it was tense between them. While Jackie had accepted money to stay with Jack, that didn't mean she was happy. It was good he was on the road most of the year, because she really didn't want a lot to do with him. He was always tense and angry after coming home from one of his trips, stressed out about whatever had occurred out there, and she had no patience for any of it. They fought constantly. He could never do anything right, and neither could she. They would make public appearances, smile for the cameras and seem to all the world to be a happy couple, but then return home to their separate bedrooms. Under those circumstances, when Janet wondered how her daughter intended to have a baby and get the money she'd signed up for; Jackie didn't have an answer. When she saw her son-in-law on television taking a high moral stance while grilling some mobster, she could only think, *What a hypocrite.*

Since his wife seemed to want as little to do with him as possible, Jack continued his affair with Joan Lundberg, not just in Los Angeles but in other cities across the country. According to her diary, they were in New York in January, Albany in February, Baltimore in March, and Lynchburg in April. While he wouldn't allow her onto the Caroline for fear of raising questions, Jack always flew her out on other airlines to meet him as long as she promised to keep a low profile. He picked up all her expenses, sending her money in advance for tickets. People began to think she was part of the family. "She told me, 'I never worry about trouble when I'm with Jack because I pass for his sister, Pat, all the time,'" said Joan's sister, Linda Lydon. "Their coloring was similar, they had the same teeth, a gorgeous smile."

Jack's handlers, especially Dave Powers, catered to Joan's every need. She had begun to think he was a very caring person until it occurred to her one day that his job was really to keep her from engaging with others. He was "handling" her, as was everyone else around the senator. The intention was to make sure Joan didn't want for anything, lest she approach someone to ask for it. Jack's managers were also adamant that she never be photographed with him. Once, a photographer snapped a quick shot of Joan talking to the senator as he held a baby in his arms. Dave went over to the lensman, grabbed the camera from his hands, ripped out the film, and hurled the camera to the ground, smashing it to pieces. Later, one Kennedy associate reported seeing Jack and Joan sitting side by side and having a whispered conversation while also pretending to read newspapers.

Linda Lydon, seventeen at the time, recalled an occasion when she and Joan were visiting their parents in Park Ridge, Illinois. She answered the phone and a man with a Bostonian accent asked to speak to Joan. He said his name was "Mr. Smith." After Joan took the call, she told Linda it had actually been JFK. The two were planning a trip to Omaha, Nebraska, on May 17 and she suggested Linda accompany them. "He's got a brother you'd really like," she said. "His name is Teddy." Linda said she wasn't interested; she already had a boyfriend. "After that, Jack Kennedy called all the time," Linda said, "always using the very unoriginal pseudonym 'Mr. Smith.' I got very used to hearing that voice." She said their father, Charles Lundberg, disapproved of JFK because he was Catholic: "We were Lutheran, so a Catholic? My God, no! And married? My God, no! And a Democrat? *My God, no!"*

Joan later recalled that she and Jack got along well, "aside from normal lovers' tiffs between two high-spirited people." Given his strained relationship with his wife, Jack began to enjoy a kind of domestic intimacy with Joan that actually resembled a marriage. They started to delight in the little things. For instance, it made her laugh that he always flushed the toilet before he finished urinating. Their favorite alcoholic drink was a Greyhound—grapefruit juice and vodka. They had fun together, spending hours on the beach and in the ocean. They loved dingy beach-town restaurants, places where diners couldn't believe their luck in running into *the* Senator Kennedy, places Jackie would never patronize. He would read about politics while Joan read about show business. They watched a lot of television together, mostly *Gunsmoke* and *Wagon Train,* programs Jackie would never watch. Joan also challenged his sense of privilege. For instance, he'd never taken a taxi cab and had no idea how to even pay the cabbie. "Either I drive, or I have drivers," Jack told her, "always have." They often discussed his political career, with him starting off sentences with, "When I'm president . . ." He was cocky, certainly not given to much self-doubt when it came to his ambitions. She later wrote:

> *I always demonstrated my faith in his destiny, and my firm conviction that he would one day become President.*

When it came to his private self, however, Jack did have serious doubts. When Joan told him she could sense he was a good man, he disagreed. He said he didn't think that was at all true. "I'm not good," he said, his tone distant. "I'm anything but good." He said he was "stuck in himself" and couldn't seem to break out to be a better person. He just was who he was, he told her, and had no choice but to accept it because there was no way he could change it.

About eight months into the relationship, Jack finally told Joan the truth about the rift in his marriage. It wasn't over a miscarriage, as he had earlier said. He confessed that Jackie had suffered a stillbirth of a baby girl and that he hadn't been there for her in the days that followed the tragedy. This was difficult for Joan to believe. She would recall having to take a moment to decide how to react. She now suddenly better understood why he'd been so ostracized by his family and, in particular, his wife. She recalled,

"He said, 'This ugly deed will haunt me forever. It's what I deserve, but not what she deserves, meaning Jackie.' He said he'd give anything to see that little girl grown so that he could get down on his knees and apologize to her. When he said these things, I knew there was goodness in him and that he needed understanding, not judgment. He'd already judged himself harshly. My biggest fear was that he'd lose faith in himself over it. I didn't want that to happen."

One night in May, after a speech to the Overseas Press Club in New York, Jack and Joan were sharing a cigarette in bed when, according to what she later wrote in her unpublished memoir, he suddenly asked her, "Tell me the truth, Joan. Do you think Jackie is screwing other guys?" She was surprised and wanted to know why he'd ask such a question. He explained that Jackie was "so great," he couldn't imagine her not having someone else in her life. At the beginning of the year, he said, they'd started having sex now and again, but it wasn't very good—"there's too much left unspoken between us," he said—and he just hoped she was being better loved by someone else. He said that recently after having sex, she'd asked him, "What you do with me in bed? Is that what *she* likes?" obviously meaning Joan. He could see the "damage in her eyes," he said, "and it killed me. I felt a part of me die."

Lately, any time Jack mentioned Jackie, Joan couldn't help but feel a little jealous. Just the fact that they were sleeping together again bothered her. Did it mean that Jackie was working on forgiving him? If so, what might that mean for her? Joan had never deluded herself into believing he'd leave his marriage. She always knew divorce was out of the question and had accepted their arrangement. But still, even given everything she now knew about Jack Kennedy, she was falling for him. "I want him to know I love him," she told one of her relatives. When asked why, her answer was, "Because I think he needs to know someone does."

MILESTONE BIRTHDAY DECISIONS

On May 29, 1957, Jack Kennedy celebrated a milestone birthday when he turned forty. By this time, he had pretty much deluded himself into believing that if Jackie knew how helpful Joan Lundberg had been to him, she actually might've been grateful to her. As far as delusions go, and he'd have a good many during his marriage, this was one of his biggest. In fact, he *was* better and Joan *was* at least partly responsible. She'd certainly helped him open up and be more communicative.

With their own communication somewhat better, Jackie had suggested earlier in the year that she wanted to try again for a baby. Jack didn't think about how having a family might complicate things with Joan. He just went with it. Sure enough, right before his birthday, he and Jackie announced that she was once again expecting.

On July 28, Jackie turned twenty-eight. The plan was for her to celebrate at Hammersmith with the Auchinclosses, not with her husband. Janet and Hugh still didn't want to be around him, which concerned Jackie, especially with a baby coming. She wanted her mother to know her grandchild and realized that if Janet refused to see Jack, she'd never see the baby. Jackie further explained that Jack's family had forgiven him for the way he'd handled himself after Arabella, and that if Rose Kennedy could get past it surely Janet could too. Janet said she'd have to think about it.

On the morning of July 28, Jackie received a call from one of her Bouvier aunts telling her that her father, Jack Bouvier, was seriously ill at Lenox Hill Hospital. "She wanted to fly to New York immediately to see him," recalled her cousin John Davis. "It was to just be a day trip. She said she'd be back that night for a small birthday celebration. Her mother was worried because Jackie was six months along and doctors warned her not to fly. However, there was no talking her out of it; she had this desperate need to see her father. 'Then, I have to go with you,' Jack told her. Jackie agreed. If he hadn't offered, she would've been hurt."

Once at the hospital, the Kennedys were surprised at how ill Black Jack was; he was just sixty-six but looked twenty years older. The truth is that he had liver cancer, but his family hadn't told him, and they didn't want Jackie to know either.

While Jackie was with her father, Jack decided to call his mother-in-law to try to apologize for his behavior after Arabella's death. It appeared he was not only moved by his father-in-law's illness, he was motivated by his own milestone birthday to rectify the terrible state of affairs with Jackie's family. He told Janet he wanted things to be better between them, especially given that a baby was on the way. He also spoke to Hugh. The Auchinclosses were torn. They'd been so angry for so long, it wouldn't be easy to just forget all about it, no matter how repentant Jack seemed to be. But for Jackie's sake and that of the baby, they agreed to try.

That night, Jackie returned to Newport from New York, Jack at her side. There was a dinner for Jackie and then a birthday cake with twenty-eight candles. Things were tense, but at least they were all giving it a go. When Janet and Hugh said they were leaving for a cruise with Jamie and Janet Jr. on August 1, everyone promised to get together again as soon as they returned.

A week later, on August 3, Jackie was at the Georgetown house packing to go back to New York. This time, she intended to spend a full week with her father. While packing, she got a call that he'd fallen into a coma and didn't have much time. She and Jack ended up getting to the hospital in New York just moments after he passed away.

The funeral was on August 6 at St. Patrick's Cathedral. The next night, George and Rosemary Smathers joined the Kennedys for dinner in the suite they'd taken at the Carlyle on East Seventy-Sixth. "I think about my father and Jackie's father and they're alike," Jack told George. "My dad is a son of a bitch, and so was Jackie's. What do you think my mother will say about my father when he buys the farm?" he asked. "'Good man'? 'Good husband'? 'Tried hard'? Hell, no. She'll say, 'Here lies my son of a bitch husband, Joseph P. Kennedy. Here, let him lie. Now that he's at rest, so am I.'" Jack had paraphrased one of his favorite John Dryden poems. He said he was beginning to feel that things needed to get better between him and his wife. Otherwise, he said, "When I'm dead and buried, Jackie will probably end up saying, 'Here lies Jack Kennedy. The hell with that guy. I'm glad he's gone.'"

CAROLINE

In the middle of November, Jack and Jackie went to New York to prepare for the birth of their baby. Jackie was understandably nervous and wanted to be close to the hospital. Joe Kennedy still had his two apartments in New York at 270 Park Avenue, one for himself and one for everyone else in the family who might need it. He offered that second one to Jack and Jackie for the final weeks of her pregnancy. This time, Jack wanted to be at her side as much as possible. He was trying harder to be a better husband, and everyone noticed. "But a leopard doesn't change his spots," Janet warned her daughter.

On November 27, 1957, the day before Thanksgiving, Jackie gave birth by cesarean section to a healthy seven-pound, two-ounce baby girl. They named her Caroline after Jackie's sister, Caroline Lee, with the middle name Bouvier. Even Janet was a little taken by her son-in-law's reaction to his new daughter. She'd been angry with him for so long, but once she saw him with her little grandchild, she had to admit it—her heart melted a little.

"I'll always remember Jack's face," Janet recalled, "when the doctor came into the waiting room and told him the baby had arrived, that it was a girl and Jackie was fine and the baby was fine. I'll always remember the sweet expression on his face, the way he smiled. The sheer, unadulterated delight he took in Caroline from that first day on. He seemed perfectly at home with babies. I don't ever remember his having that stiffness or that being afraid to touch them that Hugh seems to have always had." Janet recalled Jack having to leave the next day to speak in Dallas, Texas, "and he didn't want to go. He just wanted to be with his daughter."

It would be a long recovery for Jackie; she wouldn't leave the hospital for two weeks. In the meantime, her mother found a nanny for the baby, a determined, red-headed British woman named Maud Shaw. Lee and her husband, Michael, then also moved into 270 Park Avenue to help care for Jackie, while Jack went back and forth to Washington as his Senate duties required. When Rose and Joe came to visit, they fussed over their new grandchild and took pictures with her and with her parents. Things were definitely better all around.

It seemed that some of Jack's inherent selfishness was beginning to subside as he doted over the baby. He would smile with delight, his eyes lighting up with love whenever he held Caroline in his arms. She really brightened his life. He was also being much kinder to his wife. One morning, Jackie picked up a book she'd been reading and noticed he'd written on its placemark: "I hope you have a lovely day." It wasn't much but it felt somehow . . . significant.

Now a new mother, Jackie also became more invested in her role as a wife, and it started showing in small ways. For instance, she began making fashion choices for Jack. He'd always appeared disheveled, though she hadn't wanted to complain about it since it somehow seemed part of his youthful appeal to voters. When they met he had only four suits in his closet and each looked as if it had seen better days. He also had a habit of leaving clothing in the closets of hotel rooms. Wardrobe considerations were obviously not a priority for him. So, Jackie began personally choosing his suits and ties with care so that he always looked smart. Soon, he would be considered one of the best dressed senators on the floor, and he'd have his wife to thank for it.

The couple also began establishing a few small but meaningful marital rituals. For instance, she made sure he could enjoy a fresh cup of coffee in the morning before leaving for the Senate. She'd also leave sweet notes in his pockets for him to find later in the day. He would call her whenever he had a break just to see how her day was going. When she had some trouble with her sister, he made sure to keep track of all the details no matter how much they bored him, and then sided with her in the dispute. While he wasn't as forthcoming about his feelings as she would've liked, she'd grown to accept him for who he was, and he was doing the same with her.

Jackie was never going to be a political animal, and Jack knew it. They wouldn't be having in-depth discussions about policy. He was fine with that. She understood people, however, thus she understood politicians. She knew which were hypocrites and which were allies. She could size up a person within minutes of talking to him, and there was value in that for Jack. He had once told her President Truman said, "You want a friend in Washington? Get a dog." She completely understood and agreed.

In December 1957, Jack was on the cover of *Time,* a testament to how much of an impact he'd made canvassing the country. The same week the magazine went on sale, he came home from Chicago and found a framed copy of the cover hanging in the kitchen, next to his cover of *Life* from earlier in the year.

"I made some for your parents," Jackie said proudly, "and mine, too."

He looked at it and winced. "That has to come down, Jackie," he told her.

"No," she said. "It'll come down in 1960 when you're president, and they put you on the cover again. Until then," she concluded with a kiss on his cheek, "it stays."

FALLING FOR HIS WIFE

————

T hings may have been better in Jack's marriage, but that didn't mean Joan Lundberg was out of the picture. On February 22, 1958, he was scheduled to give a speech in Tucson, Arizona, at a Democratic dinner. Since he was going to be in town for a few nights, he asked Joan to meet him. She checked into the hotel using the usual pseudonym, "Mrs. Robert Thompson."

Joan had noticed a distinct change in Jack after Caroline's birth. When she was on the phone with him, he couldn't stop talking about the baby, and also about her mother. Back in December, when Caroline was christened at St. Patrick's Cathedral, pictures of Jack and Jackie with the newborn made all of the papers. Joan stared long and hard at one of them, the image underscoring for her that she wasn't a part of Jack's life, and he wasn't really a part of hers, either. While she knew some of the people in his orbit, he knew very few of those in her life. When she'd invite him out with her friends, he usually declined. "He didn't want to be a part of her world and felt it was too risky," said one of Joan's friends who actually did meet Jack on a couple occasions. "He was very nice," said that friend, "and seemed to treat her well. But what they had was for them and them alone, and Joan knew she had to be satisfied with it. I asked her, 'When will we see him again,' and she said, 'Your guess is as good as mine.' After Caroline's birth, I think she felt the clock ticking on even the little bit she had with him. Therefore, I know she was very relieved when he wanted to meet up in Tucson. However, once they were together again, it was still all about Caroline and all about Jackie."

In Tucson, things just got worse for Joan. She began to realize Jack no longer saw Jackie as the woman he'd married only because he needed to for political purposes, the "arranged marriage" he'd once spoken of. Now that she was the mother of his only child, he seemed to be attached to Jackie in an entirely different way. He couldn't say enough about how caring she was to their daughter, and how hard she worked at making a lovely home for them. His face actually lit up with pleasure when he talked about her.

Back when they'd first met, Joan had asked him if he loved Jackie. "I don't know that I love anything," had been his dark response. It now felt to her that maybe he was actually falling for his own wife, especially when he decided he and Joan shouldn't share a bed in Tucson. That was a first. When she offered to accompany him to a speech at Denver University the next day, he declined. "What about when you come back to L.A. next month?" she asked. He was scheduled to speak at an FDR memorial dinner at USC on March 1. No, he told her, Jackie would be with him on that trip. "He really was pulling away, and she knew it," said her friend.

While Joan tried to be understanding, as had always been her role, she was getting angry. At herself. After all, she'd known what she was getting into with him. Jack wasn't hers, and he never would be. He'd never told her he loved her, for instance. Perhaps she'd been just a distraction after all. She later wrote:

I think I was now very much in love, and I was so mad at myself because I knew better. I knew better!

After Tucson, Jack and Joan began to argue on the phone. She felt unappreciated. She reminded him that it had been *her* idea that he patch things up with his in-laws. After he did so, he blew right past it without acknowledging her good advice. That hurt. While they'd again share their bed in a couple months' time, Minneapolis on April 25 and 26, things were definitely different between them.

On May 22, Jack had to make a quick trip to Los Angeles right in the middle of a very busy campaign schedule on the East Coast. He was going to be in town for just one night, and then back to Massachusetts. Once in Los Angeles, he called Joan and suggested she meet him at his sister Pat's for supper. However, a half hour later, he called back and said they'd have to meet somewhere else. Apparently, when Pat heard Joan was coming, she put her foot down. "She'd had enough of 'Trailer Park Joan,'" said an intimate of hers named Patricia Brennan, a real estate agent at the time in Los Angeles. "She was no longer going to cover for her brother by hosting Joan, or any other woman, not after Caroline was born. She was done with all of that after Caroline. That was the end of it for her. 'I'm a mother, too,' she told me, 'and this is just too much of a betrayal of another woman, my own sister-in-law.' She was ashamed of herself for ever having done it at all."

Joan wrote:

Pat just said, "No more." So, I wasn't allowed in her house ever again.

Jack decided not to make an issue of it and checked them into a hotel. While there, he mentioned he was going to go to Puerto Rico on November 15 to give a speech about Latin America. Joan wondered if she could go with him. No, he said, Jackie was going on that trip.

On June 25, according to Joan's calendar, she called Jack to ask to see him. She said it was urgent. He sent for her to meet him two days later, on June 27, in Hartford, Connecticut, where he was giving a speech for the state's Democratic Convention. That's when she gave him some shocking news.

She was pregnant.

JOAN'S UNWELCOME NEWS

Ever since Jack had become a father, Joan had felt off-kilter. She never seemed to know where she stood or what he was thinking and she was still angry with herself for having gotten in so deep with him. In her unpublished memoir, she sought to own her carelessness and be honest with the four children she'd had by the time she wrote it in the mid-1970s:

> *I want my children, even if nobody else, to know exactly how their mother has lived well, if not wisely. I'll take the Duke of Wellington's advice to Harriet Wilson: "Publish and be damned." I've committed many sins, but I've never lied . . .*

Joan would recall that her news about the baby was "like a knife to Jack's heart." He was, naturally, upset. While it was a shock, Joan wrote that they shouldn't have been so surprised:

> *I didn't like wearing a diaphragm, and Jack wouldn't wear a rubber.*

Jack couldn't help but wonder if Joan had purposely planned the pregnancy given that she'd seen his devotion to Jackie after Caroline's birth. She denied it but, still, the charge hurt. He also wondered if he was really the father. Maybe that was a fair question. After all, there had been no reason for them to remain monogamous. He claimed he couldn't even remember the last time they'd been together. She assured him he was the father and, yes, they *had* been together, in Minneapolis back in April. When he asked her how she felt about the pregnancy, she said she loved the two children she was presently raising on her own and knew she'd also love any child she and Jack brought into the world. He didn't know how to respond.

"I have no words," he said.

"*Find some,*" she told him.

He reached over and took both her hands in his own. "I'm so very sorry, Joan," he told her, and he seemed to really mean it.

"I am, too," she said.

They arranged to see each other in July, but then Jack called and canceled, saying he was going to be with family for summer vacation. When Joan finally reached him on the telephone, he said, "I don't see how this can happen."

According to what she later said, she told him, "But it's already happened, Jack."

He said he needed more time to think and promised to call her. She knew that it was over between them; she just didn't know how long it would take for him to pull the plug.

I wasn't that naïve. What else could I expect?

Back when Jack was with Inga Arvad, he'd faced the same situation. It was 1942 and Joe had already shipped Jack off to South Carolina to get him away from her. They still found ways to see each other, and one day she told him she thought she was pregnant. They were being bugged by the FBI at the time and, according to that agency report, "Kennedy had very little comment to make on the subject." The next day, Inga wanted to discuss it again, but Jack refused. The FBI then quoted her as accusing him of "taking every pleasure of youth but not the responsibility." At twenty-eight, Inga was older than Joan, had no children, and desperately wanted them. Jack didn't suggest she have an abortion. We don't know whether it was because he was opposed to it or because he knew they were being surveilled. It turned out to be a false alarm—Inga was not pregnant, after all.

One friend with firsthand knowledge of Jack's thinking about the situation with Joan said, "I knew someone was pregnant, but I didn't know who. He was distressed about it. He said he couldn't believe he'd been so stupid. This could be the end of everything, and he knew it, so close to the election for his second term in the Senate. He also knew there was no way Jackie was going to stick around if she found out about it. 'I love my wife,' he said, 'and this will kill her.' I think the soldier in him told him to keep his head down, and just keep moving. The stakes were too high. Plus, the culture was different back then. This kind of thing was really looked at as the woman's problem, not the man's. She needed to take care of it. That's the way we viewed these things back then, I'm sorry to say."

At one point in July, Jack finally called Joan to talk things over. She wanted to see him in person, but he told her it was impossible. He didn't want to see her face-to-face. Sounding edgy and not like himself, he told her he'd decided she couldn't have the baby. He couldn't do it to his wife or his family. She tried to argue, but she didn't know how. Citing his selfishness seemed futile. He always got everything he ever wanted from anyone he ever needed, so why bother hashing it out now? She'd been his pseudo-therapist for too long, anyway. He'd benefited from it. She hadn't.

Jack said that as soon as he got a break, he'd mail her four hundred dollars. After she got the envelope, he told her, "You'll know what to do, Joan. Please," he said, his tone desperate. "Being a politician is who I am," he told her. "Politics is all I know. If you take that away . . ." His voice trailed off. Before she could respond, he disconnected the line.

A week passed before Joan received the envelope in the mail. Because there was no return address, she knew it had to be from Jack. She dreaded opening it. She took a letter opener and carefully slit the top of the envelope. She looked inside. It was empty.

SOMEBODY'S DAUGHTER

Joan Lundberg spent two days trying to reach Jack Kennedy. Now she was as confused as she was frustrated. Had he changed his mind? Was the empty envelope some kind of sign? Why couldn't he just talk to her? He was more maddening than ever, and that was saying a lot.

Finally, he called her back. "Kennedy!" she exclaimed. "Did you change your mind about the baby?" No, he told her, he most certainly had *not* changed his mind. He sent her the money! Didn't she get it? When she told him the envelope was empty, he became upset. He'd assumed she'd received it and hoped she'd had the abortion by now. He became positively unhinged. Joan later wrote:

> *My God! You had never heard anybody use expletives so much in the whole history of Washington. He ranted and stormed and raved . . .*

Apparently, the cash had been stolen from the mail. However, Jack was very clear; he didn't want Joan to have the baby. Though she was now more than three months along, she didn't fight it. He wired more money that same day, and she took care of things a day after that.

Afterward, Joan couldn't imagine how she and Jack could even remain friends. Their affair had begun as fun for her and therapeutic for him during a time when he was completely ostracized by his entire family. Somehow, it had grown into something else, at least for her. She was angry and disappointed, but also realistic. He was never going to be hers, and she knew it.

"From what she later told me, Mom realized the party was over," said her son Zachary Hitchcock in 2024. "She couldn't be on the sidelines. That just wasn't Mom. When she told me all about Kennedy and everything she had gone through, the baby and all of it, I was surprised she'd been able to handle it for as long as she did. The presidency, Jackie, the abortion, and then this whole Camelot being in the offing, there was no way mother could be marginalized in that way. Not only was she too big a presence, she had way too much pride. She had to step aside. That was the only way."

It ended not in person but on the phone. When Jack called Joan to check on her, she told him, "I'm going to need to put some distance between us."

He understood. "I owe you so much," he told her, and she had to agree that he certainly did.

"One thing I want to say to you, Kennedy," she told him. "You love Caroline, and I know that, but I'm somebody's daughter, too. Remember that the next time you treat a woman the way you've treated me."

When he told her he wasn't that kind of man, she said she was sorry but she had to disagree. "Jack, look," she finally concluded, not wanting to debate it, "all I want for you is to have an extraordinary life. That's all I want now," and with that she hung up.

There was no big fight. We both knew it was for the best.

"It was hard," said Joan's sister, Linda Lydon, also in 2024. "When Joan loved, she loved hard. But how could this work? There was no way, and she knew it. It's what happens when a woman ends up in a relationship with a married man, especially when there's such a power differential. In years to come, she did what she could to get on with her life. It wasn't easy, but my sister was a very powerful woman. She would do it."

And as for "Kennedy"? Joan never spoke to him again.*

———

On November 4, 1958, Jack Kennedy won his second term in the Senate with 73 percent of the vote, which, at more than 800,000 votes, was the largest winning margin in the history of Massachusetts politics. This victory further solidified his stature as a national candidate. Now the real race was about to begin, the one for the presidency in two years.

———

* See "Joan Lundberg Hitchcock Postscript" in Source Notes.

He'd escaped a close call with Joan Lundberg, but he'd never forget it. He vowed to never allow himself to get into a similar situation. Therefore, he rethought his version of infidelity, or at least he rationalized a way to continue with questionable behavior. He told Peter Lawford, "One night here with a girl, and one night there, that's okay, I guess, but an actual relationship? No. That can only be with Jackie. I will never take a chance with my marriage again."

PART XII

A Father's Deception

LOST SISTER

A couple days after Jack's reelection to the Senate, he was out of town and Jackie and Caroline were staying with family in Virginia at the Auchinclosses' Merrywood estate. It was during this time that a painful chapter of Kennedy history became clear.

One evening, Jackie was dining with Janet and Hugh, her stepbrother Yusha, and her sister, Lee, now separated from Michael Canfield. Their guests were interior designer Sherry Parker Geyelin and her husband, Philip Geyelin. Philip, a correspondent for the *Wall Street Journal,* would later win a Pulitzer Prize while reporting for the *Washington Post.* Also joining them was Sherry's father, Colonel Chauncey Parker, a founding partner of Hugh's Washington brokerage firm, Auchincloss, Parker & Redpath.

In a 1999 interview, Mrs. Geyelin recalled, "Hughdie said something about Jack's four sisters, one of whom died in a plane crash. Jackie said, 'No, Uncle Hughdie. Jack has *five* sisters.' She then rattled off their names: 'Rosemary, Kick, Eunice, Pat, and Jean.' Hughdie looked surprised. 'Who's Rosemary?' he asked. Lee answered, 'She's the one in the nervous hospital.' Janet disagreed. 'No,' she said. 'She's the one with spinal meningitis.' Clearly, there was some confusion."

Jackie tried to set the record straight. She told the others Rosie *had* been sent away, but that Jack never talked about her. All he ever said was that she'd been hospitalized after being diagnosed as "retarded." She also recalled Ted having once told her during a holiday meal, "It's never the fullness of our table that I notice, it's the absence of three place settings—Joe, Kick, and Rosie." He added, "I used to fear that if I disobeyed my father, I'd disappear, too." Jackie said his words sent a shiver down her spine.

Jackie also recalled having asked Rose Kennedy about Rosie while she and Eunice were taking a stroll on the beach with her. Rose explained that in large Catholic families it was common for one child to have a divine calling to be a priest or a nun. Rosie was that child in their family. She said Rosie was now a cloistered nun at the Benedictine Abbey in Bethlehem, Connecticut. Cloistered sisters, Rose explained, could have no contact with the outside world, "and never see their families again." Jackie had never heard of such a thing. It sounded awful, like a prison sentence. No, Rose assured her, it was actually a holy decision to live "a contemplative life." She concluded, "Our Rosie has chosen the life of a cloistered nun, and that's a choice we must respect. Isn't that right, Eunice?"

Eunice stared straight ahead and answered in a flat voice: "Yes, Mother."

Rose's story was untrue. Her daughter had never studied to be a nun and, besides, cloistered sisters are allowed to see their families at certain times of the year, depending on the order. Jackie suspected it was all a lie, but she couldn't be sure. All she knew was that while staring at Rose as she so dispassionately told the story, she, again, had to wonder, *My God! Does this woman ever cry?*

After dinner, Janet, Jackie, Lee, and Sherry talked more about Rosie over tea. Janet recalled the time she was at the Kennedys' home and noticed a display of photographs of all nine Kennedy siblings on the grand piano. Each was in color, she remembered, except for the pictures of the ones who'd died, Joe and Kick, both in black-and-white. "And one other girl," Janet said, "also in black-and-white." She thought it over for a second. "My God, Jackie," she whispered. "Could that have been Rosie? Is she dead?"

No, Jackie said, she was sure Rosie was still alive. How then, Lee wondered, could the Kennedys just accept her disappearance and go on with their lives as if she never existed? It seemed impossible to imagine. "But it's just like Jack did with Arabella," Jackie said.

Two years before, Jackie had been unable to understand why Jack had reacted as he had to the loss of their stillborn child, Arabella. Now it began to make more sense. If he could accept the disappearance of his own sister without much grief or sorrow, how might he be expected to respond to the death of a baby he never knew? The conclusion hit like a bolt of lightning. "The baby is lost," Jackie whispered, recalling his haunting words as told to her by Bobby. "What's done is done."

BURIED SECRETS

R ose Mary Kennedy, known to her family as both "Rosemary" and "Rosie," was the first daughter born to Joe and Rose Kennedy on September 13, 1918. At about the age of seven, they were given the sad diagnosis that she was "mentally retarded," the phrase commonly used throughout the twentieth century to refer to those with impaired cognitive function. Today, of course, "intellectually disabled" is the preferred term. The Kennedys decided to keep her home rather than send her to an institution, as had been suggested. She wasn't that impaired at the time, her deficiencies manageable and often not even noticeable.

Rosie was nineteen in 1938 when President Roosevelt appointed Joe as ambassador to Great Britain. The family's subsequent eighteen months in England was an exciting time of high society affluence and popularity for them. Joe, Rose, and their beautiful, well-heeled children became international stars with extensive newspaper and magazine coverage. The eldest girls, Rosie and Kick, were even presented to King George and Queen Elizabeth. Photographs of them with their mother, all three in flowing white-and-silver satin gowns, were circulated around the world by the media.

Rose loved every second of it. *This* was the life she was cut out for. How she loved engaging with wealthy and influential people and being part of an exciting society. She even fantasized that Joe might one day be elected president of the United States if he pleased FDR enough with his ambassadorship. Overlooking their religion in this fantasy, it seemed like a real possibility. Rose definitely felt she had the right pedigree to be First Lady. This dream filled her with a kind of hope and promise for the future she hadn't had since the day she married her husband. She'd never been happier. But, then . . . it all came crashing down around her when England entered World War II and the Kennedys were forced to flee the country.

Joe's apparent appeasement of Hitler ruined him. He wanted America to just leave Hitler be and not engage with him. Or, at the very least, try to make some kind of a deal with him, as if such a thing was even possible with a madman like Adolf Hitler. There were a lot of people who believed he was right; many public opinion polls of this time showed that people didn't want America to go to war. But the tide was definitely beginning to turn toward Americans wanting to protect their allies. As a result, Joe was considered unpatriotic and pandering to America's enemies, Hitler in particular. Though that criticism painted him with a wide brushstroke, it didn't matter. Hitler was becoming so dangerous, there was no nuance to be understood in dealing with him. Therefore, the world pretty much turned against Joe Kennedy. He resigned as ambassador in November 1940; it was either that or get fired by FDR. He'd never serve in public office again.

Not only was Joe finished, so was Rose. With all her hopes and dreams up in smoke, she was furious with her husband and felt he was shortsighted and stupid. If he'd been more diplomatic—"which, I *thought,* was the job of a diplomat"—he could've found a way to express himself without alienating the president and most of the country. The real problem, at least as Rose saw it, was that Joe was too hotheaded to express his controversial views in a diplomatic fashion and, thus, he was misunderstood. "The president sent *you,* a Roman Catholic, as ambassador to London, which probably no other president would have done," she scolded him. "He sent you as his representative to the Pope's coronation. You write yourself down as an ingrate in the view of many people."

His response: "I'm not sorry for anything I did and, furthermore, I'd do it all again."

Many years later, Rose reflected on this difficult time to her grandniece Kerry McCarthy: "We had everything, but Joe didn't have an ounce of humility and refused to learn anything. He never listened, but maybe I should have said more. Afterwards, I was very angry at him. I felt he had not accomplished what we could have accomplished as a couple. He had not accomplished what he should have as a world leader, and I was made to suffer for it. I lost my friendships. We lost our prestige, and within a few years we began to lose our children. And I wonder if he ever knew how much I lost because of him."

It was against this backdrop of marital hostility that Joe devised a solution to the problem of their mentally challenged daughter, Rosie, in a way that would prove catastrophic. "In 1941, when we returned to the U.S.A., Rosemary was not making progress but seemed instead to be going backward," Eunice Kennedy Shriver recalled. "At twenty-two, she was becoming increasingly irritable and difficult. She became somber and talked less. Her memory and concentration and judgment were declining. My mother took her to psychologists and dozens of doctors. All of them said her condition would not get better."

While he was in England, Joe had researched an operation called a "prefrontal lobe lobotomy," a new and, it was thought at the time, innovative procedure touted as brain surgery to calm a patient's mental disturbance, ease their frustration, and allow them a more peaceful life. Once back in the States, Joe discussed the idea with Rose. He suggested it could benefit Rosie. Rose asked Kick to use her contacts at the *Times-Herald* to investigate. Kick learned that some patients were left with serious brain dysfunction. In fact, the *Journal of the American Medical Association* strongly warned against the surgery. Upon showing this research to Jack, he said, "Absolutely not. We can't do that to Rosie."

After Rose conferred with Joe about Kick's findings, she *thought* they agreed that Rosie, now twenty-three, wouldn't have the surgery. But then, in November 1941, Joe decided he knew better; he secretly sent the young woman off to a psychiatric hospital in Belmont, Massachusetts, for the operation. "Uncle Joe didn't discuss the details with anyone," recalled his grandniece Kerry McCarthy. "He told my grandmother [Joe's sister, Loretta] that Rosie was in need of an exciting new treatment and that he was going to see to it. Her response was 'Oh, that sounds wonderful, darling.' And that was that."

The operation went very wrong, with the result that Rosie was left profoundly impaired. After the operation, her head was tilted, she drooled, she no longer had full use of her limbs, and she couldn't walk. She couldn't care for herself and could only speak a few words. One nurse who attended the surgery was so upset about its outcome she quit nursing. Joe was horrified. "It hadn't been an impulsive decision," said Kerry McCarthy, "but rather the result of numerous conferences with physicians in whom Uncle Joe had placed his trust. He was devastated, angry, and felt he'd been lied to. But then this other part of him kicked in: damage control."

Imagine a man as proud and stubborn as Joseph P. Kennedy confessing to his wife and children that he'd permanently disabled one of their own. He simply couldn't do it. He discussed the matter with Arthur Houghton. Janine Burke recalled, "Joe wanted to keep what happened to Rosie a secret, but Arthur told him, 'No. You can't do that, Joe. Your wife has a right to know. They all do.' He begged him to come clean, but Joe was afraid of looking like a failure. He was too prideful to admit he'd made such a terrible mistake. He was sure they'd all turn on him. Rose was already furious with him for the way he'd ruined their lives as ambassador. She'd already shut him out. How could he now be vulnerable to her about what he'd done, knowing she'd judge him so harshly? He told Arthur, 'No. This secret dies here. Promise me.' Poor Arthur reluctantly made that promise. 'I will keep your secret,' he told Joe.

"Then, when Rosie didn't return home, Uncle Joe told everyone he'd sent her to a facility for therapeutic treatment," continued Kerry McCarthy. "Since she'd already spent so much of her life in and out of hospitals, everyone, including Aunt Rose, just accepted it."

As incomprehensible as it is that Joe would keep such a secret from his wife, it's just as inexplicable that Rose wouldn't press hard for more of an explanation as to what happened to their daughter. She would later claim she knew nothing about any of it, and that it would be twenty years before she learned the truth. However, she was aware that Joe had been considering the surgery. When Rosie disappeared, she must've known what happened. Years later, in her memoir, she described the operation as "a certain form of neurosurgery" and gave it just one paragraph.

The hard truth is that Rosie had always been a lot of work. Rose had dedicated herself to it, but it wasn't easy. She was barely maternal to the children who required much less, so having to give so much to Rosie was a real undertaking. Once that burden was lifted, Rose didn't fight it. In fact, she was relieved. But in time she would come to feel differently.

By 1974, the year Rose Kennedy published her memoir *Times to Remember,* more than thirty years had passed since her daughter's disappearance. Rose's secretary, Barbara Gibson, recalled, "She told me she was fine for a while but that eventually she fell into a terrible, despairing time. She felt so guilty, she barely had the courage to get up in the morning. She'd read her Bible, go to church, pray, and be dutiful about all of it, 'but I wasn't joyful,' she told me. 'I'd lost the part of me that was fun. I used to be a lot of fun, Barbara,' she insisted, 'but that was gone once I realized what I did.' Instead, she became very nervous and fidgety, never comfortable in her own skin because she hated herself so much. She told me, 'I'd fall to my knees every morning and say, "Lord, I'm ready to come home." But I always knew,' she said, 'he had a plan. I was a flawed mother who'd made a big mistake, but I knew I was forgiven. I just had to continue, no matter how much I didn't want to,' she concluded, 'and Lord knows I didn't want to.'"

HIDING ROSIE

When Jack Kennedy was elected to Congress in 1946, Joe Kennedy worried about how his future might be affected if the secret of his lost sister was ever revealed. By this time, Rosie was institutionalized at a facility called Craig House on the Hudson River, outside of New York City. It's where she'd been for five years and where Joe visited her, perhaps, three times.

By the time he was elected, it had been about five years since Jack had last seen his sister, and he was now demanding answers. He wanted to know where she was, and he also wanted to know if there were any other skeletons in the family closet he should be aware of. She was fine, Joe told him, and being treated in some hospital somewhere. No visitors were allowed. Beyond that, there were no other secrets.

One night at dinner, Jack and Arthur Houghton were surprised when Joe went into a sudden rage about it. *"Enough,"* he said as he slammed both hands onto the table. "I told you, she's fine," he said to Jack. He then swatted his dish and place settings onto the floor and stormed from the dining room. Rose stared at her son with disapproval.

Jack asked, "Can I say something?" to which she snapped, "Not unless it's a prayer."

When he rolled his eyes, Rose found it disrespectful. She walked over and slapped him hard. "I am the mother!" she said. "And if anyone should be concerned, I should be, and I am not!" Then she, too, left the room.

Jack didn't know what happened to Rosie; he only knew she was gone and that his parents became completely unhinged when he pushed for answers. If perception was reality, as his father liked to say, the perception was that they'd somehow gotten rid of his sister. Was that in fact what had happened?

By the summer of 1949, Jack was consumed with his work in Congress and no longer asked questions about Rosie. By this time, Janet DesRosiers had been with Joe for about a year. "He never mentioned Rosie," she said. "Once, I was in the attic and I found a box of photographs of her. I sat there and stared at these pictures for a long time and I thought, *My God, how sad is this? No wonder these people are the way they are, so distant and removed. It's how they protect themselves from the truth of what they allowed to happen to this poor girl.*"

After Jack was elected to a second term in the House in the fall of 1948, Joe became even more worried about the proximity of Craig House to Manhattan's news media. In June 1949, he moved Rosie to another institution, the Sisters of St. Francis of Assisi at St. Coletta School for Exceptional Children in the far-flung country town of Jefferson, Wisconsin. He also made significant renovations to that facility with an investment of hundreds of thousands of dollars, the equivalent of millions in today's money, drawn off the newly established family foundation in memory of the fallen son, the Joseph P. Kennedy Jr. Foundation. Joe even had constructed a three-bedroom house for Rosie off the main campus of St. Coletta's. It's where she would live for the next fifty-six years with two full-time nuns.

Rosie's home was called the Kennedy Cottage. How interesting is that name considering where Rose Kennedy would seek her own solitude every day—Rose's Cottage, her small shed on the Hyannis Port beach. One has to wonder if, in some part of her heart, Rose's need to isolate was her way of finding commonality with the daughter she'd allowed to be banished so long ago. While such disregard of a child sounds terrible when applied to today's standards, sadly, it's how parents often coped with emotionally disabled children at that time. They'd ship them off so that the rest of the family could go on with their lives without social shame. Sometimes, doctors would even discourage visits for fear of upsetting the patients' daily routine.

In a letter to Sister Anastasia at St. Coletta's on May 29, 1958, which happened to be Jack's forty-first birthday, Joe thanked the nun for her consideration:

> *I am still very grateful for your help. After all, the solution of Rosemary's problem has been a major factor in the ability of all the Kennedys to go about their life's work and to try and do it as well as they can.*

FULL DISCLOSURE

By 1958, Rosie Kennedy had been institutionalized for sixteen years. Twenty-three when she was locked up, she was now thirty-nine. Jack hadn't seen her in all that time. He told Jackie he didn't even know where she was living. Jackie wanted to know more, though, especially once she started drawing an equivalency between Rosie and Arabella. Maybe it was her reporter's instinct, or maybe she just wanted to better understand her husband, but she began to discreetly ask around. At first, she got nowhere. She even called the Benedictine Abbey in Bethlehem, the convent Rose had once mentioned as Rosie's home. They'd never heard of her. After a couple weeks of digging, Jackie finally got the information she needed from the one Kennedy daughter to whom the patriarch was closest: Eunice.

From 1941 until 1948, when Rosie was at Craig House, Eunice was unaware of her sister's whereabouts. After Joe moved his daughter to St. Coletta's in 1949, he confided in Eunice. We now have documentation from Rose Kennedy, a letter she penned to the administrator of St. Coletta's in 1971, that indicates Joe spoke to Eunice about Rosie's care in 1949, "when Rosemary first went to St. Coletta," Rose wrote. One of Joe's relatives familiar with his thinking said, "He confided in Eunice because he wanted her to know where Rosie was in case something ever happened to him. He didn't want anyone else to know. He swore her to secrecy, especially where her brothers were concerned, because he wanted them to have plausible deniability."

In 1953, Eunice and her new husband, Sargent Shriver, settled in Chicago. One of the most important contacts in Eunice's charity work relating to the Kennedy Foundation was with the city's archbishop, Samuel Stritch.

Stritch had previously worked closely with the Sisters of St. Francis Assisi, the order who ran St. Coletta's. With Stritch's assistance (and, apparently, without Joe's knowledge), Eunice and Sarge drove from Chicago to Jefferson several times to visit Rosie at St. Coletta's.

What a burden keeping this secret must have been for Eunice Kennedy. But she feared her father as much as she loved him. Under most circumstances, she never would've betrayed his trust, but she did so for Jackie, or at least indirectly. Perhaps to avoid a crisis of conscience, she suggested that Jackie speak to Archbishop Stritch about Rosie. Stritch then revealed to Jackie that Rosie was at St. Coletta's. Jackie was excited to have this new information and couldn't wait to share it with Jack. When she did, she was shocked to find it wasn't news to him. He'd known all along!

We don't know exactly when Jack found out about Rosie's whereabouts. He and Kick had questioned their father several times but gave up when they couldn't get answers. Once he finally knew where she was, Jack must not have wanted to incur his father's wrath by going to visit her.

"Fine," Jackie told him. "We're going now."

Jack was reluctant. He had no idea what Rosie might now be like. He could only imagine, and those were thoughts he tried to push from his mind. It was easier to just think she was being taken care of . . . somewhere. "But Jackie thought his keeping this secret for so long had really affected him," said Cybil Wright. Wright was a good friend of Yusha Auchincloss's and would introduce him to the woman he'd marry, Alice Emily Lyon, daughter of the U.S. ambassador to Chile. She continued, "Jackie was sure the secret of Rosie was the reason Jack was so cold and disconnected. He'd closed himself off from his sister and then from everyone else, too. She wanted to fix it. Her mother disagreed. Mrs. Auchincloss wanted her to stay out of it. 'Jacqueline feels she's solved a big mystery,' she told me and Yusha, 'but what she doesn't understand is that sometimes a family is held together by its secrets.'"

Of the little we know of the conversation Jack and Jackie had about Eunice, we know Jackie told him, "It's time, Jack." We know this because Janet revealed it in an unpublished interview in 1973. We also know Jackie asked Jack not to say anything to Joe that might implicate Eunice. "She did me a great favor," Jackie told him, "and now we must protect her." Nobody was to know. Indeed, the culture of secrecy around Rosie prevailed.

About a month later, on May 16, 1958, Jack planned a secret trip to St. Coletta's while he was in Madison on the campaign speaking at the University of Wisconsin. Bob Healy of the *Boston Globe* accompanied him, though not to St. Coletta's. Jack went alone to see Rosie, not even with Jackie. In the next year, he would secretly visit her several more times, including in February and then again in November after speaking at Wisconsin's River Falls State College. There remain some fascinating small-town stories from its natives about the senator's visits to Jefferson.

Maryann Gleisner, president of the Jefferson Historical Society for the last sixty years, recalls her uncle Jerome Slechta and his wife, Margaret, as having hosted a dinner to introduce Jack to local politicians.

Ms. Gleisner worked as a beautician in her mother's beauty shop, a family business for more than sixty years. While her mom styled the hair of the nuns at St. Coletta's, hidden under habits, Maryann worked on the patients, including Rosie, every week for many years. "Even as an adult, she had a deep hole in her forehead where she'd had the lobotomy," she recalled. "She would say things in opposite. If she liked flowers, she'd say, 'I hate flowers.' You'd ask, 'Rosie, do you have to go to the bathroom,' and she'd say, 'No!' which meant she had to go. In the seventies, when Rose Kennedy wrote her memoir, she sent me a signed copy and I read about Rosie's life before the surgery, how she was presented to the queen. I was so sad to know it was her father who'd done this to her."

After better understanding his sister's circumstances, Jack became committed to the passing of several disability statutes. In 1958, he was one of a group of senators who sponsored legislation to funnel more federal money to states in an effort to expand research and education for children with mental disabilities. That legislation passed both houses in Congress to become law in September 1958, four months after Jack first visited Rosie, and was known as Public Law 85-926.

Jack also supported Eunice in her 1958 mission to use the Kennedy Foundation's resources to study intellectual disabilities. In a couple years' time, after Jack was in the White House, Eunice would persuade him to establish the Committee on Mental Retardation and the National Institute of Child Health and Human Development, the former of which was established by executive order, the latter by legislation signed into law.

Christina J. Goldstone, author of *Leading with Their Hearts: The Story of St. Coletta of Wisconsin,* today has a daughter at St. Coletta's. She said, "I don't think the public is fully aware of what John Kennedy did for disability education and treatments. His other important programs, the Peace Corps for instance, are much more well known. In fact, though, he picked up the baton and moved forward with it to make a big difference in the lives of people with disabilities and their families. One thing I know for certain: the nuns at St. Coletta's loved his sister, Rosie, very much. All these years later, she's still remembered fondly there."

PART XIII

The Climb Up

Joseph and Rose Kennedy after their wedding ceremony, at St. Stephen's Church in Boston, October 7, 1914. *John F. Kennedy Presidential Library and Museum, Boston*

Father and sons. Joseph P. Kennedy proudly holds four-year-old Joseph Patrick Jr. and two-year-old John Fitzgerald Kennedy, 1919. *Kennedy Family Collection / John F. Kennedy Presidential Library and Museum, Boston*

Jack's side of the family, the Kennedys, in Hyannis Port, on July 3, 1934. Standing in back row, from left to right: Joseph P. Jr., Kathleen (Kick), Rosemary (Rosie), and Eunice Kennedy. Seated in front row, from left to right: Patricia (Pat) Kennedy, Robert F. (Bobby), Rose, John F. (Jack), Joseph P. Kennedy Sr. with son Edward M. (Ted) in his lap, and Jean (standing). *Bachrach Studios, Kennedy Family Collection / John F. Kennedy Presidential Library and Museum, Boston*

Jack Kennedy on PT-109. He started the
mission a skipper and ended it a hero.
August 1943. *Kennedy Family Collection / John
F. Kennedy Presidential Library and Museum,
Boston*

Brothers Jack and Joe Kennedy, both serving in
the navy during World War II, are pictured here in
uniform. Joseph Kennedy Jr. was tragically killed in
action on August 12, 1944. *Kennedy Family Collection / John
F. Kennedy Presidential Library and Museum, Boston*

Jackie and Jack, a beautiful couple, on their wedding
day at St. Mary's Roman Catholic Church in Newport.
Jackie was given in marriage by her stepfather, Hugh
Auchincloss. September 12, 1953. *John F. Kennedy
Presidential Library and Museum, Boston*

Janet DesRosiers, who was brought into the marriage
of Joe and Rose Kennedy in 1948, poses in front of a
happy group in Monte Carlo. 1952. From left: former Boston police commissioner, Joseph F. Timilty;
Kennedy attorney, Bartholomew A. Brickley; Rose Kennedy; Joe Kennedy; and Joe's best friend,
Arthur Houghton. *Janet DesRosiers Collection*

Janet, Jackie, and Joe Kennedy at a Hialeah Race Track outing. Janet and Joe were the real power players in their respective families and had a mutual if also begrudging respect for one another, though Janet did tell Joe's son, Jack, "If you think you'll do to my daughter what your father did to your mother, you have another thought coming." *National Archives*

Janet DesRosiers (front and center) sits next to Joe Kennedy's sister, Loretta, at the Hialeah Race Track in Miami, 1954. Behind them, left to right: Rose, Joe, and Arthur Houghton. Reflecting on her relationship with Joe, Janet, now 101, said, "I was young and swept away. I can't believe I allowed myself to become a third party in the Kennedy marriage. But I did." *Janet DesRosiers Collection*

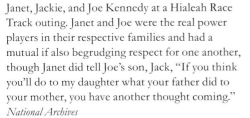

Jack and Jackie share a moment at the 1956 Democratic Convention in Chicago. Shortly after, Jackie suffered the stillbirth of their daughter, Arabella, while Jack was away on a cruise. His absence during this heartbreaking time deeply affected Jackie, a wound that lingered until she later uncovered the reasons behind his actions. *John F. Kennedy Presidential Library and Museum, Boston*

After the death of Arabella, things changed between Jack and Jackie. Similar to the way his father brought Janet DesRosiers into his marriage to Rose, Jack introduced Joan Lundburg into his own marriage. Their relationship lasted for three years, with Jackie well aware of it. "He didn't have to lie to me about her," Jackie said years later. "I was already lying to myself." *Zachary Hitchcock Collection*

Outgoing Republican president Dwight D. Eisenhower meets with Democratic President-elect John F. Kennedy in the Oval Office on December 6, 1960, symbolizing the peaceful transfer of power that has been a hallmark of American democracy. *Abbie Rowe, White House Photographs / John F. Kennedy Presidential Library and Museum, Boston*

President-elect John F. Kennedy meets with Vice President Richard Nixon, the runner-up in the closely contested 1960 presidential election, to demonstrate solidarity and unity. The meeting took place at the Key Biscayne Hotel in Florida on November 14, 1960. *Richard Nixon Presidential Library and Museum*

The new president and his First Lady, John F. Kennedy and Jacqueline Kennedy, on Inauguration Day. January 20, 1961. *John F. Kennedy Presidential Library and Museum, Boston*

Mary Pinchot Meyer was in a relationship with President Kennedy while he was in the White House. "Mary Meyer is finished," Jackie eventually told him. "It's over, Jack. It's either her, or me. You choose." Of course, Jack made the right choice—his wife. May 1963. *Robert Knudsen, White House Photographs / John F. Kennedy Presidential Library and Museum, Boston*

The Kennedys brought true elegance to the White House. Here the president and First Lady depart the National Theatre following the premiere performance of the musical *Mr. President*. September 25, 1962. *Abbie Rowe, White House Photographs / John F. Kennedy Presidential Library and Museum, Boston*

It was with the death of his son Patrick Kennedy that President Kennedy had a crisis of conscious. "It's very painful," he said of his behavior in his marriage to Jackie, "and by painful, I mean shameful." Here, he and his mother-in-law, Janet, arrive at the hospital just before little Patrick's death on August 9, 1963. *Jamie Auchincloss Collection*

The world stood still for thirteen days as President Kennedy grappled with the Cuban Missile Crisis. He spoke to the world in a White House address to draw a line in the sand and set the stage for a peaceful resolution. October 22, 1962. *National Archives*

As President, Jack faced immense challenges—the Bay of Pigs, the Cuban Missile Crisis, civil rights, and th escalating conflict in Vietnam. While his time in office was tragically cut short, his leadership during pivota moments left a lasting impact on the nation and the world. *Photo by Jacques Lowe, All Rights Reserved, The Estate Jacques Lowe*

POLITICAL OPERATIVES

In March 1959, after returning together from campaign stops in Oregon, Utah, Idaho, and Montana, Jack and Jackie had dinner in a Georgetown restaurant with their good friends Ben Bradlee and his wife, Tony. At thirty-eight, Ben was five years older than Jack. Their friendship would suffer a number of hits over the years as they attempted to navigate the unlikely relationship of a politician and a journalist. But they'd always find their way back to each other. Over this particular meal, Jack and Ben talked about setting the stage for Jack's presidential run. In a 2000 interview, Ben recalled the conversation.

"What about this Catholic issue?" Ben asked Jack.

Though the Kennedys had been deliberating over this particular subject for many years, Jackie thought it was absurd. "Jack is the worst Catholic I know," she said. She smiled off his look. "You know it's true," she teased him. "Eunice could be a nun, Bobby a priest, but they wouldn't even let you be an altar boy." She reminded him of one of the first times they went to church together, when they had just begun dating. He had to remain in the pew and not receive Communion because he wasn't in a state of grace, meaning he hadn't gone to Confession. "So there we three were—you, me, and Mummy, excommunicated because she'd divorced Daddy [Black Jack]—sitting sheepishly while your poor mother had to climb all over our knees to get to the altar for her Eucharist."

Ben Bradlee recalled, "Jack said, sure, the Catholic question could whittle away at his support, but he had bigger problems. He didn't have the full backing of farmers and unions, for instance. Also, Southerners were ambivalent about him, as were more liberal Democrats who questioned his complacency on civil rights."

Throughout most of the South, Blacks could not vote, were barred from public restrooms and subjected to violence. The legal system usually worked against them. In the North, Blacks faced discrimination in housing, employment, and education. Though the Supreme Court ruled unanimously in 1954 that racial segregation in public schools was unconstitutional, many political leaders in the South used "states' rights" to continue to justify segregation. By the end of the 1950s, fewer than 10 percent of Black children in the South were attending integrated schools. At the Fourth of July celebration at Hyannis Port in 1957, Jack told his father, Joe, and stepfather-in-law, Hugh, that Black American leaders should pace themselves, rather than push too hard for equality. "If these guys like [Martin Luther] King don't show more moderate judgement they could end up self-defeating," he said. "Many Americans are blind to it and don't want it. Whether we like it or not, people are used to a certain way."

The McCarthy issue—Jack's not having been present for a censure vote because he was laid up after back surgery—had also damaged his support among the liberal community, who cited it as an example of his lack of principles. Then, there was the Cold War. Ben Bradlee recalled, "'The Soviets are winning it,' he told me, 'and Americans don't like it. *I* don't like it. Sputnik is bad news.' He was referring to the Russian-launched space satellite Sputnik [in October 1957]. Lots of people had been sure the U.S. would be number one in space with a satellite, so when the Russians got there first it made folks pretty anxious."

On April 1, 1959, weeks after that dinner, Jack assembled a team of political operatives at his father's Palm Beach estate to seriously map out plans for a presidential run. It was decided they needed a Washington office, headed up by Jack's brother-in-law Stephen Smith, Jean's husband. He'd be responsible for keeping Jack apprised of his status with delegates and regional party leaders and what needed to be done to keep them close by for the Democratic Convention.

Later that summer, Jackie went to England to visit Lee and the man she'd just married in March, Prince Stanislaw Radziwill, known as "Stas." (She'd divorced Michael Canfield a year earlier.) Meanwhile, Jack stayed at Hammersmith with the Auchinclosses and Caroline. From there, he dictated a letter to his wife:

I went up there to Newport last Friday afternoon, and Caroline looks beautiful. Miss Shaw evidently felt rather strange for the first three or four days, but since then has spread her charm out, and seemed in great form when I saw her. Caroline was a great success on the beach and seemed to love the water. Miss Shaw is the loveliest figure actually on the beach and has a beautiful red-brown bathing suit that goes with her hair. She has let herself go, however, slightly, around the middle. I flew back Monday with your mother, who was in an excellent humor and spoke warmly of you and Lee.

After Jack's time in Newport, it was back to work. The next set of important meetings would be at Bobby's Hyannis Port house in October. Jack decided to run in the Wisconsin primary, where a Lou Harris poll showed him in good standing. The Catholic question left him no choice but to go there. Not only would a win in a rural, farmland territory demonstrate his ability to address issues vital to Middle Americans, many of whom wondered if a rich politician could relate to their needs, but would also signify that his faith wasn't a major concern. How ironic. Wisconsin was, of course, where Rosie was at St. Coletta's. That coincidence didn't escape Jackie, who mentioned to her mother the symbolism behind winning that state. She felt it wouldn't escape Jack, either.

Torbert Macdonald and George Smathers were both present that weekend in October set aside for strategy sessions. Sitting with Joe on the porch, they watched as Jack walked a stretch of sand with Bobby and Stephen Smith. His gait was so slow and laborious, Torbert, a decorated war hero in his own right with a Silver Star and a Purple Heart, couldn't believe it. "It's like he's walking in wet cement," he said.

"Not to worry," Joe told him. "He's a Kennedy. My blood runs through his veins. We use our weaknesses to our advantage. What happened on PT-109, that's public relations now. People will respect him all the more because of it."

THE CAVE

After one strategy meeting, Jack and Jackie took their own stroll on the beach to watch what promised to be a stunning sunset. They soon came across a small cave. Jack cleared away some of the brush in front of it, looked inside, and smiled to himself.

Jack told Jackie that when he was about thirteen and Kick was twelve, they discovered this particular space while playing. They went inside and huddled while their parents shouted out their names in search of them. With the passing of about fifteen minutes, their tone became more frantic. Finally, Rose demanded, "Jack and Kathleen, show yourselves immediately!"

Kick whispered, "Should we tell them we're okay?"

"No," Jack told her. "Let's just sit here a little while longer."

All he wanted was to be with his little sister. It was always such a noisy household—at this point, they had six siblings: Joe, Rosie, Eunice, Pat, Bobby, and Jean—there was no one-on-one time for any of them. If he could carve out a moment with his favorite sister, that's what Jack wanted to do.

Jack said he liked to close his eyes and take himself back to that special place with Kick. When he did so, he felt her presence strongly. He said he wished Jackie could've known her, especially since they'd both, at different times, worked at the *Times-Herald*. He told her that now, given her early death, he imagined Kick understanding the secret of life after death, the great mystery of heaven and hell upon which his family's entire religion was predicated. He was sure he'd be the one to whom she'd want to tell everything about it: *You'll never believe it, Jack!*

So much had occurred lately to make Jack open up, and Jackie was responsible for a lot of it. He was finally becoming emotionally available to her, and his emotional intimacy drew her closer to him, as well. They even discussed Inga Arvad for the first time.

Jackie remembered that Jack had wanted to add Inga to the guest list for their wedding, but that his father had vetoed it. She never asked anything more about it, though in subsequent years Jack's friends did occasionally bring the name up. When Jack finally explained the whole story to her, Jackie's takeaway was fascinating. She told him—and later her family—she believed the reason Joe didn't want Inga in his son's life was because she was a strong woman with influence, and he didn't want her to have any sway over him. Jackie felt the patriarch had just used the Nazi rumors as an excuse to get rid of her.

While Jack hadn't thought of that, he had to admit it might have been the case. He cautioned Jackie that he hadn't seen Inga in twelve years; there was no reason to be worried about her. Only Jackie would know if she felt any pang of jealousy hearing about Jack's first love. We do know—and only because she told her mother—that she was happy Jack finally felt comfortable enough with her to discuss it. It was as if she was just beginning to know and understand the sensitive, complicated, and maddening man she'd taken as her husband five years ago. She was starting to feel as if she was in a real marriage, and she knew—or at least she hoped—he'd finally begun to feel the same way.

Importantly, Jackie had forgiven Jack for his behavior three years earlier after the birth of Arabella. She believed him to now be a different man and refused to hang on to any anger and resentment. For the sake of their marriage and, as she told her family, "my own peace of mind," she felt the time had come for forgiveness. "I've learned that marriage requires hard work," she said. "You have to be willing to do it. I am willing."

Jack still had his faults, and Jackie wasn't naive to them. "Only great men have great flaws," she told her good friend Joan Braden, quoting the French Classical author François de La Rochefoucauld. "I probably don't know the half of it," she added, "and thank goodness for that. This life isn't for everyone."

"She knew Jack well, faults and all," Joan Braden said, "and she'd made her choice. Forgiving him for Arabella was her way of reclaiming her life and taking back her strength after what he'd done to her." But don't misunderstand, cautioned Joan. Jackie was also cognizant of the fact that any future with John F. Kennedy would likely have more challenges. "She knew this," concluded Joan. "She knew this very well."

"Are you happy?" Jack asked Jackie while they watched the sun go down. Jackie smiled and put her head on his chest. He gazed up at the colorful sky and, as he later told Torbert Macdonald, "I felt like maybe for the first time in my life things were going to be, I don't know . . . okay, I guess."

OFFICIALLY IN THE GAME

Eighteen years, I have been in the service of the United States, first as a naval officer in the Pacific during World War II and for the past fourteen years as a member of the Congress. In the last twenty years, I have traveled in nearly every continent and country—from Leningrad to Saigon, from Bucharest to Lima. From all of this, I have developed an image of America as fulfilling a noble and historic role as the defender of freedom in a time of maximum peril—and of the American people as confident, courageous and persevering. It is with this image that I begin this campaign.

At forty-two and one of the youngest presidential candidates in American history, Jack looked strong and vibrant in his well-tailored dark blue silk suit and his perfectly knotted tie. He'd come a long way from the days when he'd leave the house in a wrinkled outfit that had never known an iron. He also seemed healthier than ever, his face filled out even though it was mostly due to the cortisone he was taking for his Addison's. He was tan and fit, the perfect picture of a man his age at the top of his game, a war hero who could legitimately claim that distinction, unlike Humphrey, Nixon, or, likely, anyone else who might come forward as a contender. Jackie, in a sleeveless black dress, was gorgeous at his side, happy and proud. They looked like the perfect political team.

In his speech in the Senate Caucus Room to announce his candidacy for president, Senator John Fitzgerald Kennedy outlined his concerns about the Soviet gains in the arms race, which "already threaten our existence." He spoke of his cross-country campaign of the "last forty months," and his

belief in the importance of the primary system and its benefit to voters. He
made it clear he was running for president, not someone's VP, as had been
suggested in recent weeks might be a better fit for him.

The biggest criticism Jack faced at this time was that he was too young
and inexperienced for the job. While he was incredibly well-spoken, he was
often weak on detailed policy. He was poetic and compelling with plenty
of sweeping themes and aspirations, but sometimes, after the glow of his
persona dimmed, the listener would leave his speech thinking, *Wait. What?*

The ambiguity was sometimes intentional. In speaking to a voter's
emotions, Kennedy purposely used broad strokes. *We will fight Communism.
We will fight for nuclear disbarment. We will fight for lower taxes. We will fight for
equal rights.* All of it sounded good to many Americans, and certainly good
enough to sketch out JFK's so-called New Frontier. However, for some, the
question still remained: *How?*

Answers to any remaining questions didn't matter. Many voters were
compelled enough by the sheer force of JFK's personality, charisma, and
speaking skills to overlook any lack of specificity in what he was saying, certainly not unusual in political campaigns. They couldn't help but be swept
away by his handsome and youthful image and by the persuasiveness of
ideas that at least *sounded* forward thinking. People asked for his autograph
when they met him, not for his views on Russia. *Saturday Evening Post* declared, "Mr. Kennedy is the clean-cut, smiling American boy, trustworthy,
loyal, brave, clean and reverent, boldly facing up to the challenges of the
Atomic Age."

Importantly, Jack also seemed confident that he and only he could handle the big challenges facing the nation. Sometimes, that confidence mor-
phed into arrogance, but that, too, worked in his favor. Many people want
certainty in their politicians. A voter wants to feel their candidate believes
that whatever needs to be handled can be handled swiftly and without hesitation. "Kennedy is ambitious," Arthur Schlesinger Jr. wrote at the time,
"because the Presidency alone would give him the power to fulfill purposes
which have long lain in his mind and heart."

PART XIV

JFK for President

FEMME FATALE

After Jack Kennedy secured the knot on his tie, he stared at his reflection in a full-length mirror. He then opened a bottle of pills, took one, opened another bottle, took another pill, all while smiling at his brother-in-law Peter Lawford behind him. Jack had joined Peter in his suite at the Sands Hotel for, as Peter later put it in a 1981 interview, "a couple of drinks and a change of shirt, probably the fourth or fifth of the day, knowing him." It was true Jack would change shirts numerous times a day, never feeling clean, always worried he'd perspired too much.

Still taking in his mirrored image, Jack pulled his cuffs below his jacket sleeves and adjusted the dress studs on his shirt. He reached for a comb, ran it through his reddish-brown hair, then patted it in place. While doing this, he was also reading a book propped up on the bureau; he was always reading something.

"Handsome as ever," Peter said as he toasted his brother-in-law with his rocks glass.

"Do I look presidential?" Jack asked.

"Hell, yeah," Peter exclaimed.

Hours earlier, Peter was at JFK's side as he addressed a dinner reception at the Convention Center. In an hour, he would join Frank Sinatra, Dean Martin, Joey Bishop, and Sammy Davis Jr.—known collectively as the Rat Pack—for the first of two sold-out performances in the Sands showroom, where they'd be appearing for the next week or so. The fellows kept a punishing schedule, performing every evening after filming scenes for a movie they were making for Warner Bros. called *Ocean's 11*. Their show in the Sands's Copa Room was the hottest ticket in Vegas.

About a month had passed since Jack had announced his candidacy. It had been hectic, not a day off. His mother had once spoken of a "big wave that carries you from one great thing to the next and leaves you with no time for consideration." Certainly, Jack was riding it at this time.

Jack had been in New Mexico that morning of February 7 and was en route to Oregon when he decided to accept Frank Sinatra's invitation to stop off in Vegas. The two men had known each other for a few years. Both Catholics, Jack was two years younger than Frank, who was forty-four.

The Rat Pack show that night was exceptional. "Ladies and gentlemen, it gives me a lot of pleasure," Frank said during a break in the action, "to introduce my friend Jack Kennedy. He's running for president of this great country." Jack smiled, stood up, and turned around to big applause. "Good lookin' fella, ain't he?" Frank said. "Vote for him. He's one of the good ones."

Blair Clark, a friend of Jack's who worked for CBS News, recalled, "We were all seated at Sinatra's table, and after the show people kept coming and going, jumping up and sitting down, all these bimbos, showgirls, good girls, not-so-good girls. That was the night we met Judith Campbell."

Judith Campbell Exner (as she was later known after her marriage to a golf pro named Dan Exner) was twenty-five, a raven-haired beauty with full lips and dark eyes. Intelligent, charismatic, and a great conversationalist, she was born to an affluent Catholic family, lived in Los Angeles, and had married fledgling actor William Campbell in 1952 at eighteen and divorced him in '58. She dated Sinatra briefly in '59. He was the one who'd invited her to the show this evening.

"Jack, meet Judy," Frank said as everyone mingled. Jack smiled and shook her hand.

"When our eyes met, I don't know . . . it was something else," Judy later recalled. "There was such power in his look. Very strong charisma, sexual energy. I was sucked in right away."

"Goddamn!" Peter whispered to Jack. "This girl's something else, isn't she?"

Peter said Judy looked just like Elizabeth Taylor. Or, maybe even Jackie. But not to Jack. To Jack, she looked just like . . . yes, Joan Lundberg.

HIGH HOPES

The major candidates for the 1960 Democratic presidential nomination would be Senator John F. Kennedy of Massachusetts, Senator Lyndon B. Johnson of Texas, Senator Stuart Symington of Missouri, former Illinois governor Adlai Stevenson (unofficially), Governor Pat Brown of California, and Senator Hubert Humphrey of Minnesota. It would be a hard-fought battle beginning, of course, with the primary in New Hampshire, won handily by Jack on March 8 with 85 percent of the vote, a big victory. Next up, the all-important Wisconsin primary on April 5.

Jack knew he had to beat Humphrey in Wisconsin in order to neutralize him for the nomination. Therefore, the Kennedy contingent worked hard campaigning there, with Bobby, Teddy, and Kenny O'Donnell even moving their families into the Hotel Wisconsin. Jackie appeared at a Polish event in Milwaukee, too, greeting the crowd in its native language and mentioning that her sister was now married to a Pole—namely, Stas. "The crowd loved her," said John Radziwill, Stas's son. "Bobby called her their 'secret weapon.' She wanted to help because she knew Jack had never worked harder to win anything, campaigning in small Wisconsin towns from morning to night."

While in Wisconsin, Hubert Humphrey sensed something in Kennedy that was maybe a little close to home. "You have to learn to have the emotions of a human being when you are charged with the responsibilities of leadership," he said in one speech. Certainly, Jack had been accused in the past of being dispassionate and lacking in empathy, and not just in public life but at home. Norman Mailer hit it on the head when, after a press conference he attended, he wrote of Jack, "There was an elusive detachment to everything he did. One did not have the feeling of a man present in the room with all his weight and all his mind." It was as if, sometimes, Jack couldn't camouflage his real personality and character, even when acting out his role as politician.

Humphrey also castigated Kennedy for being less liberal than he let on, which was also true. JFK was actually quite conservative, often exaggerating his liberalism in order to placate the base. "But that's just something candidates do in election cycles," noted Liz Carpenter in a 1998 interview. She was a reporter who traveled with the Kennedy contingent in 1960 and later went on to become executive assistant to LBJ and then press secretary to Lady Bird. She continued, "I remember that Humphrey further revealed that Joe Kennedy had contributed a thousand dollars to Nixon's Senate campaign ten years earlier. This revelation was supposed to demonstrate Jack's conservative leanings. Again, politics being what it was, Jack's team was forced to lie and say the contribution never happened. With the entire Kennedy family out there stumping for him, Humphrey was eventually so overwhelmed he complained that it felt, and these were his words, 'like an independent merchant competing against a chain store.'"

In the end, Jack scored a big victory in Wisconsin by winning the primary there on April 5. However, it was clear that his margin of victory had come almost entirely from Catholic districts. Given as much, the worry was how he could ever hope to win the next primary in West Virginia, a state where only 3 percent of the population was Catholic. Joe had warned him not to run there, but Jack was determined. "He knew if he dropped West Virginia, particularly for the Catholic reason," Lem Billings remembered, "it would be interpreted as meaning that a Catholic could never be president of the United States."

The afternoon after the Wisconsin win, Jack had lunch with Jackie and Caroline. Even though he'd won Wisconsin, Jackie knew he wasn't feeling very victorious because of the Catholic margin. One political operative had even told her that a picture of her smoking had cost him some votes. "I hope that's not true, Bunny," she said, using the loving nickname she gave him because of his prominent front teeth. He said it was a ridiculous assertion and that she was doing "just great." She was happy for the acknowledgment. Though she had plans to fly to Palm Beach with Caroline and Maud, she offered to instead stay behind with Jack.

"No," he said, kissing her, "you go on ahead with Miss Shaw and I'll see you in a few days."

Maybe Jack wanted Jackie to stay. Or . . . maybe not. Judy Campbell, many years later, said she saw him that same night, right after Jackie left. She said that by the time Jackie was leaving with Maud, Judy herself had already checked into the Sheraton Park Hotel and had phoned Evelyn Lincoln in Jack's office to make final arrangements. "He's expecting you at N Street at 7:30," Mrs. Lincoln said, according to Judy. She offered to send a car, but Judy said no, she'd take a cab.

THE TROUBLE WITH JUDY

It would be almost fifteen years before Judy Campbell would come into national prominence. In 1975, she would be subpoenaed by the congressional Church Committee investigating CIA assassination attempts. She'd then end up being the first prominent woman to claim publicly to have had an affair with Jack Kennedy, starting before his presidency and continuing into his White House days. She'd earn quite the place of notoriety in Kennedy history because of her connection not only to him but also to Frank Sinatra and mobster Sam Giancana. According to Judy, March 7—the day before the New Hampshire primary—was when she and Jack began their affair in New York. Then, they were together a second time, she said, on April 6, at his home in Georgetown after Wisconsin.

Judy Campbell would've been better taken at her word if she didn't later prove to be a less than reliable narrator of her own life. Her situation wasn't like Joan Lundberg's. Joan was consistent with her story, had friends and relatives privy who could vouch for its truth, and wrote a manuscript about it for her children. Even Jackie's mother and stepfather and other members of her family knew about the Lundberg affair as it was unfolding. Jackie had told Janet, of course, who then told Hugh. Jack Warnecke knew about it, as well. The other side of the family—the Kennedys—heard about it from Peter and Pat Lawford. But Judy Campbell would keep changing her story over the years without any credible witnesses to support it. It's what she claimed happened on April 6 at Jack's home that especially makes one question her honesty. She said Jack had asked her about a recent trip she'd taken to Florida and she told him she'd met someone named "Sam Flood." Jack supposedly said, "Oh yeah. That's Sam Giancana, the big Mob guy."

Back in the 1950s and '60s, Sam Giancana was one of the most power-ful and feared gangsters of the Chicago syndicate, the operating boss of the Outfit. The successor to Al Capone, Sam always managed to evade the law, even though he was a known murderer who'd made a fortune from pros-titution, extortion, drugs, and loansharking. Some reports said he earned as much as $50 million a year. Law enforcement lost count of how many killings he'd ordered in the last ten years.

"Listen, Judy," Jack allegedly said, "can you help me with the campaign? I want you to take something to Sam when you go back to Chicago." She said Jack then asked her to deliver to Sam a satchel containing $250,000, the equivalent of more than $6 million in today's money, which he was to then use to help swing the West Virginia primary in Jack's favor. Judy said she took a train to Chicago that night and made the transfer to Sam Giancana.

One problem with her story is that, by April 6, Judy had only been in Jack's company three times—Las Vegas, New York, and Washington having had sex with him, she maintained, in the last two instances. How likely is it that a savvy politician like JFK would trust someone he'd met in a Las Vegas showroom just two months earlier to bribe a world-renowned gangster into helping him subvert American democracy?

She also claimed to have arranged no fewer than ten meetings between the president and Sam Giancana, one of which she said she believed took place in the White House. The idea of such a meeting occurring in such a place defies logic.

Making things all the more problematic when evaluating Judy Camp-bell's credibility is the fact that she didn't mention anything about being a courier between Kennedy and Giancana to the Church Committee in 1975 or in her published memoir, *My Story,* in 1977. These revelations didn't come to light until she was paid for a feature in *People* magazine in 1988, and then in numerous television interviews for which she was paid. In explaining why she hadn't come clean earlier, Judy said she feared for her life; after all, Giancana was murdered right before his testimony before the committee and his killer was never found. In 1988, at the age of fifty-four, Judy was suffering from cancer and felt she only had a few years left and wanted to die with a clear conscience. She did in fact lose her cancer battle in 1999.

Crime expert William F. Roemer was a former FBI agent who wrote the significant and well-reported book *Man Against the Mob* in 1989 before the 1990s onslaught of exaggerated tales about the Mob and the Kennedys. Sam Giancana's daughter, Antoinette Giancana, says her father was so used to being tailed by Roemer, he used to mock him by giving him his days' schedule in advance. In a 1991 interview, Roemer stated, "By 1960 we [the FBI] were following Sam Giancana everywhere he went and using electronic surveillance on him as well, all of which was approved by Hoover. If Exner met with Giancana, or if Giancana ever met with the president, the FBI would've known about it at the time, as would a whole lot of other people. It wouldn't have taken until Judy Campbell started being paid for stories for it to become known."

There are enough entries in White House visitor logs with Judy Campbell's name for us to have confidence that she did have a personal relationship with JFK from 1960 until the spring of 1962. "I was wrong to have an affair with a married man," she told the gossip columnist Liz Smith in 1977. "I take responsibility for all of that. It's there forever. I tried to rationalize it because I fell in love with Jack. He swept me off my feet." One wonders why that wasn't sufficient for her. It would seem that an affair with the president of the United States would be headline-making enough for any one person. Why add all the fictitious, cloak-and-dagger intrigue about mobsters?

"Beyond the relationship itself," Wiliam Roemer concludes of Judy Campbell, "everything else she ever claimed has to be taken with the proverbial grain of salt."

SINATRA

————

Frank Sinatra had had a tremendous career spanning more than twenty years. Considered by many music scholars to be the voice of a generation, he was a song stylist like no other. As was well known, he also had a complicated relationship with the underworld. When it came to mobsters, he couldn't help himself. Going all the way back to his early days in Hoboken, Frank was intrigued by notorious characters powerful enough to get away with anything. It's how he saw himself—unbound by convention whether in relation to his love life, his marriages, or his career. But it was never a simple equation when it came to Sinatra and the underworld. While he enjoyed bragging about knowing them, they also wanted to claim him as their own. After all, he was the most famous Italian American in America, maybe even the world.

Joe Kennedy was acquainted with Frank through his son-in-law Peter Lawford. He wasn't sure what to believe of Frank's much-gossiped-about underworld ties, but he knew Frank had connections of some kind. According to many people, including Frank's own daughter Tina, Joe hoped to use those relationships to his son's advantage or, as Tina so aptly put it, "Power goes to power." Worried about the upcoming primary in West Virginia and the general election, particularly in Illinois, Joe wondered if Sam Giancana might help swing things in Jack's favor. He played with the idea in his head. It was a possibility, not a fait accompli. A man who never ruled anything out, Joe wanted to at least consider it.

Joe Kennedy had some dealings with Sam Giancana in the past and had even called upon him for a few favors. However, after the Racket Committee hearings headed up by Bobby, and considering that Jack was running for president, Joe knew better than to just arrange a sit-down with the man. This is why he invited Frank to his home in May 1960. "I was thinking," he told him, "how'd you like to be ambassador to Italy?" Frank thought he was joking, but Joe said he wasn't. If Jack became president, he said, it could really happen. "But first things first," he said. "Come with me."

Rupert Allan was a famous Hollywood publicist at that time, and a friend of Sinatra's. In previously unpublished remarks from 1995, he explained, "Frank told me Joe walked him through the maze of the house, down a flight of stairs, and into the private wine cellar. Frank walked in and took a gander at floor-to-ceiling shelves stocked with expensive liquors and wines. 'Christ, almighty,' he said, 'you leave any booze outside this room for other people?' Joe smiled, closed the door, and got to the point. He said he might need some help in West Virginia and Illinois. Maybe Frank could appeal to Sam to put some pressure on the principal players there, such as the heads of labor unions? 'I can ask,' Frank said, 'but I can't promise anything. Those guys have minds of their own,' he said. 'Understood,' said Joe. 'You'll go straight to the top. Right?' Frank boasted, 'Giancana? Friend of mine goin' way back.' Then Joe said, 'Pick something out. Anything you want.' Frank pulled an expensive bottle of brandy. 'Good taste,' Joe said as he walked him out of the cellar. That one meeting was the beginning of this big and sometimes fantastic legend having to do with Frank, the Kennedys, and the Mob."

A couple days later, Frank Sinatra scheduled a golf date with Sam Giancana. Tina Sinatra recalled, "Dad said, 'I've never come to you for a favor before, Sam, but this time I have to do it.' When he conveyed Joe Kennedy's request for help in West Virginia's Mob-run unions, Giancana said he'd be happy to help."

WEST VIRGINIA

After New Hampshire and Wisconsin, Jack Kennedy continued to beat Hubert Humphrey in primary races, capturing Illinois, Massachusetts, Pennsylvania, and Indiana. Next up were Ohio, DC, Nebraska, and the all-important and much-discussed West Virginia primary, which was scheduled for May 10. It was a tough schedule, all of Kennedy's stops being made on his private jet, the Caroline, of course.

West Virginia would, as is often the case in elections, prove to be a battleground state. Canvassing that state was also a wake-up call for Jack, who was completely taken aback by the impoverished conditions. He was also forced to acknowledge that a big challenge for him was in understanding the problems of struggling working-class Americans. "Because of technological advances in coal mining, hundreds of people had lost their jobs in West Virginia and were fighting to survive financially. Uncle Jack had never seen anything quite like it," Torbert Macdonald Jr. said. "It made sense. How would he? The way he was raised? But getting out to Middle America and understanding its people was the only way a man would ever become president in this country."

Even though Jack had won Wisconsin, Hubert Humphrey had made good headway there by hitting hard with the issue of Kenedy's Catholicism. Humphrey emphasized Jack's faith as a liability in the heavily Protestant West Virginia. Eleanor Roosevelt, with whom Jack had a strained relationship, said, "We wouldn't want the Pope in the White House, would we?" It didn't help that former president Truman, who supported Symington, felt Jack was too young and inexperienced to hold high office. He was also worried about the father's influence in the White House. He had a great line:

"It's not the Pope I'm worried about. It's the Pop." Truman thought Jack was probably a better fit for VP. Jack felt that if he settled for VP it would prove right the naysayers who believed a Catholic could never be elected president.

Jack decided to deal with the question of his faith head-on in West Virginia and cite it as a personal strength while also making it clear that he always put country above everything else, even religion. "Nobody asked me if I was a Catholic when I joined the United States Navy," he said. "Nobody asked my brother if he was a Catholic before he climbed into an American bomber plane to fly his last mission."

One problem Humphrey faced was that he hadn't served in the military, having reportedly been rejected because of a hernia. Or . . . maybe not. There were rumors that he'd done some underhanded things to get out of serving, and Lem Billings—who was working in West Virginia for Jack—years later came right out and called him a "draft dodger" in his oral history. There was some discussion in the Kennedy camp about whether to mention that Jack had been rejected for service, but that it hadn't stopped him from serving. Would this prove his determination? However, his team realized it might also open the door to questions about how Jack had managed to get into service. Since the answer, which was that Joe had falsified Jack's medical records, could just make things worse, it was decided not to focus much on Humphrey's war record. Even without the Kennedys pushing it, rumors about Humphrey's lack of service were enough to give Jack a real leg up. At a debate on May 4 in Charleston, Humphrey couldn't land any good blows. Jack easily won it, even if it had been an uphill battle.

Finally, a week later, on May 10, the West Virginia primary took place. Jack flew to Washington to wait for the results. The night of the primary, the Kennedys were joined at their N Street home by Ben and Tony Bradlee. To ease their nerves, the foursome went to see a terrible low-budget movie called *Private Property*. Ben recalled Jack jumping out of his seat every fifteen minutes to go to the lobby and call Bobby in West Virginia for updates. "Nothing yet," Jack would then solemnly report to Ben upon returning to his seat.

After the foursome got back to N Street, Jackie was in the kitchen getting ice cubes when the phone rang. "Suddenly," she recalled, "I heard this war whoop of joy. It was Bobby. He told Jack, 'We won West Virginia. *We did it!*'" Jack had ended up defeating Hubert with over 60 percent of the vote, an important victory because it proved he *could* win in a heavily Protestant state. "We now knew there was no way Catholicism was going to keep him out of the White House," Lem Billings said. "This issue was buried in West Virginia, forever. Everybody was quite aware that night that the biggest milestone had been passed." In fact, after that particular loss, Hubert Humphrey ended his campaign.

Even today, the question remains: Did Sam Giancana, at Frank Sinatra's behest, help swing West Virginia? There's no solid proof that either man had anything to do with the win other than the assertions of people in Frank's life, like his daughter Tina. She says Frank told her he absolutely did approach Sam, who promised to help in any way he could.

In fact, there were questions about this West Virginia win from the very beginning. Analysts began investigating it within weeks of the victory to see how much "vote buying" had been in play. Topper Sherwood, who co-wrote the book *Just Good Politics: The Life of Raymond Chafin* (a leading union official in West Virginia), noted, "Investigations were carried out by the U.S. Justice Department, the FBI, anti-Kennedy Democrats, the *Wall Street Journal,* local newspapers, and Washington journalist Jack Anderson. Invariably the conclusion was, as one former state governor declared [intending no apparent irony], that Kennedy had 'sold himself' to the voters, not bought them."

This isn't to suggest that there wasn't a lot of cash being thrown around in West Virginia. Playing some of his famous backroom games, Joe Kennedy worked behind the scenes to pay off sheriffs, district attorneys, councilmen, mayors, and anyone else of influence he could convince to support his son. Charlie McWhorter, who was well-connected in national and state Republican politics and also a native of the state, said in 1998, "The way the Kennedys paid people off was like nothing I'd ever seen before or since. They just wanted to win, didn't care what they had to do, whose pockets they had to line. They tore through the state with wads of Joe Kennedy cash. It was something to see, all right."

In fact, it would seem the Kennedys really didn't need Sinatra's or Giancana's help. They already knew how to play down and dirty with the best of them. "What was the Mob going to give him?" asked Joe's biographer David Nasaw. "He had all the money he needed to ship to West Virginia, and he did. I found one of his accountants who talked about bringing satchels of money to West Virginia to buy votes. Humphrey was also buying votes, but he just didn't have as much money."

―――――――

After the win, the Kennedys and Bradlees flew down to Charleston on the Caroline for Jack's victory speech. As the party was underway, Jackie stood awkwardly in the background, appearing to not want to take up much space. Occasionally, she tried to make eye contact with her husband, but he was busy. It wasn't that Jack was intentionally rude as much as he was just swept up in all of the excitement. "Someone needs to teach him the fine art of the PBO," Jackie once said. When asked what she meant, she explained, "The polite brush-off." In fact, though, Jack was too busy turning on what he always called the ol' BP—"big personality"—to give much thought to the PBO. This was a victory for him, a big one for them all, and she knew it.

Eventually, Jackie went to a pay phone to call her mother. Janet was asleep, but Hugh answered. "Did you see?" Jackie asked. Hugh said he saw it all and offered his congratulations. He told her Jack was sure to get the nomination now, and that it probably meant they were headed to the White House. He asked if she could believe such a thing was happening to them all. She said she couldn't imagine it yet, but she had to agree that it was now a very real possibility.

After that call, Jackie went back to the party. Someone tapped her on the shoulder; she turned around. It was Jack. "I've been looking for you," he said, a twinkle in his eye.

"What a big deal this is for you, Bunny," she told him.

"Big deal for *us*," he said. "We're going all the way, Jackie. Hold on tight," he told her, "and enjoy the ride." He reached out and took her hand, seeming very happy to have her at his side. "How about you and I go out there now and turn on the ol' BP?" he finally asked her. With that, they drifted back into the crowd.

THE CANDIDATE

I am fully aware of the fact that the Democratic Party, by nominating someone of my faith, has taken on what many regard as a new and hazardous risk . . . and you have, at the same time, placed your confidence in me, and my ability to render a free, fair judgment . . . and to reject any kind of religious pressure or obligation that might directly or indirectly interfere with my conduct of the presidency in the national interest.
                    —*JFK's acceptance speech, Los Angeles Memorial Coliseum*

After competing in ten primaries, Jack Kennedy snagged the nomination of his party for president on July 13, 1960, during the Democratic Convention in Los Angeles. It was no surprise; he'd secured the needed delegates for the nomination before the convention had even opened. What was surprising, though, was his decision the next day to choose Senate Majority Leader Lyndon Baines Johnson as his running mate, a choice made to assuage the concerns of Southerners about his liberalism. Plus, Jack suspected that if he snubbed LBJ, the man would likely stand in his way of getting any piece of legislation passed—"what with his enormous ego, so thwarted and bitter," as Jackie said of Johnson.

George Christian, a noted reporter who'd later join both Texas governor John Connally and LBJ as press secretary, recalled, "Kennedy had wanted Senator Stuart Symington from Missouri. The way I heard it, the poor guy, Symington, heard about it and actually started writing his acceptance speech. But when Jack was told he needed LBJ, he made the switch."

Joe Kennedy agreed LBJ was the man for the job; he actually knew him better than Jack. Bobby, however, hated LBJ, like a lot of others in his brother's circle, especially since Johnson had trash-talked both his father and brother in the past and was even rumored to have been behind a plot to reveal Jack's Addison's to the public during the 1956 convention (which the Kennedy team had quickly denounced as a total lie). "He's a very difficult man to be around," said George Smathers of LBJ in his oral history, "because he doesn't play golf, he doesn't play cards, he doesn't go fishing, he doesn't care about the seashore, he doesn't care about sailing, he doesn't care about anything, he just likes politics and he talks about it morning, noon, and night."

Jackie didn't take LBJ that seriously, not at this point, anyway. She later remembered Jack telling her how Johnson would show off to reporters on the Senate beat, "that he could—I don't know—play squash and have sexual intercourse once a week." Later, she would remember how dutiful his wife, Lady Bird, always was in his presence. "Anytime Lyndon would talk, Lady Bird would get out a little notebook. She was sort of like a trained hunting dog. He'd say something as innocent as, 'Does your sister live in London?' and Lady Bird would write down Lee's name and 'London.' I mean, she had every name, phone number—it was a—*ewww*—sort of a funny kind of way of operating." (Later, though, Jackie would actually become very fond of Lady Bird and the two would enjoy a close friendship.)

"I'm forty-three years old," Jack told Kenny O'Donnell in speaking of LBJ. "I'm not going to die in office, so the vice presidency doesn't mean anything." LBJ had a slightly different take, or as he told the former congresswoman Clare Boothe Luce, wife of *Time* founder Henry Luce, "I looked it up," he said. "One out of every four presidents has died in office. I'm a gamblin' man, darlin', and this is the only chance I got."

Now that Jack was the first senator since 1920 to be nominated for the presidency, he was eager to tackle the rest of the campaign against the Republican presidential nominee, his old friend Richard Nixon. Privately, though, he was a little worried he didn't have the stamina to get to the finish line. "I'm tired and not feeling that great," he confided in his stepfather-in-law, Hugh Auchincloss, during one phone call. He said he'd been in a foul mood for weeks, that no one wanted to be around him, and that he was "just plain disgusted" with politics.

"The senator's disposition definitely changed as the campaign progressed," said Janet DesRosiers. "He was done, fed up, over it. I didn't think he could take much more. I didn't think any of us could, actually. It was hard work. Jackie, who was pregnant again by this time, would just burst into tears for no reason, the stress getting to her as it did all of us."

Hugh told his stepson-in-law to rest up as much as he could. He was sure Jack had what it took to get to the finish line as a winner. Always the scholar, he quoted a 1940 speech of Jack's hero Winston Churchill: "Victory at all costs. Victory in spite of all terror. Victory however long and hard the road may be." Jack loved the sentiment and was calmed by it; anyone who quoted Churchill to him was sure to win him over. Hugh then put his daughter Janet Jr., who'd just turned fifteen a month earlier, on the line. She told Jack how good he looked on TV, "like a movie star, even," before handing the phone to Jackie. "I'm so nervous," his expectant wife told him, "and so very proud of you."

Janet DesRosiers, who'd known Jack since he was nineteen when she was hired by his father, wrote him a note that meant a lot to him:

I'll always be thinking of you and praying for you and I'll be remembering a tall, very thin, slightly stooped young man with rumpled hair (and sometimes a suit to match) who drank milk and liked cupcakes, who was shy and simple but brave and noble and great—just as great as he is now with all the trimmings. A young man who needed no one. That was my Jack Kennedy. I hope he'll live forever.

Jack was so moved, once he returned to the Cape he asked Janet to be his secretary if he won the White House. She agreed.

"Do you think I can do it, Janet?" he asked her.

"I *know* you can do it," was her answer.

Very early the next morning, Janet DesRosiers watched as the candidate walked along the Cape Cod shoreline alone. He stopped at the breakwater, bent over, and cupped cold salt water in his hand. He threw it onto his face, flung his head back, and looked up at the promising sun.

KICK HIM IN THE BALLS

The first-ever televised debate between presidential candidates with the Democratic nominee John F. Kennedy going up against the Republican choice, Vice President Richard Nixon, was historic. Janet DesRosiers, doubtless one of the only firsthand witnesses still alive, recalled, "Everyone was bouncing off the walls in the studio, but it was so exciting and I'll never forget the electricity in the air. Bobby, with a phone glued to his ear, asking me to get this person or that person; Ted Sorensen, Pierre Salinger, Richard Goodwin, and other guys on team Kennedy scuttling about while also pounding answers to questions into Jack's brain; and poor Jack pacing back and forth shirtless, a look of gloom on his face."

Over the course of this one and then the three subsequent debates, the candidates would address a wide range of issues, including agriculture, education, economy, medical care, and foreign policy. Nixon had seven years of recognition value as vice president, whereas Jack was popular in Massachusetts. Even with his high profile, he was still a relative newcomer to many Americans. The stakes were high.

While Jack was in Chicago, Jackie was at their home in Hyannis entertaining Boston politicians. According to photos taken on the day, she wore a simple black maternity shift and white pearls with her hair in a bouffant style. "Perfect strangers in the home sitting on your antique furniture?" Janet asked her as she scanned the crowd of visitors. "It *is* a new world, isn't it?"

Janet and her close friend Carolyn Baldridge were both staying at Jackie's to help her, now seven months pregnant, prepare the nursery for the baby. Carolyn was one of Janet's bridge-playing partners; her husband,

Edward, worked in the finance business with Hugh. Her son, Julian, also present that night, recalled, "Mrs. Auchincloss couldn't stop talking about how sure she was that Jack would win the debate. 'You don't know him like we do,' she told us. 'He's the man for the job. I think he has the love and support of the American people,' she said, 'and we couldn't be prouder.'

"When the senator called, Jackie was so eager to talk to him she grabbed the phone right out of Mrs. Auchincloss's hand. She was saying things to him like, 'The whole country is behind you, Jack. You must remember that.' She thought he had a good platform. 'He wants to make the country great,' she said, 'and he knows just how to do it.'"

Backstage in Chicago, Jack Kennedy sat staring at himself in a mirror as a light coat of tan makeup was applied to his face. His jaw set, he looked determined, ready for battle. He didn't want to talk to anyone. His prep over, it was too late to absorb any more information. He knew all he needed to know. Now he just wanted to stare at his reflection, think about how far he'd come and where he was headed. "He opened a small satchel, took out a bottle of pills, put one in his palm, and swallowed it without water," Janet DesRosiers recalled. "Then, another bottle and another pill, again with no water. Bobby finally poured him a glass and handed it to him for the rest of his pills. 'Kick him in the balls, Jack,' he told his brother as he walked him out onto the stage. Jack just chuckled."

"I looked at him as he came out onto the stage, tapping his teeth the way he did when he was focused, and I thought, *My God, he's going to annihilate Richard Nixon,*" Ted Sorensen remembered, "and I also remember thinking Nixon didn't have a clue, the poor bastard."

It was a lively debate and most people agreed Jack was the winner. He was confident and charismatic compared to Nixon, who seemed pale, not only in skin tone but in character and personality.

Seventy million people watched that first Kennedy-Nixon debate, a huge audience even by today's standards. It's not hyperbole to say it really changed politics. It's been said that JFK was a product of a new age where TV image could shape a campaign. In fact, he actually prompted that era with this debate. From 1960 onward, presidential candidates not only had to have a grasp of policy in a debate against their opponent but they also had to be compelling in a telegenic way because almost every voter in America would have a television in their living room. It wouldn't be easy for every politician, either. Many were just not camera-ready back then, and some still don't have the talent for it. Jack once said that what fascinated him most was "not so much the ideas of politics, but the mechanics of the whole process." By mechanics, he meant the manner by which messages were delivered and, in 1960, that definitely meant television . . . and Jack Kennedy was good at it.

Though Jackie's guests sat silent throughout the hour-long broadcast, when it ended they all jumped to their feet and applauded. Julian Baldridge, who was twenty-five in 1960, recalled, "Fifteen minutes later, the phone rang. *'It's him!'* Mrs. Auchincloss said as she ran to pick it up, *'It's him!'* A hush fell over the room as she handed the phone to Jackie. 'Listen to this, Jack,' Jackie said as she pointed the receiver at the people in the room. We all started cheering, whooping, and hollering. Jackie then had a brief conversation with the senator and we heard her say, 'I'm so proud and excited for you, Jack. We all are. Mummy is over the moon. You were just great.'"

As people milled about, the phone rang again. This time it was Rose Kennedy. Jackie took the call. Rose was "a basket case, as usual," Jackie later told her mother, because she feared Nixon had won. Jackie told Janet, "I said, 'Don't you dare tell that to Jack. He was very good.' And do you know what she said to me?" Janet waited. Employing her best shaky-voiced Rose Kennedy impression, Jackie said, "Being just good, my dear, is not good enough."

The impression might've been humorous, but Jackie's brief conversation with Rose was deflating. She walked to a bench in front of the fireplace and sat alone, suddenly looking tired.

"Is there anything I can do for you?" Carolyn Baldridge asked her.

Jackie leaned in and whispered, "Yes, Mrs. Baldridge. Please help Mummy get all these people out of my goddamn house."

OCTOBER SURPRISE

O n October 19, eleven days before the presidential election, Dr. Martin Luther King Jr. was jailed in Atlanta for taking part in a sit-in protest at a racially segregated department store lunch counter. In a 1998 interview, Helen Thomas, the noted White House UPI correspondent, explained, "At that time in Atlanta, Blacks had to use separate water fountains, bathrooms, and other public spaces. They were also banned from being served at lunch counters. Incredibly, because of a ridiculous previous traffic violation, MLK was quickly sentenced to four months of hard labor. At the suggestion of Jack's brother-in-law Sargent Shriver, he [Jack] telephoned King's pregnant wife, Coretta, to offer his support. Mrs. King then told the press how appreciative she was of the senator's concern, and didn't hasten to also mention, 'I have noticed that Mr. Nixon has been very quiet. What does that tell you?'"

Initially, despite being sympathetic to King, Bobby was upset that Sargent had gotten Jack involved at all. This wasn't the best time to risk alienating voters not inclined to support civil rights. Joe Kennedy, in Palm Beach, was furious. He, Arthur Houghton, and the family's physician Dr. Robert D. Watt and his wife, Madeline, were in his library in Palm Beach as the discussion grew tense. Joe called Jack. "Maybe you'll get the Negro vote, sure, but those governors in the South will throw their support to Nixon," he told him, practically screaming into the phone. "You'll lose those states, Jack!" he exclaimed before slamming down the phone. "My faith in him is less than full right now," he told the others. "He needs to get his head out of his ass. There's no profit in forgetting that the Negro vote isn't worth sacrificing the white vote."

"Bobby realized the injustice of jailing Martin Luther King and personally called the judge to get him released," said Helen Thomas. "Plus, of course, he knew it was just the kind of thing that could turn an election. In the end, it would prove to be very, very helpful to the Kennedy campaign, and it happened at the last minute, a true October surprise, if you will. Like it or not, Joe Kennedy would later have to admit that the Negro vote really made a very big difference in what was about to be a close election."

"I earnestly and sincerely feel that it's time for all of us to take off our Nixon buttons," the civil rights activist Reverend Ralph Abernathy said. "Since Mr. Nixon has been silent through all this, I'm going to return his silence when I go into the voting booth."

It should be noted, though, that MLK did not come out and endorse Kennedy, though this "October Surprise" definitely energized the Black vote. An oft-told story, which seems to have originated with Arthur Schlesinger's 1965 book, *A Thousand Days: John F. Kennedy in the White House*, has Martin Luther King Sr. saying, "I had expected to vote against Senator Kennedy because of his religion. Now he can be my president, Catholic or whatever he is." Jack found the comment amusing. "Imagine Martin Luther King having a bigot for a father," he said. "Well, we all have our fathers, don't we?"

<hr/>

By the end of October 1960, Jack Kennedy had done everything he and his campaign could to win the presidential election for his party. He was exhausted and on edge, but it had been worth it. "He told me, 'You know what? I gave it my all,'" said Janet DesRosiers, "'and now it's up to the American people. This is the United States of America and in this country we get to choose. If they choose me, great, I deserve it. If they choose Dick Nixon, so be it. Bad choice; however, that's democracy at work, isn't it? But,' he added with a gleam in his eye, 'you know what Dad says. "In this country, it's either the palace or the outhouse." I've never used a goddamn outhouse in my entire life,' he said, 'and you can be sure I'm not gonna start using one now.'"

The Inaugural Committee
requests the honor of your presence
to attend and participate in the Inauguration of

John Fitzgerald Kennedy

as President of the United States of America

and

Lyndon Baines Johnson

as Vice President of the United States of America
on Friday the twentieth of January
one thousand nine hundred and sixty-one
in the City of Washington

Edward H. Foley
Chairman

John Kennedy's campaign for the presidency culminated in his election in November 1960 as the thirty-fifth president of the United States and his inauguration on January 20, 1961. *John F. Kennedy Presidential Library and Museum, Boston*

President Kennedy's handwritten notes for his historic inaugural address, which included the iconic line, "Ask not what your country can do for you—ask what you can do for your country." *John F. Kennedy Presidential Library and Museum, Boston*

Camelot Days. Jackie and John Jr. watch Jack's chopper take off from the South Lawn of the White House, and, already, John-John misses his daddy. October 11, 1962. *John F. Kennedy Presidential Library and Museum, Boston*

THE WHITE HOUSE
WASHINGTON

November 3, 1962

Dear Mother:

    I signed today the pictures from Krushchev.

    Would you be sure to let me know in the future any contacts you have with heads of state, etc. concerning requests for pictures, signatures, etc. Requests of this nature are subject to interpretations and therefore I would like to have you clear them before they are sent.

    Needless to say the picture is most interesting and will be highly regarded.

Love,

Jack

Mrs. Joseph P. Kennedy
Hyannis Port
Massachusetts

Refers to a photo of him & Jackie with Kruschev & Mrs K. which I requested him to autograph RK

In 1962, Jack's mother, Rose Kennedy, wrote to Soviet premier Khrushchev requesting an autographed photo. When Jack found out, he sent her a note asking that she consult with him before corresponding with heads of state. Interestingly, this occurred shortly after the Cuban Missile Crisis. In her witty reply, Rose wrote: "I understand very well your letter, although I had not thought of it before. When I ask for Castro's autograph, I will let you know in advance!" *John F. Kennedy Presidential Library and Museum, Boston*

Janet and Hugh Auchincloss, Jackie's mother and stepfather, were almost as close to Jack as his own parents. Circa 1960, the White House Years. *John F. Kennedy Presidential Library and Museum, Boston*

Senator Jack Kennedy with Janet and Hugh's son, Jamie, age seven, in 1954. One of the last survivors of the Camelot generation, Jamie says of JFK, "I knew him from the time I was six until his death. I saw him with Jackie. I know that what they had was real, and I know they had it on their own terms." *Jamie Auchincloss Collection*

LEFT: Janet DesRosiers, Joe Kennedy's secretary and longtime companion, in 1955 at Hyannis Port. "You have to start living the life of the woman you want to be," Jackie's mother, Janet Auchincloss, told her. *Janet DesRosiers Collection*

TOP RIGHT: Unable to resist Gunilla von Post, Jack saw her just before he married Jackie—and afterward, too. *National Archives*

Joan Lundberg with her son Zachary, circa 1963. "You love Caroline, and I know that," Joan told Jack, speaking of his daughter. "But I'm somebody's daughter, too. Remember that the next time you treat a woman the way you've treated me." *Zachary Hitchcock Collection*

Marilyn Monroe with Jack's brother-in-law Stephen Smith (Jean's husband) after her "Happy Birthday" performance for JFK at Madison Square Garden. May 19, 1962. *John F. Kennedy Presidential Library and Museum, Boston*

One of the earliest photographs of John Fitzgerald Kennedy as an infant, taken in 1917, the year of his birth. *John F. Kennedy Presidential Library and Museum, Boston*

Jack at about age five, playing make-believe as a cop. *John F. Kennedy Presidential Library and Museum, Boston*

U.S. Navy ID card for Lt. John F. Kennedy, USNR. 1942. *John F. Kennedy Presidential Library and Museum, Boston*

John Fitzgerald Kennedy

35th President of the United States
Born May 29, 1917
Inaugurated January 20, 1961
Died November 22, 1963

He was already on his way to becoming a better man and president. Who knows what JFK might have been like as an elderly statesman? *John F. Kennedy Presidential Library and Museum, Boston*

BOOK II

The Presidency

PART I

Mr. President

ELECTION VICTORY

It was morning in Cape Cod and Jack Kennedy, now forty-three, awakened early. His morning grogginess quickly gave way to the realization that this was it. This was the day he and his loved ones had been dreaming about for the last twenty years. Being elected president had been the goal for him and his father ever since he was a young man. With the passing of the years, they eventually invited his brother Bobby to dream along with them, then Teddy, and then, of course, his mother and sisters. What better way for the family to honor their fallen son and brother, Joe Jr., than to win the presidency he had hoped one day to win.

Jack was battle-tested and ready for the Oval Office thanks to his many trips overseas on fact-finding missions, his time in the war, and then his years in Congress and in the Senate, where he learned how to govern. Even marrying Jackie had been part of the master plan. Everything might've been for naught had his relationship with Joan Lundberg come to light. It never did. From all available evidence, Jackie never found out about the abortion, either. He had somehow emerged unscathed. If he thought too long and too hard about any of it, he told one of his friends, "it paralyzes me, so I push it out of my head and take it as a lesson learned." He missed Joan, though. She had been good to him at a time when he really needed someone in his life like her, and he'd never forget her. He also knew better than to ever try to contact her.

The early returns came in fast and strong in Jack's favor. It looked pretty good. The surge didn't last long, however. Pennsylvania was good, but Ohio, not so much. At Bobby's house, as Jack watched the returns come in on television, he began to lose heart.

"But we were supposed to win Ohio," he murmured.

Jackie nodded, her eyes glued to the TV. "That is surprising, Bunny," she said softly.

At one point, Jack slipped off to take a walk and drop in on Larry Newman, a Hyannis Port neighbor since about 1945; he had the same name as one of Jack's Secret Service agents. The two men sat down in Larry's kitchen as he popped open a couple of Heinekens. He always had a frosted glass waiting for his friend. Surprisingly, Larry had voted for Nixon. Jack wasn't offended, though. It was a different time. Most people didn't hold a man's vote against him back then, figuring everyone had a right to an opinion. "This is America," Jack said. "We all get to choose in a democracy. That's what it's built on." However, he added that if he had a successful first term, Larry had better vote for him in 1964. They laughed and shook on it.

Throughout the night, Midwest states one after another started turning on Jack. When Wisconsin seemed as if it was going to Nixon, Jackie gave him a look of surprise. Nebraska was another disappointment. "We could see that Jack's religion was the thing people couldn't get past," Jackie said years later. "I remember thinking, *No, this can't happen, this can't be it. It can't be because of* that!" At one point, she saw Rose nervously fingering her rosary and praying, her trembling lips mouthing the words. She remembered thinking, *Pray harder, Rose. Pray harder.*

As the night wore on, things began to change again and now Jack was ahead, though not by much. By 10:30, it looked pretty good and Jackie decided to go to bed. "It was so sweet," she recalled. "Jack came up and sort of kissed me goodnight—and then all the Kennedy girls came up, and one by one we just sort of hugged each other, and they were all going to wait up all night."

At about three in the morning Richard Nixon told a crowd of supporters that if things continued as they were, Jack would likely become president, "and he will have my wholehearted support." Some pundits thought otherwise, however; they still predicted a loss for Kennedy. By about four, the candidate had had enough of the roller-coaster ride and decided to join Jackie in bed. "Wake me if anything happens," he told Pierre Salinger.

Dave Powers was surprised. "How can you sleep now?" he asked.

Jack shrugged. "It's too late to change another vote," he said.

When the Kennedys awakened hours later, Jack was president. Richard Nixon had conceded—sort of:

> *I want to repeat through this wire the congratulations and best wishes I extended to you on television last night. I know that you will have the united support of all Americans as you lead the nation in the cause of peace and freedom during the next four years.*

Jack couldn't help but be a little irritated by the concession. The protocol was to do it on television with a speech, not with a telegram read by a press secretary, in this case Herb Klein. Today some Democrats might argue that Nixon's way was better than no concession at all.

AS REAL AS REAL GETS

It was close. Historically close. In fact: 34,226,731 votes for Kennedy to 34,108,157 for Nixon. It was the tightest election of the twentieth century when measured by popular vote, the closest, in fact, since 1884. Jack had squeaked into high office with just 118,574 votes out of 69 million cast, fewer than one-fifth of 1 percent. Because narrow margins in several critical states had carried him to his win, ten states were decided by fewer than 10,000 votes. In the Electoral College, the win was more handy: 303 to 219.

Of course, back then, just as today, no election that close is ever going to be viewed by some of the losing party as anything but an outright steal. At the time, the *Chicago Tribune* wrote, "This election was characterized by such gross and palpable fraud as to justify the conclusion that Richard Nixon was deprived of a victory." The paper then provided a myriad of reasons to justify its conclusion, including the overnight disappearance of ballots, the use of phony names to vote, as well as votes logged in by dead people. Even back in 1963, and in years prior, conspiracy theories relating to elections ran rampant. There would always be people who believed Jack Kennedy's ascension to high office had been somehow rigged and that Joe Kennedy and his big bank account had paid for it.

In the end, credit for JFK's success at the polls, as slim as it was, went to the man himself. He ran a tight campaign and never strayed from message. It was simple, direct, and one people could embrace. Even if it sometimes lacked specifics, it wasn't lacking in heart. Many people agreed with him that the country had been losing ground to Russia and other external forces, especially in regard to the arms race. Voters decided Jack was the man to set it straight, to confront the Soviets, and to put America back on the right track.

Also in his favor was the way Jack Kennedy wore his idealism on his sleeve. He believed not only in his country but also in its people as he urged all Americans to contribute to its greatness. It's not that he was starry-eyed, either. Arthur Schlesinger said, "I once asked him how he'd define himself and he said, 'An idealist without illusions.' He felt in his heart what many Americans felt in their guts, that they had a real stake in their country. That brand of optimism wasn't an act. It was who he was at his core. Folks sensed it and liked it. They say that in politics it all comes down to this: Do you like the guy, or do you hate the guy? People liked the guy. I think that's why he became the youngest man to ever be elected to the White House. It was new and exciting, something to look forward to." Later, in 1964, Jackie put it this way: "Before Jack, politics was just left to all the corny old people who shouted on the Fourth of July and, you know, all the things that made me so bored with politics."

JFK's win was far from a mandate, and it concerned him and his father. He'd basically just barely squeaked into high office, and the Kennedys would've preferred a complete landslide. In talking later about the slim margin, Joe quipped, "Did you think I was going to pay for a landslide?" He was joking, of course. Or was he?

According to what Hugh Auchincloss later remembered, Joe Kennedy once told him he wished it had been a much bigger win. "The American people didn't rally behind Jack as they should've," he said. "It's like they tossed a coin, someone called heads, Jack came up heads, Nixon came up tails. They didn't give a mandate to either guy. But we won," he said with a chuckle, "so, the hell with 'em, I guess." Hugh agreed and mentioned that Abraham Lincoln also had a tight election, less than 40 percent of the popular vote, but that didn't stop him from enacting his policies. Joe added that at least Jack would get along better with the Democratic Congress, something that he felt would've caused Nixon "an early death." He and Janet were "overwhelmed and very proud," Hugh said. While it was almost impossible to believe that such a thing could happen in their family, he'd told Janet they'd all better get used to it, "because it's as real as real gets." Both he and Janet were very excited and proud.

AN UNLIKELY MEETING

Joseph Kennedy had a great idea in the days after the election, one very much like that of an experienced diplomat. Because the election had been so close and there was such controversy about its legitimacy, Joe thought the political opponents should have a meeting and photo opportunity. It would go a long way toward easing tensions and uniting the country.

Jack had mixed emotions about Dick Nixon. While he'd admired him during their Senate days, after the campaign he told Ben Bradlee he believed him to be "mentally unsound," and "sick, sick, sick." It's the rare politician who comes out of a heated campaign with warm feelings about the opponent who has just dragged him through the mud. Still, Jack was willing to meet with Nixon. He agreed with his father that it might actually do the country some good and unite even those voters who had been against him.

Nixon also agreed to the visit, though he was very depressed about losing and felt the election had been fixed. In a few weeks, at a Christmas party, he'd tell guests, "We won, but they stole it from us." However, as a true statesman and public servant, at least at this time in his life, he was unwilling to inject himself into any kind of controversy over the election, nor did he want to contest it. As he later put it, "The bitterness that would be engendered by such a maneuver on my part would've done incalculable and lasting damage throughout the country."

Because Richard Nixon was staying at the Key Biscayne Hotel in Miami-Dade County while, at this same time, Jack was in Palm Beach, the logistics worked. With Arthur Houghton in his office, Joe called his friend, former president Herbert Hoover in New York, who he knew had Nixon's ear. "It would be good for the country," Joe told him. "Tell Dick to do it, and he will." When he hung up, he said to Arthur, "It'll happen. If Nixon refuses, I'll have Jack call him. The world needs to see this. *Russia* needs to see that *this* is America."

After Hoover talked to Nixon, Joe called him personally. Then Jack decided to call him as well. Soon after, Pierre Salinger issued a press release saying that Jack planned "to congratulate the vice president on his campaign, and restore their cordial relations."

Jack and Dick agreed to meet the Monday after the election. Kennedy would go to *him,* not the other way around, which also speaks volumes for JFK and his not wanting to stand on ceremony as some winners might've done. Nixon was still the sitting VP, which also played in the decision that Jack should go to him. Lem Billings accompanied him to Miami. "This was one of the first times I had gone outside the house with him after he was president-elect," Billings recalled. "This visit to Nixon was a good example to show how difficult it was to adjust to my different role."

Lem and Jack flew to Miami on the Caroline. "I'd ridden to the airport with him in his car and I had been with him all the way down on the plane, so I was just thinking the way I normally did about the way we'd always been when traveling," Lem recalled. "A car was waiting there beside the plane and there were a lot of people at the airport to meet him. I automatically got into the car." Jack slid in next to Lem, realized how comfy his old friend was in his seat, and said, "So, where would you like the mayor of Miami to sit?" Lem flushed with embarrassment, got out of the car, and walked over to another vehicle in the motorcade. "I realized that from then on I was never going to ride with the president in the car that met him," Lem said. "But this was also the first time I rode in a convoy of the president of the United States, so it was terribly exciting."

When Kennedy pulled up in his motorcade in front of the Key Biscayne Hotel, the long string of black vehicles with flags attached and blue-and-red lights flashing, Nixon was waiting for him along with a boisterous crowd of well-wishers. As soon as Jack got out of the car, he and the vice president shook hands heartily. Liz Carpenter recalled, "They were alone together for almost an hour, without Secret Service. Nixon assured Jack he had no intention of contesting the election. Contrary to rumor, Jack hadn't offered Nixon a post in his cabinet, but he did say he wanted to bring in some Republicans so he could get the opposing point of view in any decisions he'd have to make as president."

"Ladies and gentlemen, the vice president and I had a very cordial meeting," Jack told the assembled media when he emerged. "I was delighted to have a chance to see him again," he said. "We came to the Congress the same day fourteen years ago, and both served on the Labor Committee of the House of Representatives. So, I was anxious to come here today and resume our relationship, which had been," he added with a jokey grin, "somewhat interrupted by the campaign."

When he was asked whether he and Richard Nixon talked about how the campaign went, Jack Kennedy quipped, "I asked how he took Ohio, but he didn't tell me. I think he's saving that for 1964."

TRANSITION

Unlike his predecessors Truman and Eisenhower, President John F. Kennedy didn't appoint an official chief of staff. The closest anyone came to that role was Kenny O'Donnell, whose official title was "assistant and appointments secretary." Kennedy didn't want a chief of staff for one reason: he said he wanted his aides to report to him, no one else.

Jack's intention from the start was to emulate Truman and Eisenhower in another way, though, by awarding important appointments to Republicans, a concept he felt was in the interest of national unity. Kenny O'Donnell was a little worried about it, but said Jack told him, "If I string along exclusively with Harvard liberals, they'll fill Washington with wild-eyed ADA [Americans for Democratic Action] people. I can use a few smart Republicans. Anyway, we need a secretary of the Treasury who can call a few of those people on Wall Street by their first names." His GOP choices included McGeorge Bundy for national security adviser, Robert McNamara for secretary of defense, and C. Douglas Dillon as secretary of the Treasury. In truth, Bundy and McNamara were barely Republicans; both had voted for Kennedy. Only Dillon was a true partisan, having served Eisenhower as undersecretary of state. Ted Sorensen, of course, would also be at Jack's side as special counsel to the president. Adlai Stevenson was to be U.N. ambassador and Arthur Schlesinger special assistant.

Even after Jack was president, his old friends remained in his life—Billings, Smathers, Bartlett, Spalding, Bradlee, and the rest. Certainly, "the Needle," Torbert Macdonald, still gave as good as he got. "Once, he and the president had a fight about something," his daughter Laurie recalled. "I'm fourteen. The phone rings and I answer it and the operator says, 'The White

House is on the line. The president calling for the congressman.' I yell out, 'Dad! Uncle Jack's on the phone!' My father moans, 'Oh God!' He comes in, takes the phone, and says, 'How'd you get this number? It's unlisted.' I thought to myself, *Oh, I don't know, Dad, he's the president, so I think he didn't have a problem getting your number.* They were in a big fight about who knows what, and my dad didn't want to hear from him. They were still equals, which had always been true of them. I actually think these two old friends got even closer once Uncle Jack was in the White House."

It was important to Jack that Americans felt the transition to his new administration be seamless. To that end, he asked both J. Edgar Hoover and Allen Dulles, directors of the FBI and CIA, respectively, to continue. He obviously didn't like Hoover at all, especially after the espionage accusation involving Inga Arvad almost twenty years ago. He'd often wondered about the tapes Hoover had of his and Inga's private moments. In a sense, keeping him around would help ensure they'd never see the light of day. In addition, Hoover was a longtime friend of Joe's, which also helped guarantee a level of discretion. Jack and Bobby would always keep an eye on him.

Often Jack would meet with his staff in the White House swimming pool, which always confused some people. Why the pool? One reason was because it was a way of soothing his bad back. There was another explanation, though. "The president had gotten very concerned about people overhearing what he might say," said George Smathers. "He used to say he had one sure method of knowing people were not recording his conversation. 'I take them swimming, take off all their clothes, put them in a pair of trunks, and then I feel reasonably safe about it.'" The irony is that Jack immediately had a recording system installed in the Oval Office that allowed him to tape almost every private conversation he ever had without anyone's knowledge other than Bobby's and Evelyn Lincoln's. Lincoln was responsible for changing out the tapes every morning. She said later, "I think it was for his memoirs, or that's what he said. No one knew. When he was out of office in '63, the first thing Bobby did was come to me and say, 'Get those goddamn tapes out of there,' because he didn't know what was on them. He knew whatever it was, though, probably wasn't good."

As for Jack's father, now that his dream was realized? Joe would try to keep a low profile in his son's new administration rather than risk anyone thinking he was influencing policy. There were stories he and Rose planned to move into the White House, but they were untrue. While Jack respected his father's opinion, he'd often not heeded his advice, especially in recent years. That wouldn't change. "You're *listening* to me, but not *hearing* me," Joe would charge. "*Fix that!*" Jack would never forget how important Joe had been to his political ascension. And he knew Joe would never let him forget either. Gore Vidal once asked Jack why the patriarch had worked so hard to get him into high office. Jack's answer was, "For his ego. Not mine."

By this time, Jack was the proud father of his own son—John Jr., six pounds, three ounces, born on November 25, 1960. Jack was in Palm Beach when Jackie went into premature labor in Washington. "I'm never there when she needs me," he lamented on the plane as he made his immediate return to her. His sense of duty and responsibility to his wife was now strikingly different than it had been just four years ago when she gave stillbirth to Arabella. Also, having a son seemed very important to him, or as Jack told his neighbor Larry Newman, "Dad's a pain in my ass, but if I can do for my son half of what he did for me, that'll be a whole hell of a lot."

FAMILY PRIDE

There has obviously been a lot written about the inauguration of President John Fitzgerald Kennedy. There was a sense that day that something greater was happening in our country, more than just the inauguration of a new president. Jamie Auchincloss, who was at the inauguration, recalled, "You could sense a new era for Washington, for the nation, for the world. It was more than just a changeover of administration and a party victory. It was the official proclamation of a brand-new American dynasty, the Kennedys."

After all that's been said about the inaugural celebrations and balls, including the acclaimed, star-studded event expertly produced by Frank Sinatra, what stands out is President Kennedy's inaugural speech, his call to Americans to become part of something bigger than just themselves, a call to arms, if you will:

> And so, my fellow Americans: ask not what your country can do for you—ask what you can do for your country. My fellow citizens of the world: ask not what America will do for you, but what together we can do for the freedom of man.

It's also easy to forget that this was a day that was important to two families, Jack's and Jackie's. Jamie Auchincloss, again: "Maybe some people thought we took it for granted as a family, or just went along with the flow without realizing how monumental it was, but we were actually acutely aware of the great privilege and responsibility. There's a picture that stands out in my mind of Jack and Jackie in the moments after he was sworn in. She has her hand on his chin and he's looking at her with tears in his eyes. You can see in that one photo how honored he was that the American people had chosen him and entrusted him with their welfare. 'Serving as president will be the honor of my life,' he told me after he was sworn in, and I know he felt that very strongly."

"Mr. President," Janet Auchincloss formally intoned as she approached her son-in-law with her extended hand. He gave her a quizzical look. She told him that they could no longer think of him as a man. They now had to think of him as "the office." He smiled at her as he kissed her hand. Their relationship had always been a complicated one. She'd agonized over his behavior in the past and had disapproved of him for years. But he was president now and she couldn't help herself, she was very proud.

A couple of months earlier, right after he'd won the election, they'd had a conversation during which he said, "You and I have been on quite a journey, Mummy, haven't we? I'm sorry. I hope you know it." While that was good to hear, she wasn't sure she could trust him. "But I think I need to be free of this anger in my heart," she confessed to Hugh. So, she was trying. She told Jack she believed they all had to just move forward with their lives, "because that's what families do," she said. "Families endure. *We* endure."

After the inauguration, Jack and Jackie along with Lyndon and Lady Bird departed for the Old Supreme Court Chamber of the Capitol for a joint congressional luncheon. Meanwhile, the Kennedys and Auchinclosses enjoyed their own meal in a private room at the Mayflower Hotel.

All of Jack's siblings—Bobby, Teddy, Eunice, Jean, and Pat—smiling and jubilant, were at the luncheon flanked by their spouses. His very excited and proud parents, Joe and Rose, were also there. Hugh and Janet joined the circle, along with Hugh's sons Yusha and Tommy and his daughter Nini (from his previous marriages). Jamie and Janet Jr. were present as well. Jackie's sister, Lee, wasn't there, having just endured a difficult birth of a baby daughter in England. She remained in that country with her husband, Stas. There were also a few Bouviers, relatives of Jackie's late father, but they always seemed to recede into the background whenever there were Auchinclosses around.

Janet chatted with Rose about her first official duty as the mother of the First Lady. It had occurred two days earlier on January 18, when Janet substituted for Jackie at the Reception of Distinguished Ladies at the National Gallery. She was in good company with Rose's daughters, Eunice, Jean, and Pat. It'd be the first of many times Janet would take Jackie's place at a function that the First Lady hoped to avoid.

Janet wondered if Rose and Joe would be spending the night in the White House. No, Rose told her, they'd been renting a house in George-town for the week. "But, Rose," Janet exclaimed. "I should think you would want to stay in the Queens' Bedroom! Your son is president now. Tell him to put you up in the Queens' Bedroom!"

Rose had stayed at the White House once or twice during Joe's am-bassadorship, but never in the Queens' Bedroom. Later that night at the inaugural ball, she looked royal in a vintage white lace gown trimmed in silver-and-gold beads that had been created for her in 1938 by the famous British designer Edward Molyneux. It was the same gown she'd worn when she and daughters Kathleen and Rosie were presented to King George VI at Buckingham Palace. That had certainly been one of her proudest mo-ments, and she could still fit into the gown twenty-two years later. It's a good thing Rose passed on staying in the Queens' Bedroom, though. Little did Janet know that Jackie, the new First Lady, planned to spend the night there herself.

The question was raised as to where protocol would have Rose and Joe stand while in the receiving line at formal White House functions. Rose said she'd recently learned their place would be behind the president and First Lady, behind the vice president and his wife, behind the Speaker and his wife but ahead of members of the Senate, the House, and the cabinet.

"And where does the mother and stepfather of the First Lady stand?" Janet asked.

Rose drew a blank; she hadn't thought to ask. "Probably in the kitchen," Hugh answered, a twinkle in his eye.

Later Joe, seventy-one, pulled aside Hugh, sixty-two, to consider the road traveled so far by both families. The two men were very different kinds of patriarchs. Joe, who had never served in the military, was a controversial ambassador who'd made his fortune in the stock market and movie industry while raising a future president. Hugh had served as a sailor in World War I, in the Commerce and State Departments, and in the navy. As an heir to the Standard Oil fortune, he was known for his sensible decisions while raising a future First Lady. They were both getting older and realized that the next generation would soon be taking over.

Hugh reminded Joe that Jackie was only thirteen when she moved into his Merrywood estate in Virginia with her dog, Cappy, right after he mar-ried Janet proudly dressed in his white naval uniform. The year 1942 was a "tough year for our country," he added, referring to the war. Joe smiled, a distant look on his face. It also happened to be the year he had Jack shipped off to South Carolina to get him away from Inga. It was at least in part because of that fateful decision that Jack ended up in the Pacific, his life in peril on PT-109.

"The fact that we've lived long enough to see this incredible moment means everything, doesn't it?" Joe asked Hugh as their two families left the Mayflower Hotel to watch the inaugural parade.

Hugh didn't disagree. "Comes once in a lifetime, this kind of thing," he said, "and even then, only if you're the luckiest people on this earth."

HONOR THY PARENTS

R ose Kennedy couldn't forget what Janet Auchincloss suggested about spending a night in the Queens' Bedroom of the White House. Though she had been reluctant about it, she was still intrigued. The day after the inauguration, she decided she *did* want to enjoy those "royal" accommodations. When she called Jack, he was in the East Room for the swearing-in ceremony for cabinet members. He returned her call immediately and was surprised but also delighted to learn she wanted to take him up on his offer. Rose said she first had to go back to Florida with Joe. However, she would return in a few days. About a week later, Jack had Evelyn Lincoln call housekeeping to get the room ready for his mother.

The Queens' Bedroom on the second floor of the White House was named in honor of its many royal guests over the years, such as the queens of Norway, Great Britain, Greece, and the Netherlands. Elegantly designed in the Federal style, the walls were rose-colored with two north-facing floor-to-ceiling windows, each framed by heavy Scalamandré drapes. There was also a comfortable sitting room. It was the eight-by-six-foot Sheraton four-poster bed with its rosewood headboard and floral pink-and-green canopy that most distinguished the space. Donated around 1902, this bed, which supposedly belonged to Andrew Jackson, was first used in the Lincoln Bedroom across the hall before being moved to the Queens' Bedroom.

Jack couldn't wait to escort Rose to her room when she arrived. He opened the door and, with a sweeping arm, welcomed her to the Queens' Bedroom. She stood in place and gazed about at the surroundings.

"Do you like it?" he asked.

"Well, it's . . . nice," she said with some hesitation. She went to the

window, looked down at the South Lawn, and noted that the view of the
Washington Monument from the Lincoln Bedroom was better. She opened
her small suitcase and took out a sweater. The White House was certainly a
lot colder these days, she said, than it was back in the '40s.

After dinner with Jack and Jackie and others, Rose retired for the night.
Now alone, she realized the Queens' Bedroom definitely wasn't to her taste.
She couldn't even lift the heavy drapes in order to open the windows and
let in some air. When she did manage to crack one, she became immediately
chilled and closed it right away. She also later complained of hearing strange
sounds throughout the night and said she imagined "dead kings and old
queens walking about the hallway." The next morning, she wasn't able to
apply her makeup because the room was so dim. She couldn't even see well
enough to select her jewelry.

Rose was packed and ready to leave before Jack was even awake. When
she ran into Jackie on the way out and told her the room was "not fit for a
queen," Jackie had to laugh. Later, Janet asked her how Rose had enjoyed
the accommodations. "I can assure you," Jackie said, doing her humorous—
and, by this time, family famous—impression of Rose's tremulous voice,
"that room is *not* fit for a queen."

Just as he had tried to honor his mother after taking high office, Jack
wanted to do the same for his father. About two months after the inauguration, Jack called his father and asked him to come to the White House.
He said he wanted to share something special with him. One night after the
dinner hour, Joe appeared with Arthur Houghton. After greeting them, the
president asked Arthur if he'd mind chatting with Janet DesRosiers, who
was working late as usual, so that he might have a private moment with his
father. He then pointed to an imposing, glossy white door and said, "Shall
we go into the Oval Office, Dad?"

Of course, Joe had been in the Oval Office during FDR's administration. However, to now be asked to enter such a sacrosanct space with his
son, the new president, had to have been incredibly moving considering all
he'd done to make it happen for himself, for his son, and for their family.
After they walked into the president's private office, Jack closed the door
behind them and, there, father and son remained for about half an hour.

MATERNAL BREACH

A small breakdown in communication between the mother of the president and the mother of the First Lady occurred during the inaugural luncheon. Though it was minor, it turned into a real fracture in their relationship.

Jackie hadn't been at all well that week, still recovering from giving birth to their son, John. She was very pale and sickly-seeming after taking heavy doses of Dexedrine for her anxiety, which only served to make her edgy and even more tired. "I wish I had been better so I could have been there for Jack," she later said. "But I was just so sick."

Rose had her eye on her daughter-in-law the entire day and night, less out of concern and more in judgment. She'd had nine children, she kept telling people, and had recovered quickly after each birth. That's just how Kennedy women were. She couldn't understand why Jackie wasn't able to pull it together. When one of the cousins on the Bouvier side of the family overheard Rose's criticism, she duly reported it back to Janet. Janet was upset and pulled Rose aside. The two women then had a whispered discussion. Why, Janet wanted to know, was Rose being so critical of her daughter?

Rose Kennedy was no match for Janet Auchincloss. Rose was tiny, skittish, and always seemed overwhelmed, whereas Janet was tougher with nerves of steel. "Have you ever had a cesarean delivery?" Janet asked.

Rose was taken aback. "No, I haven't," she answered.

John's premature delivery had been Jackie's third cesarean in four years, Janet said, counting Arabella and Caroline. If Rose hadn't even had one, she allowed, "then, you don't know what it's like, do you?" It would be best, she concluded, if Rose kept her opinions on the subject to herself.

"Fine, Mrs. Auchincloss," Rose said. "You've made yourself perfectly clear."

The two women angrily walked off to their respective corners.

"Family tensions aren't unusual in heightened moments," Janet's stepson Yusha wrote later. He added that when the stakes were as high as they were on that particular day, it was only natural that "nerves be frayed." Janet was upset about it, though. She let it go for the inaugural ceremonies, but when everything calmed down she felt the need to call Rose and continue their discussion. Jackie asked her not to do it. It could only lead to more trouble, she said, and, "can't we all just be happy for once?" Janet wasn't happy and she wouldn't be until she defended her daughter. She made the call.

We don't know the details of the conversation between the matriarchs, just its general framework. As they spoke, Janet began to feel Rose was not only questioning Jackie's strength and resolve, but also Janet's mothering skills. Rose suggested that Jackie would've been a lot healthier for the inauguration if Janet had taken better care of her. By the time they hung up, they were done with each other.

"Jackie didn't want to get in the middle of it," said one of Janet's family members. "Janet didn't understand it because all she was doing was defending her. That's what the fight was about, she said. 'No, it wasn't,' Jackie told her, 'the fight was about who's the better mother. You or her.' Jackie said she had enough on her mind with the transition. If her mother and Jack's mother were now to be enemies over something she thought was so silly, there was nothing she could do about it."

PART II

Commander in Chief

NEW FRONTIER

A s with all incoming presidents, John F. Kennedy had some immediate goals for his first hundred days in office. His friends Charlie and Martha Bartlett became privy to some of his plans when they spent time with the Kennedys after they moved into the White House. The experience of visiting Jack and Jackie in America's home was a heady one for the Bartletts. After all, they were responsible for introducing them to each other so many years ago.

Over dinner, the Kennedys talked about saving the buildings around Lafayette Square, across from Pennsylvania Avenue. Mr. Bartlett recalled, "This was something Jack had been interested in doing going back to when he was a senator. He'd already contacted an architect [John Carl Warnecke] to get it started, someone he'd met during his time at Stanford. Jackie said Eisenhower was going to tear down these historic buildings and construct a new executive office building and court of claims. If he'd been in office just one more year, she said, that would've happened. 'The old goat got out just in time,' she told us. She also said she was planning to restore the White House, which she said looked like a bad Holiday Inn in the Midwest. I remember chuckling to myself and thinking, *When was the last time you were ever in a bad Holiday Inn in the Midwest?*"

Jack talked a little about the Peace Corps. With his idealism always his North Star, he explained his intention of having American volunteers work in other countries to assist in humanitarian efforts. "Sargent is going to handle it for us," Jackie said. Charlie was struck by her usage of the word "us" and recognized that Jackie thought of herself as an important part of these goings-on, and not just a witness to them. She also mentioned that Jack first offered the position to Lem Billings. However, Lem was afraid that if he joined the administration, it would change his friendship with Jack, hence why Sarge ended up with the appointment. The president intended to sign the Peace Corps into law in March, granting $40 million for its first year's operation.

Another pivotal move the new president made in his first days in office had to do with civil rights. Acclaimed Kennedy historian James DiEugenio noted, "On the day Kennedy was inaugurated, he had speechwriter Richard Goodwin call Doug Dillon in the Treasury and ask why were there no Black faces in the Coast Guard parade. When Dillon didn't know, Goodwin told him to find out. It turned out that the Coast Guard hadn't admitted an African American in years and that there were no African American cadets in line, either. Kennedy was dismayed and at the first cabinet meeting he requested that every secretary bring a graph of how many people of color were in each department and where they were located. When the president received the report, he was shocked both that there were so few and that they were all located near the bottom rungs of government."

On March 6, 1961, Jack signed the first affirmative action order in American history, establishing the President's Committee on Equal Employment Opportunity. It required federal contractors to "take affirmative action to ensure that applicants are employed, and that employees are treated during employment, without regard to their race, creed, color, or national origin." James DiEugenio added, "That order was then extended to any company doing business with any branch of the government. For the first time, textile mills in North Carolina had to hire workers who were African Americans since they were making uniforms for the navy."

Historians have often felt JFK could've done a lot more for Blacks during his time in office. In fact, the president had to walk a tightrope when it came to this issue for fear of offending staunch conservatives while at the same time not wanting to jeopardize liberal votes for his proposed civil rights legislation. "But I still don't think forty-five days is such a long time to start acting on civil rights," concluded DiEugenio.

FAMILY BUSINESS

———

Is it nepotism to bring Bobby in as attorney general?" Jack asked his Auchincloss in-laws one winter afternoon at Merrywood. Because Janet and Hugh had just sold the estate and were preparing to move into a home in Georgetown, boxes of possessions were scattered about the dining room. Jackie, Lee, Janet Jr., as well as Julian Baldridge and his mother, Janet's friend Carolyn, were in the process of packing things up. According to Julian, Hugh didn't feel it appropriate to weigh in.

"This is a big decision, son," he said. "You know what they say about nepotism, don't you?" Jack waited with a smile. "Nepotism is appointing your grandmother to office for the good of the party," Hugh said with a wink. The quote came from the famous writer and Civil War veteran Ambrose Bierce.

"Yes, of course it's nepotism," Janet said. "But so what, Jack?" she asked. "You're the president. You get to do what you want!"

By the time Jack was elected, thirty-five-year-old Bobby Kennedy wanted out of politics, due to its confrontational nature. "I had been chasing bad guys for three years," he said, "and I didn't want to spend the rest of my life doing it." His father had different ideas. He wanted Bobby at his brother's side. "I witnessed a family squabble that took place around the family pool in December 1960," said Janet DesRosiers. "Joe insisted Jack appoint Bobby as his attorney general. His argument was that he owed it to Bobby because of his hard work during the campaign. He also knew Bobby would protect Jack and do anything he could for him. 'I believe in him,' I heard him tell Jack, 'and I'm asking you to believe in him, too.'" But Bobby hadn't even tried a case in court yet, so JFK wasn't sure. He also feared it would cause a very big controversy so early in his administration.

Joe felt he had good reason to be concerned about tough times in the offing. After all, it was the beginning of the 1960s, with civil rights and organized crime at the forefront of domestic concerns, and the ongoing Cold War and nuclear disarmament on the international stage. On the personal front, Joe worried about Jack's propensity for indiscretion in his personal life. He'd never cared what his son did privately until he was a presidential candidate. Then, he cared a lot. He believed Bobby could keep Jack on the straight and narrow. Like his mother, Bobby was a staunch Catholic and Joe hoped his devotion to his faith might somehow influence Jack.

At Merrywood, as the family members talked it over, Janet recalled the way Bobby had stayed with her during one of the worst moments of her life. Though she wasn't specific, everyone knew she was referring to the death of Arabella. The younger brother had stood in for the absent brother not only at Jackie's bedside but also at Janet's side at the cemetery. She said she'd never forget his goodness and strength when she needed it most. The hidden secret about Bobby, she said, was his compassion. People believed he was a brute, but that wasn't true. He was someone they could always count on, and someone Jack could trust with any important job, and if that job was attorney general, she said, so be it.

Jack certainly couldn't disagree about Bobby's dependability. But he worried that many policy decisions relating to civil rights would be even more difficult for conservative Southerners to stomach if made by a couple of white siblings. "But whatever anyone does in that respect will be hard for racists to handle whether made by white brothers or not," Jackie said. She wondered what Rose Kennedy thought of it all.

Jack explained that Rose never weighed in on important matters like this one. He knew her response would be, "What does your father think?" Jackie couldn't help but smile to herself. The fact that Jack trusted her family with such an important decision meant a lot to her.

Jack eventually did decide to entrust Bobby with the role. At the end of the year, he announced that his younger brother would be his new attorney general. While there were the expected protests, they were relatively mild, which would almost certainly not be the case today if a president appointed his brother to such an important position. President Kennedy seemed almost immune to criticism, at least at this stage in his administration. It was a honeymoon phase for him . . . and it would soon be over.

BAY OF PIGS

In 1959, Fidel Castro came into power in Cuba by overthrowing its dictator, Fulgencio Batista, in an armed and bloody revolt. The CIA had had its eye on Castro for at least ten years, concerned about his Communist ties. Castro's later allegiance to Soviet premier Nikita Khrushchev was particularly dangerous because Cuba, located about ninety miles off the coast of Florida, was a strategic concern for the United States. Thus, it would've been easy for Khrushchev to attack the U.S. mainland, and Castro certainly couldn't be trusted to keep that from happening. The U.S. was also concerned about human rights abuses in Cuba before Castro came into power, cruelty he not only allowed to continue but had made worse. In short, he was a tyrant and had to go. Hopefully, he could be replaced by someone more beneficial to Cuba's people as well as friendly to the U.S.—and someone who wouldn't assist Khrushchev in spreading Communism throughout the rest of Latin America. A 1960 CIA memo was clear about the U.S.' intentions. In it, President Eisenhower was quoted as saying of Castro, "I want him sawed off."

All sorts of wild CIA plans were employed to eliminate Castro during the Eisenhower administration, ridiculous plans that included exploding cigars and microphones poisoned with LSD. One woman was even recruited to slip Castro a poison pill while on a date with him. However, the pill dissolved in the jar of cold cream in which she hid it. When Castro became suspicious of her, she confessed to him that she was a hired assassin. He handed her a gun and said, "Fine. Do it!" Instead, they ended up having sex. That's how crazy these times were and how inept the CIA was when it came to offing Fidel Castro. The agency's many failed attempts only served to warn Castro that the U.S. was trying to get rid of him, which just caused him to more closely align with the Soviet Union. "You know how you kill the bastard?" Joe Kennedy asked. "You walk right up to the son of a bitch, you pull out a gun, and you shoot him in the head. Why is this so hard?"

In March 1960, Eisenhower approved a top-secret CIA plan to train Cuban exiles for an invasion of their homeland in hopes of finally overthrowing Castro. The plan was for two nighttime air strikes against Cuban air bases, during which paratroopers would disrupt transportation and push back the Cuban forces. A smaller force would then land on Cuba's south coast, specifically the Bay of Pigs.

By the time JFK was elected, the CIA had already set up training camps in Guatemala, and a small army had been trained for the invasion. If it succeeded, José "Miró" Cardona, a former member of Castro's government, would take over presidency of Cuba in a way that would be friendlier to, and better controlled by, the U.S. Jack learned of the plan in November 1960, during his first post-election briefing. At first, it seemed like a good idea, a way to eliminate Castro early on so that Jack wouldn't have to deal with him throughout his administration. Besides, if he backed out of a plan to liberate Cuba of Castro and the world found out about it, how would that make him look?

Arthur Schlesinger, one of the few people who spoke out early against the raid, later wrote, "The Agency [CIA] had given Kennedy to believe that if the exiles, after landing, managed to establish a beachhead in Cuba, public dissatisfaction with Castro might generate a national uprising that would topple the dictator and put the exiles in power—and that if they failed, they could 'melt into the mountains' of Cuba as guerrillas." The plan was anything but secret, though. As a result of predictably sloppy CIA security, Castro learned of the training camps in Guatemala a month before even the incoming president. By this time, the CIA had also enrolled powerful mobsters like Johnny Roselli and Sam Giancana in their campaign to remove Castro. The Mob eagerly signed up for this duty in order to reclaim the power and influence it had enjoyed in Cuba's casinos back in the fifties before the Castro regime banned them from Cuba. The Underworld's plan was to take care of the Cuban revolutionary by at least spring of 1961. However, true to form, Castro continued to evade death.

On Saturday, April 15, eight bombers left Nicaragua to bomb the Cuban airfields. Jackie remembered that she and Jack were planning to spend the weekend at Glen Ora with her mother and stepfather and Jack's sister Jean and her husband, Stephen Smith. Glen Ora was the estate the Kennedys had recently leased in Virginia for their weekend getaways. Lem Billings was also present.

Jack was preoccupied; he already knew things were not going well in Cuba by the time he and Jackie joined the others at Glen Ora at one o'clock. When Jean asked Jackie what was going on, she explained that there was a crucial mission unfolding in Cuba that seemed to be falling apart. She said she was worried about Jack because she felt that being president was more complicated than they'd imagined. She feared that, in some ways, he felt like a fraud. "But it's not true," she said. "It's the people around him who are the frauds," she concluded, suggesting, for the first time, that she believed the president was being misadvised. When Jean asked if perhaps she or Steve should speak to him, Jackie said no, he couldn't speak to anyone other than his cabinet.

Jean then told Jackie a story. She said that when Jack was young, he and his brother Joe would play catch on the Hyannis Port beach with their father, the three of them casually tossing the ball back and forth. Occasionally, when the sons would least expect it, the father would suddenly hurl the ball at one of them at full speed. It would catch him off guard at first, and hit him hard until, finally, he learned to expect it. "My brother was raised to expect the unexpected," Jean told Jackie. "The country needs a leader right now," she added, "so you tell Jack his sister said to expect the unexpected." Jackie told her she'd pass on the message.

On Sunday afternoon, April 16, Jack took a call from Secretary of State Dean Rusk in his bedroom. "I was in there and he was sitting on the edge of the bed," Jackie recalled, "and it went on and on, and he looked so depressed when it was over." Indeed, the battle in Cuba was raging, and it looked dire. Jack was determined not to send in American troops. His mind was made up. *He was not going to send in troops.* But as things deteriorated, it became clear that without that American military and their air strikes, the invasion would be doomed and many lives would be lost.

The main reason Jack had even allowed the mission to go forward was because he'd counted on the seasoned men he'd inherited from the previous administration, such as Allen Dulles, the first civilian director of the CIA, to know what they were doing. Some of the president's own people—like Secretary of Defense Robert McNamara, Secretary of State Dean Rusk, and National Security Adviser McGeorge Bundy—had also endorsed the plan, or at least didn't speak out against it. JFK, who usually questioned everything before making a decision, apparently hadn't asked enough questions.

The fact that Jack had asked to take the plan home and study it, and Dulles wouldn't let him, probably should've put him on guard about Dulles. Perhaps Dulles—considered by historians as a bit of a "master spy" and someone who had long hated Castro—knew that if he'd allowed the plan to be studied by a former military man like Kennedy, he might've found fault with it. Or . . . maybe Dulles knew he and Jack basically disagreed about Cold War strategy. In 1956, Dulles made his position clear when he referred to it as "brinkmanship." He viewed it as a strategy having to do with "the ability to get to the verge without getting into the war. If you cannot master it, you inevitably get into war. If you try to run away from it, if you are scared to go to the brink, you are lost." Jack definitely would not have agreed with the idea of *purposely* going to the brink of war just to see who would blink first, and Dulles had to have known it.

"I said, 'What is it?'" Jackie continued as she recounted the events of that Sunday afternoon. "Jack sat there on his bed and shook his head and just wandered around that room, really looking in pain almost, and you just knew he knew what had happened was wrong. Usually, he made his decisions easily and would think about them before, or once he'd made them be happy with them. That's the one time I just saw him, you know, terribly, really low. It was an awful weekend. The invasion beginning and then no air strike, half doing it and not doing it all the way, some awful thing that had been landed in his lap that there wasn't time to get out of."

While the invasion unfolded, Bobby Kennedy had a speaking engagement in Williamsburg, Virginia. "I don't think it's going as well as it should," Jackie confessed to him on the phone once she and Jack returned to the White House. The younger Kennedy immediately took a plane back to Washington. "I've got to be with Jack," he told Ethel. "I know he needs me."

Surprisingly, Bobby didn't learn the details of the invasion until his return. Even Jack's friend Chuck Spalding knew about it before Bobby since Jack had confided in him. Chuck knew before Bobby? How was that possible? However, in his capacity as attorney general, maybe it could be argued it wasn't in Bobby's purview to know about the raid. But as Jack's protective brother, he probably should've been informed. "I should've had him involved from the beginning," Jack later told Lem Billings of Bobby.

"Up until that time, Jack had more or less dismissed the reasons his father had given for wanting Bobby in the cabinet as more of a tribal, Irish thing," Lem Billings said. "But now he realized how right the old man had been. When the crunch came, family members were the only ones you could count on. Bobby was the only person Jack could rely on to be absolutely dedicated. Jack would never have admitted it, but from that moment on, the Kennedy presidency became a collaboration between them."

Concerned about his state of mind, Bobby asked Jackie to keep an eye on Jack. "Please stay very close to him," she recalled him as having told her. "Just be around all afternoon. Don't leave anywhere, just sort of comfort him because he's so sad." Jackie also said Bobby then related a childhood story to her. After Jean's softball tale a couple days earlier, it was becoming clear to her that one of the things that most bound the Kennedys in crisis was their shared history.

Bobby said that when he was about four, Rose left him locked in a bedroom while she took his sisters out shopping for clothes. He recalled his panic rising as he kept trying the locked door. He started to cry and he continued doing so for about an hour, sitting in a corner, alone. Finally, he heard someone unlocking the door. His heart began to race. It opened and there stood Jack, who was about twelve. He'd found the key on the doorway ledge. Bobby said he was never so happy to see any one person. "He rescued me, and I never forgot it," he told Jackie. "A stupid, simple thing like that made such an impression on my dumb little four-year-old mind." In that moment, Bobby said, he vowed to always be there for his brother. "He needs us both now," he told Jackie.

"My goodness!" Jackie exclaimed. "When Rose found out what happened, she must have been beside herself with tears." Bobby looked at her and shook his head.

A congressional reception was scheduled that same Tuesday evening, April 18, a white-tie affair for congressmen, cabinet members, and their wives. The White House doorman, Preston Bruce, whose job it was to escort the president and First Lady down to meet their guests, couldn't help but notice that Jack wasn't himself. Jackie also seemed distracted. "Tough day," she told him.

Earlier in the day, someone who worked in Evelyn Lincoln's office had told Jackie a woman had been repeatedly calling for Jack. Given the ongoing crisis, Evelyn wouldn't put her through.

When Jack was first inaugurated, Jackie installed a spy in Mrs. Lincoln's office to keep her abreast of any suspicious calls made to her husband. Jackie's "agent" was a secretary hired by the White House at her suggestion, a woman she knew through her half sister, Janet Jr. This woman spoke in 2024 on the condition of anonymity. Jackie's instructions to her, she said, were simple: "Just keep me posted of anything that perks your ears." At this time, as all hell was breaking loose in Cuba, Jackie was told that a Miss Campbell was repeatedly calling for Jack. Of course, this must have been Judy Campbell, who Jackie had never met. "She thought it was absurd that any woman would try to track down the president of the United States at a time like that one," said Jackie's spy. "She told me, 'It's so dreary, these women vying for Jack's attention. Imagine what their lives might be like if only they had husbands of their own.'"

George Smathers recalled dancing with Jackie in the East Room during the congressional reception. "She was hopping mad about Cuba," he said, "and talking about what she felt Jack needed to do to get in control of his cabinet. These men she said, 'work for him and don't seem to know it.' She told me, 'The president shouldn't have agreed to any of this nonsense unless he knew he'd have air cover.' I was surprised. 'Cuba is what? Fifty miles off our shore?' she asked, angrily, 'how could they bungle this thing so badly?' [It was actually ninety miles.] I had never heard her talk like that before. 'He's the goddamn president,' she said, 'and he needs to remind those guys who's boss.' I asked if she'd told him as much and she said, 'No, senator, he doesn't need to hear this from his wife. He has enough on his mind without my little opinions.'"

Smathers continued: "As we were talking I got a tap on my shoulder. It was Bobby. I thought he wanted to cut in, but he motioned me to a corner. 'The shit has hit the fan in *Cuber*,' he whispered in the thick Boston accent all the Kennedys had. 'What can I do to help?' I asked. 'Pray,' he said. I told him, 'You gotta send in the marines, Bobby! Tell Jack he's got to fight. That's what Ike would do.' At the mention of Ike, Bobby walked away. He obviously didn't think much of the idea, and no one else did, either, even though I know Bobby passed it on. They always thought of me as a war monger, especially in relation to Cuba."

While he was never an official policy adviser, Senator Smathers was someone with whom Jack had often engaged on Latin American issues. He had such a particular knowledge of the region, especially Cuba, which he and Jack talked about long before he was president, he was sometimes referred to as "the senator from Latin America." But after his advice vis-à-vis the

Bay of Pigs, Jack never wanted George to bring up Cuba again. "We were later having dinner and I said something about Cuba and he threw his fork down so hard it actually cracked the plate right down the middle," Smathers recalled, "and he said, 'That's it. You and I should never discuss *Cuber* again. Got it?' I did. We never discussed *Cuber* again."

During that congressional reception, Jack was summoned into the Cabinet Room. Studying a map, he told Admiral Arleigh Burke, chief of the U.S. Navy, "I don't want the United States involved in this," to which Burke replied, "Hell, Mr. President, we *are* involved." Jack then allowed six jets from the USS *Essex* to fly over the invasion area for about an hour, but that was the extent of what he would authorize.

MOVED TO TEARS

President John F. Kennedy sat on the edge of the bed in his private bedroom at the White House, a breakfast tray pushed to the side, toast with marmalade, poached eggs, orange juice, and coffee with skim milk. He dropped his head into his hands. Jackie, standing before him, didn't quite know how to respond. She knew her husband well, and this wasn't like him. "He started to cry, just with me," Jackie later recalled. "He put his head in his hands and sort of wept."

Jack was rarely given to outward displays of emotion. Lem Billings, who'd known him from about the age of fifteen, was emphatic about it. "I never saw him cry in my life," he said. Jackie recalled seeing him brought to tears only once before. "It was the winter he was sick in the hospital," she said, "you know, just out of sheer discouragement, he wouldn't weep but some tears would fill his eyes and roll down his cheek." In the past, she'd certainly wanted him to express sorrow and had even agonized over why he seemed unable to do so. She'd always felt that empathy might be a great asset to him as a politician. But he didn't seem to have any. Now, she began to see that he was changing. It had been a slow but definitely consistent emotional evolution taking place over the last few years. Certainly coming to terms with his sister Rosie's fate had been key to it. By the time Jack got to the White House, he was better equipped to feel and express real emotion.

Jack was capable of dealing with his own suffering, as Jackie had witnessed in the past. But now he had to face the loss of men on his watch, the result of a disastrous failure unfolding just months into his presidency. "It was so sad," Jackie recalled, "this awful thing to happen. And he cared so much . . . all those poor men who you'd sent off with all their hopes high and promises that we'd back them, and there they were, shot down like dogs or going to die in jail."

When he was running for the presidency, the biggest criticism of JFK was that he was too inexperienced to handle the job. However, he himself was confident he'd be able to deal with anything thrown at him. "Sure, it's a big job," he'd told *Time-Life*'s John Steele after he was elected and before he took office. "But I don't know anybody who can do it any better than I can." Of course, that kind of posturing isn't unusual in candidates and in newly elected politicians. The truth is that mistakes will be made. When they happen in the first hundred days of an administration, a time frame historically considered critical, it can be devastating not only to the office of the president but also to the man holding it.

Facing his first test, it looked as if Jack had not only fooled himself into thinking he was fully capable but had let America down, too. Jackie, upset about all of it, felt strongly that Jack didn't have the proper support from anyone around him, his cabinet, the generals, the CIA, and anyone else involved. "What else can a new president do but put his trust in his advisers?" she asked. "Who knows how to be president until he is one?" Still, she wasn't going to allow him to be indecisive, not at this critical juncture. "The President Kennedy I know wouldn't sit here and just be defeated," she told him, according to what she later told her mother. "The President Kennedy I know would figure this goddamn thing out." She was being tough on him and that wasn't her usual tone. She was already growing into her new role, though. When it mattered most, she would find her power and motivate him into action—and this was definitely one of those times.

That evening, when Jackie couldn't find Jack in the residence, she searched the White House for him. It was very late, no one was around, and it was blessedly quiet for a change. She went down to the Oval Office. It's door was cracked open. She peered in and there he was, the president of the United States, her husband and father of her two children, sitting behind his massive desk and staring up at the ceiling, deep in thought. She wanted to join him, but she knew better. She had known him long enough to know that what he needed most in that moment was to be just as alone as he could possibly be.

———

There have been reams of historical reporting about the Bay of Pigs over the last sixty-plus years, picking it apart moment by moment, every decision analyzed, many of the conclusions very critical of the president. However, some facts are consistently overlooked.

As stated earlier, the idea of the invasion hadn't been President Kennedy's. It had been foisted upon him from the previous administration, as often happens. While it unraveled, there seemed no solution available to him other than to send in American troops. But Jack had been clear from the beginning that wasn't an option. If he did, he reasoned, what would stop Russia from retaliating in alliance with Cuba? Most of the important decisions he had to make during his time in office were made with many different scenarios in mind. His leadership always had to take seriously its global responsibilities. With his own war experience always top of mind or, as he put it, "tempered by war," he wasn't willing to start a new one. Therefore, he had to make a hard choice, the hardest of his presidency so far. He chose defeat rather than send in troops. Tragically, Cuban lives were lost in the process, 1,500 men either slaughtered or captured. That made JFK look incompetent and America look foolish. Charles de Gaulle of France called Jack "inept." (de Gaulle had once been Jackie's "hero," but after the Bay of Pigs she felt he was "just so full of spite.") Nikita Khrushchev of Russia said Jack was "a soft, not very decisive young man."

Even JFK's staunchest admirers were surprised. "The realization dawns in Washington that the President isn't always the cold-blooded operator he seemed to be while directing his presidential campaign," wrote Kenneth Crawford for *Newsweek*. "The discovery that he's fallible, after all, comes as quite a jolt to some of his admirers."

ACCOUNTABILITY

The Bay of Pigs marked a defining moment in the political and personal transformation of President John Fitzgerald Kennedy in that it made indelibly clear the full weight, scope, and responsibility of the office. Failing could not be an option, Jack now realized, especially when the whole world was watching.

It wasn't just embarrassment. What enraged Jack even more was Castro's boasting of his victory, his making sure the world knew Cuba had bested the new, young, and inexperienced American president. His bragging that his forces had crushed the U.S. Army helped solidify Castro's support more than anything else ever had in the past. It made him appear even more invincible, and Jack was furious about it. In May 1961, the White House commissioned a report on Cuba from which the conclusion was clear: "There's no living with Castro."

Still, from a political standpoint, Bobby felt Jack had to reconcile the Cuban misadventure with the American public. "You have to own up to it," Bobby told him. "People will forgive you. They always do if you own up to your mistakes." Jackie disagreed. She said she thought all of it was, as she put it, "fishy," and believed Jack should do a thorough investigation before issuing any apology. About two years later, she would tell the architect John Carl Warnecke, "When Jack was in office, the CIA was full of egotistical quacks and head cases who shouldn't have been advising him on his wine list let alone on world events. They could not be trusted."

Where the invasion was concerned, Jackie forcefully expressed her opinion that Jack shouldn't take any responsibility at all, at least according to an undated letter her mother, Janet, wrote to her Newport society friend Eileen Slocum:

> *Please excuse my language, this is certainly not of my liking, but last night Jacqueline told Hughdie and me—"Not one goddamn thing should come out of the President's mouth in terms of admitting anything in relation to it [Cuba]." We all know our Jack and we all know this is not entirely his fault—though, as presidents must and have always done, he insists on taking punishment from all quarters. It isn't fair but as a stewart [sic] of the people, Hughdie says—and I must say I agree—the President has little choice in the matter.*

Jackie's words, as related by her mother, had indeed been strong coming from a First Lady. They were echoed by her father-in-law. "The president does not apologize," Joe roared. "*He's the goddamn president!*" Joe also felt there was more to the story and he didn't want Jack to take responsibility until everything the CIA knew, or didn't know, was revealed. However, Jack knew those conclusions wouldn't be reached until the agency's report was completed, as well as an independent one he'd personally commissioned. Nothing could be finalized for months, probably not until the end of the year. Settling the matter for the American people couldn't wait that long. Jack knew he had to take responsibility and put the whole thing behind him. He agreed with Bobby; he had to fall on his sword. "There's an old saying," the president told the world at a State Department press conference on April 21, "that victory has a hundred fathers and defeat is an orphan. I am the responsible officer of this government." While Jack took full responsibility, he didn't give details about the raid, even after being asked by reporters for a full accounting. He explained that more information might jeopardize national security, but the truth was that he felt the less known about the failed enterprise, the better.

It would appear that the Kennedy brothers were right about coming clean to the country. After that press conference, Americans rallied around JFK and gave him the highest Gallup poll approval ratings of his presidency—83 percent. Liz Carpenter, who was working for LBJ by this time, noted, "I think the reason was because people actually *liked* Jack Kennedy. He was young and inexperienced but the sense was that he was at least trying while under pressure and learning on the job. If it had been

Nixon, older and more experienced, I'm pretty sure the public would've turned on him, thinking the man should've known better." Despite the bump, Jack was still discouraged, so much so that he even contemplated not running for a second term. In his diary, Lem Billings wrote from Glen Ora on April 30:

> *President Kennedy hates to read the news—paper editorials, etc. now—as he finds it depressing. In fact, when he saw a recent copy of* Time *magazine, he threw it into the fire to avoid reading it . . . All during the weekend, he said he certainly wasn't interested in a second term—that this was the most unpleasant job existent. I told him that I heard that the Vice President's every action was based on 1968. [Here, Billings means everything LBJ ever did was with an eye toward running in 1968.] He said he [LBJ] could have it in 1964. When we talked about his presidential library Jack said he didn't think anyone would be interested in building it as this looked like it would be a rather tragic Administration.*

When NBC correspondent Elie Abel mentioned to Jack that he was thinking of writing a book about the first year of the Kennedy administration, Jack retorted, "Who would want to read a book about disasters?"

After the Bay of Pigs, Jack had no choice but to dismiss the CIA's top echelon, an unprecedented move at the time, which meant Allen Dulles had to go, as well as Richard Bissell and Charles Cabell. Dulles was replaced as head of the CIA by John McCone in November 1961.

Years later, in 1984, a scholar named Lucien Vandenbroucke reviewed Allen Dulles's notes about the invasion, which were stored in the Princeton Library. These writings reveal that Dulles knew full well the invasion would never find success unless JFK sent in troops. He admitted that he'd deceived the president into thinking things would work out well, just as they had with a similar CIA plan in Guatemala in 1954. Dulles figured that when the invasion began to fail, JFK would finally understand the "realities of the situation" and be forced into reversing his position. Dulles wrote, "We felt that when the chips were down, when the crisis rose to reality, any action required for success would be authorized rather than permit the enterprise to fail."

Again in a letter to Eileen Slocum, Janet Auchincloss wrote a line so clear-eyed in its simplicity it truly captured her son-in-law's experience of the Bay of Pigs, and she wrote it more than twenty years before Dulles's notes were even found. She wrote:

> *A President's job is to protect and serve America. To the best of his ability. Even when misadvised. I believe our President did precisely that—BECAUSE he was misadvised.*

For the duration of the Kennedy administration, there would always be covert CIA operations designed to assassinate Fidel Castro, such as the ill-fated Operation Mongoose overseen by Bobby at Jack's direction from November 1961 into late 1963. These enterprises included more bizarre plots to kill the Cuban dictator, none of which succeeded. Castro's people began to think of him as having been ordained by God because he seemed invincible. It became so farcical a situation that, at one point, Castro was asked if he had a favorite sport. "Yes," he answered, "avoiding assassinations."

Meanwhile, back in Washington, one thing had become painfully clear to President John F. Kennedy: Nikita Khrushchev and Fidel Castro had been emboldened by America's failure in Cuba. As a result, the threat now posed by these two Communist leaders was greater and deadlier than ever before, and the U.S. was most certainly in their sights.

JACK'S MIRACLE DRUG

You won't believe it," Jackie told her mother and sisters. "Jack's a new man. His back is great. He's happy. He's rested. It's a miracle."

While Jack was meeting with former president Dwight Eisenhower in Maryland at Camp David, Jackie, Lee, and their half sister, sixteen-year-old Janet Jr., were in Newport helping their mother prepare Hammersmith Farm for the summer season. Janet Sr.'s secretary, Adora Rule, stood by with her trusty clipboard, taking instructions from the matriarch about everything from the ordering of culinary foods for the kitchen to the distribution of linens for the bedrooms. Janet wondered about the nature of Jack's treatment. She said she hoped it didn't involve the silly chiropractic nonsense she'd read about in *Time*. No, Jackie said. Jack was actually getting injections from a doctor. She didn't know what kind, she admitted, but she speculated they had to do with vitamins. When she said the name of the doctor, Max Jacobson, Lee had heard of him. Her friend Truman Capote was a patient and told her about the shots, which he said made him feel like Superman. She said her husband, Stas, had been considering the treatment for himself. Jackie then surprised everyone by revealing that the doctor had treated Jack immediately before each of the Nixon debates. He'd then used Jacobson's services many times in the subsequent months.

Sixty-year-old Max Jacobson was recommended to the president by his friend Chuck Spalding. "I'd been having trouble in my marriage," he recalled, "and someone suggested I see this guy. I let him give me a shot and it filled me with such energy, I left in a great mood thinking it had been terrific. Of course, I was high as a kite. Higher, even." Spalding said Jacobson called his treatment an "IV Special," "which was 15 percent vitamins," said

Spalding, "and 85 percent speed." Soon, Dr. Jacobson would be known to his patients as Dr. Feelgood.

Janet Jr. was worried. A strange doctor giving injections to the president of the United States didn't sound like a good idea to her. She knew young people in her school who were hooked on drugs and had seen the damage done to them. Her mother reminded them all that in the 1940s, Jack Bouvier, Jackie and Lee's father, had been given an injection by a shady physician that turned out to be heroin. He ended up in the hospital for two weeks and almost died. Despite these warnings, Jackie didn't care. In fact, she said she was considering the shots for herself.

Recent months had been hard on Jackie. She was already tired, stressed out, and fed up, and then the Bay of Pigs happened. Seeing Jack so overwhelmed had been hard on her, causing her to sink deeper into a depression or, as she put it, "just one jump away from tears." She was also having more bouts of anxiety. Surprisingly, she was being given weekly CIA summaries of briefings at this time, which just made things worse. While it's not common for the wives of presidents to receive such summaries, she had asked for them, saying, "I'm the First Lady, I should be aware." Her motivation was that she didn't trust the CIA, especially after the Bay of Pigs. Jack was impressed by her initiative and told McGeorge Bundy to accommodate her. "But, finally, I couldn't bear to read through those anymore," she later said of the briefings. "They put me in such a state of depression."

When her mother asked why she felt she needed Dr. Jacobson's bizarre treatments, Jackie's eyes dampened. "Because I'm not used to failing," she said. She suddenly got dizzy and seemed almost about to black out—another of her anxiety attacks had come on and very suddenly. She rushed to the bathroom and could then be heard retching. When Janet Jr. went to the door and knocked, Jackie said, "Go away. Leave me alone!"

In the end, Janet believed Jackie was suffering from "baby blues," 1960s' parlance for postpartum depression. Not only had Janet experienced it after giving birth to all of her children, Lee had, more recently, suffered so badly after giving birth to her daughter Tina that she was practically incapacitated. That's why she'd been absent from Jack's inauguration. Of course, this was probably part of it, but Jackie's anxiety certainly didn't make things any easier for her.

When she emerged from the bathroom, Jackie apologized and said she'd been in such a rut lately, she'd even taken to spending her mornings crying in the shower.

Lee sighed. "I've been crying in the shower ever since I was a teenager," she said.

From the harsh way Janet looked at her daughter, she didn't think the remark was very helpful.

DR. FEELGOOD

In May, the president and First Lady were scheduled to make their first foreign trip, the initial stop being Ottawa, where they'd be welcomed by Prime Minister John Diefenbaker. Two weeks later, they'd be off to Paris, where they'd be hosted by President Charles de Gaulle. Next would be Vienna for an important, historic meeting with Premier Nikita Khrushchev. In what had amounted to a sort of second State of the Union address in May, almost as a reset of his presidency after his one hundred days were ruined by the Bay of Pigs, the president said he wanted to meet with the Soviet leader, "to make clear America's enduring concern is for both peace *and* freedom, that we are anxious to live in harmony with the Russian people, that we seek no conquests, no satellites, no riches, that we seek only the day when nation shall not lift upward against nation, neither shall they learn war anymore."

Before they could leave the States, however, Jack had to figure out what to do about Jackie. She was still listless and unwell.

On May 12, according to Dr. Max Jacobson's unpublished memoir, he was summoned by the White House to fly to Palm Beach and meet with the president. "He came right to the point," the doctor wrote of Jack. "He was very much concerned about Jackie's condition following her last delivery. She suffered periodic depression and headaches. He wanted to know whether she could endure Paris and Vienna. I said, 'I will be better able to judge after seeing the patient.' She seemed to be unhappy and complained of a severe migraine. After a brief conversation, I said, 'The least I can do for you is to stop your migraine.'" Jackie decided to try one of his injections. "This broke the ice," wrote the doctor. "Her mood changed completely.

After the president saw this, there was no further discussion over the feasibility of a trip."

Chuck Spalding was in Palm Beach with the president. He recalled that they went to the Palm Beach Country Club to play golf and that by the time they returned Jackie was in a much better mood. Apparently, the injection had done its promised thing; it made her feel happy and carefree—maybe a little too much. Spalding reported that when she called her mother, Jackie sounded so giddy that Janet asked if she'd been drinking. Jackie then explained that she'd been treated by Jacobson. Upset, Janet said she thought she and Jackie had agreed this wasn't the way to deal with her problem. Of course, they'd had no such agreement.

Jackie had several more injections at the White House before leaving for the trip. Jack was then given an injection on Air Force One just before they took off. "Max Jacobson and his wife, Nina, followed the Kennedys to Paris on an Air France jet so as to not draw the attention of the press," said Chuck Spalding. "Jacobson then treated the president and First Lady numerous times during their time away." In fact, from this time onward, Jacobson would be a fixture in the Kennedys' inner circle, often at the White House, where gate logs show more than thirty visits in 1961 and 1962, or at Glen Ora.

Where the doctor's injections of Jackie were concerned, Jack's thinking was maybe understandable, if reckless. He was worried about her. Lem Billings said, "Jack married a girl who had these ups and downs. To have her moody really drove him out of his mind. He couldn't stand it. He spent a great deal of his time, when she was in these moods, cheering her up, and he worked very hard at it." At one point, Jackie told him she felt as if she were trying to dig herself out of a hole. It was alarming and he wanted to help her. He viewed the physician's treatments as a solution to her unhappiness. After all, the shots were given by a licensed doctor and Jack himself had never felt better than after taking them. He wanted the same for Jackie.

Once the Kennedys were in Paris, they were greeted by massive crowds waving French and American flags on the motorcade route, all the while shouting out, "Jacquiii! Jacquiii! Jacquiii!" It was clear that the First Lady, and not the American president or even the French president, was the real attraction. It was the first time in her eight-year marriage that Jackie caused more of a frenzy in public than her husband, and she liked it. It raised her spirits. "I'm the man who accompanied Jacqueline Kennedy to Paris," Jack famously told the press at that time, "and I have enjoyed it."

Back in the States, Jackie's mother knew just by watching the television news coverage that her daughter was high. After Jacobson's treatments, Jackie always ended up appearing glassy-eyed. She'd speak slowly and deliberately in a manner that would actually become her public persona during the Kennedy years. She soon began to rely on the injections almost as much as did Jack, who was getting as many as four a week. When Jackie's social secretary, Tish Baldrige, objected to it in Paris, Jacobson set out to prove it was safe. He injected her and, as she later recalled, "I went flying."

Janet was about to call Rose Kennedy to discuss her son's relying on Jacobson's shots, but Hugh convinced her not to do so. The two hadn't spoken in four months, not since their argument at the inauguration. A couple of weeks after the inauguration, Janet and Hugh planned to be in Palm Beach. Jackie insisted Janet try to heal the breach. Janet begrudgingly wrote to Rose to invite her to lunch. Rose wrote back on January 30, 1961:

> I should love to see you. However, my schedule is very crowded and it would be much better for me to wait until a later date. My love to you, dear Janet, and I hope Joe and I catch a glimpse of you and Hugh next week.

A glimpse? Janet was insulted, despite Rose's expression of affection. At a family gathering a few weeks later, the matriarchs made it a point to stay clear of each other. For Janet to now call Rose just to criticize her son's judgment would only make things worse. Hugh was wise to talk her out of it.

THE WOMAN SHE WANTS TO BE

———

As the president soaked in the tub of the Chambre du Roi (King's Room), the suite he occupied in the French Ministry of Foreign Affairs, the Quai d'Orsay, he called out for Dave Powers and Kenny O'Donnell. He often had meetings with his advisers while easing his back in a hot bathtub; he called them "tub talks." He wanted to discuss with them the address he was to give that morning at SHAPE—the Supreme Headquarters Allied Powers Europe. Much to his surprise, the men arrived with a guest, Janet DesRosiers. "You'll excuse me if I don't get up to shake your hand," Jack told her, smiling.

"I understand perfectly, Mr. President," she said, blushing.

———

After Jack was elected president, he promoted Janet DesRosiers from head attendant on the Caroline aircraft to his co-executive secretary in the White House with Evelyn Lincoln. She started with him in that capacity even before the inauguration. "I was charged with answering the phones, placing his calls, and setting up his appointments," she recalled. "Before moving into the White House, he'd set up quarters in his father's Hyannis Port house. I once found him staring at photos of Secret Service agents and flipping the pictures over to read their names on the back. I asked what he was doing. 'If these men are willing to lay down their lives for me,' he said, 'I should at least be able to address them by their names.'"

Janet's first week at the White House was challenging, especially when she realized the hours were to be 8:30 in the morning until 10:00 at night, or even later. "I was beyond fatigued, so much so that I was becoming almost oblivious to my surroundings," she recalled. "I wanted and needed a life of my own. I felt I'd served the president well during those frantic campaign years and didn't want to become a White House prisoner, for that is what you are when you work there with Secret Service agents standing every few feet and creating a jail-like atmosphere. Bill Lawrence [of the White House press corps] came into the Oval Office one day and offered me a pill. It was an upper, totally unfamiliar to me. I took it out of desperation and, as the time bomb took effect, I floated higher and higher off the floor. The campaign was fun; this wasn't.

"Evelyn Lincoln and I had adjoining desks," she continued. "When an article appeared in the *Washington Post* implying the president was going to dump her for me, it became tense between us. I was sure she resented me. If she only knew I was losing interest in my own job, let alone wanting hers."

The primary reason Janet left Joe Kennedy's employ was because she wanted to marry and have children. The White House, she soon learned, was no place for a thirty-eight-year-old woman who was trying to settle down; it was a place teeming with lecherous men looking for conquests. Also, word got around that she'd been with the fearsome Joseph Kennedy, which definitely tended to frighten off any potential suitors. After about a month, Janet walked into the Oval Office to tell Jack she wanted out. He smiled and said, "To be honest, if I knew how hard this job was going to be, maybe I wouldn't have worked so hard for it."

Jack realized that for Janet it wasn't just the workload, it was the impossibility of meeting someone in what he called "this den of thieves." Jack had always liked her very much, even if he didn't approve of his father's relationship with her. He couldn't deny she'd been very good to him for many years. He wanted to help her move forward with her life. When he asked about her plans, she said she wanted to relocate to Paris for a year to study. Her parents were French, she explained, and she'd always wanted to live there. It gave him an idea. What if she became the secretary to General James M. Gavin, who he'd just appointed as the American ambassador to France? "In five minutes," Janet recalled, "I had the job."

"Thank you for your loyalty to my parents all these years," Jack told Janet on her last day at the White House. Jackie stood at his side. With a smile, he said he realized it couldn't have been easy. He then kissed her on the cheek and told her the time had come for her to have her own life. "You're a good person, Janet," he said.

Jackie then added, "You have to start living the life of the woman you want to be."

My God, Janet thought. Those were the exact words Jackie's mother had said to Janet on the day the Kennedys were wed. She caught her breath in surprise. "Thank you, Mr. President," she told him, "and thank you, Jackie. I'm going to do just that."

Now, while in the bath, Jack explained to his surprise guest, Janet, that he'd thrown his back out while planting a ceremonial tree in Canada. He said that Dr. Janet Travell had shot him up with Novocaine, but it didn't work. He didn't mention that Jacobson had also injected him. While the pain didn't go away, after that injection Jack did say he cared a lot less about it.

"I'm so sorry, Mr. President," Janet said.

"You can call me Jack, you know," he told her.

"No. I just can't, Mr. President," she said. Though she'd known him for twenty years, he was still the president, even if, in this moment, he was naked and soaking in a bathtub. He smiled at her in a boyish way she'd never forget. Indeed, it was the last time she'd ever lay eyes on him.

While living in Paris, Janet discovered a whole new world, one in which she actually fit, one that didn't revolve around the reflected glory of a powerful, wealthy family patriarch with whom she could never have a future. Three years after her awkward conversation with that man's son in a bathtub, Janet DesRosiers married Edgar Benjamin Fontaine, who was on the board of directors of Delta Steamship Lines. Married for twenty-one lovely years, they'd raise two sons, "Benji," from Ben's first marriage, and their own, Andrew.

As of this writing, Janet DesRosiers is happy, healthy, and 101 years old.

KHRUSHCHEV'S THREAT

W hile in Paris, President Kennedy got along well with General de
Gaulle, who advised him to keep his wits about him during his upcoming meeting with Khrushchev, especially where West Berlin was concerned. The Soviet leader had proposed a separate treaty between the Soviet
Union and East Germany that would strand Berlin within the Russian-
allied German Republic. Since millions would likely seek to escape Communist dictatorship by fleeing west through Berlin, Khrushchev wanted to
close off that route. This was unacceptable, said de Gaulle, and he felt there
should be no negotiating over the fate of Berlin. He strongly suggested Jack
hold firm. Jack took his advice to heart, though later Jackie would report he
viewed de Gaulle as "an egomaniac."

Once Jack got to Vienna, the meetings with Khrushchev were tough-
going. None of what was discussed was new terrain for the Soviet leader.
He had talked to Eisenhower about America pulling out of West Berlin for
some time, and Eisenhower was determined not to give in to his demands.
Some progress had been made during talks at Camp David in 1959, but then
things went downhill a year later when the Soviets shot down an American
U-2 spy plane over Soviet territory. That event ruined any chance for more
talks; Khrushchev decided to wait for the next president to reopen the discussion. During their meeting, the Soviet leader basically condescended to
Jack while lecturing him on the socialist agenda. Jack quickly grasped that
Khrushchev was a dangerous man whose only real interest was in heighten-
ing Cold War conflicts.

Khrushchev made it clear he was determined to control West Berlin,
ending the shared occupation of that city by the Americans, the British, and

the French. When Jack pushed for continued American and other allies' access, Khrushchev pushed back. When the president tried to address a possible treaty over nuclear testing, Khrushchev wasn't buying that, either. It was now clear that the failure of the Bay of Pigs had caused him to believe that America's young president was a novice and easily cowed. This was exactly what Jack feared would happen.

"It is up to the U.S. to decide whether there will be war or peace," the Soviet leader said.

"If that's true," Jack famously responded, "it's going to be a cold winter."

"I never met a man like this," Jack later said of Khrushchev to Hugh Sidey from *Time*. "I talked about how a nuclear exchange would kill seventy million people in ten minutes, and he just looked at me as if to say, 'So what?'" In off-the-record comments to *New York Times* columnist James Reston, Jack said of the summit, "Worst thing in my life. He savaged me. I've got two problems. First, to figure out why he did it, and in such a hostile way. And second, to figure out what we can do about it."

One has to wonder about Jack's state of mind during this crucial summit, considering that Max Jacobson was treating him on a regular basis. "The meeting may last for hours," Jack had told the doctor. "I can't afford any complications with my back." There were already people in the press who thought he wasn't ready for a match-up with Khrushchev, and many Republicans felt Jack was too green for such an important meeting. Even Hugh Auchincloss, a Republican turned unofficial Democrat for his stepson-in-law, worried about whether Jack was up to the task. "He's as wily as they come," Hugh said of Khrushchev, "and even Ike had his work cut out for him with that bastard." Still, Jack was president. What was he to do? Back away from it? All of which brought him to an important question . . .

Was Berlin worth a nuclear war? Jack really had to consider his options in this regard. The United States had informally agreed with the Soviets to ban nuclear testing back in 1958, but, lately, Americans were becoming more fearful and public opinion had begun turning toward a resumption of nuclear testing. People remembered that it wasn't until America dropped the atomic bomb on Hiroshima and Nagasaki that the Japanese surrendered and World War II ended. Going all the way back to World War II, Jack had always believed America had to fight hard to protect its interests. But after the Bay of Pigs, he clarified, "We're not going to plunge into an irresponsible action just because a fanatical fringe in this country puts the so-called national pride above national reason."

On the way home to the United States on Air Force One, the president remained shaken by his meeting with Khrushchev. He suddenly worried that his critics might have been right. Jackie recalled, "Khrushchev thought he could do what he wanted with Jack. Jack was really quite depressed after that visit. I think the meeting was so much worse than he thought it would be." Jack realized that there'd always be people who felt he, as a young president, didn't know what he was doing. But this face-to-face insult from the Soviet leader was a real blow to his ego. "I only saw him really upset once in my life and that was after he confronted Khrushchev," said Lem Billings, who was also on Air Force One with Jack. "I was particularly surprised and worried to see him so upset. There is no question the president had never come face-to-face with such evil before."

The confrontation made Jack wonder how equipped he'd be to take care of America through whatever might happen with the Soviets. He took out a pad and scribbled on a sheet of paper a quote from Abraham Lincoln that he sometimes used in campaign speeches:

I know there is a God and I see a storm coming; If He has a place for me, I believe I am ready.

THE BERLIN WALL

On July 25, 1961, President Kennedy gave a memorable and historically important address to the nation:

We cannot and will not permit the Communists to drive us out of Berlin, either gradually or by force. We will at all times be ready to talk if talk will help. But we must also be ready to resist with force if force is used upon us.

In terms of "force," what the president then declared sent chills down the spines of millions of Americans:

Tomorrow, I am requesting of the Congress new funds for the following immediate objectives: to identify and mark space in existing structures—public and private—that could be used for fallout shelters in case of attack; to stock those shelters with food, water, first-aid kits, and other minimum essentials for survival . . . and to take other measures that will be effective at an early date to save millions of lives if needed.

That was certainly frightening rhetoric, even though a lot of people thought it was as much for Khrushchev's consumption as it was for the American population.

Within weeks of that speech, the East Germans found a troubling solution to stop the tide of refugees fleeing to West Berlin. At first, it was a barbed-wire fence separating West Berlin and East Berlin. As a result, in the early morning hours of August 13, 1961, thousands of people suddenly found themselves stuck on either side of this barrier, unable to cross to go to work, return to their friends or, worse, their families as East German guards with machine guns threatened their lives. This barricade, which was soon expanded to include cement walls and guard towers, would became known, of course, as the Berlin Wall, one of the most iconic images of totalitarianism and the Cold War.

It would be eighteen hours before the president knew anything about the barrier, that's how poor communications were in 1961. But was he surprised? No. In fact, from the time of his meeting with Khrushchev at the Vienna Summit two months earlier, Jack, along with Bobby, had been sending clear messages to the Soviet leader that they could actually live with a border closure. Some historians even believe the brothers used back channels to encourage a barricade to stop the flow of refugees in hopes of discouraging Khrushchev from further confrontation. That theory is buttressed by a conversation JFK had with his economic adviser, Walt Rostow, a week before the closure. "Khrushchev is losing East Germany," Jack said. "He cannot let that happen. If East Germany goes, so will Poland and all of Eastern Europe. He will have to do something to stop the flow of refugees. Perhaps a wall. And we won't be able to prevent it." As if picking and choosing his battles with Khrushchev, Kennedy had other priorities, such as the ongoing negotiations relating to the nuclear test ban. He felt nuclear disarmament was a more urgent concern than the freedom of East Berliners, which wasn't in his power to defend anyway. Once the wall was a fait accompli, JFK decided not to publicly denounce it so as not to risk further escalation with Khrushchev. "It's not a very nice solution," he told Kenny O'Donnell, "but a wall is a hell of a lot better than a war."

The president's conversations with Rostow and O'Donnell were private. If Americans had known Kennedy didn't completely object to the wall, it would've appeared as if he was appeasing Khrushchev which, no doubt, would've been politically damaging, especially after the Bay of Pigs. In the days after the wall was built, Jack sent Lyndon Johnson to West Berlin to assure its citizens that the the United States would defend their rights. Though LBJ would be the highest-ranking American official to visit Berlin since the end of World War II, he really didn't want to go. "There's gonna be a lot of shootin' going on, and I'll be in the middle of it," he said. "Why me?" It was later learned that he even feared the Russians might shoot down his plane. Most people in the Kennedy camp had a dim view of LBJ by this time, even Jackie who, in 1964, recalled of him, "He wanted the panoply that goes with power, but none of the responsibility."

Once in Berlin, however, LBJ did make a strong impression before almost half a million cheering Berliners. He gave an impassioned speech drafted by Walt Rostow but which JFK had practically written line by line to, as Bobby Kennedy said, keep LBJ from "talking nonsense." Said LBJ:

> *To the survival and to the creative future of this city we Americans have pledged, in effect, what our ancestors pledged in forming the United States—"our lives, our fortunes, and our sacred honor." The President wants you to know and I want you to know that the pledge he has given to the freedom of West Berlin and to the rights of Western access to Berlin is firm. . . . This island does not stand alone!*

While LBJ spoke for JFK in this instance, the president rarely spoke for himself in regard to the Berlin Wall. The noted historian Michael Beschloss observed, "Between August 1961 and the day of his death—except for his visit to West Germany in June 1963—Kennedy mentioned the Wall in only three speeches. Each reference was merely in passing and consisted of no more than a sentence. Americans were less questioning about foreign policy in 1961 than they are today. Back then, most people believed the president was in charge and knew what he was doing, not like today where we are more demanding of information."

As it would happen, JFK's effort to contain Khrushchev by tolerating the Berlin Wall wouldn't work. In fact, and maybe it should've come as no surprise, Kennedy's behavior only served to further embolden the Soviet leader to try to get away with more. For instance, in August, he unilaterally decided to resume nuclear testing. This was a surprise; Jack had thought Khrushchev was at least unofficially in alignment with him but, clearly, that wasn't the case. "Fucked again," he famously exclaimed.

In October 1961, about a year after the Soviets stepped up their testing, they set off the biggest bomb in history, Tsar Bomba, thousands of times more powerful when it was tested than the Hiroshima bomb. While Jack refused to participate in any public tit-for-tat where nuclear testing was concerned, he had instructed Defense Secretary Robert McNamara to begin testing underground. Few knew, as was the case with the Berlin Wall, what JFK was doing behind the scenes, which is customary with all presidents. There really can never be total transparency. It wouldn't be safe or prudent if everyone knew the details surrounding each and every decision made by its leader to protect America's interests.

PART III

All That Glitters

ADVISE AND CONSENT

THURSDAY, SEPTEMBER 21, 1961. WASHINGTON, DC.

Because everyone in President Kennedy's circle knew of his fascination with show business, it wasn't a surprise when he agreed to host an unofficial White House luncheon for the cast of the movie *Advise and Consent*, based on the novel by Allen Drury about American politics, which was filming in Washington. It was as a favor to Peter Lawford, one of the stars of the movie. According to Evelyn Lincoln's datebook, the president and First Lady were scheduled to host twenty-one guests for a three-hour luncheon, including director Otto Preminger, Mr. and Mrs. Walter Pidgeon, Henry Fonda, Peter Lawford, Ethel Kennedy, and Eunice Shriver. On JFK's official diary, the event is described in capital letters as "OFF THE RECORD."

Jackie thought the luncheon might be an opportunity for her mother and mother-in-law to reconcile their differences. She personally invited both but didn't tell one the other would be present. This strategy had already proved unsuccessful, though. About a month earlier, she invited both families out on the *Marlin* in Hyannis Port, thinking it might be a chance for Janet and Rose to talk. When Rose figured out what was going on, she sat in the bow of the boat with her daughters and purposely didn't speak to Janet. It made for a very uncomfortable day. Now, for the luncheon, when Jackie called and invited Rose, she agreed to come. Jackie then invited Janet. The first question from Janet was, "Will Rose be there?" Jackie didn't want to lie; she admitted that Rose would be present. As a result, Janet said she wouldn't attend.

Another problem presented itself two days later when Tish called Peter Lawford to make final arrangements with him. Because Frank Sinatra happened to be in Peter's room, Tish felt there was no way to avoid inviting him. The problem was that, following the patriarch's lead, the Kennedys had distanced themselves from Frank after the election.

Frank Sinatra was frustrated that the Kennedys refused to acknowledge what he'd done for Jack, particularly given the narrow margin of victory. He hadn't done any probing into the Mob's true involvement, he just knew Jack had won and he believed his entreaty to Sam Giancana had been the reason for it. His later boastings would go a long way toward sparking decades of speculation about the Mob's influence on this election. Unfortunately, Frank—who was, basically, nothing more than a means to an end for the Kennedys—would end up paying a big price in terms of access to the president for ever having gotten involved in Joe Kennedy's power games with the underworld. Whether or not the entertainer had been integral to Jack's victory didn't matter. He became persona non grata just by virtue of the question being posed by so many. Years later, Tina Sinatra would report that her father had only one private visit with the president at the White House after Jack was elected. Because there's no other record of it in the official logs, it would appear that his attendance at the *Advise and Consent* luncheon was, in fact, the one time he was there.

Jack was pleasant enough, but markedly not as excited to be with Sinatra as he'd once been. When Jack mentioned he might be in California in March, Frank eagerly offered to have him stay at his home. Jack said he'd consider it, but his heart wasn't in it.

"There needed to be an extra woman on the guest list for the luncheon, someone to pair with Frank," recalled Ben Bradlee. "The last thing Jackie wanted to think about was who could best entertain Frank Sinatra. It was Jack's idea to invite my divorced sister-in-law, Mary Meyer."

Mary Pinchot Meyer was an acquaintance of Jackie's; both had attended Vassar, though Mary was there five years before Jackie. In 1956, they had been neighbors in McLean, Virginia, when Jack and Jackie lived at Hickory Hill. Mary had been unhappily married to a man named Cord Meyer, who worked for the CIA. When they divorced in 1958, she vowed to never wed again. However, the divorce didn't break her spirit. She was a pretty blonde, fun and interesting, someone to whom men seemed to gravitate. She'd actually found her way to a few White House galas in recent months. When Jackie hosted a dinner to honor Lee and Stas back in March, Jack wanted to be sure Mary was invited. Jackie thought it odd. "She's a friend of Bobby's," he explained, "and besides, you know Mary. She's harmless, just another divorcée." That night, Lee couldn't help but notice Mary leaning in closely while talking to her brother-in-law. She was wearing a low-cut dress displaying ample décolletage. "She's not much of a mystery, that one," Lee told her husband, Stas. When she reported it all back to Jackie, Jackie said she couldn't be insecure about every voluptuous woman who ever looked at her husband, or "I'll end up in the nervous hospital."

At the luncheon, Jack seemed even more fascinated by Mary than he'd been at the previous dinner, cornering her and talking to her. She was in an expansive mood, animated and laughing. At one point, Jackie walked over to them with a plate of food. Casting a frozen smile at Mary, she handed the plate to Jack, gave him a look, and walked away. He got the message and moved away from Mary.

––––––––––

Beginning on September 26, Jack and Jackie spent a restful week at Hammersmith Farm in Newport with Caroline, John, and their nanny, Maud Shaw. Janet's friend Oatsie Charles recalled, "Because Mr. and Mrs. Auchincloss were abroad and Jamie and Janet Jr. were away at boarding school, the Kennedys had the run of the place. I visited them at this time, me and my husband, Thomas.

"The president clearly enjoyed Hammersmith, the boating, fishing, and golfing at a nearby resort or going to Bailey's Beach. Bobby and Ethel drove down for a day with their children. We all went out on the *Honey Fitz,* and Jacqueline got up on her water skis. We cheered as she skied behind the boat. The president was a delight. 'Look at Mummy go!' he told the kiddies. 'Look at Mummy go!' Then, of course, Ethel had to get up on her skis, too. At one point, the brothers began discussing Khrushchev. Jacqueline said, 'No, no, no, you boys, there'll be no talk about that awful man on such a gorgeous day.' It was such a gay time. I thought, *Two men with such responsibilities to have fun and be so relaxed? What a rare thing this must be for them.*"

On October 1, Jackie wrote to her mother from Hammersmith:

You could never guess what this vacation has done for Jack. It was the best he ever had. Here we sit for hours on the terrace just looking at the bay and drinking in the beauty, and all one's strength is renewed. Jack was much tireder [sic] than I ever thought. So, you can't imagine what you have done for the country in allowing Jack to come here for a rest.

As the difficult year of 1961 came to a close, though, the president had a lot more on his mind than "drinking in the beauty of Hammersmith." He wanted to keep open the lines of communication with Khrushchev after their disastrous summit. On December 29, 1961, Khrushchev wrote to the American president:

> *The Soviet people regard the future optimistically. They hope that in the coming New Year, our countries will be able to find ways toward closer cooperation for the good of all humanity.*

To which JFK responded on December 31:

> *It is my earnest hope that the coming year will strengthen the foundations of world peace and will bring an improvement in the relations between our countries, upon which so much depends.*

THEIR WORLD CHANGES

=======

TUESDAY, DECEMBER 19, 1961. WASHINGTON, DC.

The president was at the White House in a National Security Council meeting when the call came in that would permanently change his life and that of his family. His father had been rushed to a hospital. While no one was quite sure what had happened, Jack was told it might be a stroke. It seemed impossible to imagine. He had just seen Joe that same morning when Joe accompanied Jack to the West Palm Beach Airport for the flight out of Florida to DC. Jackie and the children stayed behind, and Jack was scheduled to join them for the weekend. His first reaction was that Joe, now seventy-three, had to be fine. How could he be otherwise? He was one of the strongest, toughest, most resilient men Jack had ever known. Nothing had ever been able to beat him down.

After seeing his son off at the airport at a little after 9 A.M., Joe went to his regular morning golf game at the Palm Beach Country Club. He was with his niece Ann Gargan when he started to feel unwell. She got him home right away. Once there, a physician ordered him to St. Mary's Hospital, where doctors soon confirmed that he'd suffered a massive stroke. It was thought he might not survive. The president cut short his meeting so that he could get back to Palm Beach with Bobby and Jean. Eunice flew down from Washington separately, Ted from Boston, Pat from Los Angeles.

After Air Force One touched down at about eight that night, the president was taken straight to the hospital, where the First Lady awaited. Eventually, the couple, along with Attorney General Bobby, was able to see the patriarch. He wasn't coherent.

"Dad, how are you?" Jack asked.

Joe held up his right hand, which was already showing the effects of the stroke. "*Nooo!*" he shrieked. "*Nooo!*"

It was horrible. They all stared in disbelief as a nurse rushed into the room to give him a sedative. Afterward, Jack appeared dazed as he sat straight in a chair in the waiting room, trying to comprehend what had just happened.

"He'll be fine," Jackie kept saying, trying to reassure him. "He's strong and stubborn. He'll be fine, Bunny."

The next morning, which was Wednesday, December 20, Joe was close to death and a priest even administered last rites. Bobby was then asked by doctors if the family wanted to cease efforts to keep him alive. "No," the son said, "let him fight for his life." Jack and Jackie then arrived at the hospital to visit before going to St. Edward's Church, where they'd spend an hour in prayer, a ritual they'd conduct twice more that same day.

As usual, there was work to be done by the president; an important conference with Britian's prime minister Harold Macmillan in Bermuda was scheduled for Friday. While Jack was there, a woman kept calling the house asking for him. When Jackie heard about it, she asked Rose's secretary if it was a "Miss Campbell." She was told the caller wouldn't leave her name. She just said she'd call again later. When she did, Jackie happened to be in the kitchen and grabbed the phone from the secretary. "Who is this?" she demanded to know. The line went dead. "The next time she calls," Jackie told the secretary, "tell her the First Lady is having the Secret Service track her down. Tell her Mrs. Kennedy promises hell will rain down on her if she ever calls this number again looking for the president." The secretary was surprised and reluctant. "I said, tell her!" Jackie insisted. "*Do as you're told.*" It was already a tense time and Jackie was in no mood to be challenged. Two hours later, the secretary reported back to Jackie that the caller had again tried to reach the president. When she passed on the message, the woman became unglued and said, "Tell the First Lady I'm very sorry!" before hanging up. She never called again.

It was just one small matter in the course of a very difficult day, but Jackie was very annoyed by it. When Rose asked her about it, she was honest. She said some woman had been calling Jack, and she put an end to it. Rose wondered if it was a stalker. "They're all stalkers," Jackie told her. A few hours later, Jackie was driven to the West Palm Beach Airport to meet Jack on his return from Bermuda. Of course, she didn't mention anything about the mystery caller. She was photographed happily greeting Jack on the tarmac after which, hand in hand, husband and wife walked to the president's limousine.

Before meeting Jack, Jackie had called her mother and stepfather in Virginia to tell them about Joe. "Our world has just changed," she told Hugh. Alarmed, the Auchinclosses immediately flew to Florida with plans to spend one night before returning to Merrywood on Christmas Eve to be with their children. Bobby was surprised when Janet and Hugh walked into the St. Mary's Hospital waiting room. "After everything we've been through," Janet told him, "you're family."

Everyone was concerned about Rose, who was now seventy-one. It was true that her emotions toward her husband were complex and had been for almost twenty-five years, ever since he lost his ambassadorship and made critical, life-changing decisions about their daughter without consulting her. Plus, there were his infidelities. There were days when she couldn't even stand to look at him. Still, he'd been her husband for almost fifty years and they had a shared history, not to mention nine children.

Jackie had recently told her mother about one of Jack's childhood memories. When he was about six, Rose was annoyed with him, or maybe jealous, because he always went to his father for advice. She pulled him aside and said, "Someday your father will be dead. What'll you do then, Jack? You'll have to figure things out on your own, won't you? You may as well start now."

Jack became frightened, started to cry, and asked, "What's the point of having a dad if you can't go to him?"

Rose looked at him with disapproval. "Don't you dare cry," she said. "We never cry in this family."

While Jackie thought it was an awful story, it wasn't a surprising one. Now, as she looked at Rose, she could feel only sympathy for her. If she would cry even once, Jackie later recalled thinking, maybe she'd allow herself to *feel* something. Or . . . maybe if she felt something, she would cry even once.

"She's in shock," Janet said of Rose as she watched her gazing at Jack from across the waiting room. By this time, it had been almost a year since the matriarchs' argument. How silly and trivial it all felt now. Janet went over to Rose and placed her hand on her shoulder.

"I'm scared," Rose murmured to her.

"I know you are," Janet told her. "I'm scared, too, Rose. Come. Sit with me."

Janet took Rose by the hand and guided her to a chair. The two women then sat side by side, staring straight ahead while Rose nervously fingered her rosary.

CARING MAKES YOU WEAK

O nce Joe was home from the hospital, Janet DesRosiers flew to Hyannis Port to visit him. Their last communication had been a letter from him, dated September 21, 1961. He wrote that he'd hosted her boss, Ambassador James M. Gavin, and his wife, Jean, to dinner at Hyannis Port:

> *He and his wife were very enthusiastic about you, and the ambassador told the president that you were taking care of the important people. The president said no one could do it better, and Mrs. Gavin chirped in with her boasts also. There was no question in their minds about how well stood you remain with the Kennedy family. As for Jack's presidency, I have everything I have always wanted for him. Alas, it is a hectic world now, dear Janet. Not much fun, I'm afraid. Not much fun, at all.*

It was heartbreaking for Janet to see this very powerful man she'd once loved now so fragile and weak. There he sat looking vacant, on the same porch where he'd once regaled her with exciting stories about his incredible life and times. Propped next to him was a black-and-silver walking cane given to him by his daughter-in-law, inscribed: "To Grandpa, with love, Jackie." Janet recalled, "I can't count the number of times he told me he never wanted to be an invalid. 'When I go, I just want to go,' he used to say. He never wanted to be a prisoner in his own body. So, for Joe to end up this way was a fate worse than death. It was cruel."

As Janet walked up to him, Joe began to point at her, thrusting his finger and shouting out, "Noo! Noo!" She was stunned. In fact, it wasn't directed at her. After the stroke, it was all Joe could ever say to his wife, his children, his caretakers. From his very first minutes in the hospital onward, his protestations of "Noo!" would just get louder and angrier as the day wore on.

"I sat with him and reminded him of one particular moment during Jack's inaugural parade," recalled Janet DesRosiers. "Joe had been in the stands with Rose as the president and First Lady passed by in their bubble-top limousine. Jackie blew him a kiss while Jack stood up and tipped his top hat to him. Joe returned the gesture. It was his proudest moment as a father. When I reminded him of it, his eyes filled with tears. That's how I knew he was still in there, somewhere. I knew it for sure.

"I felt sick as I left him that day," Janet concluded. "This lion of a man dissolving into tears as I walked away was more than I could handle. 'You don't have to worry about him,' Rose told me as we parted company. I said, 'But, Rose, I will always worry about him.' She looked at me with those incredibly sad eyes of hers and she said, 'You know, dear, it's caring that makes you weak.' That took my breath away. I knew her so well, though. She had already fortified herself against what had happened. She'd turned all of it over to God so that it would no longer be her burden to carry. Otherwise, she wouldn't be able to live with it. If strength is handing all your problems over to God then, yes, she's the strongest woman I'd ever known. But if strength is actually dealing with them, then no, she's the weakest."

A month later, Joe's best friend, Arthur Houghton, along with his physician, Dr. Robert D. Wyatt, came to visit Joe. The two men had been best friends for forty-five years, since 1917. Arthur was now in his eighties and unwell. "He could barely walk because of such bad arthritis," said Dr. Wyatt in 1994. "When he saw Joe, he began to cry. Then, of course, Joe also started to cry. Arthur sat next to him, put his hand on Joe's, and they just stared out at the ocean. Joe's sister, Loretta, happened to be visiting. She'd usually dote over Joe and he'd want her with him, nobody but her, definitely not Rose. On this day, though, when she tried to sit with him and Arthur, Joe dismissed her with an angry wave of his hand. He just wanted to be alone with his friend.

"Jack and Jackie were in the parlor, and Loretta and I joined them. The four of us sat and watched Joe and Arthur for about an hour. 'I hope I have a friend like that when I'm old,' Jack said. 'But I'm pretty sure I'm never going to get that old.' When I asked what he meant, he said, "I'm going to die young, Dr. Wyatt. I won't make it to fifty.' I was surprised. 'My God, Jack, don't say that,' I told him. Loretta then whispered to me, 'It's okay, doctor.

He's been saying that ever since he was a boy. First, he wasn't going to make it to twenty, then thirty, then forty, now, fifty. He'll probably outlive us all.'"

Later that night, Jackie saw Jack sitting alone on a rock out on the beach, the glow of his flashlight dancing on the water. As always in these situations, she had to make a decision: Join him? Or leave him be? This time, she decided to go to him. She went into the bureau by the door and got a flashlight. She then walked out of the house and slowly and carefully made her way down to the beach. When she reached Jack perched on his rock, he jumped off and held his hand out to her. She took it. Then, as husband and wife stood in the darkness and watched the waves come and go, he said something he'd said more than a few times of late. "Don't let that be me," he told her, talking about his father. "I want no prayers or anything else to extend my life if it's not worth living."

Jackie promised, as she always did, that if anything ever happened to him she wouldn't pray he lived, not unless she knew for sure he'd have a happy and healthy life. She vowed that she'd let him go.

There was a long silence before he asked if she wanted to know the truth. Of course she did. He then confided in her that he wished God had taken his father's life but, "instead, he took his soul."

Jackie later recalled her mouth dropping open as the thought of karma hit her hard. "Just like Rosie," she whispered to her husband.

He nodded and whispered back to her, "Just like Rosie."

PART IV

His Sexual
Waywardness

SCARS AND ALL

The days slipped into weeks and soon it was the end of January 1962. What a mixed first year President Kennedy had had in office. Still, *Time* selected him as its annual "Man of the Year," giving the year a lot more credit than the man himself had when he talked about it with intimates. The editors said Jack had "made 1961 the most endlessly interesting and exciting presidential year within recent memory. [He] has always had a way with the people. . . . His popularity has remained consistently high. . . . 78% of the American people said that they approved of the way he is doing his job. . . . [He is] the most vigorous President of the 20th century and in his first year as President, John Fitzgerald Kennedy showed qualities that have made him a promising leader. Those same qualities, if developed further, may yet make him a great President." That was a lot of praise to take, and Jack told Jackie he had to read it a few times just so that it might sink in. Thanks to Castro and Khrushchev, it had been a tough year, but maybe not as brutal as he believed it to have been, at least politically. Privately, though, his father's stroke had taken a lot out of him.

For more than a month, ever since the beginning of Joe's medical emergency, Jackie had been at his side, loyally providing comfort and consolation. While he was grateful to her, he was still the man he'd always been. Mary Meyer, the woman he'd flirted with back in September at the *Advise and Consent* luncheon, was still on his mind.

On Monday, January 22, Jackie was scheduled to host a luncheon for the wives of the Securities and Exchange Commission. However, Jack had a different plan in mind for her. He suggested she continue to relax at their Glen Ora home in Virginia with her sister, Lee, and the children. Any time she got a reprieve from dining with Washington wives, Jackie happily accepted it. Jack then called his mother-in-law to ask her to substitute. First thing that morning, Jack left his wife at Glen Ora and flew back to the White House for a full day of meetings. At 6:45 P.M., he left the Oval Office for the private residence. On his way up, he ran into Janet Auchincloss. Apparently, the luncheon had run very late and she was still at the White House. Realizing Jackie was in Virginia, she asked if Jack might be interested in joining her and Hugh for dinner. He declined, saying he had other plans.

Janet then went to visit with Evelyn Lincoln. While the two women were talking, the Secret Service called to say Mary Meyer was standing at the visitors gate. Evelyn directed them to send her through. Ten minutes later, Mary appeared in Evelyn's office looking for the president. Evelyn told her he'd gone up to the residence. Janet said hello, vaguely remembering her as having once been Jackie's neighbor. After Mary departed, Janet's suspicions were aroused. "What is she doing in the residence when my daughter isn't home?" she asked. "I'm going up there right now to find out." Evelyn urged Janet to stay put and, of course, provided no answers. She was well aware of Jack's indiscretions, though; she was actually the one who scheduled most of them, and she knew that he'd been expecting Mary.

According to Mary Meyer's later recollection, this night in January was the one during which she and the president were first intimate. She would remain in Jack's life for about the next year and a half. What's astonishing is that they were able to keep the relationship from her sister, Tony, who was married to Jack's good friend Ben Bradlee. The Bradlees continued to spend a great deal of time with Jack and Jackie, sometimes even with Mary. They later said they didn't have a clue about the affair and felt betrayed when they finally learned about it, years after the fact.

"Jackie knew all about Mary Meyer and the president," said Secret Service agent Anthony Sherman in a 1998 interview. Sherman was assigned to the White House from 1961 to 1963. "Very little got by the First Lady," he said. "If it wasn't her spy in Mrs. Lincoln's office, it was someone else filling her in on what the president was doing. She was not naive to any of it, trust me."

Why did Jackie allow Jack to continue with Mary Meyer at the White House after she had specifically demanded discretion from him years earlier? We now know that one reason, at least as it applied to Mary Meyer, was that Jack had sworn to her that Mary only offered him oral sex, nothing more. Many women of the 1950s and '60s believed that sex of that particular nature wasn't "real sex," and Jackie and Lee agreed with that premise. "Jackie took a dim view of Mary because of the way she knew she serviced Jack," said one of her family members. "She had no respect for her. 'If that's the kind of reputation she wants around here,' she said, meaning the White House, 'that's her problem.' She also felt Mary was jealous of her. 'She wants all of this,' she told me, motioning to her surroundings, 'but she'll never have it. Maybe someone should tell her that easy women don't find husbands.'"

What really bothered Jackie about Mary was that she was divorced. She was intrigued by any woman who managed to extricate herself from a bad marriage. However, she also couldn't help but stand in judgment of a woman who so blatantly flaunted convention and left her husband. "She was all over the map when it came to divorced women," said her family member. "She once told me, 'I can't help it. I always have this feeling a divorced woman is on the prowl. My own mother and sister have been divorced, so I wrestle with it.' She said she'd talked to other married women about it and knew she wasn't alone."

During the White House years, as far as her marriage was concerned, Jackie continued to move forward with what her mother once called "mechanical compliance." It was certainly on display when she was interviewed by Charles Collingwood for her "Tour of the White House" broadcast. "I suppose the most important thing," she said, looking stiff and uncomfortable, "is to really love your husband. Then, any sacrifices or adjustments she has to make are only a joy." However, many years later, she told a family member, "I was doing my best with the cards I'd been dealt. I loved Jack. I know he loved me. I had to ignore the rest of it. My marriage was like a deep black hole and I knew if I looked down, I'd fall in."

In the sixty-plus years since President Kennedy was in office, a legion of women have come forward with stories of their affairs with him, everyone from White House interns and secretaries to female friends, a few of whom would even write books and give television interviews about their memories of what would later be called Camelot. Arthur Schlesinger concluded of Jack, "His sexual waywardness does not constitute JFK's finest hour." But maybe his mother-in-law, Janet, said it better in talking about his deep lack of character in this regard. "So many women," she said, "so little sense."

Those who knew him well believed Kennedy's sexual mischief had to do with his rising power and influence as a politician. If, as they say, power corrupts, that was certainly the case with Kennedy, especially after he was elected. "I shook hands with eleven presidents," said Senator George Smathers, "and the only ones who were totally, one hundred percent faithful to their wives were Nixon and Truman. That's it. The rest of them? No."

Some physicians have speculated that the testosterone-based anabolic steroid Jack was taking to treat his Addison's increased his libido, causing sexual compulsion or hypersexuality. That's the opinion of Dr. Nassir Ghaemi, who was given permission to review JFK's medical records. Others would speculate that maybe Jack was an untreated sex addict, a psychological dysfunction not really recognized until sometime in the 1980s.

There are a lot of theories but, if anything, Jack Kennedy was a man of his time. The culture's enablement of misbehaving men back then gave them license to surrender to their demons. That said, the plethora of stories reported about him and his women does defy belief. Could a man as sick as he was, taking as many medications as he was taking while also carrying the burdensome responsibilities of high office engage in such constant sexual activity? Surely, much of what has been reported has been exaggerated. Agent Joseph Paolella said, "I remember overhearing the president's mother say something that stuck with me. 'That many women?' she said to her daughter Eunice. 'I seriously doubt it. Not that many women and Khrushchev, too.'"

Jamie Auchincloss concluded, "What I knew back then and what I know today is that there was only one woman Jack truly loved, to the extent that he was capable of love, and that woman was Jackie. Whereas others speak of him obliquely and speculate about him, I actually knew him from the time I was six until his death. I was at his wedding. I saw him with Jackie, with their children, countless times. I know that what they had was real, and I know they had it on their own terms."

Kennedy had a telling conversation with George Smathers in early 1962. "Do you worry Jackie will find out about the other women?" George asked him.

Jack became instantly frustrated. "Other women?" he asked. "There are no other women, senator. I've never told any other woman I love her. Not one. There is only Jackie. Besides," he said, "we could all be blown up in an atomic war tomorrow. That's what worries me. Not this bullshit."

Years later, in 1999, George Smathers said, "He was clear with me.

'Jackie knows everything,' he said. 'There's not one goddamn thing she doesn't know. She and I have no secrets. She knows I'm not perfect. She knows I've tried everything to escape myself. She knows I just can't do it,' he concluded, 'and she loves me, anyway. Scars and all.'"

CHANGING TIDES

Back on May 25, 1961, President Kennedy delivered a historical speech to a joint session of Congress, entitled "Special Message to Congress on Urgent National Needs." It mainly concerned the Cold War with the Soviet Union and ways to beat them at it. The speech is most remembered, though, for what Jack had to say about the space race between the two superpowers.

Many Americans had been concerned when the Soviet Union moved ahead of the United States and put the first man into orbit. Jack's new, bold initiative to have America get a man in space and maybe even to the moon rested on the success of astronaut Alan B. Shepard's brief suborbital space-flight on May 5, 1961, on *Freedom 7*. He was the first American in space. It was only fifteen minutes but still a big deal, big enough for Jack to request that Congress expand funding of space activities. He proclaimed:

> *I believe that this nation should commit itself to achieving the goal, before this decade is out, of landing a man on the moon and returning him safely to the earth. No single space project in this period will be more impressive to mankind, or more important for the long-range exploration of space; and none will be so difficult or expensive to accomplish.*

On February 20, 1962, JFK's plan took a leap ahead when astronaut Colonel John H. Glenn Jr. became the first American to orbit the Earth. He circled the planet three times on *Friendship 7* over a period of about five hours before safely landing in the Atlantic Ocean. This was just the boost the nation needed in its race for superiority to the Soviets in conquering space. Everyone could stop worrying about the arms race, if only for this one triumphant moment, and focus on this achievement. "You did it, Jack," Jackie told him. "What a victory for you." He beamed at her, clearly happy to share the moment with her and the family.

At this same time, in the winter of '62, Bobby's ongoing investigation of gangsters like Sam Giancana and his ilk—Johnny Roselli, Mickey Cohen, Jimmy Hoffa, and others—had tied Frank Sinatra to some of their more unsavory underworld activities. In February, Bobby's initial investigation was completed and a report was compiled by the Justice Department. Basically, it implicated Sinatra in all sorts of illegal activities and noted that "no other entertainer was mentioned so frequently with racketeers." It also stipulated that Giancana had spent "a number of nights" at Sinatra's desert home.

While most of this information was part of an FBI report, a great deal of it was based on unnamed Justice Department sources and on extremely sketchy intelligence. Most of these reports are composed of reams of information gathered from anonymous sources with large swatches of information heavily redacted. Today, one can barely make heads or tails out of most of the FBI's memoranda relating to the Kennedys, Sinatra, and the Mob, three sentences on a page with the rest of it all blacked out.

Bobby decided his father had had the right idea in distancing the family from Frank Sinatra after the election, and that they should continue to do so. But during that *Advise and Consent* luncheon back in September, Jack had mentioned to the entertainer that he might be in California in March. Frank had offered his home to the president, and Jack said he'd consider it, so an excited Frank began to spend a small fortune remodeling his house in anticipation of the president's stay.

While Frank supervised his extensive remodel, the Secret Service had a communication with Ben Bradlee telling him that Sinatra's estate would be impossible to secure. The Secret Service asked Bradlee to intervene. A better location, the agency suggested, would probably be Bing Crosby's Palm Desert home in the Silver Spur Ranch area. Ben called Crosby's brother and business partner, Gary, to ask if it was possible for the president to stay there.

Bing was recovering from kidney stone surgery, so Gary called back a half hour later and said his brother would host the president but wouldn't be present. Frank was out, Bing was in.

Soon after that decision was made, Evelyn Lincoln called Ben Bradlee to tell him that Peter Lawford was very distraught. Ben recalled, "She said Peter was climbing the walls because he knew Frank would be furious about the switch. 'Who cares?' I said. 'If the Secret Service wants to change the president's location, that's its call, not mine.' I called Jack and told him about it. He said, 'And why exactly do I need to know this?'"

On March 12, 1962, twelve days before the planned presidential visit to California, Peter called Frank to tell him about the change of plans. He implied it was because of Frank's "connections." Frank didn't take it well. In his mind, he'd done exactly what he'd been asked to do by Joe Kennedy, which was to approach the Mob for help in securing the presidency. Now he was being punished because of those very same ties? "I thought Jack had more class than that," he complained to his valet, George Jacobs. "I thought he was better than that." He was inconsolable.

None of this would've happened, said Mob expert Scott M. Burnstein, had Joe Kennedy not been so compromised by his stroke. "It was all very ham-fisted, not elegant," Burnstein said. "If Joe had been in charge, it would've been better finessed. Rightly or wrongly, Frank thought he had influenced the election. Rightly or wrongly, the Mob thought they'd bought themselves a president. To shatter all of that without an eye toward consequences wasn't something Joe would've done. He would've been more artful about it."

On March 13, the *Desert Sun* reported that at the end of the month the president would be staying at the Crosby estate in Palm Desert. "President to Linger at Bing's" was the headline. That same front page also ran with another headline: "Jacqueline Hands Out Lollipops to Kids in India Hospital." The First Lady happened to be abroad on an unofficial diplomatic mission with her sister, Lee, and good friend Joan Braden. The trip entailed visits to Rome, India, Pakistan, and London.

On March 15, the Secret Service logged a visit to the White House from "Mrs. Meyers [*sic*]"—Mary, of course.

A week later, on March 22, the president's schedule included a luncheon with FBI director J. Edgar Hoover. According to his official log, he met with Hoover in the residence, not in the Oval Office, and Kenny O'Donnell attended the meeting. "We later learned there was conversation about the Mafia, most of it having to do with Judy Campbell and her ongoing association with Sam Giancana and Frank Sinatra," recalled Secret Service agent Larry Newman. "The president didn't like the sound of it, and coming from Hoover, who he pretty much hated, didn't make it easier to take."

Years later, Judy Campbell would add to her story that she was being used by the Kennedy brothers to deliver money to Sam Giancana to help finance the CIA's and Mafia's assassination of Fidel Castro. She said Bobby would sometimes come over to her while she was lunching at the White House, squeeze her shoulder, and ask, "Judy, are you okay carrying these messages for us to Chicago? Do you still feel comfortable doing it?" Again, the idea that the Kennedys would ever enroll Judy for this kind of duty is pretty far-fetched. Even the notion of her having lunch at the White House cannot be proven. Yet, even without these alleged courier services, she did pose a real problem simply because she was a friend of a leading mobster and was also sleeping with the president. The potential for blackmail couldn't be overlooked.

When Bobby told Jack he should end it with Judy, Jack agreed. She'd just been a lark anyway. It wouldn't be that difficult to let her go. Judy, apparently, had more trouble breaking things off. She continued to call until the end of the year and either she and Jack talked during those calls (her version) or they didn't (his), but by December it was definitely over.

MARILYN

Much has been written about President Kennedy's relationship with Marilyn Monroe, most of it imaginary and inaccurate but all of it a major contributor to the myth-making of both people. But now the question has to be raised: Were they ever really intimate? The story has always been that they had sex at Bing Crosby's home in March of 1962, and that this was, likely, the only time. Fresh research, however, does cast some doubt on it.

First, a little backstory:

In the winter of 1962, one of Jack's and Jackie's friends, a socialite named Louise "Fifi" Fell, hosted a black-tie party at her Park Avenue home in New York. The president was invited. It was there that he met the very famous actress Marilyn Monroe, who'd lately found herself drawn into the Kennedys' inner circle. About six months earlier, Jack's sisters Pat and Jean had partied with her after a Frank Sinatra concert in Las Vegas. Pat struck up a close friendship with her. Afterward, her husband, Peter, invited Marilyn to dinner at their Santa Monica home in honor of Bobby and Ethel. Marilyn, very excited about it, exaggerated the night to close friends, claiming it was a "date" with Bobby. It wasn't. It was just a meal with at least a dozen others.

If Marilyn is to be believed, Jack asked for her number while the two were at Fifi Fell's home. He told her he was planning to be in California in March and invited her to join him there. Of course, this was a busy time in his life; there's never any lag time in a president's schedule. In the winter of '62, he was in a dispute with the United Steelworkers of America, a conundrum on his mind as he huddled with advisers the morning of Friday, March 23, before departing Andrews Air Force Base for California.

After a few diplomatic stops in the Palm Springs area (fifteen miles from Palm Desert), Jack arrived at the Crosby residence at about 8:15 P.M., accompanied by Dave Powers and the Secret Service. His schedule notes: "No further activity this date."

Mildred Geary's mother, Evelyn, worked at the local desert boutique called City Flowers. She recalled, "Kathryn Crosby used the floral shop for big occasions and had ordered dozens of birds of paradise as centerpieces for that night. My mother delivered them. She remembered seeing Bob Hope smoking out at the pool.

"As Mother left, Bobby Kennedy breezed by. [RFK had arrived in Los Angeles a day earlier for a speaking engagement at the California Crime Prevention Conference.] When the presidential motorcade suddenly pulled up, Mom had to wait for the hubbub to die down before she could leave. There were California Highway Patrol officers and county sheriffs and deputies and Secret Service agents. It was a wild scene. The president got out of a black Lincoln and, along with his agents, walked into the estate. As he went by my mom, she shouted out, 'President Kennedy, pray for me.' Many people thought that because he was Catholic he had some kind of special communication with God. He stopped and asked, 'What do you want me to pray for?' She answered, 'Pray I live a long life, Mr. President.' He said, 'I'll do that.' They shook hands and he moved on."

On Friday night, there was a poolside dinner at 9:30, no press allowed. Reporters who'd followed the president's plane to California in aircraft of their own were entertained elsewhere at a party hosted by the Desert Press Club. After dinner, some of the houseguests adjourned to the screening room for a showing of the Crosby and Hope film *The Road to Hong Kong,* which was scheduled to be released in a week in the UK. Others lounged at the pool. At about midnight, Jack was shown his sleeping quarters, one of six bedroom suites with its view of Joshua Tree's mountains and the Coachella Valley.

On Saturday morning, Pierre Salinger and General Chester Clifton met JFK at the Crosby estate and motored with him to the Eldorado Country Club residence of his predecessor Ike Eisenhower. The two presidents visited for about an hour in what was described as a "courtesy call," during which they discussed the ongoing steelworkers crisis. Jack then returned to the Crosby estate and spent the day golfing and then baking in the sun.

On Sunday morning, March 25, JFK and Dave Powers departed the Crosby residence for the Sacred Heart Church in Palm Desert to attend Mass. They returned an hour later, with no further official activities scheduled. At about 11 P.M. that night, the presidential party departed the Crosby estate. It rendezvoused with the rest of his contingent at the Palm Springs Airport and then, at 11:30, took off for Washington, DC.

On April 2, 1962, President Kennedy wrote to Bing Crosby:

Dear Bing: You will never know how much I enjoyed my weekend at your ranch. I can truthfully say that my stay there was one of the most pleasant and restful that I have had for a long time. I therefore want to thank you for making this possible. With warmest personal regards to you and Kathy, I am . . . Sincerely, Jack.

The question remains: Did President Kennedy have a rendezvous with Marilyn Monroe at Bing Crosby's, as per many books published over at least the last forty years, as well as documentaries and television shows? It's always been the same three or four sources attesting to a sexual encounter, including the actress herself. In truth, though, Marilyn was never the best narrator of her life, known for her sometimes wild imagination. The story of her and the president has always been anecdotal at best, people hearing it from other people who claimed to know about it.

Marilyn's masseuse Ralph Roberts, who wasn't actually present at Crosby's that weekend, was one of the primary sources. He claimed Marilyn called him from Crosby's and then, to his surprise, put Jack on the line. Jack didn't identify himself, Roberts said, but he recognized his Boston accent. It begs the question, would the president of the United States hop on the phone with a total stranger while having what was supposed to be a secret rendezvous with Marilyn Monroe? That scenario has always seemed suspect. Afterward, Marilyn was said to have told Roberts she "made Jack's back feel better." However, if one traces the anecdote back to the 1960s, it shows up in one of the first respectable books about Marilyn, *Norma Jean* by Fred Lawrence Guiles in '69. He quoted Ralph Roberts in his work as saying Marilyn "made Jack's back feel a lot better" after a sexual encounter at the Carlyle Hotel in New York. Guiles doesn't even mention Bing Crosby's estate. To confuse things even more, that encounter at the Carlyle can't be substantiated, either.

Then, there was Los Angeles County assessor Philip Watson, who, in countless books, was said to have claimed to have seen Marilyn and the president together at a guest cottage on Crosby's estate. However, when interviewed in 2024, his daughter, Paula McBride Moskal, says her father never mentioned it to her or to her other family members. She was fifteen in 1962 but, throughout her father's entire life, she says, it never came up. "I can only say that if my dad ever saw the president of the United States hanging out with someone as famous as Marilyn Monroe," she said, "it would be a story I sure would've heard a lot growing up."

Paula Moskal does say Jack Kennedy was discussed in her household, but only because her father didn't believe a Catholic should've ever been elected president, "and that was something he and my mother, a pro-Kennedy Democrat, argued about all the time." Surely, Watson would've used as a defense for his position the fact that he'd caught the Catholic president cheating on his wife with the likes of Marilyn Monroe. "Never came up, ever," insists Mrs. Moskal.

Similar holes can be found in the stories of other sources, inconsistencies galore. It's not worth deconstructing each and every account. Some notable writers didn't even include the weekend in question in their works, such as Pulitzer Prize–winning author Seymour Hersh, in his 1997 book about Kennedy, *The Dark Side of Camelot*. The highly critical tone of Hersh's book suggests that if he believed it to be true, he most certainly would've included it. He spent five pages on Marilyn and JFK without ever mentioning that particular weekend.

Shedding the most doubt on the rendezvous, though, is Pat Newcomb, also interviewed for this book in 2024. As one of Marilyn's closest intimates, she was present for nearly every major event in the actress's life from 1960 through 1962. For instance, it was her idea that she and Marilyn slip off to Juarez, Mexico, on January 20, 1961, to obtain Marilyn's divorce from playwright Arthur Miller, "because the press and the whole world was focused on the inauguration and we could get in and out without anyone noticing." She'd spend the night before Marilyn's death as a guest in her home and would also be there the morning after her death. "I have to be honest with you and tell you that I don't know anything about Marilyn ever being at Bing Crosby's home for any reason whatsoever, let alone to be with the president," Newcomb said. "I certainly never heard about it at the time. I only heard about it years later from all of the books and movies about Marilyn, but definitely not at the time it supposedly happened. I don't even think I know where Bing Crosby lived."

Pat Newcomb is, today, ninety-five years old. A sensible, rational person, she wasn't the least bit defensive when interviewed. While she was eager to help, she's also not inclined to dwell on the life and times of her long-gone friend and client. "Who sits around remembering what people in their lives did sixty years ago?" she asked. "I'm sorry, but that's not me." The event in question isn't just another moment in a busy life of fleeting moments. When your friend, one of the most celebrated women of all time, spends the weekend with the president of the United States, that seems like something you'd remember. Moreover, as Marilyn's publicist, Ms. Newcomb likely would've somehow been involved in the planning of any such weekend. Granted, she's known for her discretion and loyalty to Marilyn. Much of the Marilyn fan community, in fact, is uncertain of her for that very reason, always believing she's holding something back. Still, one might imagine she'd simply decline to comment on the Crosby weekend if she wanted to hide something.

Since the public has been hearing about President Kennedy and Marilyn Monroe at Bing Crosby's estate for decades, it's understandably difficult to consider the possibility that perhaps it never happened. The point of fresh research, however, is to flesh out history. As new information comes to light, historical accounts sometimes change, offering fresh perspectives and deeper understanding.

What's especially worth noting, at least where President Kennedy is concerned, is that there's no substantiated record of him ever being alone with Marilyn Monroe between March 1962, when he was at Bing Crosby's, and August of that same year, when Marilyn died. If the rendezvous at Crosby's never actually happened, it stands to reason that perhaps these two celebrated people were never alone together, ever!

Of course, it may still be true that Jack Kennedy had sex with Marilyn Monroe—absence of evidence is, as they say, not evidence of absence. We may never know for sure what the truth of the matter is. Based on our present knowledge of the situation, though, it's certainly not a proven fact.

WHEN MARILYN CALLS

W e can't know what was going through Marilyn Monroe's head where JFK was concerned after she, at the very least, met him at Fifi Fell's home and then became acquainted with his brother at Peter Lawford's. We do know she had emotional problems that sometimes caused her to imagine things that weren't true. Even her closest friends and staunchest defenders acknowledge it.

In April 1962, Marilyn attempted to call Jack in Hyannis Port on the Kennedys' private line in their bedroom. Jackie answered. "Is Jack home?" Marilyn asked.

Jackie said he wasn't home—he was actually at Camp David with Dwight Eisenhower—and asked who was calling.

"Marilyn Monroe," came back the answer. "Is this Jackie?" she asked.

When Jackie identified herself, Marilyn asked if she'd tell the president she'd called. When Jackie asked what it was regarding, Marilyn said she just wanted to say hello. Jackie said she'd pass on the message and then hung up, very surprised.

The fifteen-second call caused a real stir on Jackie's side of the family as everyone wondered if it had really been Marilyn or perhaps someone playing a practical joke. When Jackie told Jack about it, he said it had to have been a crank call because he'd never given her their private number. Even Jackie's sister, Lee, didn't have it. Would he call her back? He said he didn't have her number and even if he did, why would he?

Ten years later, Jackie would learn from a therapist treating her who'd also once treated Marilyn, a psychiatrist named Marianne Kris, that it really *had* been Marilyn. Considering the timing of the call, it's likely she was calling to talk to Jack about her recently confirmed booking to sing at his forty-fifth birthday celebration at Madison Square Garden on May 19; his actual birthday was May 29. The booking was confirmed on April 11 by Kenny O'Donnell, who sent the actress a letter:

> *Your appearance will guarantee a tremendous success for the affair and a fitting tribute to President Kennedy.*

Even given the brevity of the call, Jackie was troubled by Marilyn's voice. "It was like talking to a ghost," she said. Lee happened to know the actress socially and told Jackie she was dependent on prescription medications, which may have been what Jackie detected in her voice. What the Bouvier sisters didn't know was that Marilyn had actually suffered an overdose on April 11, the same day as O'Donnell's confirmation of the New York booking.

It was later reported that during the summer of 1962, Marilyn began to pepper the president with calls at the White House, which went unanswered. Supposedly, Jack dispatched Bobby to tell her to stop. That's when Bobby was said to have taken up with her.

Marilyn's supposed swapping of one Kennedy brother for the other is another story that's persisted for decades. It first got national traction in 1973 with Norman Mailer's book *Marilyn: A Biography*. However, in an interview with Mike Wallace, Mailer admitted he didn't believe it but had included it just to sell books. The problem in verifying it is that Marilyn made the claim to a number of trusted friends who, in turn, passed it on to serious journalists. Her prevarication about her relationships with both Kennedy brothers, combined with the willingness of legitimate reporters to take her at her word, would keep the tale alive for decades. The true extent of Bobby's relationship with her seems to involve a number of phone calls she made to the Justice Department, calls verified by Arthur Schlesinger; Bobby's publicist, Edwin Guthman; and his secretary, Angie Novello. Novello was the one who routed them to the attorney general's office through the DOJ's switchboard. In a rare 1984 interview, she said Bobby was a sympathetic person who allowed Marilyn to unburden herself, but that was the extent of it. Eventually, he stopped returning her calls.

There are people who will always believe that Bobby Kennedy and Marilyn Monroe had an affair. However, George Smathers was emphatic:

"Bobby didn't mess around. Period. Him and Marilyn? That's all a bunch of junk."

Ethel Kennedy met Marilyn at the same time as Bobby at Peter Lawford's in the winter of 1962. Six months later, in May, Marilyn called Hickory Hill looking for him. Ethel had less patience with her than Jackie did when the actress had telephoned Hyannis Port a month earlier. Though Bobby was home, Ethel declined to put him on the line. One of her secretaries at the time, who asked for anonymity, reports that Marilyn said, "Mrs. Kennedy, I'm such a big admirer of yours," to which Ethel responded, "Thank you, Miss Monroe, but I don't need fans," and hung up on her. Ethel then asked Bobby why she was calling. He told her it must have something to do with the upcoming Madison Square Garden show, and that he and Jack didn't take it very seriously.

Though the Kennedy brother viewed Marilyn's enrollment in the birthday celebration as not a big deal, Jackie disagreed. She believed Marilyn had problems and said, "I think she's a suicide waiting to happen." One woman who worked for Jackie throughout her time at the White House and for years afterward overheard a conversation between the First Lady and the president in the East Wing. Jackie reportedly told him, "I want you to stop it, Jack. This one's different. This one worries me. This one's trouble." The source said the president denied being anything more than just an acquaintance of Marilyn's. He wouldn't let it go, though, typical of Jack. He wanted to convince her of his clean hands where Marilyn was concerned. However, Jackie didn't want to argue about it. She felt that he and Bobby were intent on exploiting the actress and she wanted them to stop. Marilyn had obviously been trying to reach out to them, she pointed out, and they had continually rebuffed her. Either they wanted her in their lives, or they didn't. "How would you feel if someone treated Caroline the way you are treating Marilyn?" Jackie asked him. "Think about that."

Jackie's words had to have made some impression on Jack. It was much the same point Joan Lundberg had made in their last conversation. "I'm somebody's daughter, too," she had said. "Remember that the next time you treat a woman the way you treated me."

TWISTED

Instead of participating in the Madison Square Garden extravaganza, Jackie decided she wasn't going to go to the celebration at all. Instead, she'd compete on the same day in the Loudoun Hunt Horse Show in Leesburg, Virginia. Her decision sent shockwaves through the family, mainly because her mother didn't agree with it. Janet believed the First Lady's place was at the president's side, especially given the significance of the occasion. "This decision's not noble," she told Jackie, "it's selfish. Remember who you are. You are the First Lady of the United States. She's just an actress." Her mother's opinion didn't matter, however. Jackie's mind was made up. She wasn't going.

Julian Baldridge, son of Hugh's brokerage firm employee Edward Baldridge, recalled an incident at Hammersmith during the time Marilyn was such a sore subject. It was early morning and the staff were doing their chores, preparing the house for the day as Janet gave instructions. Three women in crisp white uniforms rushed busily around the large Deck Room, so called because it'd been built to resemble an upside-down ship, the beams of the ceiling like the ribs of a sea vessel. The women were busy fluffing pillows, dusting, vacuuming, and arranging flowers. While all of this was going on, Marilyn's name came up in reference to her movie *The Misfits*. There was some talk among them about who the actress was sleeping with and what her private life might be. "The First Lady happened to be walking by," recalled Julian Baldridge. "I remember she looked terrific in a smartly tailored white pantsuit with a wide leather black belt. She stopped at the doorway. 'Enough about Marilyn! I mean it! Stop gossiping about her!'"

Everyone was taken aback; this kind of outburst was so out of character for Jackie. While it was certainly clear that she was tired of hearing about Marilyn, she also seemed to be defending her honor. Still, her tone was sharp. Mr. Baldridge remembered, "Mrs. Auchincloss looked at her with surprise. 'We need this room,' she then said. 'Everybody out.' We all rushed onto the patio and quickly closed the French doors. We could then see mother and daughter through the windows having what appeared to me to be a heated conversation. Mrs. Auchincloss grabbed her by the shoulders, Jackie pushed her away. A few minutes later, Jackie walked off, upset. Mrs. Auchincloss then came out onto the patio. 'I apologize for the outburst,' she told me, and then to the servants she said, 'I'm paying you to work, aren't I? Get back to work.'"

Later that day, Jackie saw the same maids having lunch on the patio. She walked up to them. "Submitted for your approval," she said, standing before them. "The contrite First Lady who woke up on the wrong side of the bed." She was mimicking Rod Serling's opening introduction to the then-popular science fiction television program *The Twilight Zone*. The staff was delighted. Jackie then sat with them and chatted.

About twenty minutes later, Julian Baldridge watched from the Deck Room as Jackie gyrated her hips and swung her arms trying to teach the women how to do the Twist, the country's latest dance craze. "Believe it or not," he recalled, "the Twist was thought at the time to be very daring. Some people were even shocked it was being danced in the White House. When Mrs. Auchincloss saw Jackie out there with the maids, she said, 'It's a new world, all right, when the First Lady of the United States is teaching the help how to do the Twist.'"

———

Jack had no problem with Jackie's decision not to attend the Madison Square Garden birthday celebration. It was her choice and he wasn't going to force her to go. He did have some concerns with the alternative plan to compete in a public horse show. He feared she'd appear spoiled and pampered while racing her prize horse in her expensive riding gear. He asked her to change her mind about it, but she refused. Jackie had actually become a lot like her husband in recent years, digging in when facing opposition instead of acquiescing to it. When he got nowhere with her, Jack called Jackie's stepbrother Yusha, who was working in Beirut at the time while serving with the U.S. delegation to the United Nations. Because Yusha had always been so close to Jackie, Jack thought he might influence her to give up the horse show. However, Yusha wasn't able to make any headway with her. Jack was then concerned enough to consult with his national security adviser, McGeorge Bundy, not in an official capacity but as a friend.

Jack was close to Bundy, always jokingly calling him "Mac Bundy." Jack said he feared Jackie's participation in the horse show would make them look "like a couple of swells" (slang for a wealthy person). Bundy responded later with, of all things, a poem:

> *Shall I let her in the Horse Show? / The President was gloomy / "Will our critics strike a worse blow than on Steel or Trib or Phoumi?" . . . So smothering doubts the President shouts, 'I who decide say, Let her ride!' I can't say No—on with the Show.*

"Steel" was a reference to Jack's recent dispute with the steel industry. "Trib" referred to the *Herald Tribune* newspaper, the subscription of which Jack canceled because he was upset by some criticism of him, and "Phoumi" referred to Phoumi Nosavan, the Laotian military leader who'd recently suffered a major loss at the hands of the Pathet Lao. Jack got the point. Though most everyone thought it odd that the First Lady wouldn't be at the president's side for such a high-profile birthday celebration, he decided not to fight Jackie on it.

On the night of May 19, 1962, Jackie enjoyed a cookout with her family at Glen Ora in Virginia. Meanwhile, about three hundred miles away in Manhattan, the JFK birthday gala was in full swing at Madison Square Garden. A highlight, of course, was Marilyn's cooing of a seductive but campy "Happy Birthday" in a skintight, see-through gown. Jack seemed a little embarrassed, but game. It was all in fun and he didn't take it seriously. He later told Jackie not to worry about any of it because, in a month's time, no one would even remember it had happened.

Less than three months later, on August 4, Marilyn Monroe died of a drug overdose. Peter Lawford gave Jack the news, calling him from Los Angeles. Both Jack and Bobby were sad, but not surprised. It somehow seemed inevitable. "There's a big difference, however, between wanting to die," Jackie said later, according to two people close to her, "and running out of reasons to live."

Like millions of young women, Janet Rutherford Auchincloss—Janet Jr., Jackie's half sister—was overcome with grief over Marilyn's sudden death. She was seventeen, about to graduate from Miss Porter's School, which had also been attended by her half sisters, Jackie and Lee, and would soon enroll at Sarah Lawrence. She couldn't stop crying about the fallen star, identifying with her the way many women did at that time. According to Janet's friend Stella Brenton, who later attended Sarah Lawrence with her, she cried to her sister and her mother, "The world destroyed Marilyn."

Jackie didn't agree. "No, Janet," she said. "The world didn't destroy Marilyn. The world built Marilyn up. It was the men in her life who destroyed Marilyn."

THE JFK/MARILYN CONTRACT

In August 1995, more than thirty years after Marilyn Monroe's death, the author Seymour Hersh obtained a stash of three hundred secret documents that he hoped to use in his book *The Dark Side of Camelot*. One was purportedly a 1961 agreement between Jack and Marilyn that had to do with keeping their relationship confidential. In return, $600,000 was supposed to be deposited into a trust fund for Marilyn's mother, Gladys Baker Eley, confined at that time to a mental institution. Hersh said he obtained the contract from a collector named Lawrence Cusack, and it was supposedly witnessed by none other than . . . Janet DesRosiers.

"When Seymour Hersh tracked me down, I told him the signature wasn't mine, and that I had never met Marilyn Monroe," Janet DesRosiers recalled in 2024. "He was so angry, he stormed out. My God, he wanted more than anything for that contract to be authentic. He, apparently, had a lot riding on it. Whoever forged it must've figured, Jack is long gone, Marilyn is long gone, Janet must be long gone, too. But guess what? Janet was alive and well." She was seventy-two at the time.

After millions of dollars were spent developing television specials based on this "contract" and other documents like it, it was finally determined that Lawrence Cusack had forged all of it. The material was then pulled from Hersh's book. Cusack was arrested, convicted of fraud and forgery, and sentenced to nearly ten years in prison.

COLLATERAL DAMAGE

By spring of 1962, as the Kennedys tried to figure out how to handle Marilyn Monroe, Jack's sister Rosie had been confined to St. Coletta's for twenty years. She'd had a good life there, made even better with the emergence of a special woman in her life, Sister Paulus, a St. Francis of Assisi nun who'd taken a real interest in her. Sister Paulus's niece Elizabeth Koehler-Pentacoff wrote an excellent book about her aunt and Rosie called *The Missing Kennedy*. "It was as if my aunt was born for the role," she said. "She and Rosie bonded quickly. Rosie was troublesome at first, my aunt told me, because she had a lot of anger. But she soon calmed down when my aunt began working with her, relating to her, caring for her, and, most importantly I think, treating her like an equal." In 1961, shortly after Joe had his stroke, Sister Paulus became Mother Superior at St. Coletta's.

Once Jack became president, he never returned to St. Coletta's. Arranging a visit was just too complicated and risked too many questions from the press. He kept saying that in his second term he'd figure out a way to visit again. Eunice continued to go to St. Coletta's quite often with her husband, Sargent Shriver.

Back in October 1961, President Kennedy announced a national plan relating to mental retardation. The program featured a commission on how to treat and prevent intellectual disabilities, obviously designed with Rosie in mind. A year later, Eunice wrote a groundbreaking article, "Hope for Retarded Children," for the *Saturday Evening Post*. In it, she described how her mother "took Rosemary to psychologists and to dozens of doctors. All of them said her condition would not get better and that she would be far happier in an institution. It fills me with sadness to think this change might not have been necessary if we had known then what we know today." While this was obviously a reimagining of painful family history, Eunice was at least . . . trying.

In the spring of 1962, Jack decided that his mother had a right to see her daughter, but only if that's what she wanted. But Eunice was reluctant to bring Rosie into the family fold. After all, that wasn't at all what her father ever wanted, and Eunice was still loyal to her father and his wishes. Given that Joe was now so incapacitated, she felt she should protect him and pushed back hard against the idea. Once Jack became president, however, he had the final say in all family matters, especially after Joe's stroke, and everyone accepted it. He was not only leader of the free world, he was now leader of the family. He felt Rose should become more involved in Rosie's care, but in small steps, starting with Rose calling St. Coletta's to speak to the staff. With Eunice on the other line, that call was made.

What Rose learned during her call to St. Coletta's came as a terrible shock. She was told that Joe had been advised by doctors that anytime Rosie mixed with outsiders she became very combative. Therefore, she was to have had no contact whatsoever with the outside world, and that had been the status quo for the last twenty years. It's ironic that when Rose lied and told Jackie her daughter was living a cloistered life, it wasn't far from the truth. "Mrs. Kennedy was shaken by what she learned about her husband's edicts, shocked by his beliefs," said Elizabeth Koehler-Pentacoff. "She wanted changes made immediately. She wanted the nuns to take Rosemary shopping, out to restaurants and to social outings. No longer sequestered, Rosemary began living a broadened life."

Finally, in the spring of 1962, Eunice and Rose flew to Wisconsin to visit Rosie at St. Coletta's. Rose hadn't seen her daughter for over twenty years. The last time she had, Rosie was slow and sometimes emotionally volatile, but she certainly wasn't physically disabled. Therefore, Rose didn't know what to expect. Imagine Rose Kennedy, as tense and anxious as she always was about everything going on around her, making the decision to finally face her long-lost daughter. It had to have taken a tremendous amount of courage.

After getting off the plane, Rose and Eunice walked into the waiting area. They spotted Rosie, accompanied by two nuns. Now in her early forties, she was tall and buxom and certainly looked very different than she had as a younger woman. She had brown, naturally curly hair and freckles. Her face was round, and she wore large square-shaped glasses. Noticeable were her long, elegant, tapered fingers, her nails manicured and painted pink to match her lipstick. "When Rosemary saw her mother, she ran to her," Elizabeth Koehler-Pentacoff reported. "The nuns quickened their pace, their dark robes flapping after them. Mrs. Kennedy opened her arms in greeting as Rosie raised her one good arm. The reunion then took an ominous turn."

Instead of embracing her mother, Rosie began to pummel the tiny and fragile seventy-one-year-old matriarch with her closed fists. She screamed at her, not words but just loud, guttural sounds. Like her father Joe after his stroke. Rose was nearly pushed off her feet and would've been had Eunice not been standing directly behind her. The nuns had to pull Rosie away. Everyone then stood frozen in place, shocked by what had just occurred. "The lobotomy hadn't erased the past twenty years from Rosie's memory," concluded Elizabeth Koehler-Pentacoff. "She knew her mother had not been with her when she needed her most."

About ten years later, when Rose Kennedy recounted this same story to her secretary, Barbara Gibson, she said, "I deserved it. I was collateral damage to what Joe had done so many years ago, that stubborn, stubborn man. I deserved exactly what my poor Rosie dished out to me that day. I deserved every little bit of it. God help me, Barbara, I deserved it."

PART V

The Other Side of Camelot

WELLSPRING

O n Friday, August 24, 1962, Jack Kennedy tracked down his mother-in-law at the Colony Club in New York. She was lunching with Betty Tuckerman, mother of Nancy Tuckerman, Jackie's former roommate at Miss Porter's School, who would, in about six months, replace Tish Baldwin as her social secretary. Jackie was away in Ravello, Italy, with her sister, Lee, on vacation. She had taken Caroline with her but left little John at Hammersmith in Janet's and Maud Shaw's care. Jack told Janet he was lonely and wondered if he might spend a couple days with them.

Despite the many issues she had with him in the past, Janet continued to do whatever she could to have a rapport with her son-in-law, especially after he was elected president. She'd once said the family would "endure" and she'd meant it. "There's good in the worst of us," she reasoned when talking about Jack to her friend Eileen Slocum, "but bad in the best of us." Of course, she'd be happy to host him.

The rapport Jack had with Janet was very different from the one he had with Rose. Sometimes, he and his mother would sit in total silence, trying to think of something to say to each other. "I'm the president," he'd muse, "so one might think there'd be *something* for us to talk about." However, he often enjoyed their quiet times together. At least at the end of a tough day when he was with Rose, he knew he wasn't going to be challenged on some political matter. She always thought he knew best and would never engage him on that level. If he really wanted peace and quiet, he knew where to find it. They could sit in blessed silence, staring at the beach or up at the stars, and all was well in their little world. Rose knew it, too. She realized how much her son treasured those moments with her and wanted to be sure they had them, that she was there for him.

With Janet, it was different. With her, there was always lively talk about family, politics, and current events. Jack enjoyed that kind of exchange, as well, two sides of a maternal coin, as it were. Janet could go on and on about Jackie's childhood, regaling him with all sorts of stories. Once, he saw her sprinkle a bit of perfume on her brush before running it through her hair.

"My gosh! Jackie does the same thing," he exclaimed. "I always wondered why."

Janet smiled. "Now you know," she said.

It was just another of their family traditions. She could also talk about history and the American Civil War for long stretches and, especially, about Robert E. Lee and her familial ties to that Confederate general, all of which Jack suspected weren't really true. Notwithstanding, he loved every second of it.

In a sense, Jack and Janet were contemporaries; Janet was only ten years older. "I never had a dull moment with him," she said. "He always called me Mummy. He thought that was so funny, the word 'Mummy.' Then, you know, the children started calling Jacqueline 'Mummy,' too. He loved that, though I'm not so sure she did. Loneliness is the price of the presidency," Janet concluded. "All his ties to the outside world were severed out of necessity, and that left him with just family."

Jack said he'd arrive on August 25 and stay just two days. Janet remembered later, "It wasn't easy to have the president spend the weekend because all sorts of furor ensued. The Secret Service appeared and ninety-nine telephones were pulled in and out, the Newport police went into a tailspin and put little phone booths here and there, and the Coast Guard whizzed around the dock."

When the president's green-and-white chopper landed on the gravelly beach in front of Hammersmith, the Auchinclosses ran out to the blue water's edge to greet Jack and his Secret Service agents. "He immediately presented a gift to his mother-in-law," recalled agent Larry Newman. Newman usually worked for Jackie but because he had not gone to Ravello with her, he ended up on the president's detail for this trip. "She unwrapped it to find a Princess telephone, new and popular at the time," he recalled. "When the receiver was lifted, it lit up for easy dialing. Mrs. Auchincloss had recently said she wanted one. 'Turquoise,' she exclaimed. 'The perfect color.' She couldn't have been happier with it."

The president then spent two days sailing on the *Honey Fitz* on Narragansett Bay, playing golf at the Newport Country Club, and swimming at Bailey's Beach. He also spent a few hours at work at Hugh's desk in the study. Later, Jackie would hang an oil painting of the president there with an American flag above it. "He slept that weekend in the guest room at the top of the stairs," Janet recalled. "I went in there one afternoon and it was absolutely boiling hot. When the wind goes the wrong way, that room only has one exposure. He never complained about it, though. Not once."

When the Auchinclosses had friends over for dinner the night of August 26, Janet had one of Jack's favorite and most simple meals served: rare roast beef with asparagus and mashed potatoes. However, protocol was always a complicated affair whenever he was in his presidential role at the table with friends of his in-laws, as opposed to when he was just "Jack" with family. As president, Janet felt it only right he be served first. Then, as he ate his meal, everyone else's was dished out. Of course, since he'd had such a head start, he'd always finish first. Janet then felt it inappropriate for him to sit before an empty plate while waiting for the others. Therefore, she'd ask the help to clear all plates as soon as he was done, which usually meant the others didn't get to finish their meals. Because of this particular rule on the part of the hostess, what had already been a very tense and difficult meal with no one knowing how to relate to the leader of the free world as he sat eating his mashed potatoes at the head of the table, became even more awkward.

Years later, Janet would ask a reporter, "Did you know the president's Secret Service name was Lancer? Jackie's was Lace. Caroline's was Lyric, and John's was Lark." Even Merrywood had a code name—"Hamlet," she said, as did Hammersmith, "Hamlet 2." The White House, she noted, was "Crown." The Kennedys' Hyannis Port home had no moniker, though, which Janet felt was odd. She continued, "We were walking on the beach when the president suddenly said to me, 'Mummy, I think you should have a code name.' He thought about it for a moment and finally announced, 'I think your name should be 'Wellspring.' I said, 'But why, Jack?' And he said, 'Because "wellspring" means the source of everything good.' My goodness! Why, I blushed like a schoolgirl. 'Oh my,' I said, 'thank you, Mr. President.' My God," she concluded, "he really did steal my heart that day, I must say. He really did steal my heart."

FATHERLY CONCERNS

On Sunday evening, as the sun began to set, Jack, Hugh, and Yusha took little John for a stroll on the beach. The president walked with an Irishman's Blackthorn cane, which he kept at Hammersmith for those times, like this one, when his back troubled him. Maud Shaw and two Secret Service agents followed close behind. Then, as John built sandcastles, Jack sat on a nearby bench and chatted with Hugh, Yusha, and the agent Larry Newman.

Jack pointed at the stunning Narragansett Bay. "See, out there?" he told Yusha. "That's where I trained on the PT-109." He noted that Melville, Newport, was the site of a PT boat office training center during World War II. He recalled that he'd see "this grand house in the distance," which he imagined was "the most beautiful place in the whole world. So, to be here with you now," he said, "is a real honor. In fact," he added, "being a part of your family has been a real honor for me."

What a thing to say and coming from the president! Yusha teared up. "We've always been honored to have you, Mr. President," he told him.

"Thank you again for the flags," Hugh added. Earlier in the day, Jack had presented his stepfather-in-law with a glass encasement of two flags, the president's and America's, both of which had flown at Hammersmith during his first presidential stay back in 1961. Its gold plate was inscribed:

The President's Flag Flown at Hammersmith Farm, Newport, Rhode Island, Presented to Hugh Dudley Auchincloss by John Fitzgerald Kennedy, President of the United States—1961.

In previously unpublished remarks from a 1998 interview, Larry Newman recalled, "As we watched John play, the president mentioned that he'd recently hosted one of his heroes, General Douglas MacArthur, at the White House. 'He's got some kind of cockamamie idea about arming soldiers with a nuclear device that could blow up a hundred men,' he said. 'It's a dangerous world to raise your children in, that's for sure.' The subject then turned to fatherhood. I didn't have any kids yet. I had just met my wife that year. But Mr. Auchincloss had raised five—Yusha from his first marriage; Nini and Tommy from his second; and Jamie and Janet Jr. from his present marriage to Mrs. Auchincloss. 'What's your secret?' the president asked him."

Hugh said he was far from the perfect father, but that maybe the "secret" was in being available to his children whenever they needed him. "You get busy," he told Jack, "and there are times when you're too busy to help your kid with a problem, but you have to stop and you have to be there. You just have to." He said he wasn't always present for his first three children and regretted it. He was trying to be better for Janet Jr. and Jamie, but if one were to ask them, he mused, they'd both probably say he still fell short. "Don't let your family slip away from you, son," he told Jack.

Jack said he was frustrated because his present duties often made it difficult for him to be available to his children. He said he really wanted the memory of being a good father. He added that he looked forward to the completion of his second term so that he could then spend more time with Caroline and John.

"If you don't mind me saying so, you can't wait that long, sir," offered Larry Newman. The agent noted that by the time Jack's second term was finished, John would be eight. His impression of his father would be set in stone by then.

Hugh concurred: "Remember, Plato said, 'Of all the animals, the boy is the most unmanageable.' You have to manage him now, Jack."

Jack knew they were right. By the time he was eight, he'd already had an indelible impression of his own father.

"As we walked back to the main house, the president took John's hand," recalled Larry Newman. "'Tell me a secret,' he said as he stopped and knelt before him. John whispered in his ear, the president put on a face of mock surprise and exclaimed, '*You don't say!*' They laughed and started walking again, the boy not taking his eyes off his father for a second. The president reached into his pocket for a stick of spearmint gum, unwrapped it, and handed it to him. 'Don't tell Mummy,' he warned him. 'Which one?' John asked as he stuffed it into his mouth. 'Neither,' said the president.

"As we continued along, John asked, 'Where does the ocean go, Daddy?' The president answered, 'It goes on forever and it's always there. You can count on the ocean, Sam,' he said, using a favorite nickname for the boy. Then, putting his big hand on John's little shoulder, he said, 'The ocean will always be there for you, Sam.'"

At the end of the lovely two-day visit, Jack's chopper returned to the stretch of pebble-covered sand along the shoreline. As he and his agents got ready to board, Janet hurried over to him. He extended his hand to shake hers. She took it but then, surprising him, she pulled him in for an embrace. "You'll be back for America's Cup, won't you?" she asked, practically shouting now because of all the helicopter noise. The popular boat race and show was scheduled in about a month's time and, yes, the plan was for Jack, Jackie, and the children to return to Newport to watch it from aboard the USS *Joseph P. Kennedy Jr.* However, Jack wondered if perhaps he could come back even sooner.

"Of course," Janet said.

He asked, "Next weekend?"

She said she'd love it.

"And then he said to me, sort of hesitantly," Janet recalled, "'Do you think if I come back next weekend, I could have the old room on the third floor?' That was the room Jackie had as a girl. He was trying to get out of the hot room I'd put him in. I said, 'Mr. President, you *must* have our room [hers and Hugh's].' He absolutely refused. He said, 'I just don't want you to. I wouldn't be comfortable if I thought you had moved out of your room for me.'" Janet said they'd work it out later. "Needless to say," Janet concluded, "when he came back, I put him in our bedroom."

"I'll see you next weekend," Jack told his mother-in-law just before getting into his helicopter, the wind blowing his auburn hair as he started up the steps. Just before he got into the chopper, he turned around and hollered out at her: "Take care of yourself." Then, with a wink he added, "Wellspring."

FLASHPOINT

H e was a man who enjoyed a warm relationship with his in-laws, unlike some other husbands, especially fascinating given how Jack Kennedy sometimes behaved in his marriage. He was also president of the United States with all of the heavy burdens and demanding responsibilities inherent in that office. Therefore, after Newport, it was back to the White House for JFK and then, shortly thereafter, to the handling of another national crisis.

In September, a historical civil rights crisis unfolded when the African American air force veteran James Meredith sought admission to the state-funded University of Mississippi in Oxford, Mississippi. There was no way his admittance would ever occur in segregated Mississippi without a big fight. Even though the Supreme Court had ruled in 1954 that segregation in public schools supported by taxpayers was unconstitutional, every Mississippi school district remained segregated, unlike the learning institutions of most other southern states.

A now well-known story that bears repeating has it that in May 1961, Jack and Bobby took a secret meeting with Martin Luther King Jr. at the White House. The Kennedys urged MLK to focus on voting rights instead of on desegregation. They argued that those rights would be easier to pass through Congress and that, in the end, they'd ultimately end segregation, anyway. Thinking pragmatically like most politicians, Jack and Bobby saw voting and desegregation as thorny issues, especially in the segregated deep South. They felt they had to proceed with caution, one step at a time.

No, the civil rights leader argued, he wanted to fight for both voting rights *and* desegregation, and he was disappointed in the Kennedy brothers, especially in the president. Afterward, MLK said that at the time of his original support of JFK for high office he'd felt he had "the intelligence and the skill and the moral fervor to give the leadership we've been waiting for and do what no president has ever done." But now, he said, as a result of that meeting, "I'm convinced that he has the understanding and the political skill but so far I'm afraid the moral passion is missing."

The truth was that Jack really was conflicted about civil rights. While he obviously knew it was time for Black Americans to be treated equally and had even initiated policy to that effect early in his administration, for some activists the question remained whether or not he had a real appetite for the cause. But Jack was a product of his times. When he was younger, back in 1946 when he was a congressman, he and his family held very casual views of the difficult race problem confronting the country.

JFK's Black chauffeur George Stevens told a story to the JFK Library about Jack and Eunice having invited campaign volunteers to a restaurant in Cambridge, "and they'd invite them to eat anything they would like," he said. Meanwhile, the siblings "would send up to the colored girls back in the office some sandwiches." Stevens recalled, "I told Jack, they're all giving their time. They're all human beings. Why segregate in this way? You can't take the colored girls down to the restaurant with the white girls? Instead, you're going to feed them upstairs? I don't think it's fair."

Jack responded, "George you're thin-skinned. That's one of the things of the time." In other words, it was normal for the present culture and Jack didn't think much of it one way or the other. George was so put off by his blasé attitude, he told the Library, he quit Jack's employ after ten loyal years with him.

That was fifteen years ago. Many things had changed in the intervening years, and Jack had certainly grown. Yet, it seemed to some civil rights activists that he still didn't have the moral imperative to really fight for equality. Just as interesting, it felt to some that he didn't even clearly understand the reasons for recent escalations of racial tensions. The president recently had gone to his closest Black adviser, the newspaper publisher Louis Martin, the man who Sargent Shriver turned to in 1960 to act as a conduit between the Kennedys and Coretta Scott King after MLK was jailed, and said, "Negroes are getting ideas they didn't have before. Where are you getting them from?" Martin's response: *"From you!"* James Meredith later said he'd been inspired to be the first African American to enroll in a segregated school precisely because of Kennedy's inaugural address.

Louis Martin's succinct answer was a real wake-up call for Jack. He was beginning to realize that his personal idealism had an impact more far-reaching than he even knew. This knowledge made him stop and really question, perhaps for the first time, his resolve and commitment to civil rights.

When the University of Mississippi refused to allow James Meredith to enroll, the state's governor, Ross Barnett, sent in state troopers to support the college. It became clear that the federal government would need to become involved. Jack was willing to use troops, if necessary, but he'd rather avoid that course of action if he could. But, still stung by the Bay of Pigs fiasco, he knew leadership mattered at such a critical juncture. Though he was reluctant to make the decision to intervene, he told the Mississippi National Guard to get ready to act.

On the evening of September 30, thousands of violent demonstrators protested James Meredith's registration in what's now known as the "Ole Miss Riot" of 1962, also the "Battle of Oxford." It was clear that the governor, Ross Barnett—an Ole Miss alumnus who'd previously declared, "No school will be integrated in Mississippi while I am your governor"—had no interest in containing the situation. He'd earlier even had Meredith charged and imprisoned for accidentally writing "1960" instead of "1961" while registering to vote; the Fifth Circuit quickly ordered his release. Later, it would be alleged Barnett was working *against* the Kennedy administration by secretly pulling state troopers off duty whose jobs should've been to keep James Meredith safe.

The culture was so contaminated with racism, Jack and Bobby feared the Mississippi National Guard would actually be sympathetic to the rioters. The president felt he had no choice but to invoke the Insurrection Act of 1807 (as he would twice more in 1963 during similar civil rights conflicts) and order up thirty thousand federal troops, the most for a single disturbance in American history. In the clash, two men were killed and scores of others wounded, including twenty-eight marshals who were shot.

By the morning of October 1, the situation was neutralized. "The responsibility for this unwarranted breach of the peace and violence in Mississippi rests directly with the president," was the twisted way Ross Barnett put it. Wanting to save face, Barnett actually made an offer to the Department of Justice that the state of Mississippi would pay for James Meredith's entire education if he'd just enroll in any other college in the country. The offer was refused. Meredith then became the first Black student to enroll at the University of Mississippi.

Though the crisis would later be considered a real flashpoint in the civil rights movement, President Kennedy wasn't eager to claim its resolution as a victory because he didn't want to appear as though he was "triumphing" over the South in a way that would deepen divisions. Making matters worse, Jack had even given a nationally televised speech from the Oval Office during the crisis to thank Mississippi for "the progress of our democratic development" without understanding the scope of what was going on and how dangerous it had become. How could that have happened? Bobby said the fault lay in the communication between Secretary of the Army Cyrus Vance and the Oval Office, which provided the president with poor and misleading advice. After a call for impeachment from the Mississippi Senate in November for "inciting riot," there was even concern that the uproar could jeopardize Jack's reelection chances.

No one seemed happy, neither Blacks nor whites, with the way things had been handled. However, in the end, James Meredith was successfully enrolled in the University of Mississippi resulting in the desegregation of Ole Miss—the first integration of any public educational facility in the state—and that would be the true legacy of this explosive and historical melee.

MEDICAL COUP D'ÉTAT

By the fall of 1962, the president was undergoing a major change in his medical treatment. For years, Jack Kennedy had been on heightened doses of testosterone-based anabolic steroids to control his Addison's. This is literally the same drug used by bodybuilders that is banned in most sports. "The steroids were making Kennedy manic," said Dr. Nassir Ghaemi in 2024, the first psychiatrist given permission to access JFK's medical records. "While it may have given Kennedy the creativity, energy, spark, flair, and charisma we associate with his personality, it also had a boomeranging effect which wasn't good, and the reason they decided to lower the dose."

There was more than just a decrease in Jack's medications taking place, though. In his research, Dr. Nassir Ghaemi learned that Dr. Janet Travell had been repeatedly injecting the president with procaine, also known as Novocaine, for muscle spasms. Procaine is also an analog of cocaine, with some of the associated euphoric highs and deep lows. At the same time, he was being shot up with amphetamines and barbiturates by Dr. Max Jacobson. Obviously, all of this "medication" was doing him more harm than good. It's actually difficult to imagine how he was even able to function as commander in chief! However, according to JFK's medical records, by the fall of 1962 both Travell and Jacobson were on their way out. Dr. Ghaemi refers to their exodus as a "medical coup d'état."

Dr. Jacobson's eventual downfall was precipitated by Bobby after he ordered an analysis of his injections and then warned Jack of their danger. One of Jack's other doctors, Captain Dr. George G. Burkley, also cautioned him that the shots shouldn't be taken by "responsible individuals who at any split second may have to decide the fate of the universe." At his and RFK's insistence, then, another doctor joined the medical team, the orthopedic specialist Dr. Hans Kraus. "My husband and Dr. Burkley both put their foot down," said Kraus's widow, Madi Springer-Miller Kraus, in 2024, "and told them that Dr. Feelgood had to go, and they weren't happy with Dr. Travell either, whose treatments were suspect. So, they got rid of her, too." Still, Travell publicly retained her official title as the president's physician. Surprisingly, she also continued to treat Jackie and the children.

"My husband prescribed a regimen of daily exercises in addition to swimming, and the president would then be in better shape than ever," said Madi Kraus. "His muscles would improve so much that he could sit up straight without the corset. He didn't need it any longer, but he did continue to wear it. I think maybe he felt insecure without it."

In October 1962, Jackie returned to the States after her Italian vacation. She then spent a few weeks at Hammersmith with her mother and confided to her that Jack was finally done with Jacobson and would never go back to him. "Through fire and water," she declared, "I will fight to keep him out of our lives." She said she was very sorry she'd let it go on as long as it had, and also regretted that she'd ever allowed herself to be injected by him. "Please, Mummy, don't tell me 'I told you so,'" Jackie said.

Janet smiled at her tolerantly. "Now, that's asking a lot, dear," she admitted.

ROSE BOWL

It was just to be a small dinner hosted by the First Lady the day after she returned to Washington from Newport following her Italian vacation. In fact, that's precisely how it was described in the official White House appointment book: "A small dinner at eight o'clock."

Jackie had seven guests: Najeeb Halaby Jr., head of the FAA and father of Lisa Halaby, who would later become Queen Noor of Jordan, and his wife, Doris; James Truitt of the *Washington Post* and his wife, Anne, a sculptor; artist William Walton, a family friend; along with Mary Meyer and John Carl Warnecke. She'd purposely included Mrs. Meyer, Jack's "other woman," and Mr. Warnecke, a man on whom she'd recently developed a bit of a crush. Jackie later admitted that she was "intrigued" by the complication such a guest list presented, almost as if she was bored by the tedium of White House living and wanted to spice things up. Or, as her sister, Lee, once put it, "What is very true of Jackie is that she was attracted to drama. She would sometimes arrange things in the most theatrical fashion just to see what might happen as a result. I'd do the same from time to time. I think we inherited this trait from Mummy, the most theatrical woman we'd ever known."

John Carl Warnecke had recently been hired by the president to work on the Lafayette Square project, restoring original buildings and constructing new ones in a complementary style. In meeting with Mr. Warnecke over the last few weeks, Jackie couldn't help but find herself attracted to him. "Jack," as he was known (as if she needed another in her life), was a handsome man with the physique of a football player, six-foot-three, about two hundred broad-shouldered pounds. He was forty-two and recently divorced from the mother of his four children. A graduate of the Harvard School of Design, he was also quickly making a name for himself, his recent design of the American embassy in Thailand and the Hawaiian State Capitol elevating him to stardom in the architectural community.

Warnecke and Kennedy met in September 1956 at the Fairmont Hotel in San Fransisco, where Jack was campaigning for Adlai Stevenson in his run against Dwight Eisenhower. JFK liked to call Warnecke "Rose Bowl," a nickname first given to the architect by his old Stanford classmate Paul "Red" Fay in commemoration of the victory Warnecke's football team enjoyed in 1941 at the Pasadena Rose Bowl. Fay introduced the two men just weeks after Jack began his affair with Joan Lundberg. "Because this woman named Joan was so much on his mind, he wasn't interested in another girl Red Fay was trying to hook him up with," recalled Jack Warnecke, "an Italian American brunette named Lita di Grazia. What struck me, though, was how easily Red Fay tried to arrange things with Lita, and that his wife, Anita, was in on it, too. I figured it was just the way things were in the Kennedy marriage. It must be an open relationship, I decided."

Jack Warnecke returned to Jack Kennedy's life in March 1962 when Red Fay brought him to the White House. It was then that the two men started discussing Lafayette Square. Jackie, who was already deeply committed to renovating Lafayette, was in India at the time. By the time she returned, Kennedy had already hired Warnecke for the job.

The president had actually intended to be at Jackie's dinner but was reminded by Evelyn Lincoln that he had to give a speech in Baltimore at the Fifth Regiment Armory. For the most part, the pleasantries that evening were all, as Jackie later put it, "Fake, fake, fake, just like all of those White House dinners you think might be fine but are ruined because you invited that one person who ends up being the fly in the ointment." Apparently, Mary Meyer was "the fly" that night. During dessert, as Italian music played on the Victrola, Jack Warnecke reached over to light Jackie's filtered cigarette as Mary watched with interest. Warnecke, years later, remembered Jackie gazing at him a bit longer than necessary, as if to make sure Mary got the message . . . and might pass it on to the president? Jackie took a deep drag on the cigarette and, as she exhaled, whispered to Warnecke that Mary should take a picture, it would last longer.

Later in the evening, Mary mentioned to Jackie that she understood that she and Jack were redecorating Lafayette Park. Jackie corrected her. "*Restore,* Mary," she said with acerbity. "I do not redecorate. I *restore.* And it's Lafayette Square, Mary. Not Park." Warnecke concealed his amusement as he took in the icy moment. New to these parts, he wasn't familiar with palace intrigue.

As Mary got ready to take her leave, she went to shake Jackie's hand. Instead of taking it, the First Lady smiled and handed her an empty champagne glass. "Thank you," she said, as if speaking to a servant. She then turned and walked away, leaving Mary holding the glass. "Oh, I cut her dead, all right," Jackie said, later. Indeed, if it was drama she wanted that night, it would seem she got it.

On October 15, a week after that White House dinner, Jackie and Jack Warnecke became even better acquainted during a function at the British embassy. The president wasn't present then, either; it wasn't even on his schedule. Therefore, Jackie spent the night dancing with the architect.

"Are you happy?" he asked her.

"Oh, Jack, now what kind of question is that?" she whispered as she gazed into his eyes.

He was forward and playful with her, even suggesting that one day they might travel the country together and restore buildings for the sake of what he called "a better, more beautiful America." She asked about the president. Would he be going with them? Warnecke smiled. "Do you really want him to?" he asked.

The next day, October 16, was the day Warnecke was scheduled to present his plans for Lafayette Square to the Fine Arts Commission. "Nervous?" Jackie asked as they danced. When he said he didn't get nervous, she whispered back that she was nervous all the time.

The presentation to the Fine Arts Commission went well. Jack Warnecke had been so convincing he obtained the majority vote of approval he needed from the seven-body committee.

Fate does sometimes have a way of rearranging things. In about a year, the president would be gone and his widow would hire Jack Warnecke to design his memorial grave at Arlington. She'd then find herself having to make some tough choices. However, by that time things would be very different in the former First Lady's life and the decisions she'd make relating to the man her husband called "Rose Bowl" would be the first chapter of a new and very different story.*

But all of that was yet to come . . .

---

* See "John Carl Warnecke Postscript" in Source Notes.

PART VI

"Cuba, Cuba, Cuba"

CRISIS IN CUBA

Long before he was president, John Fitzgerald Kennedy's greatest fear for America was the possibility of all-out nuclear war. While it now seems difficult to imagine, people alive at the time remember that in the 1950s and early to mid-1960s the threat of atomic warfare was almost always on their minds as they went about their daily lives. Millions of Americans had contingency plans in place in case of a worst-case scenario, their basements converted into bunkers with canned goods and other stockpiled necessities. Television news analysts calculated the time it would take for a missile sent from Russia to destroy New York City—a half hour! Schools were even required to have drills to teach students as young as five to take cover under their desks in case of an invasion, as if that would do them any good.

To be leader of the free world during this frightening time in our history was a burden perhaps unmatched by that of any other period, and it weighed heavily on President Kennedy. It wouldn't take much, even an unintentional slip, to set off a total cataclysm. Almost every major decision he made was in anticipation of how it might affect Germany and the delicate balance between the two superpowers, the United States and the Soviet Union.

Further complicating things was Fidel Castro's deepening relationship with Nikita Khrushchev. After the Bay of Pigs and the many failed assassination attempts on him, Castro had become even more closely aligned with the Soviet leader. Castro was now firmly aligned with the Soviet empire, that rare leader who'd actually welcomed Communism, rather than being forced into it by having his country seized and overtaken.

In the aftermath of the Bay of Pigs, Khrushchev warned Kennedy that any further attacks from the U.S. on Cuba would be considered a strike at West Berlin. It was obvious to Jack that the Soviet leader was essentially trying to goad him into attacking Cuba just so he'd have an excuse to invade Berlin.

Ratcheting up concerns, Khrushchev now also figured that getting missiles into Cuba would even out the nuclear arms playing field. In the past, the U.S. had always been confident it could destroy the U.S.S.R. by launching missiles against it from nearby Turkey. However, Khrushchev thought that if the U.S.S.R. could launch against the U.S. from Cuba—just ninety miles off the coast of Florida—he'd effectively be able to target many of the continental states, which would result in at least partial, if not total, annihilation. Castro was amenable to the idea. He reasoned that accepting missiles from the Soviets could later help him defend himself and his regime, especially given how provocative the U.S. had been toward him.

It seemed like just a matter of time before there'd be some sort of explosive confrontation between President Kennedy and these emboldened leaders, Khrushchev and Castro. That fuse was lit on October 15, 1962, when a U-2 spy plane captured aerial photographs of what were believed to be Soviet offensive missile bases under construction in Cuba. When Bobby took a look at the reconnaissance pictures, his response was, "*Shit! Shit! Shit!*" The next morning, McGeorge Bundy informed Jack of the startling development. Soon after, Jack convened his top foreign policy advisers, the Executive Committee of the National Security Council, which was a special group organized by Bobby and known as the "Ex Comm."

Jack's Joint Chiefs of Staff immediately began to campaign for a surgical air strike against the nuclear missile sites before they could become operational. Kenny O'Donnell recalled, "It was thought that U.S. bombers could swoop in, eliminate the sites, and fly away, leaving the problem swiftly and magically ended. But further questions proved the solution to be illusory. First, no cruise missiles or smart bombs existed in those days to ensure the precision and success of the strike. The air force acknowledged that it could be certain of eliminating only sixty of the missiles, leaving the others free to fire and destroy us."

Obviously, Khrushchev wouldn't just turn the other cheek if the United States invaded Cuba. "If he doesn't take action in Cuba," Jack said, "for sure, he will in Berlin, and then America will have to shoulder the blame for that." On the other hand, how would it look if the U.S. did nothing? The president had told Americans during his campaign that he'd take a strong stand against Khrushchev. He couldn't back down now. It would amount to political suicide. He also had to show strength to the world. He could never allow himself to be viewed as weak on Cuba, not again, not after the Bay of Pigs. All of those concerns about image and reputation aside, the real threat was to America's shores and its citizens. Was President Kennedy really going to allow a war and mass devastation on his watch?

Jack always knew that where Cuba was concerned it would come down to these kinds of tough choices, a crucible he'd one day have to face. "It's all he ever thought about," Jackie would later say. "It was always *Cuba, Cuba, Cuba*."

SEEN, NEVER HEARD

On Friday, October 19, Jackie's sister, Lee, arrived at the White House with her children to attend a dinner the next Tuesday for the Maharaja of Jaipur. Lee's friend Terrance Landow recalled in 2016, "Lee said as soon as she got to the White House she could feel impending doom. Jackie said the dinner was off and added, 'We'll be lucky if we can reschedule it. I suggest erasing all future plans from your calendar because it's all very much in doubt. We could all be gone tomorrow,' Jackie said, 'and then none of this will matter. Not any of it.'"

With anxiety rising on the home front, Jack thought it best if his wife and sister-in-law, along with nanny Maud Shaw and Bobby's wife, Ethel, took all the children to Glen Ora for the weekend. An interesting dichotomy of Jackie's character revealed itself at this time. During the Bay of Pigs, she'd been very forceful with her husband. "The President Kennedy I know wouldn't sit here and just be defeated," she'd told him. "The President Kennedy I know would figure this goddamn thing out." During this latest crisis, she took a more measured approach in dealing with him. It was as if she decided, in this instance, she should stay out of it, or as she recalled later to Arthur Schlesinger:

> I remember one morning, there was a meeting in the Oval Room. I went into the Treaty Room to fiddle through some mail. I could hear them talking through the door. I went up and listened and eavesdropped. I guess this was a rather vital time because I could hear Robert McNamara saying something like, 'I think we should do this, that, this, that.' McNamara was summing up something and

then Roswell Gilpatric was giving some summary, and then I thought, well, I mustn't listen! And I went away.

A family friend from Ireland, Dorothy Tubridy, a marketing executive for Waterford Crystal, also happened to be visiting the White House at this time. In a 2000 interview, she made note of a White House culture in which women were to be seen, never heard. "I remember all of us girls hiding in the corners, asking each other questions but certainly not asking anything of the men we'd see rush urgently by. If you saw the president or attorney general, my goodness, you wouldn't think to ask anything of them. I regret now that I didn't stand up and just say, 'What in the world is happening?' but a little person like me? My goodness, no. I remember running into Jackie and asking, 'Do you know what's going on?' She shrugged and said, 'All of that is up to Jack and Bobby. Take my advice, Dot. We girls need to stay out of it.'" Dorothy was not a girl, however. She was about to turn thirty-eight.

"*Demand* to know," Jackie's mother insisted in a phone call that Friday. "It's your *right* to know. You have children! He's not your boss, he's your husband." Jackie didn't agree. She felt Jack had enough on his mind and she wouldn't press him. She wasn't Eleanor Roosevelt teaming up with Franklin on decision-making, she said. "The job of the president is to protect the people. It's not incumbent upon the president to explain to the First Lady how he goes about it."

Even though she didn't know exactly what was going on, Jackie obviously sensed it was urgent for her to stay at the White House with Jack. He was insistent, however, that she go to Glen Ora. He wasn't going to be in Washington, anyway. He was scheduled to go to Cleveland and Chicago for speaking engagements. Ethel declined to go and insisted on staying with Bobby at the White House. But Jackie packed up and took off for Glen Ora with Lee, Maud, and the children.

After Jackie was gone, the president found Ethel in the Treaty Room reading a book while waiting to dine with Bobby. Jack walked in and sat down heavily into a chair.

"Jackie gone?" she asked.

He nodded, glumly.

"You know she wanted to stay, don't you?" Ethel noted.

"I know that," he said.

Ethel studied him closely. "Heavy is the head that wears the crown, brother-in-law," she said.

He smiled at her wearily. He then asked if she was aware that the line was actually "Uneasy lies the head that wears a crown."

No, she said, she didn't know that, but did it really matter?

"Not right now it doesn't," Jack said as he tilted his head back and closed his eyes.

"GRAB YOUR BALLS!"

―――――――

The two most clear options for America were an airstrike against the Cuban missile bases or a naval blockade of Cuba, preventing the transport of missiles. Jack didn't want an all-out strike, and neither did Robert McNamara. They both, along with Bobby, supported the idea of a blockade, even though the term "blockade" was considered by international law to be an act of war. Instead, at Dean Rusk's suggestion, they would use the word "quarantine."

Before Jack left for his brief trip, new aerial photographs revealed even more missile sites in Cuba. Frighteningly, these could serve intermediate-range missiles that could travel about 1,300 miles to New York faster than even previously anticipated. Now, the Joint Chiefs were more adamant than ever: the United States *had* to attack. While he was in Chicago, Jack got a call from Bobby. A decision had to be made. Was the president going to go with his hawkish advisers and strike at Cuba? Or not?

"It's your call, Mr. President," said Bobby.

"No, it's ours," Jack told him. He wasn't going to make a move without his brother; he'd learned that lesson the hard way during the Bay of Pigs misadventure.

Bobby had changed so much right before Jack's eyes, from the scrappy and impulsive brawler he'd been in the 1950s while grilling mobsters on television to the more reasoned and logical thinker he'd become by 1962 in the Situation Room. Now much more aware of the complexities of the world, he was someone who clearly had what it took to be a leader in his own right one day. The third brother, Ted, was kept in the dark about the current crisis. He'd been the first senator to ever be elected while his brother was president, and actually did better in some areas of Boston than Jack had done during his own terms. Though Ted was smart and savvy in many ways, the present crisis wasn't within his purview. Ironically, Ted had a general speech about Cuba in the planning stages and called Ted Sorensen to discuss it. Sorensen told him, "Better find another topic."

After speaking to Bobby on the telephone, Jack told his press spokesman Pierre Salinger to tell the media he had a cold and was returning to Washington. When Pierre asked if something else was going on he should know about, the president told him, "You bet something else is going on, and when you find out, grab your balls."

CRUCIAL DECISIONS

P resident Kennedy well understood the military mindset. With the eyes of a soldier, he could relate to their impulse to attack. That's how they were wired; move forward or die.

McGeorge Bundy, who served in the army before becoming Kennedy's national security adviser, was ready to go into Cuba, Pearl Harbor style, with blazing guns and blasting bombs. His plan of attack even had an informal name, "the Bundy Plan," and the backing of the U.S. military. But Jack realized a president needed to think first, weigh his options, wait until every possibility was exhausted, and then and only then consider going to war. *Maybe.* In an ironic sense, isn't this exactly what his father would've advised? Joe had wanted America to stay out of World War II and, because he'd taken that position, had been accused of appeasing Hitler. While Jack's present dilemma was very different from what Joe had faced as ambassador back in the 1930s, at moments it almost seemed as if Joe, the ardent dove, was whispering in his son's ear: *No war. Find another way.* Bobby, of course, agreed.

In the end, the Kennedy brothers took into account some of their father's thinking of the past and combined it with their own experience of the present to come up with what they believed to be a sound plan. The United States would blockade all offensive weapons headed to Cuba. But would it work? Or would Cuba counterattack, and then the Soviet Union follow suit? If that happened, then, yes . . . there would have to be war. There'd be no way around it, and it would be cataclysmic. The stakes couldn't have been much higher.

Jack was scheduled to announce his decision in an address to the American people on Monday night, October 22. The Sunday before, he called

Jackie at Glen Ora and asked her to return to the White House. "There was something funny in his voice," she recalled. "I could tell something was wrong."

Jackie and Lee packed up and, along with the four children and Maud, left Virginia for DC. That same afternoon, Lee's husband, Stas, arrived. "When Lee called him in Europe a day earlier to tell him what was going on, Father decided then and there he needed to be with the family," said Stas's son John Radziwill. "He never would've wanted them so far away during such a crisis. 'They have all the hospitals on high alert,' she told him, as if there'd be any hospitals actually still standing after the bomb hit. She seemed very sure it was the end of the world, though. Of course, he had to go to her and the children. It was almost impossible to get a flight out, though. Everything was a real mess; transportation, communication, phone lines were tied up. The world was in a real panic. I think people today don't realize the fear people felt during that particular time in our history."

Later that same day, Janet joined her daughters and grandchildren at the White House, leaving Hugh behind at their Georgetown residence with their daughter, Janet Jr. The rest of Jack's family—his mother, siblings, and their spouses—kept their distance from the White House to make sure they didn't distract the president as he struggled to make tough decisions. Bobby and Ethel remained at the White House.

On Monday, October 22, JFK met with congressional leaders who strongly opposed the blockade and demanded a stronger response. The president certainly could have buckled at this point, but instead he stood strong. His intention was to deliver the nationwide televised address that night on all major networks to announce the discovery of missiles and missile sites in Cuba and put forth his plan.

At about 6 P.M., as the president prepared to go on the air, Jackie pulled him aside. While she still was unaware of all the details, she sensed that war could be imminent, and she didn't want Jack to send her away again. "I'm done hiding," she said. "Enough, Jack. I'm your wife, not someone you can just stick in a drawer somewhere. My place is here with you. If you love me, you'll want to be with me, just as I need to be with you."

She later recalled, "I said, 'Please don't send me anywhere if anything happens. We're all going to stay right here with you. Even if there's not room in the bomb shelter at the White House,' which I'd seen, 'then I just want to be on the lawn when it happens. I just want to be with you. I'd rather die with you and the children, too, than live without you.' He said he wouldn't send me away, and he didn't really want to send me away."

At 7 P.M., EDT, President Kennedy addressed the nation in a dramatic, historic eighteen-minute speech from the Oval Office. "I was the only one in there with the president outside of the cabinet men," said Senator George Smathers. "What a moment that was. What an incredible moment as the president explained as much as he could to the American people."

> *Each of these missiles in short is capable of striking Washington, DC, the Panama Canal, Cape Canaveral, Mexico City, or any other city in the southeastern part of the United States, in Central America, or the Caribbean area. . . . It shall be the policy of this nation to regard any nuclear missile launched from Cuba against any nation in the Western Hemisphere as an attack by the Soviet Union on the United States, requiring a full retaliatory response upon the Soviet Union.*

He further stated that in order to halt the buildup of missiles, he was initiating a strict quarantine of all military equipment being brought into Cuba. Any ship bound for Cuba from any nation would be turned back if it contained cargoes of weapons. As much as he didn't want war, just as his father hadn't on the eve of World War II, Jack understood what Joe had not—if it was necessary, it was necessary, and America would not back down from it:

> *The 1930s taught us a clear lesson: aggressive conduct, if allowed to go unchecked and unchallenged, ultimately leads to war. This nation is opposed to war. We are also true to our word. Our unswerving objective, therefore, must be to present the use of these missiles against this or any other country, and to secure their withdrawal of elimination from the Western Hemisphere. . . . The path we have chosen for the present is full of hazards, as all paths are—but it is the one most consistent with our character and courage as a nation and our commitments around the world. The cost of freedom is always high—and Americans have always paid it.*

"Right after the speech, we walked outside," recalled George Smathers. "I congratulated him on making one hell of a speech. He wasn't at all nervous, upset, or agitated. It was just a feeling that what was done was done and let's just hope for the best. He said, 'We're really up against it now, aren't we, senator?' We visited for a minute, and I said, 'Okay, Mr. President, I'm going now.' He invited me to stay for dinner, but I thought he should be with family. Only God knew how much time we all had left to be with family."

AN UNWELCOME GUEST

President Kennedy's speech that evening in October was as chilling as it was memorable. He had definitely drawn a line in the sand and there was no telling how it might work out for the United States, indeed for the world. Most Americans went to bed that night in a very troubled state. Meanwhile, in the Kennedys' private world that same evening, there was a bit of unrest having nothing to do with the public crisis, but rather with what was going on behind closed doors.

After Jack's address to the nation, Jackie hosted a dinner for some of their closest friends and relatives. As well as the president and First Lady, at the table were Bobby and Ethel; Lee and Stas; Janet and Yusha Auchincloss; Jackie's wardrobe designer, Oleg Cassini; British diplomat David Ormsby-Gore and his wife, Sylvia; family friends Benno and Nicole Graziani; Dorothy Tubridy and Deborah Cavendish, the Duchess of Devonshire; and William Walton and his date, Helen Chavchavadze. Jackie was the last to be seated. As she took her place, she suddenly realized that, sitting right next to Ethel was . . . Mary Meyer. She'd had no idea Mary would be at the table.

Why Jack would allow a woman with whom he was involved to dine with friends and family on such a sensitive evening remained a mystery for many years. However, it was finally solved with the discovery of a previously unpublished 1998 interview with Helen Chavchavadze, someone else who claimed to have had a brief affair with Jack. If true, that meant there were *two* of his paramours at dinner that night.

"Mary was supposed to be Bill Walton's plus-one," said Helen Chavchavadze, "but then Bill decided to bring me, instead. We watched the speech on television at his home and then raced to the White House for dinner.

From my understanding, Mary was upset by the crisis and didn't want to be alone. Her sister, Tony, was holed up with Ben Bradlee at the press office, trying to make sense of what was going on. Therefore, in the middle of this great crisis, Mary called the president to ask if she could come to the White House. He was busy, obviously, and couldn't speak to her. She ended up talking to Evelyn Lincoln, who said yes, she could come by. It's not a thing I believe the president even knew about. I think he was just as surprised as everyone else when she showed up, and once she was there he couldn't very well send her away, could he? It's fair to say he had more on his mind than whether or not Mary Meyer should be at the dinner table."

Jackie was taken aback by Mary's presence, or as her mother later put it, she appeared "hurt and hardened." Oleg Cassini recalled, "When Jackie walked by me to her seat, she was noticeably upset. I leaned over and whispered to her, 'Are you okay, my dear?' She whispered back, 'Are any of us, Oleg?'"

After everyone was seated, McGeorge Bundy came into the dining room, leaned down to Jack, and whispered that he'd heard Khrushchev might finally come to his senses. Oleg Cassini recalled, "The president took a puff of his cigar, turned to me on his right, and whispered that now there was maybe a twenty percent chance America was going to go to war. Then, to the others, he declared, 'Look, we've done all we can do. There's pretty much nothing left.' Ethel then said that whatever happened next would be God's will. Jackie raised her glass and said, 'God bless us all, everybody.' Then this woman I didn't know [Mary Meyer], brazen as she could be, had the nerve to speak up. 'Yes,' she said, 'may he bless us all.'"

As everyone toasted, Mary reached over to clink Ethel's glass. Instead of tapping Mary's, Ethel lowered her glass and glanced over at Jackie with a look that suggested she knew exactly what was going on. It would be more than two years before she'd bring it up to Jackie, however. According to one of Ethel's secretaries, she asked Jackie what was going through her head during these emotional moments at the table. Jackie said, "My only thought, to be honest, was, *Are you kidding me with this goddamn woman?*"

RESOLUTION

━━━━

W hat followed President Kennedy's speech were days of worry and uncertainty. The entire country was on edge. "There was no waking or sleeping," Jackie recalled. "No day or night." As Soviet ships headed for Cuba, American ships awaited in a blockade some five hundred miles off the island. One of the first to arrive was the destroyer USS *Joseph P. Kennedy Jr.* "I remember saying to Jack, 'Did you send it?'" Jackie recalled. "And he said, 'No. Isn't that strange?'"

At one point the president agreed with the Joint Chiefs that if Khrushchev didn't consent to withdraw his missiles, he'd have no choice but to authorize an invasion. It could happen within the next forty-eight hours. "The noose was tightening on all of us," Bobby later recalled. Jack wanted to hold out, hoping the tide would turn. When it finally did turn, it was in the strangest way. The arrival of two consecutive letters from Khrushchev to the U.S. embassy in Moscow, on Friday, October 26, and Saturday, October 27, became the unlikely catalyst for a settlement to this frightening standoff.

The first letter from Khrushchev suggested the removal of missiles and Soviet troops in exchange for a promise from the president not to invade Cuba or support any other forces with that intention. It was a rambling missive, but conciliatory and a relief. "We can sleep good tonight," Jack said. However, the next day, another communication appeared, this one much harsher in tone and demanding that the U.S. not only refrain from invading Cuba but also remove its missiles from Turkey and Italy. This surprising change in tack suggested some sort of inner turmoil in communications between Khrushchev and Kremlin party officials. Whatever was going on, these demands amounted to public concessions the president wasn't willing to make, not only on principle but because he knew the Turkish government wanted those missiles to stay in place. Admitting that they were removed would appear as if the U.S. was selling out its ally, Turkey, which would then result in what Bundy called "the decline in the effectiveness of the NATO alliance. Besides," he added, "the United States never backs down."

Jackie, in her 1964 oral history: "I remember Jack did tell me about this crazy telegram that came through from Khrushchev one night. Very warlike. He'd sent the nice one first, where he looked like he would—Khrushchev had—where he might dismantle. Then, this crazy one came through in the middle of the night. I remember Jack being really upset about that."

At this same time, a U.S. reconnaissance plane was shot down by a surface-to-air missile and crashed in Cuba, killing the pilot. Angry Joint Chiefs now insisted an air strike must take place that Monday, October 29, followed by a full-scale invasion. This period of time was maybe the darkest of the entire crisis for the president, later referred to by his cabinet as "Black Saturday." Now, it looked as if war really was imminent. That night, Dave Powers found Jack reading Caroline a bedtime story as she nestled on his lap. Powers said he had the "strangest feeling" Jack felt this could be the last time he'd ever share a moment so precious with his daughter. "We had not abandoned all hope," Bobby later recounted, "but what hope there was now rested with Khrushchev's revising his course within the next few hours. It was a hope, not an expectation. The expectation was military confrontation by Tuesday (October 30) and possibly even October 29."

It was Bobby, most people now agree, who had what turned out to be an odd idea: Why not act as if they'd never received the second missive and just respond favorably to the first one? Jack worried Khrushchev's original offer had expired with his second demand but was willing to take that chance. It was a crazy idea, but maybe it would work, he figured. In agreeing to the terms of the first missive, he told Bobby to informally relay to Soviet ambassador Anatoly Dobrynin that the United States would *also* withdraw those missiles in Turkey and Italy as per the second communication, but *secretly* and later, possibly in five months. Jack didn't want it to appear to the world that any significant concessions had been made by the United States, just the agreement not to invade and nothing about those missiles.

Now, a deal was finally on the table. "For a moment, the world had stood still," Bobby later said, "and now it was going around again." However, Jack wasn't sure Khrushchev would take the bait. That night, his administration drew up plans for air strikes on the missile sites, and plans were also discussed for how to respond to whatever the Soviets might do in West Berlin. Meanwhile, the CIA reported new and terrifying news that missiles in Cuba pointed toward the United States were being prepared for launch.

But then . . .

. . . the deal was agreed upon by Khrushchev. JFK agreed not to invade Cuba and covertly agreed to remove all missiles in Turkey and Italy. In return, Khrushchev would remove all missiles in Cuba. It was the secrecy between Kennedy and Khrushchev about those missiles that really sealed the agreement. It definitely wasn't the unconditional surrender Americans were led to believe. If either side had betrayed the confidentiality of the deal, the deal would've been off. The missiles were all eventually removed, by the spring of 1963. Kennedy was eventually able to convince both governments that the United States was still committed to them and would provide better and more efficient munitions.

These secret dealings, though rumored for some time, wouldn't be officially acknowledged for more than twenty-five years, in 1989 at a conference in Moscow by Soviet ambassador Dobrynin and Ted Sorensen. It would appear that even Jackie didn't know about it, given her comments in 1964. "I remember thinking of the inaugural address," she recalled. "'Let's never negotiate out of fear but let us never fear to negotiate.' Because I thought how humiliating for Khrushchev to have to back down. And yet somehow Jack let him do it with grace and didn't rub his nose in it."

Of course, the reason JFK didn't want to boast about the "victory," or have his aides trumpet it, was precisely because of its secret nature. It also has to be acknowledged that Jack's belief in the power of negotiation was strongly rooted in his father's isolationist philosophy. At the root of Joe's isolationism—and Jack's, too—was always the question: "How can we make a deal? Anything was better than war." That was most certainly Joe Kennedy's mindset, going all the way back to World War II, even if people didn't really understand it back then and thought he was an appeaser of Adolf Hitler's.

Given the secret agreements about missiles, some critics of Kennedy's today feel it's a false historical premise to say he'd bested Khrushchev when Khrushchev had been appeased with a secret negotiation that wasn't made public. Objectively, it could be argued that it was not the terms of the deal that mattered as much as the fact that Jack's diplomacy averted war. When the two superpowers came closest to nuclear warfare, it was President Kennedy who'd helped the world avoid Armageddon. He'd found a way to work in tandem with Khrushchev, and it also bears noting that Castro was essentially cut out of the equation. In fact, it's been said that the Cuban leader didn't even know there'd been a resolution until he heard about it on the radio. Some historians have theorized that Khrushchev believed Castro had lost his mind when the Cuban leader sent him a letter on October 26, 1962. In it, Castro basically encouraged Khrushchev to attack the United States and implied that if Cuba was destroyed in the process, so be it, "however harsh and terrible a solution." The idea that Castro was such a war monger that he'd sacrifice his own people even made Khrushchev think twice about him.

Joe Kennedy most certainly would've been proud of his son, the president. Jack had learned a lot during his short time in high office, not the least of which was to listen to his own counsel. Putting the tragic elements of the Bay of Pigs aside for a moment, perhaps it had been the most valuable learning experience he ever could've had as commander in chief. One can't help but wonder what might've happened if the trials had been switched—if the Cuban Missile Crisis had happened first and Jack had listened exclusively to the advice of his Joint Chiefs as he had during the Bay of Pigs.

PART VII

Life Changes

THEIR LAST THANKSGIVING

We have a lot to be thankful for this year," Rose Kennedy wrote in her journal five days before Thanksgiving 1962. Especially given the recent close call in Cuba, she heard no arguments from any quarter when she invited Jackie's side of the family to Hyannis Port for the holiday. She wanted the Kennedys and Auchinclosses to come together because she felt this particular holiday to be especially significant. It was eventually decided that the families would celebrate separately on the actual day—November 22—and then unite in Hyannis Port the following Saturday, November 24.

At 7 P.M. on the appointed evening, sitting at the large fruitwood table in the Kennedys' ivory-and-gold dining room were Joe and Rose; Joe's sister, Loretta; Jack and Jackie; Bobby and Ethel; Ted and his wife Joan Bennett; and Sarge and Eunice. Jean and Steve were in New York, Peter and Pat in Los Angeles. Representing the Auchinclosses were Janet and Hugh, Lee and Stas. Jamie and Janet Jr. and Hugh's other children—Yusha, Tommy, and Nini—didn't make the trip. The family's physician Dr. Robert D. Wyatt and Jackie's designer Oleg Cassini, who'd also been a longtime friend of Joe Kennedy's, were present, as were Arthur Houghton and Janine Burke. Arthur was aged and sickly, but would still live another ten years, until 1972, when he'd pass away at the age of ninety-four.

Jack was quiet this weekend. It seemed that after the Cuban Missile Crisis he fell into a depression. It may have been the stress of the ordeal, or possibly it had to do with the dramatic changes in his medication. In the kitchen, talking to her relatives, Jackie said he hadn't had a good night's sleep since the conflict. This was unusual for him, she said. Ordinarily, he could sleep anywhere, "like a soldier in a fox hole," she noted, "when it was time to go to sleep, he just would."

Janet couldn't help but notice Jack's detachment. "Is everything okay, Mr. President?" she asked. In response he just stared at her. Oleg Cassini recalled Jackie as saying the only conversations she'd had lately with Jack had to do with the suits she'd lay out for him in the morning. According to Oleg, when Janet asked why she, and not his butler, was selecting his wardrobe, Rose answered, "Because the First Lady serves at the pleasure of the president." Janet and Jackie both just stared at her in disbelief.

After dinner, Rose mentioned that she and Eunice, Jean, and Pat would soon be going to Wisconsin to visit Rosie for the holiday at St. Coletta's. Rose had certainly come a long way in accepting and understanding her eldest daughter's circumstances. Still, she kept her at arm's length from other relatives. For instance, when Joe's sister, Loretta, said she also wanted to visit Rosie, Rose told her, "Oh, no, darling, they don't want anybody else. It's far too disruptive."

Recently, when Rose was asked by a reporter why she'd become so interested in children with intellectual disabilities, she was candid about it. "The answer is simple," she said. "We had a retarded child, born about a year and a half after the birth of our second son, Jack." She then spoke about the mandate of the Joseph P. Kennedy Jr. Foundation to support research into intellectual disabilities. Rose was also proud that Eunice was beginning a summer camp for intellectually disabled children at her Maryland home, which she would call Camp Shriver. This undertaking would be the predecessor of the Special Olympics, established in about six years' time, also by Eunice, to promote physical fitness among disabled people. After that, LBJ would sign a landmark law expanding the rights of disabled people with Medicaid.

From 1958 to 1963, on Rosie's September 13 birthday, Jack Kennedy would send flowers to his sister from Freddie Birkholtz's greenhouse in Lake Mills, according to Birkholtz's daughter, Mary Jo. Today, a framed signed photograph of President Kennedy hangs proudly at St. Coletta's. On it, the president wrote with typical sentimentality: "To the school of St. Coletta's. With the very best wishes of John F. Kennedy." Many years later, in 1989, Jack's nephew Anthony Shriver, Eunice and Sargent's son, would establish Best Buddies, an international organization dedicated to pairing a volunteer with an intellectually disabled "buddy" for mentoring purposes. Each year Best Buddies still commemorates Rosie's birthday by giving its employees the day off.

After coffee and dessert, Jackie brought out a manuscript she'd been reading. It was Joe Kennedy's memoir, *Diplomatic Memoir,* which he'd started in the summer of 1938 and continued working on for the next twenty years. After his stroke, Jackie found the typed manuscript in the attic of the Hyannis Port home and became completely immersed in it. She started carrying it around with her in a leather satchel everywhere she went, reading it whenever she had a spare moment. She felt it brought her closer to the father-in-law for whom she'd always had complex feelings but who she now missed because he wasn't the same man since the stroke. Reading about his life and times as written in his own words really meant something to her.

Jackie said she was presently reading a chapter having to do with Joe leaving the States for England in 1938 for his role as ambassador. "Read it to us," Eunice said. Everyone then started chanting: "Read it! Read it!" Oleg Cassini recalled, "She looked at the president for approval. He nodded at her, yes. So, as we all sat in the parlor, Jackie stood in the middle of the room and read a passage written by Joseph Kennedy so many years earlier, her finishing school voice somehow sounding hypnotic in those moments."

> *My last visit, before I had to tear to the airport was to Vice President [John] Garner. He expressed the wish that we could get the strongest men in the United States for the cabinet. He thought we had the worst he'd ever seen, and said he was more worried than at any time in forty years. I told him how I felt—that there was nothing the matter with the aims of the president, and the New Deal wasn't at fault, but you couldn't run an organization as big as the United States government with any but first-class men. Until the boss recognized that, he was going to have plenty of trouble. Then I grinned at the worried and obviously sincere little man and said goodbye.*

There was much more to the passage. Once she finished reading it all, Jackie looked about and realized people were staring at her. A heavy sadness blanketed the room. It was as if everyone was struck by the fact that this great man who'd had so many incredible life experiences was now sitting in a corner speechless and trapped in a wheelchair. "You're right about the need for first-class men," Jack finally murmured to his father as he walked over to him and kissed him on the forehead. "That's certainly been my experience, Dad," he concluded.

"The president then left the room," said Oleg Cassini. "Soon after, people started saying good night, wanting to cut the night short."

Despite the sudden sad turn the evening took, Rose Kennedy had been wise to insist on it. Indeed, it really had been important that both families celebrate this particular Thanksgiving. As fate would have it, it would turn out to be their last one together. In fact, exactly one year later—November 24—Jack would be dead and his accused assassin, Lee Harvey Oswald, shot and killed by a nightclub owner named Jack Ruby.

"AS OLD AS THE SCRIPTURES"

At the beginning of 1963, President Kennedy's Gallup poll approval rating was 76 percent, no doubt boosted by his handling of Cuba.

Back on December 29, there had been a celebration at the Rose Bowl in Miami for the twelve hundred soldiers, primarily Cuban exiles, captured during the Bay of Pigs misadventure twenty months earlier. They were finally released in exchange for about $50,000,000 worth of food and medicine. During the ceremony, the brigade's flag was handed over to President Kennedy who said, "I can assure you that this flag will be returned to this brigade in a free Havana." Jackie then addressed the crowd of fifty thousand with a few sentences in Spanish. What had been the first true disaster of Jack's administration was transformed into an emotional cause for celebration, which, no doubt, contributed to his popularity. If those soldiers had been killed instead of returned, how would JFK ever serve another term? As it happened, his approval went way up.

However, only a short time later, the president's popularity would drop to about 60 percent, largely because of his stance on civil rights. Jack expected it. He felt strongly that the next two years of his term would have to be about the successful passing of legislation because at least a third of what he'd sought to do in his first two years was stuck in Congress. While he proved he could campaign and inspire, he still hadn't figured out how to break the gridlock that often characterizes American governance. He'd always thought the president had all the power, until he became president. Then, he realized that, no . . . it's Congress that has all the power. His long-promised civil rights bill, for instance, would make it to Congress later in June but, as usual, the body would fail to act on it. Meanwhile, things were as complicated as ever in terms of racial relations, even in the Kennedy White House.

Jean Price Lewis, who was 105 in 2024 when interviewed for this book, was known as the "Godmother of White House Women" because she'd started working for JFK when he was in the Senate. A careerwoman and divorced mother of two, she was then appointed to set up his Los Angeles presidential campaign office, and even helped organize the 1960 Democratic National Convention. She then continued with the president to the White House and then, later, would go on to work for the LBJ administration. She recalled, "One morning, Ted Reardon [administrative assistant to JFK] said, 'Jeannie, if you'd like to take tomorrow off, that's okay.' I asked, 'But Mr. Reardon, why would I want to do that?' He said, 'Some staff people from the Boston office are coming down.' He paused and then, lowering his voice to a whisper, he said, 'They're Negroes, Jean.' I said, 'Mr. Reardon, I don't know what you've heard about Southerners, but that doesn't upset me in the least! I do *not* want to take the day off.' It just goes to show, however, what people's attitudes were like at that time in our history."

In May, another civil rights crisis exploded when the unapologetically racist Eugene "Bull" Connor, commissioner of public safety in Birmingham, Alabama, unleashed fire hoses and police dogs on African American demonstrators, including children, during the Birmingham Campaign. A month later, two Black students, James Hood and Vivian Malone, attempted to enroll in the all-white University of Alabama and were blocked by Democratic governor George Wallace. Just six months earlier, Wallace had promised in his inaugural speech, "Segregation now, segregation tomorrow, segregation forever." Intent on keeping that pledge, he said he'd stop "integration at the schoolhouse door." To that end, he actually stood in front of the university's Foster Auditorium in order to bar entrance by Hood and Malone, thus the disturbance's historical name, "Stand in the Schoolhouse Door."

This time, Jack was more prepared than he'd been during the Mississippi crisis. He quickly federalized the Alabama National Guard, putting them under the command of the president, rather than the governor. Wallace stood down, and Hood and Malone were then able to enter the building, though at a different entrance. While Alabama had managed to desegregate its university without violence, such racial unrest was becoming more commonplace and dangerous. In fact, there were 161 such incidents in June alone.

President Kennedy decided the time had finally come to speak to the nation about civil rights and, once and for all, clarify his position in a televised address not only for the country but maybe even for himself. It would be his most important speech relating to this cause, which he gave on June 11, the night of the skirmish at the University of Alabama:

The heart of the question is whether all Americans are to be afforded equal rights and equal opportunities, whether we are going to treat our fellow Americans as we want to be treated. If an American, because his skin is dark, cannot eat lunch in a restaurant open to the public, if he cannot send his children to the best public school available, if he cannot vote for the public officials who will represent him, if, in short, he cannot enjoy the full and free life which all of us want, then who among us would be content to have the color of his skin changed and stand in his place? . . . One hundred years of delay have passed since President Lincoln freed the slaves, yet their heirs, their grandsons, are not fully free. They are not yet freed from the bonds of injustice. They are not yet freed from social and economic oppression. And this Nation, for all its hopes and all its boasts, will not be fully free until all its citizens are free.

The president asked Congress to enact legislation that would protect the voting rights of *all* Americans, as well as their legal standing, educational opportunities, and access to public facilities. It was a monumental speech, one for which President Kennedy would most be remembered by civil rights activists. At last, he had met his moment in history with this important issue and had done so with not only compassion but also common sense. It was the first time he'd ever spoken of civil rights as more than just a legal issue, and it was a true act of moral passion and authority, one that Martin Luther King Jr. had previously felt was missing in the president's resolve. Afterward, MLK called JFK's civil rights proposals "the most sweeping and forthright ever presented by an American president."

Jackie was at Camp David with the children the night Jack gave his important speech. The Auchinclosses were at their Georgetown home, watching with Jack's siblings Ted and Eunice Kennedy and their spouses Joan Kennedy and Sargent Shriver. After the broadcast, they called Jackie. Everyone agreed it had been courageous of Jack to take such a strong position on civil rights since doing so could jeopardize his support in the South. Jackie said Jack told her the decision to make the speech had been sudden. She said his advisers had tried to talk him out of it because they felt that taking such a position on civil rights required more thought. However, she said, Jack was determined to give what she called "an important value statement." She was proud of him, especially since he followed his own counsel and didn't listen to his aides, not many of whom—if any—she trusted. Three months later, on August 28, 1963, Martin Luther King Jr. would give his own historic "I Have a Dream" speech on the steps of the Lincoln Memorial following his March on Washington for Jobs and Freedom. Of course, King's speech is today considered one of the all-time greatest of the civil rights movement. Jack thought it was "good, damned good." Afterward, he welcomed King and other activists to the White House. Roy Wilkins, leader of the NAACP, gave credit to the president, telling him, "You made the difference. You gave us your blessings." It was true. Jack had not only sanctioned the march, he helped plan the route to make it as short as possible in order to avoid any problems. He even authorized the language of some of the speeches, all in an effort to keep the march from jeopardizing his civil rights bill in the eyes of leery conservatives. "It was one of the prime factors in turning it into an orderly protest to *help* our government," said Wilkins, "rather than a protest *against* our government."

"I have a dream," Jack kept repeating to Jackie after that historic day. "Isn't that something?" Jackie said many years later, "I remember he thought it was so eloquent and so well put, so aspirational. In fact, he felt it resonated the way his 'Ask Not' inaugural speech had. We talked about it a lot. 'I have a dream.' It really stuck with him."

JACKIE'S ULTIMATUM

W hen they were together for 1962's Thanksgiving, Jackie told her mother that, lately, the only time she saw Jack come out of his shell was when he was with their children. She said he completely lit up whenever Caroline and John walked into the room. "You can't imagine how much he loves them," she said. She'd sometimes go into Caroline's bedroom and watch as Jack sat on the sleeping girl's bed and gaze at her adoringly while running his fingers through her curly blond hair. Her mind was made up, she told her mother. She'd decided to have another baby.

"For him?" Janet asked.

"No," Jackie answered. "For me. Or maybe for us. I don't know yet."

Six weeks later, Jackie was pregnant. It happened that quickly. At the beginning of 1963, she decided to curtail all activities, though she and Jack wouldn't make an official announcement until after Easter—on April 15, to be precise. It would be the first birth for a presidential couple since Esther Cleveland was born to President Grover Cleveland and First Lady Frances in 1893. (Remember that John Kennedy Jr. was born before his father's inauguration.)

At this same time, January 1963, there was a bizarre occurrence at an Associated Press convention in Phoenix, which was attended by prominent newspaper publishers. Phil Graham, publisher and co-owner of the *Washington Post,* got drunk and gave a mostly incoherent speech. He attacked the CIA and, in the process, obliquely mentioning Jack's affair with Mary Meyer, said that she'd once been married to a top CIA official, Cord Meyer. He joked that Mary was the president's "new favorite." Graham hadn't been well for some time, suffering from alcoholism and manic depression, now known as bipolar disease. He'd been acting erratically for some time, according to his wife, Katharine Graham, who cited his "fundamentally aberrant behavior" in her book *Personal History: A Memoir.*

Phil Graham, a longtime friend of the Kennedys, had often advised Jack on critical matters, even the idea of bringing LBJ onto his ticket in 1960. He and his wife were also close to Jackie. After his spectacle of a speech, he telephoned President Kennedy and somehow got through to him, despite the late hour on the East Coast. We don't know the specifics of their conversation, but it's believed Graham apologized for what he'd just blurted out about Jack's relationship with Mary. Jack could tell his friend was in bad shape and authorized the use of a government plane to get him out of Phoenix before he did any more damage. After Graham was safe in a private mental hospital in Washington, Katharine wrote to the president and said of her husband, "He would and will die at the thought that he might have hurt you in any way. I hope he didn't—too much . . ." (Phil Graham would die by suicide with a rifle eight months later on August 3, his body discovered by Katharine.)

The next day, fearing Graham's remarks would be reported since they were delivered to a room full of press people, Jack felt he had no choice but to tell Jackie about it. If what Graham said was about to become national news, she needed to know. She was upset, as he'd expected. She decided to hold her fire, until she had a moment to digest the troubling information. When she told her mother about it later that afternoon, she was encouraged by Janet to finally take a stand where Ms. Meyer was concerned.

"Is this the same disreputable woman who was at dinner the night Jack gave his speech about Cuba?" she asked, trying to be clear. Yes, Jackie told her. "Fine," she said. "You cannot put up with this for one more second." Surely, Janet said, all of Washington would soon be talking about the scandal. According to a later recollection, she added that she could no longer sit idly by and watch as Jackie continued to be humiliated. She had her own relationship with Jack and felt she could be straight with him about his bad behavior. But Jackie didn't need her mother to intervene. She was already fired up.

"Mary Meyer is finished," she told Jack the next day, according to someone with firsthand knowledge of the situation. "It's over, Jack," she told him. She was now drawing a line in the sand. "It's either her, or me. You choose," she said, adding that if their marriage was to survive the next year in the White House, or the next four after that, things would have to change. "The hell with it," she told him. "I mean it, Jack. I'll be out."

Whereas he once would've argued about it and been determined to have the final word, now he was willing to acquiesce. "In other words, end it with Mary," he responded.

"Not in other words," she told him, "in those exact words."

Jackie had allowed Jack's behavior to go on for years, her coping mechanism in place ever since the days of Joan Lundberg. Now, as the First Lady and mother of his children with another on the way, she apparently felt she had more influence. How would it look if she filed for divorce? It's doubtful she ever would've done so—in fact, it's unthinkable—but she had to know that the threat would have some impact, especially as Jack was beginning to strategize the run for his second term. Jack said he would take care of it.

From what Jackie later told her mother and sister, she didn't believe her husband would handle the matter. After she spoke to Jack, she called Mary herself. We don't know the details of that conversation, only that Jackie said she told her, "I want you to stay the hell away from my husband." Mary was stunned. She and Jackie seldom said a word to each other, so this sudden outburst was a surprise. Mary immediately reached out to the president. When they connected, he explained what Phil Graham had done in Phoenix. Mary didn't know anything about it, but felt it would all blow over. It didn't matter, Jack told her. They were finished. "He told me he said he could no longer do this to his wife," Jackie later told her family members. "He said he no longer wanted to be that kind of man." Janet asked if Jackie believed him. She said she did.

THE VERY WORST PARTS

Funny how fate works, the way things sometimes fall into place in a man's life at just the right time. By the beginning of 1963, Jack Kennedy was already beginning to feel remorseful about not only Mary Meyer, but any woman he'd ever had in his bed who wasn't his wife. His cousin Joey Gargan recalled, "He was asked at this time what, if he could live his life over again, would he want to be different? He answered, 'If I had to live my life over again, I'd have a different father, a different wife, and a different religion.' That made sense to me, because I think for years he blamed his father, he blamed his wife, and he blamed his religion for every bad decision he ever made."

Gargan had a point. Jack told intimates at this time that he'd been rationalizing his bad behavior for so long, it had become second nature to do so. His father was to blame, he'd sometimes reason. After all, if not for Joe, he would've ended up with Inga Arvad, someone he truly loved, instead of Jackie, someone he married for political purposes and then grew to love. Joan Lundberg, he'd often reason, had come into his life because his entire family had frozen him out after Arabella's death. Similar logic also explained, in his mind anyway, Gunilla von Post and Judy Campbell and any others who'd come along. After all, if Jackie hadn't given him carte blanche to misbehave, he wouldn't have been with any of them, or so went his tortured reasoning. Mary was *really* Jackie's fault. After all, Jackie was the one who gave him permission to parade Mary Meyer around the White House the exact same way his mother had given his father permission to parade Janet DesRosiers around the Big House.

Jack's warped logic apparently started to fall apart by early 1963. George

Smathers said, "I can't say what precipitated it, but I think it had to do with the pressures of the presidency, the Bay of Pigs, the Cuban Missile Crisis, those events putting things into perspective. I remember him telling me, 'I love Jackie. She's my whole life.' I thought to myself, *Oh yeah? Since when? Since when has Jackie ever been your whole life?* Another time, he said, 'I've never loved any woman the way I love my wife.' Again, I thought, *Really?* But he was changing. Things were different. We could all see it. I mean, every person you ever talk to about this time will say the same thing. He told me, 'Every bad decision I've ever made has been my own fault. I'm sick of being a chip off the old block.' I sure knew what that meant."

Is it possible Jack Kennedy had finally come face-to-face with a hard truth? Did the worst parts of himself remind him of the worst parts of someone else? His own father?

On Tuesday, January 29, with Jackie and the children at Glen Ora, Jack called Mary Meyer to the White House. When she arrived, he reiterated what he'd told her on the phone. Mary was now confused because, as it turned out, not one reporter wrote about Phil Graham's speech. Or, as Katharine Graham wrote, "Those who witnessed this sorry spectacle seem only to have talked among themselves. As with other outrageous behavior by noted or known persons in those days, the incident was hushed up and not reported." But that didn't matter, Jack told Mary. They really were over.

About a month later, on February 20, invitations went out for a dinner dance at the White House honoring Eugene R. Black, president of the World Bank Group. Jackie didn't have a chance to review the guest list until March 6, but there, at the bottom, was Mary's name. She was upset about it. When she confronted Jack, he said he had no idea why she'd been included. He hadn't invited her. He suspected Evelyn Lincoln had just copied the names from a previous guest list. Jackie said she wanted Jack to disinvite her, but Jack felt it unwise. They had been lucky enough to escape scrutiny when no one reported the Phil Graham spectacle, he didn't now want some reporter to notice Mary's name crossed off a guest list and start asking questions. He decided to have Evelyn Lincoln call her and invite her, instead, to the after-party dance. At least Jackie wouldn't have to sit at a table with her. Ms. Lincoln did so, and explained to Mary that the Eugene Blacks had invited too many people to the dinner.

The night of March 8 was freezing cold and snowy as guests showed up to the White House for the dinner and dance. Despite the chilly temperature, Mary Meyer showed up in a summery-looking dress with, as was often the case, more than sufficient décolletage. This was the first time she would be seen at the White House since the Phil Graham spectacle, so one might've imagined her wanting to be a little less conspicuous in case any of the press there knew about it. She was on the arm of Jack's friend Blair Clark, a political activist and journalist who now worked as a general manager for CBS News; he had been on the scene when Jack first met Judy Campbell in Las Vegas.

Just after midnight, Jack had a private conversation with Mary, during which he apparently again told her it was over between them and that she should no longer expect to be invited to the White House. Already a little tipsy, Mary became emotional and actually fled the White House in tears, and with no coat. For ninety minutes, Blair Clark couldn't find her. Meanwhile, as all of this was happening, Jackie had a completely uncharacteristic conversation with Adlai Stevenson.

While it doesn't sound like her to be quite so candid with a colleague of Jack's, if one is to believe what he later wrote in a letter dated March 10 to Marietta Tree, who worked on the UN Commission on Human Rights, Stevenson claimed Jackie told him, "I don't care how many girls Jack sleeps with as long as I know he knows it's wrong, and I think he does now. Anyway, that's all over for the present." Would Jackie have said such a thing about her husband to Adlai Stevenson? The only reason it seems possible is because Stevenson claimed she made the comment on the pivotal night of March 8, when she knew for sure that Mary Meyer was being relegated to the past.

Finally, Mary reappeared at the White House, chilled to the bone, the bottom third of her dress wet from the icy snow. Because it seemed obvious to him that she was making a scene, Jack stayed clear of her. She and her date lingered a while longer as Clark tried to warm her with his own coat and a hot drink. Finally, Jackie summoned a car for them. It showed up at the North Portico at about two o'clock in the morning.

It was a serene, peaceful night and blessedly quiet with just ambient street noise in the distance. The water splashing from the fountain was the most noticeable sound. By now, the sky was a cloudless arc of black velvet sprinkled with stars. Jack and Jackie could actually see their breath as they stood in the middle of the portico's eight stately white columns. Above them was the famous neoclassical lantern hanging by four heavy metal fetters. Everything was lit by bright spotlights, giving the scene a sheen that could only be described as cinematic as Mary and Blair got into their car. Then, in that magical setting, the president and First Lady stood and waved goodbye and—as far as Jackie was concerned, anyway—good riddance to Mary Meyer.

HISTORIC SPEECHES

A man in President John Kennedy's position could only spend so much time dwelling on self-reflection. Something about it felt self-indulgent, as if an affront to the consideration of real problems going on in the real world. President Eisenhower once privately said, "A man has to give himself up to be president. Not a lot of what he thinks or does matters unless it has to do with the welfare of those who put him in charge. Everything else waits." Jack was in the midst of sorting out a lot of personal inventory by 1963, but that didn't mean the business of running the country and being concerned about the world around it could wait for his attention.

After the Cuban Missile Crisis, Kennedy and Khrushchev both realized how incredibly close they'd come to nuclear war. As Kennedy said in a White House meeting, "It's insane that two men sitting on opposite sides of the world should be able to decide to bring an end to civilization." Khrushchev had to agree with the sentiment. "The two most powerful nations had been squared off against each other," he said, "each with its finger on the button. You'd have thought that war was inevitable. But both sides showed that if the desire to avoid war is strong enough, even the most pressing dispute can be solved by compromise." With private correspondence between the two world leaders reopened, they revived their dialogue on banning nuclear testing.

Once he was sure of the mutual commitment to this dialogue, Jack announced the new round of high level arms negotiations in a commencement address at American University in Washington on June 10, famously known today as the "Peace Speech."

Some say that it is useless to speak of world peace or world law or world disar-
-mament, and that it will be useless until the leaders of the Soviet Union adopt a
more enlightened attitude. I hope they do. I believe we can help them do it. But
I also believe that we must reexamine our own attitude as individuals and as a
nation, for our attitude is as essential as theirs.

Jack said he sought "a treaty to outlaw nuclear tests," to better the
chances not just for America's safety, but for that of the rest of the world.
He vowed that the U.S. wouldn't conduct nuclear tests in the atmosphere
as long as other nations agreed to do the same. While this wasn't a formal
binding treaty, it was at least a step in the right direction toward general and
complete disarmament. Bobby called it "one of Jack's biggest moves." Indeed, the speech generated worldwide attention; Khrushchev even allowed
it to be rebroadcast throughout Russia and published in the controlled Moscow press.

A month later, on July 25, the United States and Soviet Union agreed to
ban testing in the atmosphere, in space, and underwater. The next day, in a
television address announcing the agreement, Kennedy claimed that a limited
test ban "is safer by far for the United States than an unlimited nuclear arms
race." The Limited Nuclear Test Ban Treaty would be signed in Moscow on
August 5, 1963, the eve of the eighteenth anniversary of the atomic bomb-
ing of Hiroshima. If ratified by the U.S. Senate, this promised to be a huge
achievement for the Kennedy administration. Jack was pessimistic about its
ratification, though, given that most senators had yet to announce their support and the public's response seemed muted. There was a pervasive feeling
the treaty might somehow threaten national security and maybe even invite a
Soviet attack. People were still afraid.

From a political standpoint, if the Senate rejected the treaty it would be
a real blow to Jack's presidency and threaten a second term. However, the
Senate approved the treaty on September 23, 1963, by an 80–19 margin. The
Limited Test Ban Treaty would then be ratified on October 7 and entered
into force three days later. This was a huge accomplishment for the Kennedy
administration, arguably the biggest triumph of the president's three years in
office, alongside the settling of the Cuban Missile Crisis. Finding a way to end
the Cold War once and for all was now a goal Kennedy set for his second term,
and he knew the treaty was a big step forward in that regard. "Today, the fear
is a little less and the hope is a little better," he said. "With our courage and

understanding enlarged by this achievement, let us press onward in quest of man's essential desire for peace."

Also in the summer of 1963, the president visited Germany, Ireland, and England. Ireland, in particular, meant a lot to him given his ancestry. The response to him on this trip proved beyond a doubt that he was a stronger and more respected leader than ever before, an international figure who, before the eyes of the world, had slowly but surely grown into his presidency.

Lem Billings went on that trip with Jack. As he took his place on Air Force One, he noticed empty seats all around him. "Some of the Secret Service agents didn't want to sit next to the guy because he was gay," recalled agent Larry Newman. "Terrible, yes, but that's the way it was back then. I mean, if you want the honest truth, those were the times. The guys were like, no way. We're not sitting next to Lem Billings. Sorry."

Of the visit to Germany, Lem once recalled, "I'm sure this was one of the high points of the president's life as far as a personal feeling of accomplishment. I don't know in history whether there'd been anything like that before. The real excitement about a man and the fantastic adoration of a man. Of course, he was realistic enough to know it wasn't himself as much as it was that he represented the United States. He was the leader of the powerful country in favor of keeping Berlin free. But whatever the reasons were, it was a hell of an experience to witness the acclaim of a multitude of that size. You couldn't possibly have squeezed another person into that square. The sound of human voices all roaring 'KEN-NE-DY' at the same time was almost deafening. He was certainly overcome. We all were."

President Kennedy's speech that June 26 would most certainly be another one for the history books. Prior to this moment, he'd held his fire where the Berlin Wall was concerned. Now, he would make clear his opposition in his speech, widely known as "Ich bin ein Berliner," which translates to "I am a Berliner," his way of denoting solidarity with West Berliners and condemning the Soviet Union and the Berlin Wall:

> *There are many people in the world who really don't understand, or say they don't, what is the great issue between the free world and the Communist world. Let them come to Berlin. There are some who say that Communism is the wave of the future. Let them come to Berlin. And there are some who say in Europe and elsewhere we can work with the Communists. Let them come to Berlin. And there are even a few who say that it is true that Communism is an evil system, but it permits us*

to make economic progress. Lass' sie nach Berlin kommen. *Let them come to Berlin. . . . Freedom has many difficulties and democracy is not perfect, but we have never had to put a wall up to keep our people in to prevent them from leaving us. All free men, wherever they may live, are citizens of Berlin and, therefore, as a free man, I take pride in the words,* 'Ich bin ein Berliner.'"

The Berlin Wall would remain in place until November 9, 1989, two and a half years after President Ronald Reagan gave his famous speech on June 12, 1987:

General Secretary Gorbachev, if you seek peace, if you seek prosperity for the Soviet Union and Eastern Europe, if you seek liberalization: Come here to this gate! Mr. Gorbachev, open this gate! Mr. Gorbachev, tear down this wall!

———————

By Wednesday, August 7, President Kennedy was back at the White House and chairing a meeting in the Cabinet Room about the Nuclear Test Ban Treaty. At about noon, he walked into Evelyn Lincoln's office while she was on the phone with someone from his household staff on Squaw Island. He heard Evelyn ask with alarm, "But why did she go to Otis?" She then put her hand on the receiver and told Jack that someone had just told her Jackie had been airlifted to the hospital at Otis Air Force Base in Falmouth, Massachusetts. While the plan had always been for her to give birth at Walter Reed Hospital in Washington, in case of an emergency a suite had been readied for her at Otis, and now she was headed there. Evelyn said she was still trying to figure out exactly what was going on.

Jack was alarmed. "It's too early," he exclaimed. He then picked up a phone and called his air force aide, Godfrey McHugh, to ask how long it might take to arrange a flight for him to get to his wife. Air Force One was being serviced, he was told, and LBJ was using the backup plane. Therefore, it would take thirty minutes to arrange a Lockheed Jetstar. "I want to fly right now, so get it ready," Jack told him.

At that point, Dr. Janet Travell called to confirm to Jack that Jackie had, indeed, been rushed to the hospital. "How about the baby?" Jack asked her.

"Fifty-fifty," was her response.

"That's it," he declared as he hung up. "We've got to get to Otis. Now!"

PART VIII

Patrick

CUT TO THE BONE

On the flight out of Washington en route to Maryland, the president was contemplative, not wanting to talk, worried. "He kept sitting and staring out of the window," recalled Jackie's press agent Pamela Turnure, who accompanied him, "and obviously his thoughts were completely with Jackie, and it was a very quiet trip, getting there as soon as possible." Jack had told Turnure that he and Jackie had already decided that if the baby was a boy, they'd name him Patrick Bouvier after Jack's grandfather and Jackie's father.

When Jack finally arrived at Otis at about 1:30 P.M., Jackie's obstetrician Dr. John Walsh told him that the baby had been born. He was a boy suffering from "hyaline membrane disease," now known as "neonatal respiratory distress syndrome," common among premature infants. At just four pounds, ten and a half ounces, the infant's survival was in question. In light of Patrick's frail condition, Jack decided Jackie should see him and had their son wheeled into her room in the incubator. As Jack and an attending physician watched, the crying mother placed her hands in the portholes of the isolette and adjusted her infant's blanket. She held his hand. The physician then told her the baby would have to be transferred to Boston for more specialized care, without giving many details. "Don't forget, John was premature," Jack told her. "He was in an incubator, too, and look at him today."

Janet Auchincloss and her daughter Janet Jr. arrived at the hospital just as the president and physician were leaving Jackie's room with the baby. "Jack!" Janet exclaimed when she spotted him. As she rushed to him, he reached out for an embrace. She took him in her arms. "Jack, please let me see him," she begged, pulling away. As she leaned over the incubator to gaze at the fragile baby, she became faint. Reaching out to steady her, Jack told her he was sure Patrick would be fine. "I've got to go and make plans to get him to Boston," he said.

"Where's Rose?" Janet asked. "Will she be coming?"

Jack said he had no idea where his mother was, possibly in Europe.

"But she knew Jackie was almost due," Janet said.

Jack nodded, thanked her for being with him, and then rushed off. As he did so, Janet Jr. suddenly had a thought and called out. "Jack! What if something happens to the baby in Boston and Jackie hears about it on the television?"

Jack nodded, turned around, and said, "Good thought."

"At just that moment, an air force medic happened to be walking by," recalled Secret Service agent Larry Newman. "'What do you know about televisions?' the president asked him. He said all he knew for sure was how to turn one on and off. When the president told him of their concern, the medic promised to handle it. I later heard he slipped into the First Lady's room, pried the back off the TV as she slept, and broke one of the tubes with a screwdriver."

The next day, Thursday, August 8, Jack and Janet waited at Boston Children's Hospital as doctors worked on Patrick. It was decided to place the infant in a hyperbaric chamber in hopes that the pressurized oxygen might assist his breathing. Janet later recalled, "I remember Jack saying to me in the hospital in Boston that day, when Patrick was in the little incubator and then before we went down in the iron lung room, which they tried as a last resort, I remember his saying to me, 'Nothing must happen to Patrick because I just can't bear to think of the effect it might have on Jackie.' I could see the effect it might have on him, too." It should be noted that Patrick was placed in a hyperbaric chamber, not an iron lung, as Janet had said. They were two different kinds of equipment that basically did the same thing in terms of oxygen transmission.

While Jack's sisters, Jean and Eunice, stayed behind to be with Jackie at Otis, Jack and Janet spent the night at Children's Hospital. Janet had just started to fall asleep when, at about four in the morning, she awakened with a start, sensing something was wrong. She got out of bed and padded into the hall, where she saw Bobby hugging Jack. As she struggled to come to grips with what she knew was happening, she leaned against the wall. She then watched as Jack cried and walked off, his brother's arm slung around him: "I remember thinking to myself, *Oh, my God. No. Please God.*" In her oral history for the JFK Library, Janet added, "The doctors released Patrick from the lines and tubes, and President Kennedy was able to hold his son in his arms for the first and last time. That was the one time I saw Jack genuinely cut to the bone."

"After he dressed, the president found a boiler room, a storage place for the hospital's furnace and other mechanical equipment," recalled Larry Newman. "He slipped inside, closed the door, and wept. We could hear him crying on the other side of the door."

On Saturday, August 10, the Kennedys and Auchinclosses attended the Roman Catholic funeral for Patrick Bouvier Kennedy in the residence chapel of Cardinal Richard Cushing. Jackie, still in the hospital at Otis and in no condition to be released, wasn't able to attend the service. According to what she later remembered, Jack had fallen to his knees, sobbing at her bedside upon telling her of the tragic news. She barely knew how to react. Her shock over Patrick combined with Jack's outward display of emotion had been almost more than she could bear. "There's just one thing I couldn't stand," she whispered to him. "If I ever lost you."

Rose wasn't at the funeral. As Jack had anticipated, she was in Paris. Neither was Joe, who was too debilitated to attend. All of Jack's siblings and their spouses (except for Peter Lawford, who was in Los Angeles) were present. His mother-in-law, Janet, was present with her daughters Lee and Janet Jr., as Hugh stood with Jamie. "The casket was closed, just as the president had directed," recalled Larry Newman. "He opened it slightly to slip a money clip into it which was fashioned from a St. Christopher's medal the First Lady had given him at their wedding."

"When the casket was closed again, Jack was so overwhelmed, he just folded himself over it and wouldn't leave," Janet Auchincloss recalled. "My heart broke. I'll never get over it."

Cardinal Cushing tried to restrain the grieving father, who now had one arm around the small casket, unwilling to let it go. "Come on, Jack. Let's go," the priest told him. "Let's go. God is good. Nothing more can be done for Patrick. Death is not the end, it's the beginning." Janet's son Jamie, who was sixteen at the time, recalled, "That triggered us all to tears. I told Daddy, 'It's so unfair. Why do these things have to happen?' This was my first experience with death. Daddy looked at me sadly and, with a choked voice, said, 'It's not our place to question God. It's our place to be there for your sister when she gets out of the hospital. That's our place.'"

Patrick Bouvier Kennedy was buried that August 10 in a family plot in Brookline, Massachusetts, at the Holyhood Cemetery, purchased by Joseph P. Kennedy before his stroke. Little Patrick was among the earliest members of the Kennedy family interred there.

SOME CHANGES ARE FOR GOOD

Jack Kennedy was known by friends and family to be a stoic person, like all Kennedys. That's why so many people in his life were so surprised by his depth of feeling at the death of his son. It was as if something in him had opened up. By 1963, he really was a different man than the one who hadn't even attended Arabella's funeral. Few, other than his wife, had been privy to the changes in his character that had slowly taken place over the last seven years. For instance, his private emotional state during the Bay of Pigs and Cuban Missile Crisis, and the tears he'd shed during those agonizing times, were known mostly only to Jackie and, sometimes, Bobby. With Patrick's death, his outpouring of genuine grief understandably surprised them. "I felt he was not only weeping for Patrick but for Arabella, too, and maybe even for himself and for Jackie," said Jamie Auchincloss. "It was very moving. I felt so much for him. I think it was the first time I saw Jack's true humanity, and I never forgot it."

At this same time, Jack continued to grapple with his own mortality. He had often questioned God's choices and was now doing so once again. "He couldn't understand how God could take Patrick, and what it meant in terms of his own life," said agent Larry Newman, who remained at Jack's side after the funeral. "How had he managed to escape so many scrapes, yet his son was taken from him? And how does one go on after such a tragedy?"

The night of Patrick's funeral, Jack had a heartfelt and memorable conversation with a most unlikely confessor, his twenty-seven-year-old sister-in-law Joan Kennedy. She would prove to be pivotal and helpful. Ted married the blond, blue-eyed beauty Joan Bennett from Bronxville in 1958. Jack had always admired her, called her "the Dish" because of her great beauty, and saw her as an underdog when compared to the other women in the family. Joan, like Jackie, had a difficult time fitting in but, unlike Jackie, longed to be accepted. However, the way Ted treated her in their marriage rivaled Jack's sometimes callous treatment of Jackie.

Dave Powers, who was with Jack at Squaw Island, recalled, "The first night after the funeral, it was Joan who sat with the president for a long time just to talk. There was no religious orthodoxy. No talk about how Patrick was in heaven, but rather just warm, human, simple talk."

As Jack and Joan chatted in the parlor, Dave Powers and Larry Newman heard her say there was no explanation as to what had happened to Patrick. "I'm not like Ethel," she said, "so, I don't know that all things happen for a reason. I just know that things happen, and when they do we have to somehow go on." She told him she knew they had the strength to continue despite any adversity that came their way. "It's in every one of us," she said, "that strength, which is our birthright."

Jack choked back tears as he told Joan he felt he was now being punished. Surprised, Joan asked him to explain. He said he'd made some big mistakes along the way that he believed had caused God to now take retribution on him. "I haven't been the best husband, and it's very painful," he told her, "and by painful, I mean shameful."

Joan said she didn't believe that was God's nature. "Think about it," she said. "What has Jackie ever done to deserve God's punishment?" She insisted that God loved them no matter what, and that he was also, above all, a forgiving God.

"I just want to stop lying to the people I love," Jack said.

At that, she took his hands. "You might be the one to break the cycle, Jack," she told him. He didn't have to ask what she meant. He knew. Could he really change, and would it last? "Yes," she said, "some changes are for good." The double meaning of her words was perhaps unintentional, but profound just the same, and it didn't escape him. He smiled and nodded, tears in his eyes.

"The president said he wasn't sure what would happen next," recalled Larry Newman, "but he was happy Joan was with him in that moment. 'We stick it out,' she told him. 'That's what family does.' Then, she added, 'You're the president. You can make a difference so that maybe what happened to little Patrick won't happen to other babies.'"

"Jack was deeply moved," concluded Dave Powers. "Joan left at eleven that night. He walked with her out to the driveway. 'You know,' he told me when he returned to the house, 'she's such a great girl, that Joansie is. I admire her so much.'"

Maybe because it had come from such an unlikely source, Jack was inspired by what Joan Kennedy had to say to him that night. According to her, the two had never had such a heartfelt, intimate conversation, and never would again. It meant a lot to both of them. Later, President Kennedy signed into law a large grant authorizing $265 million (about $2 billion in today's money) to be used primarily for newborn research. The grant would be sponsored by the National Institute of Child Health and Human Development, which was strongly supported by Jack and Eunice.

PART IX

Vietnam . . . and Beyond

GROWING PROBLEMS AT HOME
AND ABROAD

O n Monday, August 19, 1963, President Kennedy, still shaken and upset over Patrick, returned to work at the White House, leaving Jackie at Squaw Island under the care of the family nurse Luella Hennessey. Jackie was struggling, having fallen into the deepest of depressions. There seemed no way to ease her pain, both physical and emotional. She was cold one moment, hot the next, dizzy the next, and vomiting shortly after that, all of it brought on by the undiagnosed anxiety from which she'd been suffering since 1955. As a leader with a full slate of pressing responsibilities, Jack had to figure out how to juggle those duties while also making sure his wife was being properly cared for. It wasn't easy, especially since he, too, was grieving. Still, there was work to do. There was always work to do.

Atop JFK's concerns at this time was the escalating crisis in Vietnam. He had long been concerned about its growing unrest, going all the way back to 1951, when he and Bobby went on their fact-finding tour of the Middle East and Asia. While he was in Saigon, Jack was heavily influenced by a man working for the State Department, Edmund Gullion, who'd prove vitally important in helping him understand the complexities of the crises in Laos and Vietnam (and who Jack would recruit into his White House in 1961 as ambassador to the Republic of the Congo). With Gullion's help, Jack came to believe that only a truly independent Vietnamese government had any chance of survival.

When the French surrendered in 1954, Vietnam was divided in two with Ho Chi Minh ruling the Communist North and Ngo Dinh Diem the independent South. With the passing of the years, Kennedy found Eisenhower and Nixon's policies relating to Vietnam and Algeria, the first a former French colony, the second a French colony seeking independence, shortsighted and he gave one of his most controversial speeches on the Senate floor in 1957, specifically criticizing their administration's strategies. Now that he was in office, Jack was determined to find a way to contain what seemed like an inevitable conflict between North and South Vietnam, one he feared might end up involving the U.S. He had always been cautious about the U.S. staying out of Vietnam. He was as clear about it as he'd been about not sending troops into Cuba during both the Bay of Pigs and the Cuban Missile Crisis. Here, he was his father's son, once again. Just as Joe would not have endorsed the idea of sending troops to fight and to die in Vietnam, neither would Jack.

Every time President Kennedy approved any increased military aid to the Ngo Dinh Diem regime, he did so under pressure. In the spring of 1961, the Joint Chiefs of Staff urged him to send thousands of combat troops to Vietnam. Instead, he opted to increase the number of "military advisers"— U.S. personnel assigned to train South Vietnamese forces. While JFK was willing to provide aid and training, he was determined not to directly commit American forces to fight South Vietnam's war.

JFK actually respected Ngo Dinh Diem, a fellow Catholic, and felt he'd held his country together and maintained its independence under the worst of circumstances. The problem, though, was that the beleaguered Diem was becoming increasingly corrupt, influenced by his sinister brother, Nhu, and sister-in-law, Tran Le Xuan—South Vietnam's de facto First Lady, known as Madam Nhu. She was vindictive, power-hungry, and dangerous.

Fighting Communist guerrillas was one thing, but when Nhu and Madam Nhu began endorsing attacks on Buddhist monks with hand grenades, that was unconscionable. Soon, police raided Buddhist pagodas, some killed, others arrested, while religious monuments were destroyed. As Diem declared martial law, imposed a curfew, and closed airports, the unrest that had been festering for a long time quickly escalated. After an elderly monk doused himself with gasoline and set himself on fire to protest Diem's repressive policies, Madam Nhu referred to him as a "barbecue." *"Jesus Christ!"* Jack shouted as he bolted from the Situation Room after seeing a photograph of the monk engulfed in flames. How could the United States support such barbaric behavior?

Jack now felt that his having increased the number of military advisers in the region had been a mistake. He told Mike Mansfield he intended to bring them home at the end of 1964 after he was reelected. He feared that if he made any big moves now, he'd be under such fire from conservatives it might actually cost him that election. He *had* to be reelected, he said, otherwise whichever Republican got into the Oval Office after him would most certainly commit American combat troops to South Vietnam and drag the United States into war. He had no doubt about it. "We'd better make damn sure I *am* reelected," he concluded.

ONASSIS

On Wednesday, August 21, the president was in meetings at the White House when Luella Hennessey called to tell him the First Lady wasn't doing well. She felt he should return to Squaw Island immediately. Jack agreed to leave Washington that afternoon, after having been there for just two days. His sudden decision was confusing to some of his advisers because he rarely left Washington for Squaw Island in the middle of the week. Especially given the Vietnam crisis at hand, they found it a little perplexing. However, Jack said he needed to be with Jackie and his children, and that was the end of it for him. He was definitely prioritizing his wife and family.

That Saturday, Jack's friend the artist William Walton showed up at Squaw Island to visit for the weekend. He later recalled "a deep, very deep sense of sadness in the household" and said, "The weather was terrible and we were locked up in the house. Jack and I spent hours in his study as he read condolence letters and cards and talked about how to respond to each. 'Look at what the Pope wrote,' he'd say, giving it equal weight to a card from some housewife in Minnesota. He seemed distracted and not himself, completely unable to focus on anything."

When Bill and Jack went sailing, Rose came by the house and found Jackie sitting on the stairs crying, her head in her hands. Alarmed, she called Janet and told her she believed Jackie should never be alone while Jack was in Washington. She felt she now needed round-the-clock supervision. Janet agreed and quickly decided Jackie should spend a couple of months with her and Hugh, possibly through Christmas. The problem, however, was that Hammersmith Farm in Newport was ordinarily closed for the season on October 1, and there wasn't ample security at the Auchinclosses' new

Georgetown residence to protect the First Lady. Therefore, they'd probably have to keep Hammersmith open, which meant extending the agreements of the household staff through the winter. That promised to be costly. Rose, however, offered to pay for the entire staff, a generous offer from a woman generally known to be parsimonious.

In the midst of this family discussion, Jackie's sister, Lee, sent a telegram to Jack, which he received on August 24. She had another idea: What if Jackie vacationed with her and the Greek industrialist Aristotle Onassis?

At this time, Lee was having an affair with Onassis. "Because she was in such a high-profile marriage to Stas, a beloved public figure and father of her two children, the Kennedys were worried about how, if discovered, this thing with Onassis might impact Jack's reelection chances," said Lee's good friend Taki Theodoracopulos. At the time, Taki was a tennis pro but he'd go on to become a popular entertainment columnist. "I know the president asked the First Lady if there was any chance that they were wrong and that Lee's relationship with Onassis was only platonic," he continued. "When Jackie asked her mother what she thought, Janet was clear. 'Don't be ridiculous,' she said. 'Men and women cannot be friends.'"

Besides the family's disapproval of Onassis, there was also some complicated illegal business having to do with a fleet of ships he'd purchased from the U.S. government, an imbroglio that set him back $7 million in fines. That was just the tip of the iceberg, Bobby Kennedy felt, as he searched for other ways to bring the mogul down. Again, from Taki: "Lee told me, 'My God. The Kennedys are in such an uproar about me and Ari and'—this was very much like her—'I love it because, finally, these people are paying some attention to me instead of to my sainted sister.'"

After he got her telegram, the president called Lee in Athens to hear her out. She said she thought the cruise would do Jackie a lot of good, away from prying eyes, where she'd be able to recuperate on the high seas.

"What about Stas?" he asked.

"He's going, too, of course," was Lee's response.

Jack thought that was odd; however, he wasn't about to question the parameters of anyone else's marriage. After he discussed it with Jackie, the cruise was set for October.

LOSING CONTROL OF HIS GOVERNMENT

It was in the summer of 1963, while still swamped with grief over the death of his son and struggling to take care of his wife, that President John Kennedy would lose control of his government, and the ramifications of his missteps at this time would reverberate for years to come.

On Saturday, August 24, while the president was at Squaw Island with his family, Vietnamese generals sent word to the White House asking where the administration might stand if they decided to remove Diem's brother, Nhu, from government. Because Nhu had been largely responsible for the campaign against the Buddhists, Averell Harriman, who was undersecretary of state and who'd proven himself to Jack during his negotiations with Khrushchev on the limited nuclear testing ban a month earlier, agreed with Roger Hilsman, assistant for Far Eastern affairs, that the U.S. should move against him immediately. Michael Forrestal, deputy national security adviser, telephoned Jack at Squaw Island to get his approval of a cable—which was later to be known as Cable 243—to be sent to Henry Cabot Lodge Jr., Jack's U.S. ambassador to South Vietnam.

Many historians would later view JFK's appointment that summer of his former political rival Henry Cabot Lodge as one of the biggest mistakes of his administration. Lodge had lost his Senate race to JFK in 1952. He then served as Eisenhower's ambassador to the United Nations before joining Richard Nixon's losing ticket in 1960. He wasn't Jack's first choice. He'd originally wanted his friend and ally Edmund Gullion, who'd long held the opinion that the U.S. should stay out of Vietnam. However, Secretary of

State Dean Rusk disagreed vehemently about Gullion. Jack's first mistake? Listening to Dean. All these years later, it's difficult to understand why he didn't either stand up to Rusk or find someone for the job who wasn't such a historical Republican adversary. Bobby knew it, too, and he warned Jack. Jack's second big mistake? Not listening to Bobby. Instead, he went forward with Lodge. As it would turn out, Lodge had a mind of his own, and the president would be hard-pressed to control him.

The language of the cable Michael Forrestal wanted to send to Henry Cabot Lodge was quite clear:

> *US Government cannot tolerate situation in which power lies in Nhu's hands. Diem must be given chance to rid himself of Nhu and his coterie and replace them with best military and political personalities available. If, in spite of your efforts, Diem remains obdurate and refuses, then we must face the possibility that Diem himself cannot be preserved.*

If Diem refused to remove Nhu, the cable went on:

> *You may also tell appropriate military commanders we will give them direct support in any interim period of breakdown central government mechanism.*

This was huge. If the president signed off on the sending of this telegram, he'd effectively be signing off on a military coup d'état, because there was simply no way Diem was going to turn on his own brother. This was a problem that couldn't have landed on Jack's desk at a worse time. Not only was he still distraught to the point of distraction that weekend about his lost son and traumatized wife, much of his cabinet wasn't available to him, and that included Dean Rusk, Robert McNamara, McGeorge Bundy, and CIA director John McCone. All of them were away from the office for the weekend, though Jack was able to have a phone call with Bundy. Running the ship in Washington was a small faction who favored the toppling of Diem and Nhu, and that included Averell Harriman, Roger Hilsman, and Michael Forrestal.

Jack wondered why the cable couldn't wait until Monday when the important players—including himself—were set to return to the White House. Forrestal insisted the situation was too volatile; the telegram needed to go out right away. "Fine. Go see what you can do to get it cleared," Jack said, "starting with McCone." Jack probably wanted Forrestal to go to CIA director John McCone, who he'd appointed to replace Allen Dulles after the Bay of Pigs fiasco, because he knew McCone favored Diem and probably wouldn't approve the telegram.

There's no way to look at what happened next other than as yet another betrayal of the president comparable to the Bay of Pigs. Basically, Michael Forrestal went about the business of contacting other senior officials who, in turn, approved of the cable but with the misunderstanding—or, maybe better stated, the *false impression given to them by Forrestal*—that their colleagues had also signed off on it, and that so had the president! For instance, Forrestal called Roswell Gilpatric and told him the president and Dean Rusk approved of sending the telegram, which was definitely not true. But Gilpatric said he wasn't going to be the only one to dissent, so what did he do? He signed off on it.

After more calls with more people who had been similarly misled, Michael Forrestal called Jack to tell him that the measure had been roundly approved by all of the important parties. Jack then gave him the go-ahead to send the cable, which CIA director John McCone had never approved, either. It turned out he, too, was out of town. His deputy director of plans, Richard Helms, a CIA careerist who also wanted Diem out, approved it instead.

Making important decisions while reeling from loss is never wise. It would certainly seem that this is what President Kennedy was doing that fateful summer. It would also seem there were people in his cabinet who understood he was off his game, and exploited it to achieve their hidden agenda. "What was particularly unfortunate was that Jack had really admired Michael Forrestal," Chuck Spalding noted. "Ordinarily, he had a suspicion of the motives of anyone who was particularly zealous. The more excited they were, the more suspicious he became. Unfortunately, he [Jack] didn't realize Forrestal had become one of the zealots about whom he was usually so cynical."

After Jack sailed with the family on the *Honey Fitz* that day, the cable went out on Saturday night, August 24, 1963. In that moment, the president of the United States had effectively authorized a coup.

At one point in his blinding grief, Jack had even told Henry Cabot Lodge he'd leave the entire Vietnam situation "in your hands." He rescinded that offer later, but the damage was done. Lodge now felt *he* was in charge, not the president. The day after Cable 243 went out, Jack got a telegram from Lodge advising him to take things even further. Since Diem would likely not turn on his brother, Lodge suggested they take their demands directly to renegade generals. He said the U.S.'s position should now be that it would accept Diem without Nhu, but it would be up to the generals as to how to deal with Diem, whether to keep him in power or not. In other words, Lodge had his own ideas about how to do things, and they were a lot more aggressive than what he'd originally outlined in the cable! Jack had given his arrogant ambassador the proverbial inch and he took a mile. Now, the mission was geared not only to get Nhu out of power, but Diem, too.

At noon on Monday afternoon, with the president now back at the White House, there was a lot of infighting and finger-pointing about Cable 243, and whether or not it ever should've been sent. Dean Rusk, Robert Mc-Namara, and others, including chairman of the Joint Chiefs of Staff General Maxwell Taylor—who hadn't even seen the text of the telegram until after it was sent—felt the president had been utterly duped by the Michael Forrestal contingent, and now Henry Cabot Lodge was making things even worse. Vice President Lyndon Johnson, who had met with Diem in South Vietnam in 1961 as Jack's emissary, was also against the action. How had this happened? "My God," Jack exploded. "This shit has got to stop. My government's coming apart!" When Forrestal offered to resign, Kennedy shot back, "You're not worth firing. You owe me something."

The arguments would continue for the next two weeks with Jack now fearing he'd made a big mistake. Could he call it off? Henry Cabot Lodge told him he couldn't, saying, "We are launched on a course from which there's no turning back." Jack said he still felt that, as president, he had the right to "change course and reverse previous instructions." Lodge said that if the generals in Vietnam gave "the go signal," it would be out of Kennedy's hands. If and when they chose to proceed, there was nothing the U.S. could do about it. JFK *had* lost control.

"MY GOD! HOW SHE LOVES ME"

I am having something you can never have—the absence of tension—no newspapers every day to make me mad. I wish so much I could give you that—I never realized till I got to another country how the tension is—But I can't give you that. So I give you every day while I think of you—the only thing I have to give & I hope it matters to you . . . I miss you very much, which is nice though it is also a bit sad—because it is always best to leave someone when you are happy & this was such a lovely summer . . . but then I think of how lucky I am to miss you . . . I waited till 3 AM for your call—then they said it was an imposter . . . that happened again at 6 AM. I would love to talk to you—& if you have called & haven't gotten me please know I have waited 3 hours each time & then been told they "lost connection."

That was a letter Jackie had written to Jack a year earlier, in August 1962, when she and Lee were vacationing in Ravello, Italy. Its many pages of raw emotion had really made an impact on him. He kept it in his desk in the Oval Office and would pull it out from time to time and read it. "My God! How she loves me," Jack told one of his close friends. "And my God, how much she doesn't deserve me." He then quoted Abraham Lincoln: "Others have been made fools of by girls, but this can never be with truth said of me. I most emphatically, in this instance, made a fool of myself." When his friend suggested, "Tell Jackie how you feel," Jack asked him, "Why, after all these years, would she ever believe me?" That friend answered emphatically, "*Because she'd want to.*"

While there was still no resolution to the explosive situation in Vietnam, the president feared it was just a matter of time before it would turn deadly. Meanwhile, he'd try to enjoy his time with his wife and her family and seek to push everything else aside.

The first couple would celebrate their anniversary weekend at Hammersmith Farm in Newport and the news made all the papers. Janet sent Jamie out early that Thursday morning to fetch the *Newport Daily News,* which ran with the headline "Kennedys Come Home for Tenth Anniversary." On that same front page was a photograph of Madam Nhu, First Lady of South Vietnam, in Belgrade. At thirty-three, she was a year younger than Jackie and, according to the report, called for the president to stay out of the upheaval in South Vietnam. She said that if she came to America she wouldn't even visit him (not that he'd ever invite her) because "he's misinformed about the situation in South Vietnam and should get better information. He is a politician and when he hears loud opposition he tries to somehow appease it."

It certainly wasn't Madam Nhu Janet cared about, though. It was her daughter, who arrived in Newport looking sullen and still unwell. A special occasion was being planned, Janet reminded her. Couldn't Jackie at least *try* to be happy? "Jack will be here tonight," she said. "It's not how you feel that matters. It's how you look."

Jackie told her mother Jack had recently changed in some ways, and for the better. Still, while twisting her wedding band, she said she couldn't help but wonder if in six months' time he'd go back to being "the same old John Kennedy." When Jackie said, "I don't know that I can trust him," Janet gave her a sharp look and snapped, "Trust is for the weak." Quickly she seemed to realize her comment was less than helpful. Thinking better of it, she told her daughter that nobody understood better what she was going through than she, her mother, did. "Remember that," she said.

At seven o'clock that night, the president's helicopter landed on the stretch of beach in front of Hammersmith's main house. Everyone—Janet, Hugh, Jackie, Janet Jr., Jamie, and Yusha—gaily ran out to greet him. Also present was Sylvia Whitehouse Blake, wife of the American diplomat Robert Blake; she and Jackie had been Vassar classmates and she'd also been one of her bridesmaids. She recalled in 1998, "One could sense a distinct change in the president. I felt, and I discussed it later with Mrs. Auchincloss, that he was in a better state of mind, or at least he seemed more fascinated by his wife. Customarily, there had always been a formality between them, but now I saw him being much more affectionate, holding her hand, that sort of thing." Accompanying Jack were Ben and Tony Bradlee. Ben agreed with Sylvia in recalling that Jack greeted Jackie "with by far the most affectionate embrace we had ever seen them give each other. We wondered about it, figured it was because of Patrick but, looking back, I think maybe it was more than that."

Jack couldn't hide all of his emotions. Janet Auchincloss remembered a specific moment that perhaps spoke to his hypersensitivity at this time. When he landed at Quonset Point Naval Air Station on his way to Newport, he was met there by Rhode Island's governor John H. Chafee. In acknowledgment of Jack's wedding anniversary, Chafee presented him with a small silver bowl, inside of which was a card that read simply: "The Governor of Rhode Island." As the president walked from his chopper to the house, he handed Janet the bowl and, with annoyance, said, "Mummy, here's a present for you from the people of Rhode Island." Janet looked at it with confusion. "You can have it, if you want," he told her. "I don't want it. Don't you think it's a little strange for the governor to just hand me this bowl?" Janet later recalled for the JFK Library, "He couldn't get over it. He was really hurt by this gift being given to him with no card, no engraving on it, nothing. Not 'Congratulations and many happy returns on this anniversary from John,' or, 'John and Mary,' or anything else. I'm sure Governor Chafee didn't want to hurt his feelings, but it really was rather thoughtless, like sending someone flowers with nothing but a florist's card."

The evening of celebration would include dinner and then drinks in the Deck Room, specifically daiquiris prepared by Yusha. The conversation was lively, as usual. "That night, Jack brought up a whole lot of presents, really a wonderful collection," Janet remembered, "and he kept saying to Jackie, 'Now, you can only keep one. You have to choose.' Some of them were pictures and some of them were antique Greek and Italian bracelets and ancient Greek stones. They were all strewn about on the table in the Deck Room, and Jack was saying things like, 'Now, what do you think of this one? Do you realize this is a fourth-century BC . . . something?' or 'This is a sixteenth-century gold pair of earrings,' or whatever they were. He kept saying to her, teasing her, 'Now, don't forget, you can only keep one.'"

"I could see the present he wanted me to choose the most was this Alexandrian bracelet," Jackie later recalled. "It's a terribly simple, gold, sort of a snake, and it was the simplest thing of all and I could just see how he loved it by the way he'd hold it in his hand. So, you know, he wouldn't say which one he wanted to give me, but I could tell it was this one, so I chose it. He was delighted, and so was I."

That night, Janet and Hugh watched as Jack and Jackie walked along the shoreline holding hands. She put her head on his shoulder. He ran his hand through her hair. She then clung closely to him as he put his arm around her. Janet turned to Hugh and whispered, "My, my, my. It's finally happening."

PART X

Ticking Clock

THE QUESTION OF DALLAS

Jackie left for her Greek cruise with Aristotle Onassis and Lee Radziwill on October 1, 1963. Though she intended to be gone for just a week, she ended up not returning until October 17. By then, she seemed rested and much better. Jack had missed her. The weekend after her return, he again asked her to accompany him to Patrick's grave. But she said she was finally feeling better and was worried that it might set her back. He understood and agreed to go alone while she went on to Camp David with the children.

Before she left for Camp David, Jack told Jackie that when Texas Governor John Connally was in Washington recently, the two had discussed a quick campaign trip to Texas. At this time, Jack faced a significant battle in the southern states in his reelection bid because of his pending civil rights legislation. He really needed to go to Texas to be seen there and galvanize some support. At the same time, the conservative Connally was feuding with liberal Senator Ralph Yarborough, and there was real concern that the dispute could split the party. Connally vacillated on the wisdom of joining Kennedy in Texas because the governor was up for reelection in two years and he feared that being linked to Jack might jeopardize his reelection bid. However, if the visit had to happen, he suggested Jack bring Jackie with him. "The women want to see her," he said. "They want to see what her hairdo looks like and what her clothes look like. It's important to them."

While she'd made about a dozen trips with the president abroad, the First Lady hadn't accompanied him on any official domestic trips since his election. She had to think long and hard about how she felt about it. Her trepidation had to do with the feeling she'd once had at Jack's side in the days of his campaign for Senate. Back then, she'd felt invisible and unnecessary.

Now she realized the public had really grown to know and admire her. She recognized that she was now an integral part of a powerful political team, and she liked it and felt she could really contribute to it. Time was running out on Jack's first term, and it now made sense to look toward the second. She also needed a new challenge after Patrick, something interesting in her life to keep her mind off her sadness. Therefore, when she returned from Camp David, she told Jack she'd accompany him to Texas. Because it was to be a quick trip, she felt it would be a good testing ground for what was to come on the campaign trail.

On the morning of October 26, Jack was off to Amherst College for the groundbreaking ceremony of the Robert Frost Library. Meanwhile, Jackie took the children to the Kennedys' new summer home, which they'd just finished building in Atoka, Virginia. It was a four-bedroom yellow stucco house on forty acres of meadows along with large swaths of dusty riding trails. Despite the magnificent view of the Blue Ridge Mountains, Jack wasn't fond of the place. He was sometimes allergic to horses, always allergic to dogs, and brush was an issue for him as well. Even though he tolerated it all for Jackie's sake, it was still an annoyance. Jackie christened the place "Wexford" in honor of the county in Ireland from which the Kennedys had emigrated. Maybe she thought that might help Jack become more attached to it. It didn't. "I can only do so much," she told her mother. "If he doesn't like it, that's a shame, I suppose. But I'm okay with it. I like it and so do the children."

As soon as Jackie arrived at the home, Hugh called. He said he was alarmed after having heard that the president was going to Texas, and that Jackie would be accompanying him. He thought it was a bad idea. Just a day prior, Adlai Stevenson had been booed and spat on by protesters outside the Dallas Memorial Auditorium. "Not only weren't Kennedy's civil rights policy popular in the deep South, his efforts at nuclear disarmament were viewed by conservatives as being weak," noted George Christian, at the time Texas Governor John Connally's press secretary. "There were even editorials published in newspapers calling out Kennedy as a Communist. For any president, an abundance of caution is sensible when venturing into the lion's den, and Texas was definitely a real lion's den at that time."

"There's too much hate and extremism down there," Hugh told Jackie. He said he'd had no luck reaching Jack the day before, so he hoped she'd pass on his concern. Jackie confessed that the situation worried her, too. The night before, she and Jack had chatted about Texas with Franklin Roosevelt Jr. and his wife, Suzanne. Jackie said that the Roosevelts felt it wasn't safe and urged Jack to reconsider. However, Jackie also reminded Hugh of Jack's sinking poll numbers in the South, and of the fact that the JFK–Johnson ticket had only carried Texas by a little more than forty-five thousand votes in 1960. She felt they had no choice but to go. She'd talk to the Secret Service to make sure its agents were on high alert.

"I'm proud of you for going," Hugh told his stepdaughter, "but I fear you'll really hate it down there."

Jackie couldn't help but laugh. "Oh, Uncle Hughdie," she said, "I'm sure I'll hate every goddamn second of it."

Jackie also mentioned to Janet that she was rereading a book Jack had given her back when they were dating. It was *The Raven,* a biography of Sam Houston, the American general who played a prominent role in the Texas revolution, by Marquis James. She said she was just trying to "absorb Texas, I guess," and she thought the book might help put her in the mood for the trip. "I want to be excited to be there," Jackie said. "I think that's what the American people deserve from their First Lady."

On Sunday morning, October 20, Jack paid a visit to his father in Hyannis Port. That morning, he and Joe, who remained incapacitated, went out on the boat after having breakfast together. Afterward, Jack and Jackie took a stroll out onto the beach. As their neighbors Larry Newman and his wife, Sancy, watched, Jack took a bowl of water, a can of shaving cream, and a razor and placed them on a folding chair. He positioned a small mirror on the chair. Then, sitting in a similar chair in front of that makeshift setup, he began shaving his face under the hot sun. As he did so, Jackie knelt behind him and ran her fingers through his hair. "They appeared to be such a loving couple with not a care in the world," said Sancy Newman. "It was so lovely and so intimate, I was actually a little mesmerized by it."

"Goodbye, Dad," Jack told his father on Monday morning. The two were in Joe's second-floor bedroom, parting ways. While Jack left the room, Joe's nurse Rita Dallas wheeled her patient to the doors opening out onto the balcony so that he could watch his son's helicopter lift off. With the chopper revving up on the expansive lawn, Joe watched as Jack seemed to change his mind, turned around, and walked quickly back toward the house. Had he forgotten something?

Moments later, as Joe was still gazing out the window, Jack walked back into the bedroom. Rita Dallas saw him enter, his finger to his lips. He then lightly touched his father on the shoulder. "Look who's here, Dad," Jack said as Joe turned around, surprised. It was as if Jack just needed to see him one more time.

Jack kissed his father on the forehead and then, reaching down, took his hand, brought it up to the old man's shoulder, and held it tightly. "Goodbye, Dad," he again whispered, this time with a sad smile. Then, turning to the nurse, he added, "Mrs. Dallas, take good care of Dad till I get back."

She nodded at him. "Yes, Mr. President," she said. "I will do that."

But, no . . . he wouldn't be back.

DOUBLE MURDERS

In the early morning hours of Friday, November 1, 1963, President Kennedy received word that the long-anticipated and much-dreaded coup d'état in South Vietnam was underway. His repeated efforts to withdraw his approval of the rebellion had not amounted to much, especially given Henry Cabot Lodge's determination to see it through. Lately, Jack had a concern bigger than the coup itself. He'd become certain President Ngo Dinh Diem's own life was on the line.

In recent weeks, Jack had sent Torbert Macdonald to South Vietnam to warn Diem that his life was in danger. "Uncle Jack wanted to make direct contact with Diem but didn't want to use the embassy in Saigon because he felt he couldn't trust his people there, specifically Lodge," said Torbert Macdonald Jr. "He knew he could trust my father, who had no agenda except to help." There are no written records of Macdonald's visit to Saigon; it was completely secret. He bypassed the CIA, the State Department, and Henry Cabot Lodge, flying on military planes to Saigon instead of using commercial air, all to make the trip as covert as possible. His daughter, Laurie, who was in high school at the time, remembered, "Dad sent my brother, Brian, who is six years younger than me, a postcard which said something to the effect of, you'd better study hard and stay in school because, otherwise, I have a bad feeling you'll end up in this place, meaning fighting in Vietnam. He had a strong feeling Vietnam was going to become an endless war."

Being specific with the South Vietnamese president, Macdonald told him he had a message from the American president: "They're going to kill you. You've got to get out of here temporarily to seek refuge in the American embassy. You also have to get rid of your sister-in-law [Madame

Nhu] and your brother [Nhu]." However, upon his return, Torb told Jack of Diem, "He won't do it. He's too goddamn stubborn." Torbert Jr. recalled, "My father came back to the States discouraged about the whole thing. He felt Diem was living in a Catholic fantasy that God would protect him, he was safe and secure, and people loved him. Unfortunately, it wasn't true."

For two and a half hours that November 1, Jack paced the family quarters while worrying and waiting. He'd now decided that if the coup was inevitable, it'd better be successful and install a new government. If not, he feared not only for the region but also for how it would reflect on the United States and, specifically, his presidency. For Jackie, the scene was reminiscent of the Bay of Pigs, that other time Jack felt his presidency slipping away and believed he had only himself to blame. "Usually, I was so good about not asking questions," she recalled, "but then with all those flames on television and Diem and everything, I asked him something and he said, 'Oh, my God, kid,' which was, it sounds funny but I got used to it, a term of endearment his family used. He said, 'I've had that, you know, on me all day and I just . . . don't remind me of that all over again.' And I just felt so criminal."

While it was impossible to gauge who was winning the battle from television news reports about it, Jack sent word that he insisted the rebels guarantee the safety of Diem and his family. As the fighting raged on, he decided to send Jackie to Atoka and said he'd join her there on Saturday after attending the Army–Air Force football game (which, ultimately, he didn't attend). It now felt to her as if he wanted her out of his hair, the way it felt when he'd sent her away during the Cuban Missile Crisis. However, she didn't want to argue with him about it, especially knowing how much he had on his mind. It was All Saints' Day, a Holy Day of Obligation, and, with Jackie now gone, Jack went to Holy Trinity Church to pray for about a half hour.

That same night, Jack learned that Diem and his brother, Nhu, had surrendered and were in custody. But then, on Saturday morning, he woke up to the truly shocking news that both men had died by suicide by taking poison. He immediately disbelieved it. There was no way, he felt, a fellow Roman Catholic would kill himself. Terribly upset, he went down to the Cabinet Room at 9:30 for his morning briefing. As soon as he was seated, William Forrestal handed him Henry Cabot Lodge's latest telegram. It said Diem and Nhu had, in fact, not taken their own lives. They'd both been murdered. The coup succeeded in removing Diem and Nhu, but the immediate aftermath was chaotic, with no clear leadership in South Vietnam. Stunned, Jack leaped to his feet and rushed from the room. Maxwell Taylor said he had "a look of shock and dismay on his face which I have never seen before."

Jackie recalled, "When the coup came, Jack was just sick. When Diem was murdered, Jack was—oh, he had that awful look that he had at the time of the Bay of Pigs. He was just so wounded, and he was shaking his head and saying, 'Oh! No! Why?' He said Diem fought Communism for twenty years, and it shouldn't have ended like this. He was sick about it."

Madam Nhu, spared only because she happened to be in the U.S., now projected a terrible future for Vietnam and said that, because of the U.S.'s involvement in the coup, it was in for even greater problems. "I predict the story of Vietnam is only at its beginning, and that America will regret what will happen in years to come."

The failed coup was a disaster of epic proportions and the gravity of those events would reverberate for years to come in the region and throughout the world. Publicly, it was a disaster for the president. At this same time, he was also about to enter a new chapter in his private life that would prove pivotal.

———

At noon on Saturday, with his wife in Virginia, Jack summoned Mary Meyer to the White House. She arrived an hour later. Why now, after everything that had happened between them? Was Jack so racked with guilt over the double murders that he felt the only way to alleviate his pain was to reignite their affair? Maybe he spoke to Mary of his anguish and cried on her shoulder. However, based on conversations they later had with others, he did *not* take her to his bed. He sent her home.

Senator George Smathers didn't know, when he was interviewed in 2000, that it had been Mary Meyer who Jack had called to the White House after the double murders in Vietnam. He only knew he'd called someone to his side. "He told me two weeks later [on November 18] that he had a woman at the White House, but that he'd had a change of heart," said Smathers. "He said he looked at her and had, I guess, a crisis of conscience, which he resolved by saying to himself, 'Hell, no. I'm not doing this. I'm done with this.' When he told me the story, I said, 'But, Jack, that's huge.' He shook his head and said, 'Don't say that to me, senator. That's too much for me to handle right now. Please don't put that on me.'"

Jack might not have changed overnight, but he was definitely trying. He decided not to betray his wife. As George Smathers had said, it really was "huge." However, real change only comes after repeated opportunities to consider it. Tragically, the clock on his chances for such reconsideration was beginning to run out. November 2 was definitely the last time he'd ever see Mary Meyer. That night, he flew to Atoka to be with Jackie.*

---

* Mary Pinchot Meyer would meet a tragic demise eleven months later on October 12, 1964. She was murdered while on her daily walk along the Chesapeake and Ohio Canal towpath in Georgetown. The crime was never solved.

REGRET

O n Sunday evening, November 3, Jackie invited the Auchinclosses to
have dinner with her and Jack at the Atoka house. The Bradlees were
supposed to join them, but Jackie decided to push them to Tuesday night.
Jack told her he wasn't in the mood to put on a happy face for a reporter,
even a good friend like Ben. She thought she'd ask Bobby and Ethel in their
place. Lately, Jack hadn't wanted to socialize with Bobby. He had become a
"work friend," in the sense that they saw each other all day long in times of
crisis. In his free time, the president didn't want to discuss what was going
on at "the office," and the attorney general felt the same way. Instead, Ted
and Joan joined for dinner, as did Rose Kennedy. This was her first and,
as far as we know, only time at the summer home. It would also be the last
time Rose would ever see Jack. There are no further reported instances of
them ever having been together.

Over steaks and wine, Jack spoke about the situation in South Vietnam but, as Janet later recounted, "was quite careful not to call it a coup.
He didn't like that word." Despondent, Jack asked Ted what he thought
history might say about the first Catholic president of the United States
having participated in the murder of the first Catholic president of Vietnam. Ted's opinion was that it would definitely reflect negatively on Jack's
presidency. He also said that Americans likely didn't fully understand the
ramifications of the failed coup, "even if it means a greater possibility of
us ending up in a war over there." If South Vietnam fell under the influence of Communism, its neighboring countries would follow, he said. He
referred to it as "a domino effect." Jackie said she felt all of it was terrible.

She felt bad for Jack and told him he didn't "deserve such a burden." He told her, "Yes, kid. I'm afraid I do." He was the president and this was his burden to shoulder.

What the family didn't know as they sat at Atoka was that even before the coup, the president had signaled his intentions where Vietnam was concerned by signing National Security Action Memorandum 263. The intention of 263, which had just been signed in October 1963, was a conditional withdrawal of America's military "advisers" out of Vietnam, an evacuation that was to begin in December and be completed by the end of 1965.

In his final briefing with Michael Forrester, Jack Kennedy told him he feared the chances of the U.S. winning a war in Vietnam were "a hundred to one." When he returned from Texas, he said he intended "to start a complete and very profound review of how we got into this country, what we thought we were doing, and what we now think we can do, I even want to think about whether or not we should be there." Privately, he said, "The first advice I'm going to give my successor is to watch the generals and to avoid feeling that just because they're military men their advice on military matters is worth a damn."

Unfortunately, soon after Memorandum 263 was signed in October 1963, President Kennedy would be dead. His successor, President Lyndon Johnson, would see things differently where Vietnam was concerned. In early 1965, he'd send in combat troops, a move backed by former president Dwight Eisenhower. With Johnson's fateful decision, America's long and tragic full-scale conflict in Vietnam would begin.

But all of that was to come later . . .

A little past two in the morning, on November 4, Jack called his stepbrother-in-law Yusha Auchincloss, who was in Kuwait at the time for his work with the United Nations. After the two men spoke about what had happened in South Vietnam, Jack reported back to Jackie that he felt a little better about things. He was sure, though, that he wouldn't be able to sleep.

About an hour later, Jackie stood with Janet Auchincloss in front of a large picture window and watched Jack with his own mother, Rose, on the patio, the two of them reclined on chaise lounges. The sky above was blanketed with stars that shimmered like diamonds. Mother and son just laid side by side, not speaking, as was their custom, alone together, once again.

"Shall we join them?" Janet asked.

Jackie pondered it for a second. Then, with a small, knowing smile, she whispered, "No. I think not."

––––––––

Later in the early morning hours of Monday, November 4, Jack dictated a memorandum encapsulating his true and honest feelings about what had happened in South Vietnam:

I feel I must bear a good deal of responsibility for it, beginning with our cables of early August in which we suggested the coup. In my judgment that wire was badly drafted; it should not have been sent on a Saturday. I should not have given my consent to it without a roundtable conference at which McNamara and Taylor could have presented their views. While we did redress that balance in later wires, that first wire encouraged Lodge along a course to which he was in any case inclined. I was shocked by the death of Diem and Nhu. The way he was killed makes it particularly abhorrent.

NOT PERFECT, BUT LOVELY

If John Fitzgerald Kennedy had learned anything from his first three years in office, it was that no job could fully prepare a man for the presidency except actually being president. He'd certainly learned some hard lessons along the way, about not only leadership but also accountability, both of which he knew would be demanded of anyone seeking the American presidency. The fourth year in office would have to be about remaining in power to solidify his vision for the country. Reelection was just a year away.

If Republicans had anything to say about it, there'd be no second term for President Kennedy. The GOP felt he'd blown two big chances to protect and defend America from Castro's aggression: the Bay of Pigs and the Cuban Missile Crisis. Under his constitutional duties as commander in chief, Republicans argued, the president had the legal and moral authority to remove Castro's military threat to American security. Certain well-respected generals even went on record as saying they'd been eager to destroy Castro's missiles, but a weak and hapless JFK had made some sort of sweetheart deal with Khrushchev instead. Politics being what it is, the president would never be able to do the right thing as far as the opposing party was concerned. Jack also knew that if Republicans were loud enough and persuasive enough about what they perceived as his failures, it could jeopardize his chances for a second term.

Jack and Jackie spent the Veterans Day weekend at Wexford with the Auchinclosses and Bradlees. As Jackie, Janet, and Tony went for a long afternoon walk, Jack talked to Ben, Hugh, and Yusha about his civil rights legislation, which was still gridlocked in Congress. Though worried about the chances of a Senate filibuster, he was also sure that he'd see the bill through "in my second term." In a week or so, he'd have his first major campaign reelection meeting with the same team that had been behind his first run: Bobby, Ted Sorensen, Larry O'Brien, and Kenny O'Donnell. His brother-in-law Stephen Smith would be crucially involved as well. It's worth noting that Lyndon Johnson wasn't invited to that meeting, which many people thought made a strong statement about his possible future on the ticket.

Jack figured he'd be running against Arizona's Republican Senator Barry Goldwater. "Good competitor?" Hugh asked. "Good man," Jack answered. Kennedy and Goldwater had become friendly while serving together in the Senate. Once, when Goldwater came to the Oval Office for a meeting and plopped himself down on Jack's favorite rocking chair, Jack jokingly told him, "Keep your seat, Barry. And you can have this job, too, if you want it." He was also fairly sure Governor Nelson Rockefeller would throw his hat into the ring. While Jack obviously disagreed with them both on policy, he also believed healthy discourse and disagreement to be core to the Republic. "America's differences have always been our strength," he'd say, "not our weakness. We have to look forward as a nation and we don't get there by hating each other or our opponents." He said he saw "an America where we stand together." Indeed, his long-standing personal idealism remained at the core of his character as he began to think about how to appeal to voters for a second term.

Over Bloody Marys, they discussed a recent bestselling book written by Victor Lasky, *JFK: The Man and the Myth*. This was the first notable assessment of JFK's life and times, its timeline going all the way up to March 1963. In this well-researched and often critical book, the author stated that LBJ would probably not be on the ticket in '64: "For the Kennedys, Johnson had evidently served his purpose." The author was highly critical of Jack's personal character and reported that he was cold and calculating. He even obliquely questioned his morality. In many ways, it was a more accurate portrayal of the president than people realized at the time. Kennedy shrugged it off. "People will write books," Jack said. "Ben'll probably write one, too." (In fact, Ben would end up writing two.) He laughed and said Jackie was presently reading Lasky's work and furiously tearing out page after page and throwing them into the fire.

"I can do no wrong in her eyes," he said.

Hugh smiled. "That's a good woman," he said of his beloved step-daughter.

Jack then surprised the men with news that he'd finalized a lease on a twenty-three-acre estate next to Hammersmith called Annandale Farm. The property, which had been suggested to him by his friend Rhode Island Senator Claiborne Pell, featured sweeping panoramic views of Narragansett Bay and Newport Harbor. He said he and Jackie would split their time in 1964 between the new property and Squaw Island.

"Mummy's going to be so delighted," Hugh told him, "and as for me, I'll expect more of these Bloody Marys, son."

Jack chuckled and said, "You drive a *haad* bargain," his Boston accent speaking.

How things had changed. Just seven years earlier, Hugh had refused to let Jack sleep in the main house at Hammersmith because he hadn't returned to Jackie's side after Arabella's death. The senator was forced to sleep in the servants' quarters over the garage. Now, Hugh was proud to not only call him neighbor, but son. In all fairness, it hadn't been easy for Jack to deal with Hugh, either. The older man was so oblivious to the concerns of most Americans, it sometimes frustrated Jack. "I can remember him being so disgusted," Jackie later recalled, "because once we had dinner with my mother and my stepfather, and there sat my stepfather putting a great slab of paté de foie gras on his toast and saying it was simply appalling to think that the minimum wage should be a dollar twenty-five. And Jack saying to me when we went home, 'Does he realize that laundrywomen in the South get only sixty cents an hour?'" As much as they'd always admired each other, there were differences, too.

That same afternoon, Jack spent quality time with Jackie and the children. Young John, while dressed in a military costume, shot at make-believe targets with his toy gun while Caroline sat watching, nestled on Jackie's lap. Jack gazed at them with appreciation. Tomorrow, he and John would observe the Veterans Day pomp and circumstance at Arlington National Cemetery honoring America's fallen soldiers. The president would certainly never forget that out there, somewhere in the distance, among a vast landscape of white crosses, was a simple memorial stone marker with an engraved cross of its own that said: "In Memory of Joseph P. Kennedy, Jr. Lt. US Navy 1915–1944."

Later, as the sun went down, Jack and Jackie snuggled on a hammock together, their feet intertwined, whispering to each other as they watched the sky fill with colors. As he stroked her hair, there were long stretches of contented silence between them. It was as if he finally realized that all he ever needed was right there, with him, in that moment. Who can ever know what goes through a person's mind, but maybe Jack had finally managed to free the prisoner within. Perhaps he had found some inner peace. "Don't let the moment pass," someone close to him had once advised, and maybe now he finally understood what that meant.

For her part, Jackie would recall feeling as if she were, "maybe for the first time, loved, wanted, and cared for," or, as she told her mother, "Maybe Jack and I don't have a perfect marriage but, somehow, we're perfect for each other." Later, in a letter to her good friend Eileen Slocum, Janet wrote:

Jacqueline says that perhaps things aren't always perfect, but that they are still nonetheless lovely. She and Jack are very, very happy. I must say, never have I known two people who worked harder for it and never have I known two people who deserve it more.

MEMORIES TO BE MADE

About a week after Veterans Day, Pierre Salinger made the official announcement: the president and First Lady would be headed to Texas on November 21, 1963. Salinger noted that it'd be a quick two-day, five-city jaunt—San Antonio, Houston, Fort Worth, Dallas, and Austin—in preparation for Kennedy's 1964 presidential campaign.

"Jack and Jackie would then spend a single night and next day at Lyndon's ranch outside of Austin," recalled Bess Abell, later Lady Bird Johnson's social secretary. "On the same day as Salinger's announcement, [Republican Nelson] Rockefeller became the first to officially announce his candidacy, attacking what he called Kennedy's failures at home and abroad. Then, there was a Republican dinner in West Virginia where Rockefeller said something like, 'We've got a talk-big, act-little administration.' He said President Kennedy had made a whole lot of promises in 1960 and that there wasn't one person who didn't know that all of them had been broken. The campaign was on and it would probably get pretty ugly."

The three weeks of that final, fateful November in Jack's life passed quickly. There was another restful weekend with Macdonald, Smathers, O'Donnell, and Powers in Palm Beach beginning on Friday afternoon, November 15. "We went to Florida so that the president could pay a visit to Cape Canaveral and talk more about his great mandate: *Us,* meaning the U.S.A., beating *them,* meaning the Russians, to the moon," said Senator Smathers.

All in all, it was a pleasant weekend with Jack, Torb, and George watching the Navy vs. Duke football game on Saturday and the Bears and Packers on Sunday. "These old friends who'd been through so much together, what history they saw, what history they made," observed Torbert's daughter,

Laurie. "This would've been during my father's eighth term [in Congress]. I love thinking about these public servants who cared so much about this country, this world, just sort of chilling with each other, taking a moment to just be friends. Something about it, and the fact that my dad had this in his life with Uncle Jack, warms my heart to this day."

Torbert's son Torbert Jr. added, "My father once said this time together in Palm Beach reminded him of what it'd been like before World War II when everything was so good, Jack was with Inga Arvad, and no one had any cares. Knowing my father, he probably felt there'd be many years ahead for him and Uncle Jack. But knowing Uncle Jack, he probably felt they should enjoy it now because who knew what the future might hold. If there was a memory to be made, Uncle Jack always felt you had to make it because tomorrow was promised to no one. They talked about how both their fathers had suffered strokes and how neither wanted to go out that way," Macdonald Jr. continued. "My grandfather had just died [in September 1962] at seventy-seven."

As the best friends spoke, Jack apparently fell into a melancholy mood, musing once again about the way God worked. He wondered if his own father's stroke had been some sort of divine punishment. Was Joe struck down because of what he'd done to Rosie? Had Joe been cursed into living the rest of his life as just a shell of a person because that's what he'd done to his daughter? "That's not how God works," Joan Kennedy had told Jack after Patrick's death. He hoped so, but still he had to wonder about it. If God did work that way, what then might he expect as punishment for his own sins, of which there were many, maybe even more than Joe's? What price would *he* have to pay one day? In some ways, the possibilities terrified him, but in other ways, he was intrigued. He'd always felt his time on earth was limited. Who knew what was in store? For now, with his longtime friend from college, he was just grateful for his life.

Again, Torbert Macdonald Jr.: "Uncle Jack felt so lucky to be a congressman, so lucky to be a senator, and *so* lucky to be president. He didn't take one second of it for granted. If it all ended, he'd had it all, he'd lived it all, he'd done it all. When my father asked him how, if he could, he'd choose to go, he answered quickly. 'A gun,' he said, 'because with a bullet you never know what hit you.'"

On Monday morning, in Air Force One on the way back to Washington via Miami. Jack and George Smathers chatted a little about Texas. "Jackie's going with me," Jack told him, lighting a cigar.

"That's good, Jack," George said. "America loves a good political partnership."

Jack then concluded, "I look forward to both of us getting the hell out of there in one piece."

George Smathers later said that what most struck him in that moment was the memory of what he'd said to Jack about Jackie back in 1952: "I think you can do better." But then, after Jack married Jackie, with George as a groomsman, he felt his advice had been less than helpful. Now that Jack was president and Jackie was First Lady, George had to admit that he'd been wrong. His friend couldn't have done much better than the woman he'd chosen to be his wife.

"You're a lucky man, Mr. President," he told him as they made their way back to Washington.

Jack smiled as he puffed on his cigar. "Don't I know it, senator," he concluded. "Don't I know it."

"IT'S WE WHO MADE HIM"

Before leaving for Texas, Jackie shared a surprising secret with her mother. A couple of months earlier, at the Hammersmith celebration of their tenth wedding anniversary, she and Jack privately gave each other gifts. She presented him with a new St. Christopher's medal because she knew he'd placed his own in Patrick's coffin. In turn, he gave her a gold-and-emerald ring, which, he explained, represented the same fighting spirit of the Irish he'd seen in their son's fight for survival. He slipped it onto Jackie's finger next to her wedding band. Before he did so, however, he dropped to one knee and asked her to marry him.

Jack's gesture meant the world to Jackie because he'd never actually asked for her hand in marriage. Not officially, anyway. There'd never been a real proposal, except for a few words in an airport when she returned from her trip to England in 1953. Certainly nothing very romantic. While Janet had never had much confidence in her daughter's marriage, she now saw things in a different way. *Jack* was a different man.

Later, in her oral history for the JFK Library, Mrs. Auchincloss recalled, "I felt that they were closer. I can't think of two people who had packed more into ten years of marriage than they had. And I felt that all their strains and stresses, which any sensitive people have in a marriage, had eased to a point where they were terribly close to each other. I almost can't think of any married couple I've ever known that had greater understanding of each other, in spite of Jackie's introvertness [*sic*], stiffness—I mean that it's difficult for her to show her feelings. I think one felt in those rare moments—when one could be alone with them on a quiet evening when there weren't a million pressures pending—that they were very, very, very close to each other and understood each other wonderfully."

After hearing about Jack's surprising gesture, Janet suggested that the couple renew their wedding vows. There had actually been a precedent for it in the family four months earlier when, at Janet's insistence, Lee reaffirmed her marriage vows to Stas at Westminster Roman Catholic Cathedral in London. Though everyone treated it as a joyous celebration of Lee's marriage, its real purpose was to keep Lee away from Aristotle Onassis. It worked—until Lee tried to reconcile with Ari and he refused to take her back. Then, in 1968, he went on to marry someone else, and we all know who that was. But that particular story of sisterly betrayal was yet in the future. In this 1963 moment at Hammersmith, Janet again suggested a reaffirmation of wedding vows, but not as a pretense to keep Jackie in her marriage to Jack, but rather to honor it.

Julian Baldridge, whose father, Edward, worked at Hugh's brokerage firm and mother, Carolyn, was a friend of Janet's, recalled, "Jackie thought it was a lovely idea, yet impossible. 'Jack is the president,' she said, 'so we can't very well sneak off to a church like Lee and Stas did.' Instead, they came up with the idea of having the service held privately at Hammersmith on the occasion of their eleventh wedding anniversary, September 1964. It would be an intimate affair, not announced to the press until after the fact. Jackie said she'd talk to the president about it. Mrs. Auchincloss asked my mom to help plan things simply because, at the time, we happened to be visiting her and Mrs. Auchincloss at their O Street home in Georgetown.

"The next day, Jackie returned to her mother and said Jack really wanted to do it," Julian Baldridge said. "Mrs. Auchincloss was optimistic. She asked my mother to start to compile a folder of ideas with a tentative guest list. She asked her to reach out to Rose Kennedy for her input. And, also, she wanted her to put together some ideas as to what Jackie might wear. Jackie told us she was thinking of pale yellow or light blue, something in silk, knee length. 'This time,' she quipped, 'I get to pick out my dress.'"

When he was interviewed for this book in 2024, Julian Baldridge still had his mother's work folder, marked "JBK/JFK Renewal." It included clippings from fashion magazines as well as a handwritten note from Jackie to Carolyn Baldridge, which has never before been revealed:

Dearest Mrs. B.—I loved what you said yesterday—Good fashion is for the woman with a budget. BUT High Fashion is for the woman with time &

money—my goodness, how true that is, and funny as well—We are fortunate
to have both—time & money. So, I say—let's not disappoint.

As they talked about their plans, Janet later recalled gazing at her daughter with wonder and remarking, "After everything you've been through, you really do love him, don't you, Jacqueline?"

Smiling in that enigmatic way of hers, Jackie answered, "I do." Then, after a moment's hesitation, she added what was probably a dark truth for her, but a truth just the same. "He's Jack because of us, Mummy," she concluded. "After all, it's we who made him."

PART XI

The Unfinished Life

BLOOD RED

The sun was blazing hot as the motorcade moved slowly through Dealey Plaza. Ahead was an underpass where Jackie felt it might be cooler. Jack turned to her in the Lincoln convertible and smiled, looking, as she would later remember, more handsome than ever. He then turned back to the happy faces of the admiring crowd. That's when she heard the sound. The pop of a firecracker? The backfire of a motorcycle? Jack flinched. He grabbed his throat. He lurched to the left and looked at Jackie with a puzzled expression.

There was another pop. Then, another. Three in six seconds.

Then . . . just red. Blood red.

Then . . . black.

After a mad race to Parkland Hospital, Jackie, her pink outfit ghastly with splattered blood, stood next to Jack's body. It was stretched out on a gurney and covered by a white sheet. She bent down, took his foot in her hand, and kissed it. She pulled back the sheet. His eyes were wide and staring. She gazed down at his face, which somehow seemed so young to her. "His mouth was so beautiful," she recalled.

She kissed his lips.

A DEEP LOSS

It had been so sudden and unbelievable, it felt unreal. One minute he was vital and alive, the next, gone. Instantly, everything on President John Fitzgerald Kennedy's agenda was left unfinished, all the many vital issues that had consumed him for the last three years: the Cold War, the space race, civil rights, Castro, the Soviet Union, Khrushchev, Vietnam, and, of course, Cuba, Cuba, Cuba. He still had more than a year left in his term and, he hoped, four more after that. What he might've achieved in that time, and then in the years that followed, would now never be known.

A day after her husband's murder, Jackie went into his bedroom at the White House and found a sheet of paper on his dresser, a scribbled note:

Talk sense to the American people.

After staring at it for a long time, the newly widowed First Lady crumpled it and tossed it into a trash can. "What good had any of it done him?" she later asked her mother. "What a waste. All of it. Just a waste." She likely didn't know the note was a line from a speech Jack had intended to give at the Trade Mart in Dallas:

We cannot expect that everyone, to use the phrase of a decade ago, will "talk sense to the American people." But we can hope that fewer people will listen to nonsense. And the notion that this Nation is headed for defeat through deficit, or that strength is but a matter of slogans, is nothing but just plain nonsense.

In the decades to come, there would be a myriad of conspiracy theories about what happened in Dallas, now considered one of the greatest murder mysteries of all time. In fact, trying to unwind the events of that terrible day became a cottage industry over the next sixty years, with countless books, documentaries, and movies featuring experts like pathologists, investigators, and even Secret Service agents all in pursuit of an elusive truth. The killing of JFK was, in some ways, the beginning of the deep suspicions of democratic institutions and government that is so much a part of our culture today. From the beginning, there was a sense of a cover-up, of people plotting, of "them against us" at the highest levels, or what some people today might call "the deep state."

Had it really been the act of a single gunman, Lee Harvey Oswald, as ultimately decided by the Warren Commission? Or, did it have to do with Cuba, which was Lyndon Johnson's theory. Perhaps the assassination could be traced back to the Bay of Pigs, with disgruntled Cuban rebels finally taking revenge on Jack for not having provided military ground cover during the invasion. LBJ even privately theorized that Oswald might've been a Cuban sympathizer upset with Jack's treatment of Castro.

Because he'd overseen the CIA's many anti-Castro covert actions, Bobby Kennedy also suspected rogue CIA officers. Or, maybe the murder was retaliation for Bobby's ongoing prosecution of the Mafia? Did it have to do with the fact that the mobsters like Sam Giancana felt they'd helped with the presidential election, yet still remained targets of the administration? Whether the CIA was responsible or the underworld, Bobby couldn't help but blame himself, and everyone in the family knew it.

Some in the family even felt President Johnson was involved. "He always looked at Jack with such contempt," Janet Auchincloss claimed. Jamie says his mother "believed until the day she died that LBJ had something to do with it."

In June 2023, President Biden directed the release of more than 3,600 assassination-related records, with decisions about redactions and sensitive material reviewed by the CIA and NSA (National Security Agency), who had recommended withholding certain records for national security reasons. But President Donald Trump later promised both podcaster Joe Rogan and Bobby Kennedy's son, Robert Kennedy Jr., that he'd rescind and replace Biden's order and thereby release the complete file. He's said that he's seen the material and, as he told former jurist and syndicated columnist Andrew

Napolitano, "If they showed you what they showed me, you wouldn't have released it either," strongly suggesting that the unseen files implicate the CIA in Kennedy's murder. More than sixty years later, in January of 2025, JFK's grandson, Jack Schlossberg (Caroline's son), addressed the possibility of Trump's releasing such documents in an Instagram post: "JFK conspiracy theories. The truth is a lot sadder than the myth—a tragedy that didn't need to happen. Not part of an inevitable grand scheme. Declassification is using JFK as a political prop when he's not here to punch back. There's nothing heroic about it."

Apparently, among the CIA's confidential files is an interview Jackie gave to the agency in 1964. She told her immediate family members that she refused to confirm the Warren Commission's theory that Oswald had acted alone because she had "a strong feeling," her words, "that something was being covered up." Jackie said privately that her interview with the agency was contentious because the agents kept trying to get her to agree with their theory of a lone gunman, and she refused. She had talked to Bobby prior to the interview, she said, and had been convinced that Oswald had *not* acted alone, and she kept refusing to fall in line with the CIA's story, which frustrated the interviewers. "I hated the CIA ever since the Bay of Pigs and what it did to Jack back then," she told her mother, and Janet agreed. "I will never support the CIA in anything," Jackie said. "Never."

The CIA controls the transcripts of Jackie's interview and has no plans to allow it to be released. Those secret records also contain proof, it's been alleged by people with knowledge of them, of JFK's intention to get rid of the agency after its betrayal of him during the Bay of Pigs. That was good enough reason, some felt, for the agency to act against him. There are also supposed to be files relating to Oswald making clearer his own involvement with the CIA. "I guess none of it matters," Jackie concluded to her family after her agency interview, "unless it brings back our Jack, which it won't. So, how am I to care about any of it?"

Indeed, as Jackie suggested, all possible covert criminality aside, there was a deeper loss to consider, that of a son, a brother, a father . . . a husband. "It had all been so great—Congress, the Senate, the presidency . . . our very *lives*," Jamie Auchincloss said. "Afterward, we all fell into a sort of deep depression, a darkness. As a family, we'd been at the center of everything, the center of all power. We had a certain station that was ripped from us overnight. Worse than that, of course, the nation had lost a great president, and we had lost Jack. 'How could this happen?' Mummy and Daddy kept asking. '*How could this happen?'* Jackie, at only thirty-four, had her whole life ahead of her, another thirty years as it would turn out, but it certainly didn't feel that way in 1963 while she took her place as America's tragic heroine."

One morning, just before the funeral, Janet sat with a date book in her lap and flipped back the pages. "Fifteen," she finally declared to Hugh. He looked at her, perplexed. "Fifteen weeks since Patrick," she clarified, tears welling. "How much is she supposed to take?"

ONE LAST TIME

A week after the assassination, in a conversation with her mother and stepbrother Yusha, Jackie would remember her last night with Jack. It was in Fort Worth's Hotel Texas, suite 850, after an exhausting day of campaigning. On that day, as she recalled it, she really felt as if she'd found her momentum and had grown into the role of a true political partner for her husband. By the time they got to their hotel room, they were both exhausted. They rarely slept in the same bed, though. In Fort Worth, they'd be in adjoining bedrooms in the same suite. However, before retiring, Jackie recalled Jack wanting to spend a few moments with her.

"You were great today," he told her. "How do you feel?" he asked.

She answered, "Oh, gosh, I'm exhausted."

He held her close. Realizing how tired she was, he told her she didn't have to appear for a speech the next morning at 8:30. If she could be ready by 9:15 for breakfast in the hotel's Grand Ballroom, that would be fine. "It's almost over," he told her, reassuringly. "Dallas. Then, Austin."

Jackie said she returned to her own room and laid out her clothes for the next day—the pink suit with navy collar and matching pink pillbox hat. "Tomorrow's another day," her secretary, Mary Gallagher, told her.

While brushing her hair to get ready for bed, Jackie gazed at Mary's reflection in the mirror. "Dallas," she said, whispering Jack's earlier refrain. "Then, Austin." She then retired for the evening.

At about three in the morning, Jackie awoke with a start. "Every time she nearly fell asleep, she'd awaken," Janet Auchincloss recalled in previously unpublished remarks. "She'd try to take deep breaths, but her breathing was quick and shallow. Her hands were stiff and she couldn't move her fingers. She was suddenly dizzy, all these things that used to happen to her out of the blue." Obviously, Jackie was having another of her anxiety attacks. "She knew she needed to be with Jack," Janet said. "She just knew. She didn't know how else to explain it."

Jackie went to Jack's door, tapped lightly, let herself into his room, and crawled into his bed. They then made love. "We were together as husband and wife for the last time," is how she put it to her mother and stepbrother. Afterward, she said, she returned to her own room and fell fast asleep.

DID HE KNOW?

One morning shortly after the great loss, Kerry McCarthy and her aunt Rose embarked on one of their daily Hyannis Port beach walks. After about fifteen minutes of silence, the matriarch suddenly stopped, turned to her grandniece, and said, "I was a good mother. I did all the right things, everything I was supposed to do."

"I know you did, Aunt Rose," Kerry said.

"I loved my family," Rose added.

"I know, Aunt Rose."

They resumed their walk, Rose now lost in thought. Minutes later, she stopped and, again, broke the silence. "Do you think he heard her?" she asked.

"Heard who, Aunt Rose?"

"Jackie," Rose said. "Do you think he heard the last words she said to him? Do you think he knew she was in that car with him?"

Kerry felt a sob rising in her, but she tried to suppress it. "Yes," she said. "The world stopped for them in that car, and in those last moments Jack knew one thing for sure. He knew he was loved, Aunt Rose. He knew it as much as he'd ever known anything in his entire life."

Rose gazed across the span of beach and ocean where her children had once played so very long ago. "I'm glad," she said softly. "As long as he didn't feel alone."

A BEAUTIFUL LIFE

———

I t's a blur," Janet Auchincloss later said of the state funeral for President John Fitzgerald Kennedy. "I have fleeting glimpses of Jackie with the black veil," she said, "and of Hughdie forcing back tears during the East Room service. Jamie walking to the Capitol beside Sargent [Shriver] and behind Bobby, Ted, and Jacqueline. The bagpipes and the clip-clop of horses. Rose, small and grief-stricken. I feel Joe was there, yet I know he wasn't, but somehow, in my mind, he's there. The requiem Mass at St. Mathew's. Little John saluting the casket; it was his third birthday, can you imagine? Poor, young Caroline trying to be strong for her daddy. The twenty-one-gun salute, lighting the Eternal Flame at Arlington. Jacqueline's bravery, her strength, all of it helping the nation heal after a wound so mortal. However," she concluded, "if I continue to think too long and too hard about any of it, it goes to black."

Following that day's solemn ceremonies, Jack's loved ones had the chance to come together once again at the White House. In the Yellow Oval Room, Jackie looked ashen under her black veil as she greeted Rose Kennedy. Despite her petite size, Rose had always been known for her quiet power. On this most terrible of days, she remained as stalwart and determined as ever. She'd always felt that losing her composure during such times would give license to family members to do the same, and she simply wouldn't have it. Only her closest family members knew the truth about Rose, though. Despite any veneer of strength, she was always just a hair's breadth away from a total breakdown. "Jack would want courage in this moment," she told Jackie, trying hard to hold it together, "and he'd be so proud of you."

As Janet had suggested in her memory of the day, Joe Kennedy didn't attend the funeral. For a few years after the stroke, Jackie hoped Joe would, as she once put it, "teach us all a new way to live." She had a romantic notion that maybe his stroke might somehow free the kindhearted prisoner that had been locked within for his entire life, much the same way his son had once said he was "stuck" in himself. Without his anger, Jackie figured Joe might become a different person, a gentler man who'd relish the rest of his days while peacefully surrounded by loved ones. Jack used to call this theory his wife's "fantasy version" of how things might work out. In truth, Joe was rarely, if ever, happy again. He remained a prisoner, and not an openhearted one but an enraged one, trapped more than ever in his own body. He'd live eight more lonely, frightened years—gnarled, crippled, and unable to speak—until his merciful death on November 18, 1969, at the age of eighty-one. Today, he wasn't even up to attending his own son's funeral. When Rose mentioned that she'd soon be returning to his side, Jackie asked her to give him a kiss for her.

Jackie took Rose's arm and walked her to the ornately decorated Red Room, where a reception was being held for foreign dignitaries. The Auchinclosses awaited her there: Janet and Hugh, Lee and Stas, Jamie and Janet Jr., and Yusha among them. The first thing Jackie saw was Bobby speaking to her mother, his face grim. The two had long been unlikely allies, going all the way back to the day they gave each other strength while burying Arabella. Now, Janet held his hand and whispered in his ear. As she hugged him, Bobby seemed to go slack in her arms.

As soon as he spotted Jackie, Hugh stepped forward to embrace her. "My favorite person," he said, "braver than I ever knew a person could be." Janet then took Jackie's veil, raised it over her face, and looked into her daughter's listless eyes. Seeing her struggle with words, Hugh, naturally, knew just what to say. He recited the words of Henry Wadsworth Longfellow: "There's no grief, like the grief that doesn't speak." Janet, now near tears, nodded and took her daughter into her arms. After a few moments with her "Jacqueline," she turned her attention to Rose.

The two matriarchs had always been so different. "This woman's been suffering for years because she doesn't realize she deserves better," Janet had said of Rose at the beginning of their journey. Now, in this difficult moment, she may have wanted to embrace her counterpart, but that wasn't Janet, and it certainly wasn't Rose, either. Instead, she took both her hands. "I just want to thank you," she told her. Rose gave her a curious look. "Your Jack," Janet clarified, "he gave us all such a beautiful, perfect life."

As they took each other in, Rose and Janet had to know the truth. While the life given to them by Jack had maybe been beautiful in many ways, he was far from perfect in it. Despite his many failings, though, there'd always been something so compelling about him, the way he drew people in and made them want to be in his world, those public parts of it they felt they knew so well and even the secret parts that frustrated them so. It had been a wild ride like no other, not just for him but for his loved ones. Now, in these final moments together, it was as if a family story, maybe one of the greatest family stories ever told, had come to an end.

"It really *was* beautiful," Rose said. With those four words she seemed to lose whatever it was that had kept her going. Jackie, who'd been talking to Hugh, gave her a concerned, knowing look. Perhaps Jackie was remembering her first impression of her husband upon meeting the congressman that fateful spring day in 1951:

> *I listened to what he had to say, and how he felt about people and the way he wanted to serve, I suppose, and the things he wanted to do to with his life to make things better, and I thought, my God, just look at him—those blue eyes, that hair, that face, and just the way he is . . . the way he thinks about the world and the way he talks about the world and the way he is in the world. He's just so . . . beautiful."*

Jackie took Rose's hand and held it tightly. As she did so, she studied Rose's face more closely, and that's when she saw it—the sudden glitter of moisture in her eyes. Jackie couldn't help but stare with wonder as a single tear fell. She reached out and, with the tip of her finger, traced it down Rose's cheek.

END

SOURCE NOTES

JFK—Public, Private, Secret is my sixth book documenting the lives and times of various members of the Kennedy family, the other five being *Jackie, Ethel, Joan: Women of Camelot* (2000); *After Camelot: A Personal History of the Kennedy Family, 1968 to the Present* (2012); *Jackie, Janet & Lee: The Secret Lives of Janet Auchincloss and Her Daughters Jackie Kennedy Onassis and Lee Radziwill* (2018); *The Kennedy Heirs: John, Caroline, and the New Generation;* (2019) and *Jackie: Public, Private, Secret* (2023).

A great advantage I have as a Kennedy historian is the accumulation of twenty-five years of research into the family's personal and political dynamic, and that includes hundreds of personal interviews my research team and I have conducted over those years. For this work, I explored my archives of taped interviews to listen to the memories and observations of many of those sources for stories about Jack Kennedy that weren't necessarily suitable for the other books but that are valuable to this new work, and to a further understanding of the life of the family's true standard bearer. To hear the voices of some of the sources I interviewed over the years, many of whom have now been gone for years—such as Jack's good friends Arthur Schlesinger Jr., Senator George Smathers, Charles Bartlett, Ted Sorensen, Robert C. McNamara, John Carl Warnecke, and Joseph Gargan—was such a moving experience. To now mine those interviews for stories I've never used before, many of which I've never seen published elsewhere, was equally rewarding. I hope their memories of JFK give you a fuller understanding of who he was, and maybe a bit of a vision of who he might've been had he lived.

"One day, you'll write about Jack Kennedy, a task to be undertaken by all presidential historians, I suppose," Arthur Schlesinger Jr. told me in November 1997. He said it with no small amount of trepidation in that he was incredibly protective of his friend. I was a young and intimidated reporter when I interviewed Schlesinger about an article he'd just penned for *The New York Times Magazine* regarding his presidential rankings of presidents. (He ranked JFK as "Average High," Lincoln

"Great," and Nixon "Failed"). At the time, I was writing my first book about the family, *Jackie, Ethel, Joan: Women of Camelot*. Schlesinger was agitated about a book that had just been published, *The Dark Side of Camelot* by Seymour Hersh, which painted a negative portrait of President Kennedy. Schlesinger told me, "When you finally get to the president, my hope is that you'll get it right." That's my hope, as well. With this book I can say I did my best to be truthful and honor not only President John Fitzgerald Kennedy but also his many family members.

In addition to about five hundred taped interviews with primary sources, more than a thousand friends, relatives, politicians, journalists, socialites, lawyers, celebrities, and business executives, as well as classmates, teachers, neighbors, friends, news people, and archivists, were contacted in preparation for *JFK: Public, Private, Secret*. My research team and I also carefully reviewed, as secondary sources, the many books that have been published over the last sixty years about John Kennedy and his family members, as well as thousands of newspaper and magazine articles. I'm not going to list all of them here, though I will acknowledge those relevant to my research.

I owe a special debt of thanks to the staffs of the John Fitzgerald Kennedy Presidential Library and Museum, in particular Maryrose Grossman, Nadia Dixson, and Kyoko Yamamoto, for all of their amazing assistance. Special thanks to Stacey Chandler at the National Archives and Records Administration for her help. Thanks also to William Johnson, Ron Whealon, June Payne, Maura Porter, Susan D'Entrement, Allen Goodrich, and James Hill. Thanks also to Jennifer Quan, the intellectual property manager at the John F. Kennedy Library Foundation.

As I do with all of my Kennedy-related books, I must also acknowledge David Powers, former special assistant to President John F. Kennedy, the first curator of the John Fitzgerald Kennedy Presidential Library and Museum. I was fortunate enough to interview him on January 11, 1996. He put me through a process for it, though, which included my submission of two lengthy questionnaires, the answers to which he filled out in his own hand. That was followed by a telephone conversation to gauge my personality and character before, finally, he granted me the in-person interview. Certainly, no mention of the John Fitzgerald Kennedy Presidential Library and Museum is complete without a nod to Mr. Powers, who died March 27, 1998, at the age of eighty-five.

Thanks also to the staff of the Lyndon Baines Johnson Library and Museum for all of its hard work in making so many important oral histories available to historians such as myself, including Jacqueline Kennedy Onassis's oral history of January 1, 1974, often overlooked but very important.

My appreciation, also, to the Edward M. Kennedy Institute for making so many vital oral histories available via the Edward M. Kennedy Oral History Project, including more than twenty comprehensive oral histories given by Ted Kennedy himself.

I must also thank BACM Research for providing literally thousands of documents relating to President John F. Kennedy's administration, including files relating to the Bay of Pigs, Cuban Missile Crisis, and Vietnam, far too many to list here—77,316 pages to be precise—but much of which was extremely valuable to me in telling this story.

In addition, I had access to "President John F. Kennedy: Secret White House Recordings"—102 hours of JFK's White House recordings from July 30, 1962, to November 7, 1963; President John F. Kennedy: Administration Foreign Relations Documents 1961–1963—38,415 pages of transcripts, annotations, and editorial notes of Kennedy administration foreign relations documents in twenty-seven volumes of the State Department's Foreign Relations of the United States, the official record of the foreign policy of the United States; and President John F. Kennedy: CIA Daily Briefings—5,550 pages of President's Intelligence Checklists prepared by the CIA for President Kennedy.

I've been so fortunate to work with the same chief researcher, Cathy Griffin, for the last thirty-three years. Cathy has always managed to find people to talk to for our books who have never before talked about our subjects. Since Cathy was also the primary researcher for my other bestselling books about the Kennedys, she had a terrific grasp of the subject matter and knew exactly where to go for *JFK: Public, Private, Secret* to seek our deeply reported stories.

Cathy and I value our sources. After all, my books would be nothing without them. We cultivate each one to make sure he or she knows how much we appreciate the cooperation, and how we never take it for granted. Sources sometimes risk a lot to cooperate, and so we make it a point to never let it be regretted.

Many of our sources approve their stories before publication—all they have to do is ask. I have no problem granting that approval because I understand how important it is to them that they be accurately portrayed. If someone says something they may later regret, we go back to that source to make sure it was said in earnest. Sometimes, the source wishes to rephrase it—and that's fine, too. Whatever it takes to be accurate while at the same time compassionate and empathetic, that's what we do. As a result, in all these years of working together, never has there been a person who wanted to retract his or her story or has been unhappy about the way it was told, and that's a tribute to Cathy and her rapport with our sources.

The following notes and source acknowledgments are by no means comprehensive. It is not my intention to cite each and every quote and passage in an academic manner. Instead, I sought to give the reader a general overview of the depth of my research. Also, I've occasionally provided a little more information that didn't make it into the book but may still be of interest.

Some source interviews are dated in their first appearance in these notes, when those dates were available.

"PROLOGUE: THE SECRET PLACE"

Key to these pages were my interviews with Janet DesRosiers Fontaine in 2024. Here and throughout the book, as well as in my interviews, I relied on the Papers of Janet DesRosiers Fontaine, found in the National Archives.

MORE ABOUT JANET DESROSIERS FONTAINE:

I had often heard stories about Mrs. Fontaine during the course of researching my other Kennedy books. I wondered what she'd been like, what her true story was, and how her decisions relating to Joe and Rose Kennedy impacted the rest of her life. For this book, I asked my researcher, Cathy Griffin, to try to track down one of Janet's sons for an interview so we could better understand her. Cathy came back to me one day and said, "You're not going to believe this, but I spoke to her son, Andrew, and he says his mother is still alive!" I was astonished. "But she has to be . . ." I thought aloud, and Cathy finished, "a hundred years old!" Actually she was turning one hundred in March 2024.

After Andrew Fontaine was interviewed, he was gracious enough to make his mother available to me. What a wonderful woman she is, with a crystal-clear memory of her time with the Kennedys. Much of this prologue is based on her memory, but also, so many other sections of this book relied on the telling of her experiences with the Kennedys. I am so grateful to Mrs. Fontaine for her time, and also for the photographs she provided. Her story is a good and important one, and I think most of it is told in these pages for the first time. I am so happy I had a chance to know this amazing woman, and I think you, the reader, will agree that she's one of a kind.

When Janet told me about Rose's Cottage, I was intrigued and knew immediately that it would have to be the centerpiece of the prologue of this book. After I wrote this section of the book, I came across Rose Kennedy's memory of her "cottage" in her own book, *Times to Remember*. It bears repeating here:

"I had my bathing suit and my books down there," she wrote. "I would just go down there to get away from the confusion, where I wouldn't hear any of that, and read my books or read my mail. And maybe put on my bathing suit and go swimming and take a rest afterwards." She said she craved the solitude, "because all my life I have had a great many people around me. With the children and the household staff. And we had these big storms, which came up and washed away the first one [cottage]. And it washed away the second one. And there were only two as I remember. It was the place I went to pray."

BOOK I: BEFORE THE PRESIDENCY

PART I: TIES THAT BIND

"MATRIARCH" AND "PATRIARCH"

I am so indebted to Kathleen "Kerry" McCarthy for her 2023 interviews for this book. As Rose and Joe Kennedy's grandniece, she was privy to many important moments, and I so appreciate her sharing her insight. This book is so much better for her memories in this section and in many others.

Interviews: Barbara Gibson (1997, 1998, 1999, 2000); Joseph Gargan (1998, 1999). Also questionnaires sent to Mr. Gargan by the author, which he answered in his own hand on April 1, 1999, and October 3, 2002.

I would especially like to thank Dr. Adolph "Doc" Brown (2023) for his great insight. I very much appreciate his wisdom.

I'd also like to thank Dr. Drew Pinksy (2023) for his valuable assistance.

Oral histories: Jacqueline Kennedy Onassis (LBJ Library); Arthur M. Schlesinger (LBJ Library); Joseph Gargan (Edward M. Kennedy Institute); Ann Gargan (Edward M. Kennedy Institute); Arthur Schlesinger (Edward M. Kennedy Institute); Edward M. Kennedy (Edward M. Kennedy Institute); Rev. John Cavanaugh (JFK Library).

The complete text of Jacqueline Kennedy's Oral History to Arthur Schlesinger Jr.—interviews she gave in 1964 just four months after President Kennedy's death—can be found in *Jacqueline Kennedy: Historic Conversations on Life with John F. Kennedy* by Caroline Kennedy and Michael Beschloss. For our purposes in these source notes, attribution to them will be referred to as "Jacqueline Kennedy (Arthur Schlesinger Jr.)."

Also: Kirk LeMoyne Billings (JFK Library); Joseph Gargan (Edward M. Kennedy Institute); Ann Gargan (Edward M. Kennedy Institute); Edward M. Kennedy (Edward M. Kennedy Institute).

Volumes: *A Good Life* by Janet DesRosiers Fontaine; *Rose Kennedy's Family Album* by Caroline Kennedy; *Times to Remember* by Rose Kennedy; *Rose Kennedy* by Barbara A. Perry; *Life with Rose Kennedy* by Barbara Gibson and Carolyn Latham; *Iron Rose* by Cindy Adams and Susan Crimp; *Rose* by Gail Cameron; *Swanson on Swanson* by Gloria Swanson; *Marlene* by Charlotte Chandler; *JFK: Reckless Youth* by Nigel Hamilton; *The Nine of Us* by Jean Kennedy Smith.

I also referenced here and in other parts of this book Joseph P. Kennedy's unpublished manuscript, *Diplomatic Memoir,* which was made available by the JFK Library.

There are five biographies of Joseph P. Kennedy that are exceptional, and that I referenced throughout this book. They are *The Patriarch* by David Nasaw; *The Founding Father* by Richard Whalen; *The Ambassador* by Susan Ronald; *Sins of the Father* by Ronald Kessler; and *Joseph P. Kennedy Presents* by Cari Beauchamp.

Another important read: *Prohibition* by David Okrent, which settles the matter of Joseph P. Kennedy as a bootlegger.

I also referenced Rose Kennedy's Personal Papers/JFK Library and Joseph P. Kennedy's Personal Papers/JFK Library as well as "Rose Kennedy Remembers: The Best of Times, the Worst of Times," BBC (1974). I also referred to Rose's handwritten responses to "Questions: Special to Mrs. Joseph Kennedy," from author Lucy Post Frisbee, for her book *John Fitzgerald Kennedy* (JFK Library); I also referred to "Life on the American News Front: The Kennedy Family: Nine Children and $9,000,000," *Life*, December 20, 1937. I also utilized Kirk LeMoyne Billings Personal Papers (JFK Library) throughout this book.

For this section and others relating to Rose and Joseph Kennedy, important to my research were transcripts of writer Robert Coughlan's interviews with Rose Kennedy, Ethel Kennedy, and Eunice Kennedy Shriver, more than twenty interviews in total. These interviews were conducted in the winter of 1972 for Rose Kennedy's memoir, *Times to Remember*. My thanks to the JFK Library for making this invaluable material available to historians such as myself.

I also referred to "Rose Kennedy Talks about Her Life, Her Faith, and Her Children," *McCall's*, December 1973; "My Mother, Rose Kennedy" by Ted Kennedy, *Ladies' Home Journal*, December 1975.

Additionally: The Life of Joseph P. Kennedy (Forum Transcript), JFK Library (December 12, 2012).

"A LIFE OF PRIVILEGE"

ABOUT THE MACDONALDS:

I owe a huge debt of gratitude to Torbert Macdonald Jr. and Laurie Macdonald, son and daughter of Torbert Macdonald, Jack Kennedy's very close friend. Both were interviewed in 2023 and were invaluable in helping me to understand the close, very personal relationship between Congressman Macdonald and his buddy, the congressman, the senator, and, ultimately, the president.

Torbert Sr.—who died in 1976 at just fifty-eight—was a model of discretion when it came to his close friendship with JFK. He didn't say much in his lifetime, even in his oral history for the JFK Library. I would never have been able to capture that relationship if not for his children. I am very grateful to them for their assistance.

Other interviews: Charles Bartlett (1997); Joan Braden (1998); Arthur Schlesinger (1997, 2003, 2006).

Oral histories: Jacqueline Kennedy (Arthur Schlesinger, Jr.); Kirk LeMoyne Billings (JFK Library); Torbert Macdonald (JFK Library); Joseph Gargan (Edward M. Kennedy Institute); Grace Burke (JFK Library); Charles Bartlett (LBJ Library); Rev. John Cavanaugh (JFK Library); Arthur M. Schlesinger (LBJ Library);

Arthur Schlesinger (Edward M. Kennedy Institute); Edward M. Kennedy (Edward M. Kennedy Institute). I also referenced the Clay Blair Papers, American Heritage Center, University of Wyoming, Laramie, Wyoming.

Volumes: *Why England Slept* by John F. Kennedy; *While England Slept* by Winston Churchill; *The Hitler of History* by John Lukacs; *A Concise Biography of Adolf Hitler* by Thomas Fuchs; *The Pleasure of His Company* by Paul B. Fay Jr.; *The Search for JFK* by Joan and Clay Blair Jr.; *All Too Human* by Edward Klein; *In Search of History* by Theodore H. White; *Remembering Jack* by Jacques Lowe and Hugh Sidey.

I also referenced "An Epilogue for President Kennedy" (Interview with Jaqueline Kennedy) by Theodore H. White, *Life,* December 6, 1963; Rose Kennedy's Personal Papers (JFK Library); Joseph P. Kennedy's Personal Papers (JFK Library); "The Kennedy Family" (JFK Library).

The letter from Joseph P. Kennedy to Jack Kennedy can be found in the Joseph P. Kennedy Papers (JFK Library).

PART II: PRELUDE TO CAMELOT

ABOUT JAMIE AUCHINCLOSS:

James (Jamie) Lee Auchincloss is the only son of Janet Auchincloss and Hugh D. Auchincloss, half brother of Jackie Bouvier Kennedy Onassis. He has been so invaluable to my research over the years, in particular for my book about his mother and half sisters, *Jackie, Janet & Lee,* and also for *Jackie: Public, Private, Secret.* There's no way I would've been able to write those two books, or *JFK: Public, Private, Secret,* without his memories of his parents and his siblings—his stepbrother Yusha, his sister Janet Jr., and, of course, Jackie and Lee, as well as his father's other children, Nini and Tommy.

Jamie was interviewed more than thirty times over the years between 2017 and 2022. He also provided some key photographs for this book. Since he's not yet written his own memoir, I am honored to tell so many of his stories. The times I've spent with Jamie over the years have meant a lot to me. He's a wonderful person.

In 2009, fifteen years after the death of his half sister Jackie, Jamie got into trouble with the law after admitting to possessing child pornography. He was sentenced to thirty days in jail and three years' probation. It's always been my position that this surprising and unfortunate turn in Jamie's life in no way impacts his standing in history, or his memories of growing up a chief witness to the Camelot years. He paid his debt to society.

Today, Jamie spends much of his time researching his family as well as those of other presidents. He also lectures at presidential libraries across the nation.

"MERRYWOOD ROYALS" AND "FUTURE IN-LAWS"

AUTHOR'S NOTE ABOUT JANET AUCHINCLOSS:

Janet Lee Auchincloss gave two interviews in 1972 and 1973 to a journalist who intended to sell the stories to a women's magazine. However, when she and Jackie reviewed the transcripts, they both felt they were too revealing and asked that the stories not be published. I was provided these transcripts by a confidential source. It was previously thought that these interviews were conducted in 1976. However, the dates were October 1972 and January 1973. In these source notes, these transcripts will subsequently be referred to as "Janet Auchincloss Transcripts 72/73."

Also, Mrs. Auchincloss gave two oral histories to the JFK Library on September 5, 1964, and September 6, 1964, which I have utilized throughout. Prior to those interviews, Mrs. Auchincloss gave what might be considered practice interviews on August 20 and 21, 1964. Much of what she said in these interviews was not included in her oral history. A confidential source allowed me access to this material, and I utilized it throughout this book. In these source notes, these interviews will be referred to as "Janet Auchincloss Interviews 1964."

I'd always felt Janet Lee Auchincloss was unfairly represented in American history as an uncaring woman with whom her children had a rancorous relationship, Jackie in particular. I hope that in my writings about her over the years I've been able to clarify that record and set it straight. She was a complicated woman, no doubt. But what she said to her son-in-law, Jack Kennedy, in 1953 has always stuck with me. "Clearly, you don't understand mothers," she told him. "The worry," she said, "never goes away." She said she'd never stop worrying about Jackie, "not until I'm dead and in the ground six feet under, and even then."

As well as my extensive research for my book *Jackie, Janet & Lee,* I relied on:

Interviews: Charles Bartlett (1997); Martha Bartlett (1997); Cybil Wright (2022); John Husted (1997, 1998); Maud Davis (1998); Gore Vidal (1998, 2010); Luella Hennessey (JFK Library); Kathleen Bouvier (2000); Nina Auchincloss Strait (1998); Joan Braden; Jamie Auchincloss; Charles Bartlett, Margaret Kearney; and John H. Davis.

Where John H. Davis is concerned, I also drew from his interview with Joan Rivers on *The Joan Rivers Show* (1992).

I also interviewed Hugh D. "Yusha" Auchincloss III on October 12, 1998, and November 1, 1999, and used comments from those interviews throughout this book.

Oral histories: Jacqueline Kennedy Onassis (LBJ Library); Joan Braden (JFK Library); Kirk LeMoyne Billings (JFK Library); Janet Auchincloss (JFK Library); Edward M. Kennedy (Edward M. Kennedy Institute).

Volumes: *Jaqueline Bouvier Kennedy* by Mary Van Rensselaer Thayer; *America's Queen* by Sarah Bradford; *Janet and Jackie* by Jan Pottker; *Jacqueline Bouvier Kennedy*

Onassis by Barbara Leaming; *These Few Precious Days* by Christopher Andersen; *Jack* by Geoffrey Perret; *Jack and Lem* by David Pitts; *Mrs. Kennedy* by Barbara Leaming; *Jacqueline Bouvier Kennedy Onassis* by Barbara Leaming; *America's Secret Aristocracy* by Stephen Birmingham; *Top Drawer* by Mary Cable; and *Louis Auchincloss: A Writer's Life* by Carol Gelderman.

I also referenced: "Mud Wrestling with History: Snapshots of My Life as a Brother-in-Law to John F. Kennedy" (text of a speech) by James Auchincloss; Janet Auchincloss Interviews, 1964; Diaries of Hugh D. [Yusha] Auchincloss III, 1961, 1962, 1963, and 1964 [before being publicly auctioned in 2019 and provided by an anonymous source]; "The Kennedys—American Experience," PBS Home Video, DVD, 2003.

I also referenced: "I Remember . . . Reminiscences of Hammersmith Farm" by Esther Auchincloss Blitz, Newport History (Newport Historical Society), spring 1994; "Original Manuscript of Esther Auchincloss Blitz: My Life," Newport Historical Society; "Hammersmith Farm" by John T. Hopf, Camelot Gardens, Inc., 1979; "In Living Memory: A Chronicle of Newport, Rhode Island, 1888 1988"; "James T. Lee Buys East 48th St. Site," *New York Times,* January 22, 1928; "Dr. James Lee Dies at 75," *New York Herald Tribune,* May 15, 1928; "Mrs. Auchincloss Hit by Propeller," *Washington Evening Star,* July 16, 1929; "Hugh Auchincloss Marries in Capital," *New York Times,* May 8, 1931; "Mrs. H. D. Auchincloss Asks Reno Divorce," *New York Times,* May 24, 1932; "Newport: There She Sits" by Cleveland Amory, *Harper's,* February 1948; Newport Savings and Loan Association, 1988; "How the Remarkable Auchincloss Family Shaped the Jacqueline Kennedy Style" by Stephen Birmingham, *Ladies' Home Journal,* March 1967; "Rose Kennedy Talks About Her Life, Her Faith, and Her Children," *McCall's,* December 1983; "Bouvier Estate Goes to Widow," *New York Times,* January 19, 1926; "Mrs. Janet Bouvier Weds Liet. Hugh Auchincloss," *East Hampton Star,* June 24, 1942.

I also referenced various assets of the Auchincloss Family Collection of the John Fitzgerald Kennedy Presidential Library and Museum.

I referenced "Hugh [Yusha] Auchincloss: Remembering Jackie O," NBC 10/WJAR, November 20, 2013.

Additionally, I reviewed a pictorial scrapbook compiled by Janet for Hugh when the Auchinclosses sold Merrywood, entitled "Hugh D. Auchincloss, Merrywood, 1960," and inscribed: "For Hugh D.—A Souvenir of 18 Years Together at Merrywood, with all My Love, Janet, June 21, 1960," as well as "Auchincloss Family Tree" by Joanna Russell Auchincloss and Caroline Auchincloss Fowler (Higginson Book Co., 1957).

Also: "Luncheon with Jamie Auchincloss" by Gwen Dobson, *Washington Evening Star,* December 22, 1972.

"JACKIE," "PERFECT ON PAPER," AND "FROM THIS MOMENT ON"

As well as my extensive research for my books *Jackie: Public, Private, Secret* and *Jackie, Ethel, Joan,* I relied on:

Interviews: Jamie Auchincloss; James L. Buckley; John H. Davis; Joseph Gargan; Janet DesRosiers Fontaine; Kenny O'Donnell; Cybil Wright.

Oral histories: Jacqueline Kennedy Onassis (LBJ Library); Joan Braden (JFK Library); Kirk LeMoyne Billings (JFK Library); Janet Auchincloss (JFK Library); Luella Hennessey (JFK Library); Kenneth P. O'Donnell (LBJ Library); Ann Gargan (Edward M. Kennedy Institute); Grace Burke (JFK Library).

I also referred to Janet Auchincloss Interviews 1964.

Volumes: *Camera Girl* by Carl Sferrazza Anthony; *Incomparable Grace* by Mark K. Updegrove; *The Fabulous Bouvier Sisters* by Sam Kashner and Nancy Schoenberger; *740 Park* by Michael Gross; *Ted Kennedy* by Edward Klein; *JFK Coming of Age* by Frederick Logevall; *Presidential Wives: An Anecdotal History* by Paul F. Boller Jr.; *First Ladies* by Betty Boyd Caroli; *My Twelve Years with John F. Kennedy* by Evelyn Lincoln.

I also referred to correspondence to me from Joan Braden (1990).

PART III: FIRST LOVE: INGA

"A FATED MEETING," "AN AWAKENING," AND "SLEEPING WITH THE ENEMY?"

Note: All correspondence in this book to John Kennedy from Inga Arvad and vice versa are among the holdings of the Inga Arvad Papers of the JFK Library. Also, any diary entries or other writings by Miss Arvad are also courtesy of the JFK Library.

I interviewed Page Huidekoper Wilson in 2009 for my book *After Camelot.* She was a wonderful woman with a great story to tell, which she later explored in her book *Courage and Carnage.* It's so worth reading. I wasn't able to use her comments in *After Camelot* since the premise of that book turned out to be the story of the Kennedys *after* JFK. When I called to apologize to her about it, she said, "One day you'll write about Inga Arvad, use me then." And, of course, that time has now come.

Volumes: *Kathleen Kennedy* by Lynne McTaggart; *Kick* by Paula Byrne; *Kick Kennedy* by Barbara Leaming; *Honey Fitz* by John Cutler; *The Patriarch* by David Nasaw; *The Founding Father* by Richard Whalen; *The Ambassador* by Susan Ronald; *Cissy* by Ralph G. Martin; *Hitler's People* by Richard L. Evans; *The Rise and Fall of the Third Reich* by William L. Shirer; *Kennedy and Johnson* by Evelyn Lincoln; *My Twelve Years with John F. Kennedy* by Evelyn Lincoln; *Seeds of Destruction* by Ralph G. Martin; *Sarge* by Scott Stossel; *Ambassador's Journal* by John Kenneth Galbraith.

I also relied on the best and, actually, the only book about Inga Arvad, a must-read: *Inga: Kennedy's Great Love, Hitler's Perfect Beauty, and J. Edgar Hoover's Prime Suspect* by Scott Farris.

For these chapters, as well as for all of the following that relate to Inga Arvad, I also referenced the Inga Arvad Papers (JFK Library), which includes her many letters to John Kennedy, and other personal writings.

I also referenced "Newspaper Titan: The Infamous Life and Monumental Times of Cissy Patterson," a film stored in the Library of Congress; "WWII Secrets: The Mysterious Inga Arvad" by Peter Kross, *WWII History,* May 2008; "Dear Inga, Love Jack" by Geoffrey Gray, *Alta,* July 6, 2020; "Did You Happen to See?" by Inga Arvad, *Washington Times-Herald,* November 27, 1941; "Meet Miss Inga Arvad," International News Service, March 1936; "Forgotten Love Story" by BHT Staff, British Heritage Travel, September 13, 2024.

"GOOD NEWS AND BAD NEWS," "JOE'S UNLIKELY ALLIANCE," AND "A FATHER'S SCHEME"

Much of the material here is from the unpublished manuscript *Unlikely Alliances* by Janine Burke. I'd especially like to thank Miss Burke, who was Arthur Houghton's secretary and good friend. She was eighteen years old when she was hired by Mr. Houghton in 1945. She worked for him for more than twenty years.

I spent many hours with Janine in 2023 and 2024 as she shared her memories of Mr. Houghton and the Kennedys, in particular his best friendship with Joseph P. Kennedy. She also provided photographs. Most invaluable, though, is *Unlikely Alliances.* Allowing me to access her book and the great stories she told in it, many of which are published in *JFK: Public, Private, Secret* for the first time, is so very much appreciated.

The meetings between Jack Kennedy and his father witnessed by Arthur Houghton and between Jack, Inga, and the management of the *Times-Herald* are both drawn from an unpublished essay written by Ms. Burke in March 1978, which she made available to me.

Today, Janine is in her nineties and very healthy, happy, and, as she told me, "grateful for every moment I spent with Arthur and the Kennedys."

Oral histories: Kirk LeMoyne Billings (JFK Library); Richard Flood (JFK Library).

Volumes: *Inga: Kennedy's Great Love, Hitler's Perfect Beauty, and J. Edgar Hoover's Prime Suspect* by Scott Farris; *Cissy* by Ralph G. Martin; *JFK: Reckless Youth* by Nigel Hamilton; *Sins of the Father* by Ronald Kessler; *Grace and Power* by Sally Bedell Smith; *The Kennedy Men 1901–1963* by Laurence Leamer; *Kathleen Kennedy* by Lynne McTaggart.

The letter from Paul Fejos—"There is one thing I want to tell you"—is found in the Inga Arvad Papers of the JFK Library. I also accessed the "Henry James Letters" file of the JFK Library.

"'DISTRUST IS A VERY FUNNY THING,'" "THE BIRD STOPS SINGING," AND "HOW LOVE ENDS"

Interviews: Ronald McCoy (2023); Senator George Smathers (1999, 2000, 2001, 2003); Page Huidekoper; Janine Burke.

Oral histories: Kirk LeMoyne Billings (JFK Library).

Volumes: *Kick* by Paula Byrne; *Kick Kennedy* by Barbara Leaming; *Kathleen Kennedy* by Lynne McTaggart; *Jack and Jackie* by Christopher Andersen; *The Kennedys* by Peter Collier and David Horowitz; *The Kennedys* by Thomas Maier.

I also referenced Inga Avard Papers (JFK Library) as well as "How Hitler's Nordic Beauty and JFK's Love Became the Wife of a Wyoming Movie Star" by Jackie Dorothy, *Cowboy State Daily,* August 18, 2024.

INGA ARVAD: POSTSCRIPT

I'd like to thank Inga Arvad's son Ronald McCoy for all of his time, energy, and insight into the life of his mother during his interviews of 2023 for this book. His loving memory of her is really what formed her personality and character for this work, and I appreciate it and him so much. Surely, no one knows a mother like her own son.

"Do you know what happens to a woman when she gets into her mid-thirties?" Inga asked Jack Kennedy the last time she saw him in 1947. "She becomes invisible to the world." Whereas heads once turned whenever she walked into a room, Inga told Jack she was now rarely noticed, her striking beauty faded with age. Jack, however, said he thought she was still "a looker," and maybe even better than ever. "Well, you're the exception," she said sadly.

After her time with Jack, Inga Arvad went on to a life that could best be described as ordinary or, maybe better stated, peaceful. She became a wife and mother living far from the public eye in an Arizona border town called Nogales, south of Tucson, with a population of less than eight thousand. She was active in the PTA and other civic organizations and held a part-time job in the local library. At fifty, she battled rheumatoid arthritis but was otherwise in good health. Her romance with Jack was seldom, if ever, brought up between her and her husband, Tim McCoy.

Tim McCoy became the host of a local television Western show and also toured for much of the year in his own Old West revue. While Inga's ex and his wife lived an exceptional lifestyle in the White House, her home with Tim was small, cramped, and had no central heat. One son, Ronald, slept in a walk-in closet in his mother's bedroom while the other, Terry, would curl up in a corner of his father's room. "My mother lived a simple life with my father with no adventure or thrills," said Ronald, "certainly not what she ever imagined for herself back in those fun Washington days with Kick, but maybe just what she needed.

"I can't say she was unhappy," said Ronald. "We had a nice life. I do know she hadn't talked to Kennedy since 1947. When he ran for president, that's when I first found out about the two of them. I asked my dad who he thought might win the 1960 election and he said, 'Your mother might have a better idea about it.' That's when she told me. She also told me she planned to reconnect with President Kennedy in his second term. She was going to reach out to him for old times' sake. Of course, that wasn't meant to be. She loved my dad in one way, but she loved Jack Kennedy in a whole different, more, I guess, intense way."

Inga once recalled that when she parted with Jack for the last time, she quoted Henry Wadsworth Longfellow's "The Theologian's Tale":

Ships that pass in the night and speak each other in passing.

She said Jack then finished the line:

Only a signal shown and a distant voice in the darkness.

While he took the break badly, Jack Kennedy didn't regret any of his time with Inga. "If I could fall in love with her all over again," he once said. "I'd do it in a second."

Sadly, Inga Arvard died of cancer on December 12, 1973, at the age of sixty. Years later, Ronald McCoy was finally able to review the file on her kept under lock for so many years by J. Edgar Hoover. "Mom had no idea what was in that file," McCoy said. "When I read the intelligence about her and JFK and the tape transcripts of their most intimate, private moments, it was shocking. I thought to myself, *My God, Mom would've been devastated by this.*"

PART IV: MISS BOUVIER

"GETTING TO KNOW YOU," "THE JOB DESCRIPTION," AND "'BARELY PLAUSIBLE'"

As well as my extensive research for my books *Jackie, Janet & Lee* and *Jackie: Public, Private, Secret,* I relied on:

Interviews: Joseph Gargan; Morton Downey Jr.; Kathleen "Kerry" McCarthy; Senator George Smathers; Adora Rule (2016, 2022); Terrance Landow (2016, 2022); Blair Fuller (1997); Hugh D. Auchincloss III; Nancy Tuckerman (2007); Robert Westover (2016); Nancy Bacon (1998); Maud Davis; John H. Davis (1999); C. Wyatt Dickerson (1998).

Oral histories: Jacqueline Kennedy (Arthur Schlesinger, Jr.); Jacqueline Kennedy Onassis (LBJ Library); Janet Auchincloss (JFK Library); Luella Hennessey (JFK Library); Kirk LeMoyne Billings (JFK Library); Joseph Gargan (Edward M. Kennedy Institute); Paul B. Fay (JFK Library); Rev. John Cavanaugh (JFK

Library); Nancy Dickerson (LBJ Library); Arthur M. Schlesinger (LBJ Library); Arthur Schlesinger (Edward M. Kennedy Institute); Ann Gargan (Edward M. Kennedy Institute).

Volumes: *The Fitzgeralds & The Kennedys* by Doris Kearns Goodwin; *Times to Remember* by Rose Kennedy; *A Good Life* by Janet DesRosiers Fontaine; *Janet and Jackie* by Jan Pottker; *An Unfinished Life* by Robert Dallek; *Palimpsest* by Gore Vidal; *The Kennedys* by Thomas Maier; *The Nine of Us* by Jean Kennedy Smith; *Johnny, We Hardly Knew Ye* by Kenneth P. O'Donnell and David F. Powers with Joe McCarthy; *Profiles in Courage* by John F. Kennedy; *JFK: Reckless Youth* by Nigel Hamilton; *The Bouviers* by John H. Davis; and *The Kennedys* by John H. Davis.

I also referenced "Mud Wrestling with History: Snapshots of My Life as a Brother-in-Law to John F. Kennedy" (text of a speech) by James Auchincloss; Janet Auchincloss Interviews 1964; Diaries of Hugh D. [Yusha] Auchincloss III, 1961, 1962, 1963, and 1964 before they were publicly auctioned in 2019 (these diaries were provided by an anonymous source); "Growing Up with Jackie: My Memories, 1941–1953" by Hugh D. (Yusha) Auchincloss Jr. (JFK Library); Hugh D. Auchincloss Personal Papers (JFK Library); "What You Don't Know About Jackie Kennedy" by Laura Bergquist, *Look,* July 4, 1961; and "The Secret Lives of Jackie Onassis" (BBC documentary, includes interviews with Evelyn Lincoln).

I also referenced "Rose Kennedy Remembers: The Best of Times, the Worst of Times," BBC (1974) and "The Kennedys: American Experience," PBS Home Video, DVD, 2003.

I also referred to correspondence from John H. Davis (September 17, 1998) answering my questions relating to Jackie's relationship with her father.

I referred to *Our Forebears: From the Earliest Times to the First Half of the Year 1940* by John Vernou Bouvier Jr., which was privately published.

PART V: DESTINY

"HERO" AND "TRUE MEASURE OF THE MAN"

Interviews: Janine Burke; Ann Gargan (1998); Joseph Gargan.

Oral histories: Jacqueline Kennedy Onassis (LBJ Library); Kirk LeMoyne Billings (JFK Library); Torbert Macdonald (JFK Library); Letitia Baldrige (JFK Library); Joseph Gargan (Edward M. Kennedy Institute); Ann Gargan (Edward M. Kennedy Institute); Edward M. Kennedy (Edward M. Kennedy Institute).

Volumes: *PT 109* by Robert Donovan; *Combat Diaries* by Michael Guardia; *The Sinking of PT-109* by Charles Rivers Editors; *John F. Kennedy and PT-109* by Richard Tregaskis; *Collision with History* by Robert D. Ballard; *In Harm's Way* by Iain Martin; *PT 109* by William Doyle; *Into the Dark Water* by John J. Domagalski; *Jack Kennedy* by Chris Matthews; *An Unfinished Life* by Robert Dallek; *JFK: The Man and the Myth* by Victor Lasky.

I also referenced "USS PT-109 Documents" (JFK Library), which include materials maintained by President Kennedy's personal secretary, Evelyn Lincoln, concerning PT-109 and the United States Navy reports of its sinking. Also included in this folder are newspaper clippings and magazine articles as well as JFK's letters to Lem Billings from the Pacific. I also had access to a videotape of JFK discussing his experience on PT-109 in an interview in San Diego on August 13, 1957. I also referenced Rose Kennedy's Papers (JFK Library).

The letters from JFK to Lem Billings can be found in the PT-109 Papers (JFK Library). The letter from Rose Kennedy can be found in the Rose Kennedy Papers (JFK Library). The letter from JFK to Joseph P. Kennedy can be found in the Joseph P. Kennedy Papers (JFK Library).

Additionally: "Captain of the Ship That Hit PT-109 Mourns JFK," *Stars and Stripes,* November 25, 1963.

"WHAT WE GET THROUGH"

Interviews: Ronald McCoy; Cybil Wright.

Oral histories: Kirk LeMoyne Billings (JFK Library); Paul B. Fay (JFK Library); Senator George Smathers (JFK Library).

Volumes: *Inga: Kennedy's Great Love* by Scott Farris; *Jack and Lem: John F. Kennedy and Lem Billings: The Untold Story of an Extraordinary Friendship* by David Pitts.

I also referenced Inga Arvad Papers (JFK Library); Joseph P. Kennedy Papers (JFK Library, including correspondence to and from Arthur Houghton); Lem Billings Papers (JFK Library, including letters to and from JFK); and "Tells Story of PT Epic: Kennedy Lauds Men, Disdains Hero Stuff" by Inga Arvad, *Boston Globe,* January 11, 1944.

The letter from JFK to Inga can be found in the Inga Arvad Papers (JFK Library).

The letter from Joseph P. Kennedy to Arthur Houghton can be found in the Arthur Houghton Papers (JFK Library).

The letter from JFK to Lem Billings can be found in the Lem Billings Papers (JFK Library).

PART VI: MR. AND MRS. KENNEDY

As well as my extensive research for my books *Jackie, Ethel, Joan* and *Jackie, Janet & Lee* and *Jackie: Public, Private, Secret,* I relied on:

"SOMETHING LIKE THAT"

Interviews: Joseph Gargan; Janine Burke; Robert D. Watt (1994 interview conducted by Janine Burke for her book); Jamie Auchincloss; Hugh D. Auchincloss III; Janet Auchincloss Interviews 1964.

Oral histories: Jacqueline Kennedy Onassis (LBJ Library); Janet Auchincloss (JFK Library); Kirk LeMoyne Billings (JFK Library); Joseph Gargan (Edward M. Kennedy Institute); Ann Gargan (Edward M. Kennedy Institute).

Volumes: *Unlikely Alliances* by Janine Burke (unpublished); *Kennedy and Johnson* by Evelyn Lincoln; *My Twelve Years with John F. Kennedy* by Evelyn Lincoln; *Seeds of Destruction* by Ralph Martin; *Sarge* by Scott Stossel; *Ambassador's Journal* by John Kenneth Galbraith; *John F. Kennedy* by Michael O'Brien.

I also referenced "Mud Wrestling with History: Snapshots of My Life as a Brother-in-Law to John F. Kennedy" (text of a speech) by James Auchincloss; Janet Auchincloss Interviews 1964; The diaries of Hugh D. [Yusha] Auchincloss III, 1961, 1962, 1963, and 1964 before they were publicly auctioned in 2019 (the diaries were also provided by an anonymous source); "The Kennedys: American Experience," PBS Home Video, DVD, 2003; the television programs "At Home with the Kennedys" (1952 and 1958).

"'DO. YOU. LOVE. HIM?'" AND "CRAZIER THAN A CORKSCREW"

Interviews: Jamie Auchincloss; Barbara Gibson; Adora Rule; Marion "Oatsie" Charles; Lee Radziwill; Betty Beale (1998); Hugh D. (Yusha) Auchincloss III (1998, 1999); Trina Lloyd; John Husted (1997, 1998); Maud Davis; Gore Vidal (1998); Nina Auchincloss Strait (October 11, 1998); Charles Bartlett. Lee Radziwill's reminiscences here—"Hammersmith was a serene place" "or worse, a woman!"—are from a letter she wrote to her friend Truman Capote, which was provided to me by a confidential source.

Oral histories: Janet Auchincloss (JFK Library); Kirk LeMoyne Billings (JFK Library); Jacqueline Kennedy (Arthur Schlesinger, Jr.); Arthur M. Schlesinger (LBJ Library); Ann Gargan (Edward M. Kennedy Institute).

I also referred to Janet Auchincloss Transcripts 72/73, in particular for the conversation with Jackie: "Do. You. Love. Him." Also, Janet Auchincloss Interviews 1964 for "The worry, it never goes away."

Volumes: *Life with Rose Kennedy* by Barbara Gibson; *The Patriarch* by David Nasaw.

I also referenced "The Kennedys: American Experience," PBS Home Video, DVD, 2003; Interview with Ann Lowe on the *Mike Douglas Show,* 1966. I also referred to "Ann Lowe" by Elaine Nichols with research assistance by Alexis Dixon, National Museum of African American History and Culture, and "Why Jackie Kennedy's Wedding Dress Designer Was Fashion's Best Kept Secret," *New York Post,* October 16, 2016.

Lee Radziwill's memories are culled from an email she sent to an anonymous source in 2012.

The incident at the Kennedys' home between Joseph Kennedy and a female employee—"Why not give me a little smooch"—is culled from *Unlikely Alliances* by Janine Burke, who witnessed the exchange.

"PRE-WEDDING TRYST?"

Interview: Jacob Sterling (son of Gavin Sterling), 2023.

Oral history: Edward C. Berube (JFK Library).

Volumes: *Love, Jack* by Gunilla von Post and Carl Johnes; *The Fitzgeralds and the Kennedys: An American Saga* by Doris Kearns Goodwin; *Jack Kennedy: The Education of a Statesman* by Barbara Leaming.

I also referenced "JFK's Swedish Lover (Before and After He Married Jackie) Dies Aged 79," *Daily Mail*, November 9, 2011; "'Anxious to See You'—JFK Letters to Swedish Lover Auctions," Associated Press, May 6, 2021; "You Are Wonderful and I Miss You," WBZ News, Boston, May 6, 2021; "Seductive Secrets" by Katrina Schollenberger, *The U.S. Sun,* May 6, 2021.

"SEPTEMBER NUPTIALS"

Interviews: Joseph Gargan; Senator George Smathers; Chuck Spalding; Charles Bartlett; Betty Beale; Jamie Auchincloss; Yusha Auchincloss III; Adora Rule; Janet Auchincloss Interviews 1964.

It's worth noting that Janet Auchincloss's personal assistant, Adora Rule, replaced Janet's secretary Kaye Donovan on September 12, 1953, the day of Jack's wedding to Jackie. She was brought in as a Kelly Girl temporary replacement for Donovan and stayed on for more than thirty years.

Oral histories: Kirk LeMoyne Billings; Charles Bartlett (JFK Library); Senator George Smathers (JFK Library); Senator George Smathers (LBJ Library); Charles Bartlett (LBJ Library).

Volumes: *A Woman Named Jackie* by C. David Heymann; *Sins of the Father* by Ronald Kesler; *A Good Life* by Janet DesRosiers Fontaine; *Grace and Power* by Sally Bedell Smith; *Janet and Jackie* by Jan Pottker; *Jacqueline Kennedy Bouvier Onassis* by Barbara Leaming; *Incomparable Grace* by Mark Updegrove.

I also referenced the letter from Rose Kennedy to Janet Auchincloss, which can be found in the Rose Kennedy Papers (JFK Library).

I also referenced "The Kennedys: American Experience," PBS Home Video, DVD, 2003, and "How the Remarkable Auchincloss Family Shaped the Jacqueline Kennedy Style" by Stephen Birmingham, *Ladies' Home Journal,* March 1967.

Additionally: "Kennedy Fiancé Plans Simple, Small Wedding," *Boston Traveler,* June 25, 1953; "Bride Nearly Crushed at Kennedy Wedding," *Atlanta Journal-Constitution*, September 13, 1953; "Jaqueline Bouvier, Senator Kennedy to Wed," *East Hampton Star,* July 16, 1953; "Kennedy-Bouvier License Issued," *Newport Daily News,* September 4, 1953; "What's She Like?" *Brockton (Mass.) Enterprise-Times,* June 28, 1953; "Kennedy-Bouvier Nuptials Held at St. Mary's Church Before 700 Invited Guests," *Newport Daily News,* September 12, 1953; "Kennedy-Bouvier Rites Colorful," *Danbury News-Times,* September 14, 1953; "Traffic Curbs Set for Kennedy-Bouvier Wedding"; "What Jackie Kennedy Has Learned from Her Mother," *Good*

Housekeeping, October 15, 1962; and "Getting Her Due on Doll's Dress: Designer Deserves Credit" by Samson Mulugeta, *Newsday,* January 11, 1998.

Also: Social Files/Senator's Wedding/John Fitzgerald Kennedy Presidential Library and Museum: including letters to Janet Auchincloss from John F. Kennedy (July 28, 1953) and Evelyn Lincoln (August 7, 1953, and September 3, 1953); "Suggested Lists for Jack's Wedding," for "Mrs. Auchincloss and Bobby," August 4, 1953.

PART VII: JOE

"FALLEN BROTHER" AND "SHADOWBOXING WITH GHOSTS"

Interviews: Joseph Gargan; Ann Gargan.

Oral histories: Joseph Gargan (Edward M. Kennedy Institute); Luella Hennessey (JFK Library); Ann Gargan (Edward M. Kennedy Institute); Paul B. Fay (JFK Library).

Volumes: *Times to Remember* by Rose Kennedy; *True Compass* by Edward M. Kennedy; *JFK Reckless Youth* by Nigel Hamilton; *Kick* by Paula Byrne; *Kick Kennedy* by Barbara Leaming; *Joseph P. Kennedy* by Ted Schwartz; *Hostage to Fortune* edited by Amanda Smith; *Sins of the Father* by Ronald Kessler; *The Founding Father* by Richard Whalen; *Joseph P. Kennedy Jr.* by Charles Rivers Editors; *An Unfinished Life* by Robert Dallek; *The Lost Prince* by Hank Searls; *A Good Man* by Mark K. Shriver.

The letters from Joseph Sr. to Joseph Jr. ("We were considerably upset" and "I can quite understand") and from Joseph Jr. to Joseph Sr. ("It looks like") can be found in the Joseph P. Kennedy Papers (JFK Library).

The diary entries from Rose Kennedy ("What a blow" and "What a terrible shame") and the letters from Joseph Kennedy to Arthur Houghton ("We've had a little excitement") can be found in the Rose Kennedy Papers and Joseph P. Kennedy Papers, respectively (JFK Library). The letters from Joseph Kennedy to Arthur Houghton ("I'm considering a proposition") and to Lord Beaverbrook can be found in the Arthur Houghton Papers and the Joseph P. Kennedy Papers, respectively (JFK Library).

PART VIII: THESE TIES THAT BIND

"JOE'S SURPRISING CONFESSION"

Interviews: Kenny O'Donnell; Dr. Nassir Ghaemi (2024); Barbara Gibson.

I'd especially like to thank Dr. Nassir Ghaemi (2024) for all of his assistance with this book.

Oral histories: Kirk LeMoyne Billings (JFK Library); Joseph Gargan (Edward M. Kennedy Institute); Ann Gargan (Edward M. Kennedy Institute).

Volumes: *Times to Remember* by Rose Kennedy; *Life with Rose Kennedy* by Barbara

Gibson; *Jack Kennedy* by Chris Matthews; *America's Queen* by Sara Bradford; *The Bouviers* by John H. Davis; *The Kennedys* by John H. Davis.

The note from Jackie (We have just had") can be found in the Jacqueline Kennedy Papers (JFK Library); I also referenced Janet Auchincloss Transcripts 72/73, in particular, for Joseph Kennedy's confession to Jackie, "I wished him pain."

"PROFILES IN COURAGE"

Interviews: Janet DesRosiers Fontaine; Arthur Schlesinger Jr.; Joseph Gargan; Ted Sorensen (April 1998; May 2008, in conjunction with the publication of his book *Counselor: A Life at the Edge of History*, March 2009).

Oral histories: Jacqueline Kennedy (Arthur Schlesinger, Jr.); Kirk LeMoyne Billings (JFK Library); Edward M. Kennedy (LBJ Library); Arthur M. Schlesinger (LBJ Library); Arthur Schlesinger (Edward M. Kennedy Institute); Theodore C. Sorensen (LBJ Library); Theodore C. Sorensen (Edward M. Kennedy Institute); Edward M. Kennedy (Edward M. Kennedy Institute).

Volumes: *Profiles in Courage* by John Kennedy; *Counselor* by Theodore C. Sorensen; *A Good Life* by Janet DesRosiers Fontaine.

I also referenced "A Life with JFK: Inside Camelot with Ted Sorensen" (video) and a transcript of Mr. Sorensen's speech at the Charleston School of Law (February 23, 2010).

Throughout this book, I referenced the CNN documentary series "American Dynasties: The Kennedys," 2018. I was a commentator on each of the six episodes along with Robert Kennedy Jr., Patrick Kennedy, and Kathleen Kennedy Townsend.

"BAD BLOOD"

As well as my extensive research for my book *Jackie, Ethel, Joan,* I relied on:

Interviews: Adora Rule; Janet DesRosiers Fontaine; John H. Davis; Hugh D. Auchincloss III; Janet Auchincloss Interviews 1964.

Oral histories: Jacqueline Kennedy (Arthur Schlesinger, Jr.); Joseph W. Alsop Oral History (Robert Kennedy Papers/JFK Library); Joseph Alsop (LBJ Library); Arthur Schlesinger (Edward M. Kennedy Institute).

Volumes: *America's Queen* by Sarah Bradford; *Jacqueline Bouvier Kennedy Onassis* by Donald Spoto; *Jacqueline Bouvier* by John H. Davis; *Love, Jack* by Gunilla von Post and Carl Johnes.

I also referenced Gunilla von Post interviews (ABC News); "The Kennedys: American Experience," PBS Home Video, DVD, 2003.

"JACK'S 'MISTAKE'"

Volumes: *Love, Jack* by Gunilla von Post and Carl Johnes; *Jack and Jackie* by Christopher Andersen; *Jackie* by Paul Brandus; *An Unfinished Life* by Robert Dallek; *The Kennedys* by Thomas Maier.

I also referenced: Gunilla von Post Interview (ABC News).

"THE ONLY TWO CHOICES"

Interviews: Claire Baring; Janet DesRosiers Fontaine; Janine Burke.

Volume: *Unlikely Alliances* by Janine Burke (unpublished).

I also referenced "The Indomitable Mrs. Rose Kennedy" by Eileen Foley, *Philadelphia Bulletin,* June 30, 1964. Jackie's poem ("All the things") can be found in the Jacqueline Kennedy Papers (JFK Library).

Also: "Dangerous Minds: The Kennedys," CNN (1998) and "The Kennedys in Hollywood," CNN (1998).

PART IX: THE LIFE WE CHOOSE

"FAMILY TRADITION"

Interviews: Janet DesRosiers Fontaine; Janine Burke; Cybil Wright; Janet Auchincloss Interviews 1964.

Oral history: Paul B. Fay (JFK Library).

Volumes: *Diplomatic Memoir* by Joseph P. Kennedy (unpublished); *Unlikely Alliances* by Janine Burke (unpublished); *A Good Life* by Janet DesRosiers Fontaine; *Kick* by Paula Byrne; *Kick Kennedy* by Barbara Leaming; *Sins of the Father* by Ronald Kessler; *The Patriarch* by Davd Nasaw.

I also referenced the Arthur Houghton Papers (JFK Library).

"PROTECTING THE LIE"

Interview: Senator George Smathers.

A variation of the story of Joseph P. Kennedy and Gloria Swanson on the boat was first told by Axel Madsen in his book *Gloria and Joe.* Further details provided here are from George Smathers.

Volumes: *Swanson on Swanson* by Gloria Swanson; *Times to Remember* by Rose Kennedy; *The Patriarch* by David Nasaw.

PART X: SCORCHED EARTH

"MOMENT OF TRUTH"

Interviews: Terrance Landow; Senator George Smathers; Rosemary Smathers (1999); Leah Mason (secretary to Ethel Kennedy, 1996, 1998, 2017).

I also referenced the Janet Auchincloss Transcripts 72/73.

"JACK'S DEFINING MOMENT" AND "SALT SPRAY ON HIS LIPS"

Interviews: Janine Burke; Janet DesRosiers Fontaine; Senator George Smathers; Hugh D. Auchincloss III.

Oral histories: Jacqueline Kennedy Onassis (LBJ Library); Senator George Smathers (JFK Library); Senator George Smathers (LBJ Library); Kirk LeMoyne Billings (JFK Library); Janet Auchincloss (JFK Library); Lyndon B. Johnson (LBJ Library); Edward M. Kennedy (LBJ Library).

Volumes: *Unlikely Alliances* by Janine Burke (journal printed in her unpublished manuscript); *The Patriarch* by David Nasaw; *JFK: An Unfinished Life* by Robert Dallek; *Jack Kennedy* by Chris Matthews; *A Good Life* by Janet DeRosiers Fontaine; *Lyndon Johnson and the American Dream* by Doris Kearns Goodwin; *The Bouviers* by John H. Davis; *The Kennedys* by John H. Davis.

A highly recommended book well worth reading is *JFK: Ordeal in Africa* by Richard D. Mahoney, which analyzes Kennedy's foreign policy in Africa, not dealt with in detail in these pages but still an interesting subject for any student of Kennedy to consider.

I also referenced news footage from the 1956 Democratic Convention; Janet Auchincloss Transcripts 72/73 ("Jacqueline, no!"); "The Kennedys: American Experience," PBS Home Video, DVD, 2003.

"TEMPTED"

Interviews: Zachary Hitchcock; Linda Lydon.

I interviewed Peter Lawford backstage in 1981 at CBS-TV after he recorded voice-overs for an appearance on the television show *The Jeffersons*. His memories here and in other sections of this book are from that interview.

All of Joan Lundberg's written passages and her quotes in this and other sections of this book about her and JFK are culled from her unpublished manuscript *Lovers Don't Snore*, provided to us by her son, Zachary Hitchcock. Some quotes are also from "Joan Hitchcock's Evenings with JFK" by Maitland Zane, *Oui*, July 1976.

Volume: *Lovers Don't Snore* by Joan Lundberg Hitchcock (unpublished).

"JACK'S STRANGE DETACHMENT" AND "PERSONA NON GRATA"

As well as extensive research into this dark and confusing period of Jack Kennedy's life—in particular, the death of his daughter Arabella—for my books *Jackie, Ethel, Joan* and *Jackie, Janet & Lee* and *Jackie: Public, Private, Secret*, I relied on:

Interviews: Senator George Smathers; Betty Beale; Janet DesRosiers Fontaine; Adora Rule; Nini Auchincloss; Barbara Gibson, Arthur Schlesinger Jr.

Volumes: *A Good Life* by Janet DesRosiers Fontaine; *Life with Rose Kennedy* by

Barbara Gibson; *Jacqueline Bouvier Kennedy Onassis: A Life* by Donald Spoto; *Mrs. Kennedy* by Barbara Leaming; *Janet and Jackie* by Jan Pottker; *An Unfinished Life* by Robert Dallek; *JFK: Coming of Age* by Frederick Logevall; *The Bouviers* by John H. Davis; *The Kennedys* by John H. Davis; *Remarkable Kennedys* by Joe McCarthy.

I also referenced Janet Auchincloss Transcripts 72/73 ("How could I have been so stupid" and "Let me tell you something"); transcript of interview with Michael Canfield (provided by Terrance Landow).

"OUT THERE SOMEWHERE," "'TRAILER PARK JOAN,'" "THE ILLUSION OF CHOICE," AND "RULES OF ENGAGEMENT"

Interviews: Peter Lawford; John H. Davis; Adora Rule; Laurie Macdonald; Barbara Gibson; Janet DesRosiers Fontaine.

Where John H. Davis is concerned, I also drew from his interview with Joan Rivers on *The Joan Rivers Show* (1992).

Volumes: *Lovers Don't Snore* by Joan Lundberg Hitchcock (unpublished); *Sins of the Father* by Ronald Kessler; *The Patriarch* by David Nasaw.

The story of Jack running the bath in Peter Lawford's home and Sid Kaiser's faux paus were first told by Stephen Dunleavy and Peter Brennan in their book *Those Wild, Wild Kennedy Boys.*

I also referenced Janet Auchincloss Transcripts 72/73 ("Show me some respect" and "Jacqueline and I were talking"); "The Kennedys: American Experience," PBS Home Video, DVD, 2003.

Also: "How the $1 Billion Kennedy Family Fortune Defies Death and Taxes" by Carl O'Donnell, *Forbes,* July 8, 2014; "Size of Billionaire-Bashing Chris Kennedy's Fortune a Mystery, Still" by Kim Janssen, *Chicago Tribune,* June 1, 2017; "State's Longest-Practicing Lawyer Looks Back on Drama-Filled Career" by David E. Frank, *Massachusetts Lawyers Weekly,* March 13, 2014.

New reporting regarding Hugh Auchincloss's meeting with a lawyer to discuss the Kennedy fortune and, also, the decision to have JFK sleep in the servants' quarters as well as Janet and Hugh's reaction to Joe Kennedy's offer to Jackie was derived from an anonymous Auchincloss family source and corroborated by an attorney who represented the family, Benedict F. Fitzgerald, in my interview with him on April 11, 2004.

Regarding the deal made by Jackie Kennedy and Joseph Kennedy, I referred to my extensive research about Joe Kennedy's stroke for my book *Jackie, Ethel, Joan* and the subsequent miniseries based on my book of the same name for NBC.

"A PARTING OF THE WAYS"

Interviews: Janet DeRosiers Hitchcock; Kathleen "Kerry" McCarthy; Janet Auchincloss Interviews 1964.

Volumes: *A Good Life* by Janet DesRosiers Fontaine; *Sins of the Father* by Ronald Kessler.

I also referenced Rose Kennedy Papers (JFK Library).

The letter from Rose Kennedy to Janet DesRosiers Hitchcock was provided by Janet DesRosiers Hitchcock.

PART XI: EVER MOVING FORWARD

"STUCK IN MYSELF"

Interviews: Zachary Hitchcock; Linda Lydon.

Oral histories: Jacqueline Kennedy (Arthur Schlesinger, Jr.); Luella Hennessey (JFK Library).

Volumes: *Lovers Don't Snore* by Joan Lundberg Hitchcock (unpublished); *All Too Human* by Edward Klein; *Seeds of Destruction* by Ralph Martin; *The Kennedy Men* by Laurence Leamer; *Jack* by Herbert Parmet; *JFK* by Herbert Parmet; *Kennedy and Johnson* by Evelyn Lincoln; *My Twelve Years with John F. Kennedy* by Evelyn Lincoln; *Seeds of Destruction* by Ralph Martin; *Sarge* by Scott Stossel; *Ambassador's Journal* by John Kenneth Galbraith.

I also referenced "Joan Hithcock's Evenings with JFK" by Maitland Zane, *Oui*, July 1976.

"MILESTONE BIRTHDAY DECISIONS" AND "CAROLINE"

Interviews: Adora Rule; Janine Burke; John H. Davis; Senator George Smathers.

Oral histories: Paul B. Fay (JFK Library); Senator George Smathers (JFK Library); Senator George Smathers (LBJ Library); Letitia Baldrige (JFK Library); Janet Auchincloss (JFK Library); Edward M. Kennedy (Edward M. Kennedy Institute).

Volumes: *Alliances* by Janine Rule (unpublished); *JFK: The Man and the Myth* by Victor Lasky; *Grace and Power* by Sally Bedell Smith; *Jack* by Geoffrey Perrett; *The Bouviers* by John H. Davis; *The Kennedys* by John H. Davis.

I also referenced "John Bouvier 3rd, 66, Dies," *New York Times*, August 4, 1957; "John V. Bouvier 3rd," obituary, *East Hampton Star*, August 8, 1957; "Opening Chapters: Enchanting Memories and Photos of Her Early Life with Jackie" by Lee Radziwill, *Ladies' Home Journal*, January 1973; "Joan Hithcock's Evenings with JFK" by Maitland Zane, *Oui*, July 1976.

"FALLING FOR HIS WIFE," "JOAN'S UNWELCOME NEWS," AND "SOMEBODY'S DAUGHTER"

Interviews: Zachary Hitchcock; Linda Lydon; Patricia Brennan; Peter Lawford.

Volumes: *Lovers Don't Snore* by Joan Lundberg Hitchcock (unpublished); *Inga:*

Kennedy's Great Love by Scott Farris; *Mrs. Kennedy* by Barbara Leaming; *America's Queen* by Sarah Bradford.

I also referenced: Joan Hitchcock Interview, KRON-TV news footage from July 12, 1977, with reporter Fred LaCosse.

JOAN LUNDBERG HITCHCOCK: POSTSCRIPT

I would like to thank Joan Hitchcock's son, Zachary Hitchcock, for trusting me with the story of his beloved mother and her relationship with John Kennedy. I also owe a huge debt of gratitude to him for providing me with Joan's unpublished manuscript, *Lovers Don't Snore,* which she wrote in 1976 at the age of forty-three and which was key to my understanding of her and her love for Kennedy.

I am also grateful to Joan's sister, Linda Lydon, for her time and energy in helping me tell Joan's story.

I am indebted as well to Joan's husband, Mark McIntire, for his memories of her. There are other friends and relatives of Joan's that were interviewed for this book who asked to be anonymous, some of whom provided other notes and memorandum from and by Joan. I will respect their wishes here.

Joan Lundberg never again spoke to Jack Kennedy after ending things with him during their last telephone call in 1958.

In 1963, Joan married Freemont Bodine Hitchcock, better known as "Peter," shortly before giving birth to their son, Zachary. Hitchcock was heir to a prestigious Chicago investment banking enterprise. After her marriage, Jack sent Joan a telegram typical of him in its lack of sentiment: *Happy for you—Kennedy.*

Throughout her marriage, Joan often thought of JFK and, as she recalled, "still loved, admired, and respected him, both as a man and our president." Whenever intimates would ask why they'd parted, she'd never reveal the painful truth. Instead, she'd joke, "He wanted to be president, I wanted to be rich. We both got what we wanted." Of course, she was devastated by his assassination. She wrote:

When the truth struck home, I closed my bedroom curtains and shades, and I cried, screamed, and cursed alone for hours.

In the years that followed, Peter Hitchcock grew weary of Joan's endless stories about his romantic predecessor. "Mom always joked that Dad was probably the one who shot JFK just because he was so tired of hearing about him," Zachary quipped.

Joan and Peter divorced in 1967. Three years later, he died of spinal meningitis at just forty.

After Peter, Joan married three more times, including, in 1978, Mark McIntire, who starred in a very successful one-man show called *A Time to Remember* as . . . President John Fitzgerald Kennedy. Joan was one of the show's producers.

"I looked a lot like Kennedy and I think now, looking back, maybe it was her way of reconnecting with him," said McIntire. "She had Jack back, I guess. When she spoke of him, though, it was with regret. I think she felt abandoned and used."

McIntire reports that after taking a fall down a flight of stairs, "Joan's drinking turned into downright alcoholism. She was told she'd die if she didn't stop drinking." Her sister, Linda Lydon, added, "The disease ran in our family, our uncles, cousins. It was such a shame, this demon Joan battled."

Joan, maybe not surprisingly given her outsized personality, became a popular San Francisco socialite who frequently hosted parties in her Pacific Heights manse. In 1972, she hosted a publication party at her home to honor Kenny O'Donnell and Dave Powers for their book about JFK, *Johnny, We Hardly Knew Ye*. Dave inscribed her copy of his book:

To Joan: Who remembers the "Golden Days of J.F.K." Thanks a million for a great "Book Party." My very best wishes always. Dave Powers.

In 1975, Joan ran unsuccessfully for a seat on the San Fransisco Board of Supervisors, as she did again in 1977.

While researching her book, Joan came across an envelope in a box of mementos. She remembered that it had been taped to a valise that Jack used in January 1957 when the two of them were in New York at the Waldorf. On the envelope was a scribbled note from his brother:

Jack—Do you have any clothes in this bag—If so please send them to me immediately— Bobby. P.S. Don't worry but you have no more friends in Las Vegas. I put principal above your political future as I know you would want me to—

Joan had no idea what the note meant—what it was Bobby might've done to settle something in Las Vegas for his older brother. She didn't even remember saving it, but she was glad she did. It brought her back to a time and place she sometimes romanticized as "those great, shiny days."

"Her love for JFK endured," Zachary said of his mom, "and her feelings about what she went through with him, the abortion and all that, became more fueled by alcohol. She'd get sad and would sob when we talked about him. It turned into a kind of obsession in our household. I was reading the Warren Report about the assassination and looking at autopsy pictures when I was eight or nine years old. She even put up an author in our home who was writing a biography of Bobby Kennedy's assassin Sirhan Sirhan."

Joan's sister, Linda Lydon, recalled, "My husband, Dan, was from Boston. Irish like the Kennedys. Joan would have cocktails and call him at all hours of the night saying, 'Talk like Jack, Dan. Talk like Jack.'"

"For years, I resented JFK for what he did to my mother," said Zachary Hitchcock. "It wasn't until John Jr. died in that crash that I decided to accept the Kennedys with more compassion and understanding. John-John's death somehow changed my perception of his father, and in some ways my mother, too, and I guess of Jackie, too, and what she went through."

In her book, Joan wrote of Jackie:

I do have the highest regard for her. She has been blasted and hurt from all sides, and my heart goes out to her. She must be a grievously wounded woman. I hope these memoirs will not be salt in her wounds but will reassure her of what a great man her husband was.

As much as she idealized her time with Jack Kennedy, Joan also came to reconcile her time with him in realistic terms. "She began to understand that Jack Kennedy was a man of his time," said Zachary Hitchcock, "and that there were no limits for men like him, no matter how much they betrayed the women in their lives, not just the ones who were supposed to be there like Jackie, but the ones who weren't supposed to be there, like Mom."

Joan Lundberg Hitchcock spent the final six months of her life being treated for cirrhosis of the liver in Queen of the Valley Hospital in Napa. She died on January 27, 1982. She was only fifty.

PART XII: A FATHER'S DECEPTION

"LOST SISTER," "BURIED SECRETS," "HIDING ROSIE," AND "FULL DISCLOSURE"

Most of the interviews conducted for parts of the book about Rosemary Kennedy were with sources who asked for anonymity due to the subject's sensitive nature. Of course, I will respect their wishes here.

For this section and others relating to Rosemary Kennedy, I referred to transcripts of Robert Coughlin's interviews with Rose Kennedy, Ethel Kennedy, and Eunice Kennedy Shriver. These interviews were conducted in the winter of 1972.

Special thanks to Maryann Gleisner, president of the Jefferson Historical Society, for her assistance. At the time of this writing she had been with the Historical Society for fifty-nine years! She was actually a founding member when it was just in a handful of residents' homes. Her work in Jefferson speaks for itself—her family hosted the first dinner for JFK in Jefferson to introduce him to politicians there—and I very much appreciate her contributions to this book.

I would also like to express my appreciation to Ted Behncke, the former president of St. Coletta's. He retired from the position in June 2024 after being with St. Coletta's for sixteen years, nine as president. I am so grateful to him for his assistance with this book.

Also, thanks to Christina J. Goldstone, author of *Leading with Their Hearts: The Story of St. Coletta of Wisconsin,* for her assistance. It's a terrific book. Read it!

In the hope of meeting Rosemary Kennedy, I visited St. Coletta's and the Alverno Nursing Home in 1998 as part of my research for *Jackie, Ethel, Joan: Women of Camelot.* While I was able to have a brief meeting with Rosie, I was not permitted to interview her. However, the staff there were very gracious and provided many of the details found in these sections of the book.

Interviews: Philip Geyelin; Janet DesRosiers Fontaine; Janine Burke; Barbara Gibson; Kathleen "Kerry" McCarthy; Cybil Wright; Sister Joseph Marie (2002).

Oral histories: Luella Hennessey (JFK Library); Jacqueline Kennedy Onassis (LBJ Library); Jacqueline Kennedy Onassis (Arthur Schlessinger, Jr.); Janet Auchincloss (JFK Library); Edward M. Kennedy (Edward M. Kennedy Institute).

Volumes: *Diplomatic Memoir* by Joseph P. Kennedy (unpublished); *Unlikely Alliances* by Janine Burke (unpublished); *True Compass* by Edward M. Kennedy; *The Kennedy Family and the History of Retardation* by William Shorter; *Rosemary* by Kate Clifford Larson; *The Missing Kennedy* by Elizabeth Koehler-Pentacoff; *Rose Kennedy* by Barbara A. Perry; *Times to Remember* by Rose Kennedy; *The Patriarch* by David Nasaw; *A Good Life* by Janet DesRosiers Fontaine; *Eunice* by Eileen McNamara; *Kick Kennedy* by Barbara Leaming; *Torn Lace Curtain* by Frank Saunders.

I also referenced Janet Auchincloss Transcripts 72/73; Arthur Houghton Papers (JFK Library).

The letter from Joseph Kennedy to Sister Anastasia can be found in the Joseph P. Kennedy Papers (JFK Library).

AUTHOR'S NOTE ABOUT EUNICE KENNEDY SHRIVER:

I interviewed Eunice Kennedy Shriver in the spring of 2002 for an article I was writing at the time on the Special Olympics for *Redbook,* a women's magazine. I drew from that interview for some sections of this book. Incidentally, that story was never published because the editors were unhappy since it didn't contain many personal details about Eunice's relationships with other Kennedy family members. Looking back on it, I didn't have the courage to ask her the kinds of questions the editors wanted answered. In my defense, though, prior to the interview Mrs. Kennedy Shriver specifically told me via fax that "no personal questions will be answered, whatsoever."

Six months later, I received a telephone call from Mrs. Kennedy Shriver asking for a copy of the story. "I seemed to have missed it," she told me. I had no choice but to tell her that the feature didn't run. "Why is that?" she demanded to know in a clipped tone. Reluctantly, I explained the reason as honestly as I could. "Well, good for you, then," she said, suddenly seeming happy. "I applaud you for your discretion!" She concluded, "Fine, then. Now, goodbye and I hope we meet again one day." And with that, she hung up.

PART XIII: THE CLIMB UP

"POLITICAL OPERATIVES"

Interviews: Ben Bradlee (1995, 1996, 2000, 2002); Antoinette Bradlee (1995, 1999); Senator George Smathers; Paul B. Fay (JFK Library); Janet Auchincloss Interviews 1964.

Oral histories: Arthur M. Schlesinger (LBJ Library); Arthur Schlesinger (Edward M. Kennedy Institute); Edward M. Kennedy (Edward M. Kennedy Institute); Letitia Baldrige (JFK Library).

Volumes: *A Good Life* by Ben Bradlee; *Conversations with Kennedy* by Ben Bradlee; *Jack Kennedy* by Chris Matthews; *An Unfinished Life* by Robert Dallek; *Kennedy and Johnson* by Evelyn Lincoln; *My Twelve Years with John F. Kennedy* by Evelyn Lincoln; *Seeds of Destruction* by Ralph Martin; *Sarge* by Scott Stossel; *Ambassador's Journal* by John Kenneth Galbraith.

I also referenced President John F. Kennedy Papers 1961–1963, which is roughly three thousand pages in three volumes. His dictated letter to Jackie ("I went up there") can be found in this file, though it is misplaced by date.

Additionally: "Johnson and the Kennedys: An Intimate Report" by Kenneth P. O'Donnell, *Life,* August 7, 1970.

"THE CAVE" AND "OFFICIALLY IN THE GAME"

Interviews: Arthur Schlesinger Jr.; Adora Rule; Janine Burke.

Oral history: Arthur Schlesinger (Edward M. Kennedy Institute).

Volumes: *Kick Kennedy* by Barbara Leaming; *Kick* by Paula Byrne; *Kennedy or Nixon* by Arthur Schlesinger Jr.; *A Thousand Days* by Arthur M. Schlesinger Jr.

I also referenced Janet Auchincloss Transcripts 72/73; President John F. Kennedy Papers (JFK Library); Joseph P. Kennedy Papers (JFK Library); Rose Kennedy Papers (JFK Library).

PART XIV: JFK FOR PRESIDENT

As well as my extensive research for my book *Sinatra: Behind the Legend* to which I referred for this and other parts of this work relating to Frank Sinatra, Judith Campbell, and Sam Giancana, I relied on:

"FEMME FATALE," "HIGH HOPES," "THE TROUBLE WITH JUDY," AND "SINATRA"

Interviews: John Radziwill; Peter Lawford; Liz Carpenter (1998, 2000); William F. Roemer (1995); Rupert Allen (1995); Tony Oppedisano (2010, 2018, 2020); Barbara Gibson; Leah Mason; Bill Stapley (1997, 1998); Jim Whiting (1997, 2022); Micky Rudin (1996); Jilly Rizzo (1991, 1992).

Oral histories: Lyndon B. Johnson (LBJ Library); Kirk LeMoyne Billings (JFK Library); Liz Carpenter (LBJ Library); Sargent Shriver (LBJ Library).

Volumes: *Judith Exner, My Story* by Judith Exner; *Mafia Moll* by Judith Exner Campbell; *Jack Kennedy* by Chris Matthews; *True Believer* by James Traub; *Dark Side of Camelot* by Seymour Hersh; *Double Cross* by Sam Giancana, Chuck Giancana, and Bettina Giancana; *Family Affair* by Sam Giancana and Scott M. Burnstein; *Man Against the Mob* by William F. Roemer; *Sins of the Father* by Ronald Kessler; *Sinatra* by Anthony Summers; *My Life with Frank* by Barbara Sinatra.

I would especially like to acknowledge Scott M. Burnstein, best known for his book *Mafia Prince,* an all-time classic of the genre, for his help. Scott is the author of a number of other books relating to the underworld, including *Family Affair: Greed, Treachery and Betrayal in the Chicago Mafia.* In my opinion, he's the real deal when it comes to this particular subject, thorny as it is. He serves on the "Mob Museum's" Advisory Council. For more information about him and his stellar work, visit his website at https://gangsterreport.com/.

I also referenced "20/20 Interview with Judith Exner and Liz Smith," December 14, 1996, ABC-TV; "The Exner Files" by Liz Smith, *Vanity Fair,* January 1997; "JFK and the Mob" by Liz Smith, *People,* February 1988; "The Dark Side of Camelot" by Kitty Kelley, *People,* February 29, 1988; "The Last Act of Judith Exner" by Gerri Hirshey, *Vanity Fair,* April 1990; and White House Visitor Logs (JFK Library).

Judith Campbell Exner died on September 24, 1999, at the age of sixty-five. On September 30, after publication of its obituary of her, the *New York Times* wrote an addendum to it: "An obituary on Monday reported the death of Judith Campbell Exner. It quoted assertions she had made over the years that she had had an affair with John F. Kennedy before and after he was elected President. The article reported that aides of President Kennedy's, including Dave Powers, denied the affair. But it should also have reflected what is now the view of a number of respected historians and authors that the affair did in fact take place. The evidence cited by various authorities in recent years has included White House phone logs and memos from J. Edgar Hoover."

"WEST VIRGINIA"

I'd especially like to thank Kennedy historian James DiEugenio for his time and energy in helping me understand and answer questions relating to West Virginia as well as other controversies relating to JFK's rumored ties with the underworld and especially relating to his assassination. His many books about JFK are well worth reading when framing these aspects of his life story. He is also well-versed on and has done significant research into the lives and deaths of Robert Kennedy, Martin Luther King, and many other important figures of American history. A single conversation with him always leaves a person smarter! I am so grateful for his help and direction. He's critical, too, which can be daunting, but also enriching. For more about Jim's great work, go to kennedysandking.com. In particular, be sure to read "The Kennedys and Civil Rights: How the MSM Continues to Distort History" by James DiEugenio, *Kennedys and King,* October 6, 2018.

Interviews: Lyndon B. Johnson (LBJ Library); Torbert Macdonald Jr.; Kathleen "Kerry" McCarthy; Ben Bradlee; Charlie McWhorter (1998); James DiEugenio.

Oral histories: Torbert Macdonald (JFK Library); Kirk LeMoyne Billings (JFK Library); Hubert Humphrey (LBJ Library); Edward M. Kennedy (Edward M. Kennedy Institute).

Volumes: *Hubert Humphrey* by Arnold A. Offner; *Hubert Humphrey* by Carl Solberg; *Jack Kennedy* by Chris Matthews; *An Unfinished Life* by Robert Dallek; *A Good Life* by Ben Bradlee; *Conversations with Kennedy* by Ben Bradlee; *America's Queen* by Sarah Bradford; *My Father's Daughter* by Tina Sinatra; *Frank Sinatra: My Father* by Nancy Sinatra; *Sinatra* by Anthony Summers; *Just Good Politics* by Topper Sherwood; *The Patriarch* by David Nasaw; *My Twelve Years with John F. Kennedy* by Evelyn Lincoln.

I also referenced Janet Auchincloss Transcripts 72/73, as well as Chris Matthews's interview with "The Kennedy Library Forum" of the JFK Library, November 30, 2011.

Additionally: "John F. Kennedy's Final Days Reveal a Man Who Craved Excitement" by Larry Sabato, *Forbes,* October 16, 2013.

"THE CANDIDATE"

Interviews: George Christian (1998, 1999); Carolyn Baldridge (2000); Julian Baldridge; Ted Sorensen; Janet DesRosiers Fontaine; Arthur Schlesinger Jr.; Harry Middleton (1998).

Oral histories: Jacqueline Kennedy (Arthur Schlesinger, Jr.); Senator George Smathers (JFK Library); Senator George Smathers (LBJ Library); Hubert Humphrey (LBJ Library); Theodore C. Sorensen (LBJ Library); Letitia Baldrige (JFK Library); Luella Hennessey (JFK Library); Theodore C. Sorensen (Edward M. Kennedy Institute).

I also referred to Jacqueline Kennedy Onassis's Oral History at the Lyndon Baines Johnson Library and Museum (1974).

Volumes: *Lyndon Johnson: The Passage of Power* by Robert Caro; *Lyndon Johnson: Master of the Senate* by Robert Caro; *The Kennedys* by Thomas Maier; *Mutual Contempt* by Jeff Shesol; *The Kennedy Men* by Laurence Leamer; *Johnny, We Hardly Knew Ye* by Kenneth P. O'Donnell and David Powers; *A Good Life* by Janet DesRosiers Fontaine.

Janet DesRosier Fontaine's letter to Jack Kennedy ("I'll always be thinking") was provided by Janet DesRosiers Fontaine.

"KICK HIM IN THE BALLS"

Interviews: Janet DesRosiers Fontaine; Julian Baldridge; Ted Sorensen.

Volumes: *Richard Nixon* by John A. Farrell; *Nixonland* by Rick Perlstein; *Being Nixon* by Evan Thomas; *Counselor* by Ted Sorensen; *Unlikely Alliances* by Janine Burke (unpublished).

Also: "The Night Kennedy and Nixon Were Bunkmates" by Bryan Bender, *Politico,* April 29, 2022.

"OCTOBER SURPRISE"

Interviews: Helen Thomas (1998, 2011); Janine Burke; Janet DesRosiers Fontaine; Dexter King (2020).

Oral history: Helen Thomas (LBJ Library).

Volumes: *The Autobiography of Martin Luther King* by Clayborne Carson; *King: A Life* by Jonathan Eig.

I also referenced JFK Campaign Papers (JFK Library), more than a thousand pages of campaign material including memos, correspondences, Nixon debates transcripts, drafts of speeches, and policy papers, covering Kennedy's entering into public life and campaigns for the House, Senate, and mostly the presidency.

Also: "The Kennedy Convention—Pts. 1, 2, 3" by Larry J. Sabato, Center for Politics, July 28, 2016; "JFK's Early Campaigns" (1955, 1957, 1958, 1959, 1960) (includes complete campaign schedules for each year), The Pop History Dig (website, no date).

BOOK II: THE PRESIDENCY

PART I: MR. PRESIDENT

"ELECTION VICTORY" AND "AS REAL AS REAL GETS"

Interviews: Larry Newman (1995, not the Secret Service agent of the same name); Mary Frances "Sancy" Newman (1995, 2000); Arthur Schlesinger Jr.

Oral histories: Jacqueline Kennedy (Arthur Schlesinger, Jr.); Jacqueline Kennedy Onassis (LBJ Library); Kirk LeMoyne Billings (JFK Library); Torbert Macdonald (JFK Library); Senator George Smathers (JFK Library); Pierre Salinger (RFK Oral History Project/JFK Library); Chet Huntley (LBJ Library); Arthur Schlesinger (Edward M. Kennedy Institute).

Volumes: *Richard Nixon* by John A. Farrell; *Jack Kennedy* by Chris Matthews; *A Thousand Days* by Arthur Schlesinger Jr.; *Sins of the Father* by Ronald Kessler.

The question persists: Did Sam Giancana, at Frank Sinatra's behest, help swing this election, especially in controversial Illinois—Cook County, in particular—where the so-called Outfit had the most power? Navigating decades' worth of twists and turns in Kennedy-Giancana mythology is complicated given the dearth of material published about it in the last sixty years. The discussion of Cook County becomes moot, though, with the understanding that JFK really did *not need* Illinois to win the White House. His margin in the Electoral College was more than enough to survive the loss of that state. He won 303 electoral votes; Nixon 219. If Illinois's 27 electoral votes had shifted from Kennedy to Nixon, Kennedy *still* would have won with 276 votes to Nixon's 246. (Only 269 were needed to win in 1960, as opposed to 270 today.)

The scholar John J. Binder does an excellent job of analyzing this fascinating time in American politics in his paper "Organized Crime and the 1960s Presidential Election." It's well worth reading and can be found here: https://www.jstor.org/stable /27698060. I want to thank him for his assistance with my research in this regard.

"AN UNLIKELY MEETING"

Interviews: Kirk LeMoyne Billings (JFK Library); Ben Bradlee.

Volumes: *Richard Nixon* by John A. Farrell; *Richard M. Nixon* by Conrad Black; *Conversations with Kennedy* by Ben Bradlee.

I also referenced Arthur Houghton Papers (JFK Library).

"TRANSITION"

Interviews: Laurie Macdonald; Senator George Smathers.

Volumes: *A Thousand Days* by Arthur Schlesinger Jr.; *Sins of the Father* by Ronald Kessler; *The Founding Father* by Richard Whalen; *America's Queen* by Sarah Bradford; *Janet and Jackie* by Jan Pottker; *JFK: The Man and the Myth* by Victor Lasky; *Kennedy and Johnson* by Evelyn Lincoln; *My Twelve Years with John F. Kennedy* by Evelyn Lincoln; *Seeds of Destruction* by Ralph G. Martin; *Sarge* by Scott Stossel; *Ambassador's Journal* by John Kenneth Galbraith.

"FAMILY PRIDE," "HONOR THY PARENTS," AND "MATERNAL BREACH"

Interviews: James R. Ketchum (1998, 2000); Gustavo Paredes (2016, 2018); Liz Carpenter; Nancy Bacon; Jamie Auchincloss; Barbara Gibson; Hugh D. Auchincloss III; Janine Burke; Kathleen "Kerry" McCarthy.

Oral histories: Janet Auchincloss (JFK Library); Charles Spalding (RFK Oral History); Lyndon B. Johnson (LBJ Library); Luci Baines Johnson (LBJ Library); Paul B. Fay (JFK Library); Edward Kennedy (LBJ Library); Sargent Shriver (LBJ Library); Arthur Schlesinger (Edward M. Kennedy Institute); Edward M. Kennedy (Edward M. Kennedy Institute).

Volumes: *Unlikely Alliances* by Janine Burke (unpublished); *Times to Remember* by Rose Kennedy; *Rose Kennedy* by Barbara A. Perry; *Camelot's Court* by Robert Dallek; *Torn Lace Curtain* by Frank Saunders.

I also referenced Janet Auchincloss Transcripts 72/73 ("You and I have been on quite a journey" and "Families endure," etc.); Diary of Hugh D. Auchincloss III; and Rose Kennedy's interviews with Robert Coughlin (JFK Library).

Also: "Finding Inspiration: Honoring Women at the JFK Library," National Archives, March 27, 2014.

PART II: COMMANDER IN CHIEF

"NEW FRONTIER"

Interviews: David Powers (1996); John Carl Warnecke (1998, 2007, 2008); Robert C. McNamara (2003, 2008); Arthur Schlesinger Jr.; Charles Bartlett; James DiEugenio.

Oral histories: Jacqueline Kennedy (Arthur Schlesinger, Jr.); Charles Spalding (RFK Oral History); Charles Bartlett (LBJ Library); James R. Ketchum (LBJ Library).

For this section and others relating to the Kennedy presidency, I referred to transcripts of Robert Coughlin's interviews with Rose Kennedy, Ethel Kennedy, and Eunice Kennedy Shriver. These interviews were conducted in the winter of 1972.

Volumes: *An Unfinished Life* by Robert Dallek; *Jack and Jackie* by Christopher Andersen; *A Good Life* by Ben Bradlee; *The Kennedys* by Peter Collier and David Horowitz; *Camelot's Court* by Robert Dallek; *The Presidents* by Michael Beschloss; *Presidents of War* by Michael Beschloss; *My Twelve Years with John F. Kennedy* by Evelyn Lincoln; *Designing Camelot* by James A. Abbott and Elaine M. Rice; *Jacqueline Kennedy: The White House Years* by Arthur M. Schlesinger Jr. and Rachel Lambert Mellon; *The Pleasure of His Company* by Paul B. Fay Jr.; *The Search for JFK* by Joan and Clay Blair Jr.; *All Too Human* by Edward Klein; *Counselor to the President* by Clark Clifford; *Theodore H. White* by Joyce Hoffman; *Lyndon Johnson: The Passage of Power* by Robert A. Caro; *A Hero for Our Time* by Ralph G. Martin; *A Question of Character* by Thomas C. Reeves; *In Search of History* by Theodore H. White; *Remembering Jack* by Jacques Lowe and Hugh Sidey; *Kennedy and Johnson* by Evelyn Lincoln; *Seeds of Destruction* by Ralph Martin; *Sarge* by Scott Stossel; *Ambassador's Journal* by John Kenneth Galbraith.

I also referenced Robert C. McNamara Personal Papers (JFK Library); Clark M. Clifford Papers, Library of Congress, Manuscript Division, Washington, DC.

I referred to "How John F. Kennedy and Eleanor Roosevelt Went from Rivals to Allies" by Barbara A. Perry, *Dallas Morning News,* August 30, 2020. I also studied "Eleanor Roosevelt and JFK: Transcript with Matt Porter, Barbara Perry, Jamie Richardson and Others," June 25, 2020 (JFK Library).

I also referred to "JFK: The Truth as I See It" by Arthur Schlesinger Jr., *Cigar Aficionado,* December 1998. "Let us first dispose of Camelot," Schlesinger wrote. "JFK had gone to prep school and college with Alan Jay Lerner, and liked the songs Lerner and Frederick Loewe wrote for the popular 1960 musical. But no one when JFK was alive ever spoke of Washington as Camelot—and if anyone had done so, no one would have been more derisive than JFK. Nor did those of us around him see ourselves for a moment, heaven help us, as knights of the Round Table. Camelot was Jacqueline Kennedy's grieving thought a week after her husband was killed. Later she told John Kenneth Galbraith that she feared the idea had been overdone. For that matter, King Arthur's Camelot was hardy noted for its marital constancy, and the Arthurian saga concluded in betrayal and death."

"FAMILY BUSINESS"

Interview: Janet DesRosiers Fontaine.

Oral histories: Janet Auchincloss (JFK Library); Mary McCarthy (JFK Library); Joseph Gargan (Edward M. Kennedy Institute); Clark Clifford (LBJ Library); James R. Ketchum (LBJ Library); Robert S. McNamara (LBJ Library); John Kenneth Galbraith (Edward M. Kennedy Institute).

Volumes: *Robert Kennedy* by Evan Thomas; *Robert Kennedy and His Times* by Arthur M. Schlesinger Jr.; *A Good Life* by Janet DesRosiers Fontaine; *The Founding Father* by Richard Whalen; *The Ambassador* by Susan Ronald; *Jacqueline Kennedy* by Barbara A. Perry.

I also referenced Janet Auchincloss Transcripts 72/73 ("Is it nepotism" etc.).

Additionally: "An Exclusive Chat with Jackie Kennedy" by Joan Braden, *Saturday Evening Post,* May 12, 1962; "The Public and Private Lee" by Henry Ehrlich, *Look,* January 23, 1968; "Lee Radziwill's Search for Herself" by John J. Miller, *The Column,* December 17, 1972; "Stay Tuned for the Princess" by Terry Coleman, *New York Post,* June 24, 1967.

Also: "Eleanor Roosevelt Interviews President John F. Kennedy" (video), June 4, 1962 (American Archive of Public Broadcasting).

"BAY OF PIGS"

Interviews: Senator George Smathers; Roswell Gilpatric (1990); Robert C. McNamara; David Powers; Arthur Schlesinger Jr.

Oral histories: Jacqueline Kennedy (Arthur Schlesinger, Jr.); Jacqueline Kennedy Onassis (LBJ Library); Allen W. Dulles (JFK Library); Douglas Dillon (RFK Oral History); Pierre Salinger (RFK Oral History Project/JFK Library); Maxwell D. Taylor (RFK Oral History); Maxwell D. Taylor (LBJ Library); Kirk LeMoyne Billings; Lyndon B. Johnson (LBJ Library); Roswell Gilpatric (Harry S. Truman Library); Roswell Gilpatric (JFK Library).

I also referenced the Henry Cabot Lodge Jr. Papers, Massachusetts Historical Society, Boston, Massachusetts.

Volumes: *JFK vs. Allen Dulles* by Greg Poulgrain and Oliver Stone is the definitive book about this complex relationship. Well worth reading. Also: *Fidel Castro: My Life* by Fidel Castro and Ignacio Ramonet; *Fidel Castro* by Robert E. Quirk; *A Thousand Days* by Arthur Schlesinger Jr.; *Robert Kennedy and His Times* by Arthur M. Schlesinger Jr.; *True Compass* by Edward M. Kennedy; *Edward Kennedy* by Burton Hersh; *Presidents of War* by Michael Beschloss.

I also referenced Janet Auchincloss Transcripts 72/73 ("The President Kennedy I know" etc.); Robert C. McNamara Personal Papers (JFK Library); "Documents Detail Crises of the Times," Special to *Washington Post,* January 25, 1975. The information about "Jackie's spy" was provided by a confidential source.

Importantly, I accessed "Bay of Pigs CIA-NSC-State Department Files," which contains more than 2,000 pages of CIA, National Security Council, and Department of State files covering the Bay of Pigs. I also accessed the "Bay of Pigs CIA Official History of the Bay of Pigs Operation." This collection includes more than 6,000 pages of CIA official history and closely related JFK presidential, Joint Chiefs of Staff, and Department of State compiled history.

"MOVED TO TEARS" AND "ACCOUNTABILITY"

Interviews: Senator George Smathers; Ben Bradlee; Roswell Gilpatric; Robert C. McNamara.

Oral histories: Jacqueline Kennedy (Arthur Schlesinger, Jr.); Kirk LeMoyne Billings (JFK Library); Roswell Gilpatric (LBJ Library); Letitia Baldrige (JFK Library); Robert S. McNamara (LBJ Library); Kenneth P. O'Donnell (LBJ Library); Cecil Stoughton (LBJ Library).

Volumes: *JFK vs. Allen Dulles* by Greg Poulgrain and Oliver Stone; *Fidel Castro* by Robert E. Quirk; *A Thousand Days* by Arthur Schlesinger Jr.; *Robert Kennedy and His Times* by Arthur M. Schlesinger Jr.; *Robert Kennedy* by Thomas Evan; *The Kennedys* by Thomas Maier; *The Kennedy Men* by Laurence Leamer; *Johnny, We Hardly Knew Ye* by Kenneth P. O'Donnell and David F. Powers; *Jack Kennedy* by Chris Matthews; *Camelot's Court* by Robert Dallek; *American Values* by Robert F. Kennedy Jr.; *Last Lion* by Peter S. Canellos; *JFK: The Man and the Myth* by Victor Lasky.

I also referenced *Unlikely Alliances* by Janine Burke ("He's the goddamn president!").

The two passages of correspondence from Janet Auchincloss to Eileen Slocum can be found in the National Archives. I also referenced Kirk LeMoyne Billings Diary (JFK Library); Papers of Lucien Vandenbroucke (Princeton Library); Robert C. McNamara Personal Papers (JFK Library).

"JACK'S MIRACLE DRUG" AND "DR. FEELGOOD"

Interviews: Adora Rule; Chuck Spalding; Letitia Baldrige.

Oral histories: Jacqueline Kennedy (Arthur Schlesinger, Jr.); Kirk LeMoyne

Billings (JFK Library), Letitia Baldrige (JFK Library); Luella Hennessey (JFK Library); George G. Burkley (LBJ Library).

Volumes: *Max Jacobson Memoir* (unpublished); *Dr. Feelgood* by Richard Lertzman and William J. Birnes; *The Doctor Feelgood Casebook* by Richard Lertzman and William J. Birnes; *The Fabulous Bouvier Sisters* by Sam Kashner and Nancy Schoenberger; *Jack and Jackie* by Christopher Andersen; *A Lady First* by Letitia Baldrige; *Presidential Courage* by Michael Beschloss.

The letter from Rose Kennedy to Janet Auchincloss ("I should love to see you") can be found in the Rose Kennedy's Papers (JFK Library).

Also: "Other Presidents Have Lied About Their Health, but Trump's Coverup Is Immoral" by Larry Tye, WBUR, October 9, 2020.

"THE WOMAN SHE WANTS TO BE"

Interviews: Janet DesRosiers; Andrew Fontaine.

Oral history: Janet G. Travell (JFK Library).

Volume: *A Good Life* by Janet DesRosiers Fontaine.

"KHRUSHCHEV'S THREAT"

Interviews: Sergei Khrushchev (2000); Hugh Sidey (1999); Pat Kennedy Lawford (1999); Roswell Gilpatric; Robert C. McNamara; Jacques Lowe.

Oral histories: Kirk LeMoyne Billings; Allen W. Dulles (JFK Library); Douglas Dillon (RFK Oral History); Pierre Salinger (RFK Oral History Project/JFK Library); Paul B. Fay (JFK Library); Maxwell D. Taylor (RFK Oral History); J. B. (James Bernard) West (JFK Library); Robert S. McNamara (LBJ Library); Sargent Shriver (LBJ Library); Henry Cabot Lodge (JFK Library); Roswell Gilpatric (Harry S. Truman Library and Museum); Roswell Gilpatric (JFK Library).

Volumes: *Khrushchev* by William Taubman; *Khrushchev Remembers* by Edward Crankshaw and Strobe Talbott; *Khrushchev on Khrushchev* by Sergei Khrushchev; *The Light of Power* by Michael Paradis; *Eisenhower* by Stephen Ambrose; *The Search for JFK* by Joan and Clay Blair Jr.; *All Too Human* by Edward Klein; *Counselor to the President* by Clark Clifford; *Theodore H. White* by Joyce Hoffmann; *Lyndon Johnson: The Passage of Power* by Robert A. Caro; *A Hero for Our Time* by Ralph G. Martin; *A Question of Character* by Thomas C. Reeves; *The Supreme Commander* by Stephen Ambrose; *Max Jacobson Memoir* (unpublished); *Dr. Feelgood* by Richard Lertzman and William J. Birnes; *The Doctor Feelgood Casebook* by Richard Lertzman and William J. Birnes; *The Crisis Years* by Michael R. Beschloss; *Robert Kennedy and His Times* by Arthur M. Schlesinger Jr.; *The Pleasure of His Company* by Paul B. Fay Jr.; *In Search of History* by Theodore H. White; *Remembering Jack* by Jacques Lowe and Hugh Sidey; *Kennedy and Johnson* by Evelyn Lincoln; *My Twelve Years with John F. Kennedy* by Evelyn Lincoln; *Seeds of Destruction* by Ralph Martin; *Sarge* by Scott Stossel; *Ambassador's Journal* by John Kenneth Galbraith.

I also referenced Robert C. McNamara Personal Papers (JFK Library).

JFK's musings ("I know there is a God") can be found in the John Fitzgerald Kennedy Papers (JFK Library).

PART III: ALL THAT GLITTERS

As well as extensive research for my books *Sinatra: Behind the Legend* and *Sinatra: A Complete Life*, I relied on:

"ADVISE AND CONSENT"

Interviews: Ben Bradlee; Marion "Oatsie" Leiter Charles (1999).

Volumes: *My Father's Daughter* by Tina Sinatra; *Sinatra* by Anthony Summers; *A Good Life* by Ben Bradlee; *Conversations with Kennedy* by Ben Bradlee; *Mary's Mosaic* by Peter Janney; *A Very Private Woman* by Nina Burleigh.

I also referenced Evelyn Lincoln's Datebook (JFK Library); Janet Auchincloss Transcripts 72/73; Jacqueline Kennedy Papers (JFK Library); John F. Kennedy Papers (JFK Library).

"THEIR WORLD CHANGES"

As well as extensive research for my book *After Camelot: A Personal History of the Kennedy Family, 1968 to the Present*, I relied on:

Interviews: Joseph Gargan; Ann Gargan; Larry Newman; Mary Frances "Sancy" Newman; Jacques Lowe; Kathleen "Kerry" McCarthy; Barbara Gibson; Senator George Smathers.

Oral histories: Kirk LeMoyne Billings (JFK Library); Senator George Smathers (JFK Library); Senator George Smathers (LBJ Library); Joseph Gargan (Edward M. Kennedy Institute); Ann Gargan (Edward M. Kennedy Institute).

Volumes: *Life with Rose Kennedy* by Barbara Gibson; *Times to Remember* by Rose Kennedy; *Rose Kennedy* by Barbara Perry; *The Founding Father* by Richard Whalen; *The Ambassador* by Susan Ronald; *Robert Kennedy* by Evan Thomas; *Jack* by Herbert S. Parmet; *Sarge* by Scott Stossel; *Ambassador's Journal* by John Kenneth Galbraith; *Torn Lace Curtain* by Frank Saunders; *Kennedy White House Years* by Carl Sferrazza Anthony; *Rose Kennedy and Her Family* by Barbara Gibson and Ted Schwartz; *Power at Play* by Betty Beale; *My Life with Jacqueline Kennedy* by Mary Barelli Gallagher; *A Day in the Life of President Kennedy* by Jim Bishop; *The Fitzgeralds and the Kennedys* by Doris Kearns Goodwin.

I also referenced Janet Auchincloss Transcript 72/73.

"CARING MAKES YOU WEAK"

Interviews: Janet DesRosiers; Dr. Robert D. Wyatt (1994).

Volumes: *A Good Life* by Janet DesRosiers Fontaine.

I also referenced *Unlikely Alliances* by Janine Burke ("Just like Rosie" etc.).

The letter from James Gavin to Janet DesRosiers Fontaine ("He and his wife") was provided by Janet DesRosiers Fontaine.

PART IV: HIS SEXUAL WAYWARDNESS

As well as my extensive research for my book *Jackie, Janet & Lee,* I relied on:

"SCARS AND ALL"

Interviews with Secret Service agents: Anthony Sherman (1998); Bob Foster (2000, 2002); Joseph Paolella (1998, 1999, 2000, 2001, 2012); Jack Walsh (1998); Larry Newman (1998, 1999, 2000); Robert Foster (1999); and Lynn Meredith (2005). Also: Ben Bradlee; Senator George Smathers; Dr. Nassir Ghaemi; Jamie Auchincloss; Annunziata Lisi (1999, 2000, 2015, 2021, 2022); Terrance Landow; Gustave Paredes; Gilbert "Benno" Graziani (2009, 2010); Larry and Mary Frances "Sancy" Newman (1998); Jacques Lowe (1998, 1999, 2000).

I also referenced the FBI's extensive files on JFK's infidelities, 1,700 documents of which were released by the National Archives in May 1998. As I wrote in the text, depending on the FBI's files on Kennedy for verification of anything relating to his life and times is a fool's folly. Many of the records contain information from anonymous sources, most of which is not verified, much of it redacted, all of which is included at the peril of any serious researcher or historian.

Oral history: Janet Auchincloss (JFK Library).

Volumes: *Mary's Mosaic* by Peter Janney; *A Very Private Woman* by Nina Burleigh; *An Unfinished Life* by Robert Dallek; *Conversations with Kennedy* by Ben Bradlee; *A Good Life* by Ben Bradlee; *A Thousand Days* by Arthur Schlesinger Jr.

I also referenced Janet Auchincloss Transcript 72/73 ("What is she doing in the residence?" etc.).

In considering Jackie Kennedy's coping with Mary Meyer, it's worth noting that in July 1952, she wrote a letter to Rev. Joseph Leonard in which she said of JFK: "He's like my father in a way—loves the chase and is bored with the conquest—and once married, needs proof he's still attractive, so flirts with other women and resents you. I saw how that nearly killed Mummy."

"CHANGING TIDES"

Interviews: George Jacobs (1997); Snake Jagger (George Jacobs's son, 2024); Ben Bradlee; Larry Newman; Scott M. Burnstein; Joseph T. Naar (2000).

Volumes: *A Good Life* by Ben Bradlee; *Sinatra: The Life* by Anthony Summers; *Mr. S.* by George Jacobs; *Peter Lawford* by James Spada; *The Peter Lawford Story* by Patricia Lawford Stewart; *Jack* by Herbert S. Parmet; *Sarge* by Scott Stossel; *Ambassador's Journal* by John Kenneth Galbraith; *My Life with Jacqueline Kennedy* by Mary

Barelli Gallagher; *A Day in the Life of President Kennedy* by Jim Bishop; *The Fitzgeralds and the Kennedys* by Doris Kearns Goodwin; *Kennedy White House Years* by Carl Sferrazza Anthony; *Rose Kennedy and Her Family* by Barbara Gibson and Ted Schwartz; *Power at Play* by Betty Beale; *Robert Kennedy and His Times* by Arthur M. Schlesinger Jr.; *My Twelve Years with John F. Kennedy* by Evelyn Lincoln; *JFK: The Man and the Myth* by Victor Lasky.

I also referenced: Secret Service Files (JFK Library).

"MARILYN," "WHEN MARILYN CALLS," AND "TWISTED"

I owe such a debt of gratitude to Patricia Newcomb for her 2024 interview in which she set the record straight regarding Marilyn and JFK. She doesn't grant many interviews, and so I am very grateful. I'm not sure I've ever read her views about JFK and Marilyn's supposed assignation at Bing Crosby's house anywhere else. I appreciate her so much. What an incredible life she's had!

As well as my extensive research for my book *The Secret Life of Marilyn Monroe* and the miniseries for Lifetime based on it, and on my research for *Jackie: Public, Private, Secret,* I relied on:

Interviews: Milt Ebbins (1992, 1997); Hildi Greenson (two interviews, 2000); Daniel Greenson (2008); John Miner (2005); Evelyn Geary; Paula McBride Moskal (2024); Senator George Smathers; Julian Baldridge (2025); Stella Brenton; Noelle Bombardier (2012, 2015); Josefina "Fina" Hardin (2017); Frank Mankiewicz (1998); Jeanne Martin (1998).

I also drew from author Donald Spoto's files stored at the Academy of Motion Picture Arts & Sciences Library for Milt Ebbins (1992); Patricia Newcomb (1994); Joseph Naar (1994); Rupert Allan (1995); and Ralph Roberts (1992).

Oral history: Arthur Krim (LBJ Library); Mathilde Krim (Edward M. Kennedy Institute).

Volumes: *Marilyn: A Biography* by Norman Mailer; *Goddess* by Anthony Summers; *Marilyn Monroe* by Charles Casillo; *Marilyn Monroe* by Maurice Zolotow; *Norma Jean* by Fred Guiles; *Mimosa* by Ralph Roberts with Chris Jacobs and Hap Roberts; *Ethel Kennedy and Life at Hickory Hill* by Leah Mason (unpublished manuscript); *Torn Lace Curtain* by Frank Saunders; *Peter Lawford: The Man Who Kept the Secrets* by James Spada; *Frank Sinatra: My Father* by Nancy Sinatra; *Mr. S.* by George Jacobs.

I also referenced: Papers of John F. Kennedy (JFK Library), specifically for the poem written by McGeorge Bundy; Kenneth P. "Kenny" O'Donnell Personal Papers specifically for the invitation for Marilyn to perform at Madison Square Garden (JFK Library).

For more on Dr. Marianne Kris, see my books *The Secret Life of Marilyn Monroe* and *Jackie: Public, Private, Secret.*

Ethel Kennedy's comment to Marilyn Monroe ("I don't need fans") was relayed to me by a confidential source.

Additionally, "Two Myths Converge: NM [Norman Mailer] Discovers MM [Marilyn Monroe]," *Time,* July 16, 1973; "Marilyn Monroe's Love Life . . ." by Monique Wilson, *Glamour,* September 29, 2022; "Snubs, Secrets and Sunday Mass" by Bruce Fessier, *The Desert Sun,* April 1, 2012.

"THE JFK/MARILYN CONTRACT"

Interview: Janet DesRosiers Fontaine.

Note: After her death, a popular story began to circulate that Marilyn Monroe had decided to hold a press conference to reveal information about her relationships with Jack and Bobby Kennedy, as well as other government secrets. In 1985, when Ethel Kennedy was told about the supposed press conference by an associate at ABC News during a meeting with her at Hickory Hill, she said, "Oh my God! Bobby didn't discuss those things with me unless I pushed and pushed for information—and I almost never did unless it involved the safety of the family. He would never have discussed anything like that with Marilyn Monroe. Please, let's be sensible. It's ridiculous." Ethel was right; people who knew Marilyn best confirm that she never would've considered such a press conference.

Ethel made those comments in a meeting at Hickory Hill with high-level executives at ABC-TV to voice her unhappiness about a planned segment of the show *20/20* detailing the intimate relationship between the Kennedy brothers and Marilyn Monroe. The program was ultimately scrapped, some have alleged, because Ethel used as leverage her close relationship with ABC president of News and Sports, Roone Arledge. Then, in 1997, ABC planned yet another special about the same subject based on Seymour Hersh's book. Instead of being about Marilyn and the Kennedys, the show focused on the scandal relating to the illegitimate documents referred to by Janet DesRosiers in her interview for this book.

I also referenced "CNN Talk Back Live," interview with Seymour Hersh, December 26, 1997; "Janet DesRosiers: Living Among the Kennedys," *Sedona Red Rock News,* January 10, 2012.

"COLLATERAL DAMAGE"

Interviews: Barbara Gibson; Jacques Lowe.

Oral histories: Mary McCarthy (JFK Library); Maud Shaw (JFK Library); Edward M. Kennedy (Edward M. Kennedy Institute).

Volumes: *The Missing Kennedy* by Elizabeth Koehler-Pentacoff; *Life with Rose Kennedy* by Barbara Gibson; *Eunice Kennedy* by Eileen McNamara; *Eunice Kennedy* by Victoria Chase; *The Magnificent Kennedy Women* by Stanley P. Friedman.

I also referenced "Hope for Retarded Children" by Eunice Kennedy, *Saturday Evening Post,* September 1962.

PART V: THE OTHER SIDE OF CAMELOT

"WELLSPRING" AND "FATHERLY CONCERNS"

Interviews: Jacqueline Kennedy Onassis (LBJ Library); Eileen Slocum (1998, 2000); Jamie Auchincloss; Larry Newman (1998, in particular the conversations on the beach).

Much of these chapters are drawn from Janet Auchincloss Interviews 1964. I also referenced Janet Auchincloss Transcript 72/73.

Oral histories: Janet Auchincloss (JFK Library); Paul B. Fay (JFK Library).

Volume: *Times to Remember* by Rose Kennedy.

I also referenced Yusha Auchincloss Diary (JFK Library).

Additionally: "Kennedys Come Here for 10th Anniversary," *Newport Daily News,* September 12, 1963; "City, Navy Prepare for Kennedy Vacation from September 22 to October 4," *Newport Daily News,* September 18, 1961; "Kennedy Is Facing a Busy Weekend Before Leaving Newport on Monday," *Newport Daily News,* September 30, 1961; "Kennedy Swears in Customs Official at Hammersmith Farm," *Newport Daily News,* September 29, 1961; "President at Hammersmith Farm for Weekend with His Family," *Newport Daily News,* October 2, 1961; "Mrs. Kennedy in Newport with Caroline and John, Jr.," *New York Times,* June 28, 1961; "Sunset Days of Camelot: An interview with Cecil Auchincloss" by G. Wayne Miller, *Providence Journal,* September 8, 2013.

I also referenced "Kennedys in Hollywood" (E-Channel), including interviews with Barbara Gibson, Paul Fay, Oleg Cassini, John H. Davis, and Lynn Franklin; *Joan Rivers Show,* "The Kennedy Women" with John H. Davis, Cindy Adams, and Barbara Gibson; James Bacon, 1992.

"FLASHPOINT"

Oral histories: George Stevens (JFK Library); Lyndon B. Johnson (LBJ Library); Kenneth P. O'Donnell (LBJ Library); Sargent Shriver (LBJ Library); Luella Hennessey (JFK Library).

Volumes: *James Meredith and the Ole Miss Riot* by Henry T. Gallagher and Gene Roberts; *The Autobiography of Martin Luther King Jr.* edited by Clayborne Carson; *King: A Life* by Jonathan Eig; *Robert Kennedy* by Evan Thomas; *Jack Kennedy* by Chris Matthews; *The Kennedy Men* by Laurence Leamer; *Johnny, We Hardly Knew Ye* by Kenneth P. O'Donnell and David F. Powers.

"MEDICAL COUP D'ÉTAT"

Interviews: Dr. Nassir Ghaemi (2024); Madi Springer-Miller Kraus (2024); Jacques Lowe.

Author's note: I would especially like to thank Madi Springer-Miller Kraus, widow of Dr. Hans Kraus, JFK's physician and physical therapist, for her time and consideration in helping me to understand her late husband's work with John F. Kennedy. As she explained in her 2023 interviews, Dr. Kraus prescribed a regimen of twice-daily exercises that the president performed in addition to his swimming during the last two years of his life. By October 1963, JFK's back was determined to be in the best shape it had ever been and his overall health had improved as well.

Dr. Kraus worked to wean JFK off his back brace, which he believed the president's reliance on was to his detriment. Jack had abandoned it in recent months. But then in August 1963, just a few months before the visit to Dallas, he strained his back and began relying on it again, despite Dr. Kraus's concerns. Jack promised the doctor that when he returned from Dallas he'd get out of the brace once again. "He said he wanted to be able to sit up straight in the limousine and wave to people," said Madi Springer-Miller Kraus. One theory has it that it was the brace that may have kept JFK from recoiling to the floor of his car after the assassin's first bullet to the neck, which then set him up for the shot that killed him. "We'll never know if he might've survived the assassination attempt," said Mrs. Kraus, "had he not had on that brace my husband always thought of as a big problem."

Oral history: Maud Shaw (JFK Library).

Volumes: *Office Hours: Day and Night* by Janet Travell, M.D.; *The Dr. Feelgood Casebook* by Richard A. Lertzman and William Birnes; *Dr. Feelgood* by Richard A. Lertzman and William Birnes; *Portrait of Camelot* by Richard Reeves; *A Question of Character* by Thomas Reeves; *JFK's Secret Doctor* by Susan E. B. Schwartz.

I also referenced "Johnson Vows to Help His Triumphant Rival," Associated Press, July 14, 1960; "Madi Springer-Miller to Wed Dr. Hans Kraus," *New York Times,* January 18, 1959; "Dr. Hans Kraus" (Obituary), *New York Times,* March 7, 1996; JFK's Assassination Aided by His Bad Back, Records Show" by Sandee La-Motte, CNN, November 30, 2017.

I also referred to Hans Kraus Personal Papers (JFK Library).

"ROSE BOWL"

Interviews: John Carl Warnecke (in particular, "I do not redecorate, I restore"); Margo Warnecke Merk (2016); Bertha Baldwin (2016); Harold Adams (2016); Robin Chandler Duke (2010); and Diana DuBois (1998).

Oral histories: Barbara Gamarekian (JFK Library); Evelyn Lincoln (JFK Library); Mary McCarthy.

Volumes: *In Her Sister's Shadow* by Diana DuBois; *A Very Private Woman* by Nina Burleigh.

I also relied on the extensive interviews with John Warnecke conducted on December 4, 1963, and July 10, 1964, the transcripts of which can be found in the Sargent Shriver Collection (JFK Library.)

In May 1964, six months after JFK's murder, Jack Warnecke called Jackie to ask her to dinner. By this time, the former First Lady had hired the acclaimed architect to design the memorial at Arlington National Cemetery for the late President Kennedy. "I don't date," Jackie told him, "and I never will again." No, he clarified, it was just to be dinner between friends. "Fine," she decided. But by the end of May, the couple was in a serious relationship.

In November 1964, Jackie invited Jack to Newport to spend time with her and her mother and stepfather, both of whom approved of him. But being at Hammersmith was difficult for Jackie. Everything around her reminded her of her late husband and the many happy times they'd spent there. On the third day there, Jackie said she wanted to take a drive to Hyannis Port. It was there, then, that the two first became intimate.

With the passing of the years, Jack Warnecke became Jackie's rock; they even spoke of marriage. But then, in March 1967, their relationship changed when Jack confessed to being a million dollars in debt. Cut off by the Kennedys and not in line to inherit from her stepfather's estate, Jackie knew what she had to do: she ended it with Jack and married the wealthy Aristotle Onassis. Despite his disappointment in her, Jack remained one of Jackie's closest of friends for the rest of her life.

Jacqueline Kennedy Onassis died on May 19, 1994. She was just sixty-four.

John Carl Warnecke died on April 17, 2010. He was ninety-one.

I'd like to acknowledge Jack's daughter, Margo Warnecke Merk, a wonderful woman who I am proud to call a friend. In 2021, I was asked by Margo to edit her father's autobiography, *Camelot's Architect*. This wonderful book will be published in the near future. In it, Mr. Warnecke sheds even more light on his relationship with Jacqueline Kennedy Onassis, but what's equally compelling are his vivid memories of his friendship with President Kennedy and the rest of the Kennedy family. It's also been edited by the talented writer Adam Sikes and will be well worth the read.

Also, thanks to Jack's son, Fred Warnecke, his personal assistant, Bertha Baldwin, and his trusted business associate, Harold Adams.

For much more about Jacqueline Kennedy Onassis's romance with Jack Warnecke, please see my books *Jackie, Janet & Lee* and *Jackie: Public, Private, Secret*.

PART VI: "CUBA, CUBA, CUBA"

As well as my extensive research for my books *Jackie, Ethel, Joan* and *Jackie: Public, Private, Secret,* I relied on:

"CRISIS IN CUBA"

Interviews: Senator George Smathers; Joan Braden; Charlie Bartlett; Arthur Schlesinger Jr.

Oral histories: Jacqueline Kennedy (Arthur Schlesinger, Jr.,); Jacqueline Kennedy Onassis (LBJ Library); McGeorge Bundy (JFK Library); McGeorge Bundy (LBJ Library); Kenneth P. O'Donnell (JFK Library); Averell W. Harriman (LBJ Library); Lyndon B. Johnson (LBJ Library); Edward Kennedy (LBJ Library); John Kenneth Galbraith (Edward M. Kennedy Institute); Edward M. Kennedy (Edward M. Kennedy Institute); Henry Cabot Lodge (JFK Library).

Volumes: The definitive book on the Cuban Missile Crisis is *The Kennedy Tapes* edited by Ernest R. May and Philip D. Zelikow. It's an important read. I also referenced *Thirteen Days* by Robert F. Kennedy and Arthur Schlesinger Jr.; *Robert Kennedy and His Times* by Arthur M. Schlesinger Jr.; *The Crisis Years* by Michael Beschloss; *The Abyss* by Sir Max Hastings; *Gambling with Armageddon* by Martin J. Sherwin; *The Fourteenth Day* by David Coleman; *Nuclear Folly* by Serhii Plokhy; *The Shadow of War* by Jeff Shaara; *One Minute to Midnight* by Michael Dobbs; *JFK: The Man and the Myth* by Victor Lasky; *Jack* by Herbert S. Parmet; *Sarge* by Scott Stossel; *Ambassador's Journal* by John Kenneth Galbraith; *Kennedy White House Years* by Carl Sferrazza Anthony; *Rose Kennedy and Her Family* by Barbara Gibson and Ted Schwartz; *Power at Play* by Betty Beale; *My Life with Jacqueline Kennedy* by Mary Barelli Gallagher; *A Day in the Life of President Kennedy* by Jim Bishop; *The Fitzgeralds and the Kennedys* by Doris Kearns Goodwin; *Kennedy: A Time Remembered* by Jacques Lowe; *Controversy and Other Essays in Journalism* by William Manchester; *The Kennedy Case* by Rita Dallas; *Bobby Kennedy: The Making of a Folk Hero* by David Lester; *President Kennedy: Profile of Power* by Richard Reeves; *RFK: The Man Who Would Be President* by Ralph de Toledano; *Those Wild, Wild Kennedy Boys* by Stephen Dunleavy; *In His Own Words: The Unpublished Recollections of the Kennedy Years* by Robert F. Kennedy; *A Question of Character* by Thomas Reeves.

I also referenced Personal Papers of McGeorge Bundy (JFK Library); Kenneth P. "Kenny" O'Donnell Personal Papers (JFK Library); White House Staff Files of Kenneth P. "Kenny" O'Donnell; "John F. Kennedy on Politics and Public Service" (JFK Library); "White House Tapes, Miller Center Presidential Recordings Program," University of Virginia; Maria Shriver interview with Fidel Castro, *Oprah Winfrey Show*, March 1999. (Castro told Shriver: "For such a small country as Cuba to have such a gigantic country as the United States live so obsessed with this island, it is an honor for us.")

Importantly, I had access to "Cuban Missile Crisis: Presidential-CIA-NSA-NSC-State Dept Files-Audio Recordings," which is almost 4,000 pages of files and ninety minutes of audio recordings covering the Cuban Missile Crisis. I also accessed "Cuban Missile Crisis: Robert F. Kennedy Papers," which contains about 3,500 pages of documents accumulated by Attorney General Robert F. Kennedy concerning the Missile Crisis. These documents were declassified through the National Archives and Records Administration's National Declassification Center and made available to the public on October 11, 2012.

Additionally: "Kenny O'Donnell: A Casualty of History" by Mike Barnicle, *Boston Globe,* September 9, 1977.

"SEEN, NEVER HEARD"

Interviews: George Smathers; Jacques Lowe; Terrance Landow; Janet Auchincloss Interviews 1964.

Oral histories: Jacqueline Kennedy Onassis (LBJ Library, in particular, "I remember one morning"); Janet Auchincloss (JFK Library); Dorothy Tubridy (JFK Library); Edward Kennedy (LBJ Library); Luella Hennessey (JFK Library); Kenneth P. O'Donnell (LBJ Library); Letitia Baldrige (JFK Library); Maud Shaw (JFK Library); Edward M. Kennedy (Edward M. Kennedy Institute).

Volumes: *White House Nanny* by Maud Shaw; *The Other Mrs. Kennedy* by Jerry Oppenheimer; *Robert Kennedy and His Times* by Arthur M. Schlesinger Jr.; *My Twelve Years with John F. Kennedy* by Evelyn Lincoln.

I also referenced Janet Auchincloss Transcript 72/73 ("Demand to know") and "With Kennedy" by Pierre Salinger, *Good Housekeeping,* August 1966.

Lee Radziwill discussed the Cuban Missile Crisis on the *Larry King Show* in 2001 and I utilized that transcript here.

Additionally: "Lee" by Andy Warhol, *Interview,* March 1975; "How Caroline and John Remember Their Father" by David E. Powers, *McCall's,* November 1973; "Ted Kennedy's Memories of JFK" by Theodore Sorensen, *McCall's,* November 1973; "My Mother: The Queen of Camelot" by Elizabeth Castor, *The Australian Women's Weekly,* November 2001.

"'GRAB YOUR BALLS!'"

Interviews: George Smathers; Arthur Schlesinger Jr.

Oral histories: David Dean Rusk (JFK Library); Edward Kennedy (LBJ Library); Sargent Shriver (LBJ Library); Hugh Sidey (LBJ Library); Theodore C. Sorensen (LBJ Library); Theodore C. Sorensen (Edward M. Kennedy Institute); Edward M. Kennedy (UVA Miller Center); Robert Shriver III (Edward M. Kennedy Institute); Maria Shriver (Edward M. Kennedy Institute).

Volumes: *Thirteen Days* by Robert F. Kennedy; *The Crisis Years* by Michael Beschloss; *The Fourteenth Day* by David Coleman; *Nuclear Folly* by Serhii Plokhy; *True Compass* by Edward M. Kennedy; *Counselor* by Theodore Sorensen; *JFK Day by Day* by Terry Golway and Les Krantz; *A Lady, First* by Letitia Baldrige; *RFK* by C. David Heymann; *Jack* by Herbert S. Parmet; *Sarge* by Scott Stossel; *Ambassador's Journal* by John Kenneth Galbraith; *As We Remember Her: Jacqueline Kennedy Onassis in the Words of Her Friends and Family* by Carl Sferrazza Anthony; *Lyndon Johnson: The Passage of Power* by Robert A. Caro; *A Hero for Our Time* by Ralph G. Martin; *A Question of Character* by Thomas C. Reeves; *In Search of History* by Theodore H.

White; *Remembering Jack* by Jacques Lowe and Hugh Sidey; *The Pleasure of His Company* by Paul B. Fay Jr.; *The Search for JFK* by Joan and Clay Blair Jr.; *All Too Human* by Edward Klein.

I also referenced: Dean Rusk Personal Papers (JFK Library).

"CRUCIAL DECISIONS"

Interviews: John Radziwill; Senator George Smathers.

Oral histories: Jacqueline Kennedy (Arthur Schlesinger, Jr.), McGeorge Bundy (JFK Library); McGeorge Bundy (LBJ Library); Maud Shaw (JFK Library); Senator George Smathers (JFK Library); Dean Rusk (LBJ Library); Arthur Schlesinger (Edward M. Kennedy Institute).

Volumes: *America's Queen* by Sarah Bradford; *Robert Kennedy* by Evan Thomas; *Robert Kennedy and His Times* by Arthur M. Schlesinger Jr.; *Dark Side of Camelot* by Seymour Hersh.

"AN UNWELCOME GUEST"

Interviews: Oleg Cassini (1998, 1999, 2004); Janet Auchincloss Interviews 1964.

Oral histories: Barbara Gamarekian (JFK Library); Lord Harlech (William David Ormsby-Gore) (JFK Library); McGeorge Bundy (JFK Library); Lord Harlech (William David Ormsby-Gore) (RFK Papers); Janet Auchincloss (JFK Library); Dorothy Tubridy (JFK Library); William Walton (JFK Library); Hugh Sidey (LBJ Library); Edward M. Kennedy (Edward M. Kennedy Institute).

Volumes: *A Very Private Woman* by Nina Burleigh; *Camelot's Court* by Robert Dallek.

I also referenced the transcript of a 1998 interview with Helen Chavchavadze provided by a confidential source, and correspondence to me from Oleg Cassini clarifying these moments at the dinner table after JFK's speech, October 15, 1998.

"RESOLUTION"

Interview: Sergei Khrushchev (2000).

Oral histories: Jackie Kennedy (Arthur Schlesinger, Jr.); David F. Powers (RFK Oral History); Arthur M. Schlesinger (LBJ Library); Janet Auchincloss Interviews 1964.

Volumes: *Thirteen Days* by Robert F. Kennedy and Arthur Schlesinger Jr.; *Robert Kennedy and His Times* by Arthur M. Schlesinger Jr.; *The Crisis Years* by Michael Beschloss; *The Fourteenth Day* by David Coleman; *An Unfinished Life* by Robert Dallek; *Khrushchev* by William Taubman; *Nikita Khrushchev and the Creation of a Superpower* by Sergei Khrushchev; *JFK: The Man and the Myth* by Victor Lasky.

I also referenced David F. Powers Personal Papers (JFK Library); transcript of 1989 Moscow conference with Soviet ambassador Dobrynin and Ted Sorensen.

PART VII: LIFE CHANGES

"THEIR LAST THANKSGIVING"

Interviews: Oleg Cassini; Janine Burke; Mary Jo Birkholtz; Janet Auchincloss Interviews 1964.

Oral histories: Jacqueline Kennedy (Arthur Schlesinger, Jr.); Luella Hennessey (JFK Library); Theodore C. Sorensen (LBJ Library); Theodore C. Sorensen (Edward M. Kennedy Institute).

Volumes: *Diplomatic Memoir* by Joseph P. Kennedy (unpublished, in particular Jackie's reading from it); *Unlikely Alliances* by Janine Burke (unpublished); *Times to Remember* by Rose Kennedy; *Life with Rose Kennedy* by Barbara Gibson; *Eunice* by Eileen McNamara; *Kennedy White House Years* by Carl Sferrazza Anthony; *Lyndon Johnson: The Passage of Power* by Robert A. Caro; *A Hero for Our Time* by Ralph G. Martin; *JFK Day by Day* by Terry Golway and Les Krantz; *The Pleasure of His Company* by Paul B. Fay Jr.; *The Search for JFK* by Joan and Clay Blair Jr.; *All Too Human* by Edward Klein; *A Lady, First* by Letitia Baldrige; *RFK* by C. David Heymann; *Jack* by Herbert S. Parmet; *Sarge* by Scott Stossel; *Ambassador's Journal* by John Kenneth Galbraith; *A Question of Character* by Thomas C. Reeves; *In Search of History* by Theodore H. White; *Remembering Jack* by Jacques Lowe and Hugh Sidey.

I also referenced Janet Auchincloss Transcript 72/73 (in particular, "Is everything okay, Mr. President?"); Arthur Houghton Personal Papers (JFK Library); "Hope for Retarded Children" by Eunice Kennedy Shriver, *Saturday Evening Post,* September 22, 1962.

I also drew from reporting for my three-part series on Caroline Kennedy, "Camelot's Daughter," *Woman's Day,* March 2000, as well as reporting for my series of features on Ms. Kennedy for *Entertainment Tonight,* November 2000.

"'AS OLD AS THE SCRIPTURES'"

Interviews: Dexter King (2020); Janet Auchincloss Interviews 1964.

Special thanks to Jean Price Lewis, 105 years old when interviewed for this book in 2023. She worked for both the Kennedy and Johnson administrations and continued to work in politics afterward. I so appreciate the memories she shared with me for this work.

Oral histories: Jacqueline Kennedy (Arthur Schlesinger, Jr.); George C. Wallace (LBJ Library); Maud Shaw (JFK Library).

Volumes: *Wallace* by Marshall Frady; *George Wallace* by George Wallace Jr.; *King* by Jonathan Eig; *The Autobiography of Martin Luther King Jr.* by Clayborne Carson; *Robert Kennedy and His Times* by Arthur M. Schlesinger Jr.

"JACKIE'S ULTIMATUM"

Interviews: Ben Bradlee; Antoinette Bradlee; Anne Truitt (2000); Janet Auchincloss Interviews 1964 (in particular, "Is this the same disreputable woman").

Oral histories: Senator George Smathers (JFK Library); Senator George Smathers (LBJ Library).

Volumes: *A Remarkable Woman* by Nina Burleigh; *Conversations with Kennedy* by Ben Bradlee; *Personal History: A Memoir* by Katharine Graham.

I also referenced Janet Auchincloss Transcript 72/73.

Also, I referenced the White House visitor logs at the John Fitzgerald Kennedy Presidential Library and Museum to confirm Mary Meyer's many visits.

"THE VERY WORST PARTS"

Interviews: Joseph Gargan; Senator George Smathers; Ben Bradlee, Antoinette Bradlee; Janet Auchincloss Interviews 1964.

Oral histories: Barbara Gamarekian (JFK Library); Evelyn Lincoln (JFK Library); Joseph Gargan (Edward M. Kennedy Institute); Ann Gargan (Edward M. Kennedy Institute).

Volumes: *A Remarkable Woman* by Nina Burleigh; *Conversations with Kennedy* by Ben Bradlee; *A Good Life* by Ben Bradlee; *JFK Day by Day* by Terry Golway and Les Krantz; *A Lady, First* by Letitia Baldrige; *RFK* by C. David Heymann; *Jack* by Herbert S. Parmet; *Sarge* by Scott Stossel; *Ambassador's Journal* by John Kenneth Galbraith; *Kennedy White House Years* by Carl Sferrazza Anthony; *Lyndon Johnson: The Passage of Power* by Robert A. Caro; *A Hero for Our Time* by Ralph G. Martin; *A Question of Character* by Thomas C. Reeves; *In Search of History* by Theodore H. White; *Remembering Jack* by Jacques Lowe and Hugh Sidey; *The Pleasure of His Company* by Paul B. Fay Jr.; *The Search for JFK* by Joan and Clay Blair Jr.; *All Too Human* by Edward Klein.

I also referenced White House Invitation Logs (JFK Library), Janet Auchincloss Transcript 72/73; the Adlai E. Stevenson Papers including correspondence and Arthur Krock Papers, both collections found at Seeley G. Mudd Manuscript Library, Princeton University, Princeton, New Jersey.

AUTHOR'S NOTE ABOUT MARY MEYER AND THE BRADLEES

When I interviewed Antoinette (Tony) Pinchot Bradlee in 1995 and again in 1999, she was not forthcoming about her older sister Mary Meyer's relationship with the president. However, she did provide necessary background, which I utilized in this and my other Kennedy books.

I also interviewed Ben Bradlee in 1995, 1996, 2000, and 2002. He claimed that after Mary's murder in 1964, he and his wife discovered her diary. Though JFK's name was never mentioned in it, the Bradlees felt certain Mary was alluding to their affair in her writings. The Bradlees said they couldn't help but feel betrayed and disillusioned. They simply couldn't imagine how Jack and Mary had been able to keep their affair secret considering how much time they'd all spent together, and with Jackie, too.

Tony Bradlee said she gave the diary to CIA's counterintelligence chief, James Angleton, who promised to destroy it. Years later, she learned he'd not entirely kept his promise; he'd saved some pages.

When the story of Jack and Mary ended up in the *National Enquirer* in 1976—with the primary source being James Truitt, the estranged husband of Mary's good friend Ann Truitt—the Bradlees eventually went to Angleton to demand possession of any remaining pages. Tony said she then burned them herself.

Many historians don't believe in the existence of a diary and suspect it was, instead, a date book but with no information about President Kennedy. There's really no way to confirm its existence other than to take the Bradlees' word for it. Having interviewed both, however, I can attest that neither seemed dishonest enough to invent such a story, and Ben Bradlee, especially, was known for his honest reporting over the years. He wrote about the diary in his book *A Good Life*.

Again, Mary Meyer did not name President Kennedy in her writings but, apparently, she was specific enough in her storytelling to give the impression to both Bradlees that she was referring to him.

"HISTORIC SPEECHES"

Interviews: Senator George Smathers; Janet Auchincloss Interviews 1964.

Oral histories: Kirk LeMoyne Billings; Edward Kennedy (LBJ Library); Maud Shaw (JFK Library).

Volumes: *My Twelve Years with John F. Kennedy* by Evelyn Lincoln; *The Last Brother* by Joe McGinniss; *The Shadow President* by Burton Hersh; *Living with the Kennedys* by Marcia Chellis; *We Band of Brothers: A Memoir of Robert F. Kennedy* by Edwin Guthman; *Breaking Cover* by Bill Gulley and Mary Ellen Reese; *Palimpsest* by Gore Vidal; *RFK* by C. David Heymann.

PART VIII: PATRICK

As well as my extensive research for my books *Jackie, Ethel, Joan* and *Jackie, Janet & Lee,* I relied on:

"CUT TO THE BONE" AND "SOME CHANGES ARE FOR GOOD"

Interviews: Jamie Auchincloss; Larry Newman; Dave Powers; Stella Brenton (2021, 2022); Virginia Guest Valentine (2017); Christopher Lawford (May 5, 1998; August 3, 2009; September 2, 2017; January 23, 2018); Janet Auchincloss Interviews 1964.

Oral histories: Pamela Turnure (JFK Library); Luella Hennessey (JFK Library); Janet Auchincloss (JFK Library); Jacqueline Kennedy Onassis (Arthur Schlesinger, Jr.).

I also referenced Janet Auchincloss Transcript 72/73 and Evelyn Lincoln's interview conducted by Barry Goldman for *Manuscripts* magazine, 1990.

Volumes: *Jacqueline Bouvier Kennedy Onassis* by Barbara Leaming; *America's Queen* by Sarah Bradford; *An Unfinished Life* by Robert Dallek; *Patrick Bouvier Kennedy* by Michael S. Ryan; *Counselor to the President* by Clark Clifford; *Theodore H. White* by Joyce Hoffman; *Kennedy and Johnson* by Evelyn Lincoln; *My Twelve Years with John F. Kennedy* by Evelyn Lincoln; *Seeds of Destruction* by Ralph Martin; *JFK: The Presidency* by Herbert S. Parmet; *Rose Kennedy and Her Family* by Barbara Gibson and Ted Schwartz; *Power at Play* by Betty Beale; *My Life with Jacqueline Kennedy* by Mary Barelli Gallagher; *A Day in the Life of President Kennedy* by Jim Bishop; *The Fitzgeralds and the Kennedys* by Doris Kearns Goodwin.

Joan Kennedy's memory of her conversation with Jack Kennedy is based on a letter from Mrs. Kennedy that was sold at public auction in 2019. I also referenced a Q-and-A letter with Joan Kennedy to the author, November 19, 1998. It is also based on the testimony of Larry Newman and Dave Powers.

I also referenced "2d Son Born to Kennedys; Has Lung Illness" by William M. Blair, *New York Times,* July 12, 1963, "President at Wife's Bedside" by Fred Brady, *Boston Herald,* August 10, 1963; "Family Rejoins Mrs. Kennedy," *Boston Globe,* August 10, 1963; "It Started Out as a Cape Outing," *Boston Globe,* August 9, 1963; "Mother Cool, Calm in Crisis," *Boston Globe,* August 9, 1963; "Mrs. Kennedy Awaits News on Discharge," *Boston Globe,* August 13, 1963; "Mrs. Kennedy 'Fine,'" *Boston Globe,* August 8, 1963; "Mrs. Kennedy Gets News of Death from Doctor," *Newport Daily News,* August 9, 1963; "Bibs and Bootees Flood White House" by William M. Blair, *Boston Globe,* July 12, 1963; "2d Son Born to Kennedys; Has Lung Illness," *New York Times,* August 8, 1963; "Funeral Mass Said for Kennedy Baby," *New York Times,* August 11, 1963; "President at Wife's Bedside" by Kenneth D. Campbell, *Boston Herald,* August 10, 1963; "Love Letter from Camelot," *New York Daily News,* February 27, 1998.

Additionally, I referred to transcripts of the symposiums "The Kennedy Women" and "The Literary Life of Jacqueline Kennedy Onassis" at the JFK Library, October 4, 1996, and January 23, 2012, respectively. I also referred to "John F. Kennedy and Religion," JFK Library.

Also: "JFK's Alleged Last Confession," SpiritDailyBlog.com, November 27, 2018; "How JFK's Attempt to Distance Himself from the Catholic Church Backfired" by David Nasaw, *Slate,* November 20, 2012; "Religion: Kennedy & the Confessional," *Time,* March 16, 1962.

PART IX: VIETNAM . . . AND BEYOND

"GROWING PROBLEMS AT HOME AND ABROAD"

Interviews: Robert C. McNamara; Janet Auchincloss Interviews 1964.

Oral histories: Luella Hennessey (JFK Library); Edmund A. Gullion (JFK

Library); Robert S. McNamara (LBJ Library); Edward M. Kennedy (Edward M. Kennedy Institute).

Volumes: *JFK and Vietnam* by John Newman is the definitive book with the latest and most comprehensive research relating to the subject matter. It's imperative reading. Also: *The Incubus of Intervention* by Greg Poulgrain; *The Lost Mandate of Heaven* by Dr. Geoffrey D. T. Shaw; *Vietnam's Last Revolution* by Geoffrey C. Stewart; *A Thousand Days* by Arthur M. Schlesinger Jr.; *An Unfinished Life* by Robert Dallek; *Johnny, We Hardly Knew Ye* by Kenneth P. O'Donnell and David F. Powers; *Jack Kennedy* by Chris Matthews; *Jacqueline Bouvier Kennedy Onassis* by Donald Spoto; *Janet and Jackie* by Jan Pottker; *Jack and Jackie* by Christopher Andersen; *Ethel Kennedy and Life at Hickory Hill* by Leah Mason (unpublished manuscript); *The Kennedy Women* by Laurence Leamer; *Jack and Jackie* by Christopher Andersen; *All Too Human* by Edward Klein; *The Sins of the Father* by Ronald Kessler; *Seeds of Destruction* by Ralph C. Martin; *First Ladies* by Carl Sferrazza Anthony; *Counselor to the President* by Clark Clifford; *Theodore H. White* by Joyce Hoffman; *Kennedy and Johnson* by Evelyn Lincoln; *My Twelve Years with John F. Kennedy* by Evelyn Lincoln; *Seeds of Destruction* by Ralph Martin; *JFK: The Presidency* by Herbert S. Parmet; *Rose Kennedy and Her Family* by Barbara Gibson and Ted Schwartz; *Power at Play* by Betty Beale; *My Life with Jacqueline Kennedy* by Mary Barelli Gallagher; *A Day in the Life of President Kennedy* by Jim Bishop; *The Fitzgeralds and the Kennedys* by Doris Kearns Goodwin.

I also referenced Edmund A. Gullion Personal Papers (JFK Library); "Mike Mansfield, April 1962–September 1963" (JFK Library); Evelyn Lincoln's "Daily Reports" Files (JFK Library).

"ONASSIS"

As well as my extensive research for my books *Jackie, Janet & Lee* and *Jackie: Public, Private, Secret,* I relied on:

Interviews: Barbara Gibson; Adora Rule; Taki Theodoracopulos; Kiki Feroudi Moutsatsos (2022); Thea Andino (2022); Gustavo Paredes; John H. Davis (1999); Diana DuBois; and Joseph Gargan.

Oral histories: Luella Hennessey (JFK Library); William Walton (JFK Library).

Volumes: *A Time to Remember* by Rose Kennedy; *Life with Rose Kennedy* by Barbara Gibson; *In Her Sister's Shadow* by Diana DuBois.

I also referenced William Walton Personal Papers (JFK Library).

I have written much more extensively about Jackie and Lee's 1963 trip to Greece in my books *Jackie, Ethel, Joan* and *After Camelot* and *Jackie, Janet & Lee* and *Jackie: Public, Private, Secret.* See those works for much more about this time in their lives.

"LOSING CONTROL OF HIS GOVERNMENT"

Interview: Robert C. McNamara.

Oral histories: Averell W. Harriman (JFK Library); Michael V. Forrestal (JFK

Library); Henry Cabot Lodge (JFK Library); Roswell Gilpatric (JFK Library); Charles Spalding (JFK Library); Maxwell D. Taylor (JFK Library); Maxwell D. Taylor (LBJ Library); Clark Clifford (LBJ Library); Roswell Gilpatric (LBJ Library); Arthur M. Schlesinger (LBJ Library); Arthur Schlesinger (Edward M. Kennedy Institute).

Volumes: *JFK and Vietnam* by John Newman; *The Incubus of Intervention* by Greg Poulgrain; *The Lost Mandate of Heaven* by Dr. Geoffrey D. T. Shaw; *Vietnam's Last Revolution* by Geoffrey C. Stewart; *A Thousand Days* by Arthur M. Schlesinger Jr.; *An Unfinished Life* by Robert Dallek; *Jack Kennedy* by Chris Matthews; *Kennedy White House Years* by Carl Sferrazza Anthony; *Lyndon Johnson: The Passage of Power* by Robert A. Caro; *A Hero for Our Time* by Ralph G. Martin; *JFK Day by Day* by Terry Golway and Les Krantz; *Counselor to the President* by Clark Clifford; *Theodore H. White* by Joyce Hoffman; *Kennedy and Johnson* by Evelyn Lincoln; *Ambassador's Journal* by John Kenneth Galbraith; *A Question of Character* by Thomas C. Reeves; *In Search of History* by Theodore H. White.

I also referenced "Averell W. Harriman April 1961–April 1963" (JFK Library); "Henry Cabot Lodge November 1960–June 1963" (JFK Library); Dean Rusk Personal Papers (JFK Library); McGeorge Bundy Personal Papers (JFK Library); Roswell L. Gilpatric Personal Papers (JFK Library).

"'MY GOD! HOW SHE LOVES ME'"

Interviews: Jamie Auchincloss; Sylvia Whitehouse Blake (1998, 2016); Janet Auchincloss Interviews 1964.

Oral histories: Janet Auchincloss (JFK Library); Jacqueline Kennedy (Arthur Schlesinger, Jr.).

Volumes: *In Her Sister's Shadow* by Diana DuBois; *America's Queen* by Sarah Bradford; *The Kennedy Men* by Nellie Bly; *Confessions of an Ex-Fan Magazine Writer* by Jane Wilkie; *The President's Mistress* by Irma Hunt.

I also referenced Jacqueline Kennedy Personal Papers (JFK Library); Janet Auchincloss Transcript 72/73.

The conversation between JFK and Torbert Macdonald was relayed by a confidential source.

The letter from Jackie ("I am having something") was sold at public auction in 2016.

I also referred to "The Presidency of LBJ" (Forum Transcript), JFK Library, March 26, 2012; "Jacqueline Kennedy Reveals that JFK Feared an LBJ Presidency," ABC News, September 8, 2011.

PART X: TICKING CLOCK

"THE QUESTION OF DALLAS"

Interviews: Ben Bradlee; George Christian; Bess Abell (1998, 1999); Hugh D. Auchincloss III; Larry Newman; Mary Frances "Sancy" Newman; Nellie Connolly (1998, 2007).

Oral histories: Jacqueline Kennedy (Arthur Schlesinger, Jr.); Jacqueline Kennedy Onassis (LBJ Library); John B. Connally (LBJ Library); Kirk LeMoyne Billings (JFK Library); Bess Abell (LBJ Presidential Library); Dan Rather (LBJ Library); Edward M. Kennedy (Edward M. Kennedy Institute).

Volumes: *Death of a President* by William Manchester; *Conversations with Kennedy* by Ben Bradlee; *The Kennedy Case* by Rita Dallas; *Mrs. Kennedy and Me* by Clint Hill and Lisa McCubbin; *Kennedy* by Ted Sorensen; *The Day Kennedy Was Shot* by Jim Bishop; *Killing Kennedy* by Bill O'Reilly; *From Love Field* by Nellie Connolly and Mickey Herskowitz; *The Kennedy Detail* by Gerald Blaine and Lisa McCubbin.

I also referenced Janet Auchincloss Transcript 72/73; "My 8 Years as the Kennedys' Private Nurse" by Rita Dallas with Maxine Cheshire, *Ladies' Home Journal*, March 1971.

"DOUBLE MURDERS"

Interviews: Torbert Macdonald Jr.; Laurie Macdonald.

Oral histories: Jacqueline Kennedy (Arthur Schlesinger, Jr.); Kirk LeMoyne Billings; Averell W. Harriman (JFK Library); Michael V. Forrestal (JFK Library); Henry Cabot Lodge (JFK Library); Roswell L. Gilpatric (JFK Library); Charles Spalding (JFK Library); Maxwell D. Taylor (JFK Library); Maxwell D. Taylor (LBJ Library); Arthur M. Schlesinger (LBJ Library).

Volumes: *JFK and Vietnam* by John Newman; *JFK vs. Allen Dulles* by Greg Poulgrain and Oliver Stone; *An Unfinished Life* by Robert Dallek; *Jack Kennedy* by Chris Matthews; *Jacqueline Kennedy Bouvier Onassis* by Barbara Leaming; *Mrs. Kennedy* by Barbara Leaming; *A Hero for Our Time* by Ralph G. Martin; *JFK Day by Day* by Terry Golway and Les Krantz; *Counselor to the President* by Clark Clifford; *Theodore H. White* by Joyce Hoffman; *In Search of History* by Theodore H. White; *Kennedy White House Years* by Carl Sferrazza Anthony; *Lyndon Johnson: The Passage of Power* by Robert A. Cairo; *Kennedy and Johnson* by Evelyn Lincoln; *Ambassador's Journal* by John Kenneth Galbraith; *A Question of Character* by Thomas C. Reeves; *Grace and Power* by Sally Bedell Smith; *America's Queen* by Sarah Bradford; *The Kennedy Men* by Laurence Leamer; *The Kennedys* by Peter Collier and David Horowitz; *Robert Kennedy and His Times* by Arthur Schlesinger Jr.; *The Lost Mandate of Heaven* by Dr. Geoffrey D. T. Shaw; *Vietnam's Last Revolution* by Geoffrey C. Stewart.

I also referenced Dean Rusk Personal Papers (JFK Library); McGeorge Bundy Personal Papers (JFK Library); Roswell L. Gilpatric Personal Papers (JFK Library).

"REGRET"

Interviews: Senator George Smathers; Yusha Auchincloss III; Barbara Gibson; Adora Rule; Ben Bradlee; Antoinette Bradlee; Janet Auchincloss Interviews 1964.

Oral histories: Michael V. Forrestal (JFK Library); McGeorge Bundy (LBJ Library); Roswell Gilpatric (LBJ Library); Barry Goldwater (LBJ Library); Dean Rusk (LBJ Library); Senator George Smathers (LBJ Library); Edward M. Kennedy (Edward M. Kennedy Institute).

Volumes: *A Remarkable Woman* by Nina Burleigh; *Bobby Kennedy* by Larry Taye; *Times to Remember* by Rose Kennedy.

I also referenced John F. Kennedy Papers (JFK Library); Janet Auchincloss Transcript 72/73.

JFK's memorandum dictation ("I feel I must") can be found in the John Fitzgerald Kennedy Papers (JFK Library).

"NOT PERFECT, BUT LOVELY"

Interviews: Ben Bradlee; Antoinette Bradlee.

Oral histories: Jacqueline Kennedy (Arthur Schlesinger, Jr.); Grace de Monaco, Princess Grace Kelly Rainier (JFK Library).

Volumes: *A Good Life* by Ben Bradlee; *Conversations with Kennedy* by Ben Bradlee; *The Irish Brotherhood* by Helen O'Donnell; *JFK: The Man and the Myth* by Victor Lasky; *Rose Kennedy and Her Family* by Barbara Gibson and Ted Schwartz; *Power at Play* by Betty Beale; *My Life with Jacqueline Kennedy* by Mary Barelli Gallagher; *Kennedy White House Years* by Carl Sferrazza Anthony; *Lyndon Johnson: The Passage of Power* by Robert A. Caro; *A Hero for Our Time* by Ralph G. Martin; *A Question of Character* by Thomas C. Reeves; *In Search of History* by Theodore H. White; *White House Nanny* by Maud Shaw; *A Day in the Life of President Kennedy* by Jim Bishop; *The Fitzgeralds and the Kennedys* by Doris Kearns Goodwin; *The Search for JFK* by Joan and Clay Blair Jr.; *All Too Human* by Edward Klein; *From Love Field* by Nellie Connolly and Mickey Herskowitz; *The Kennedy Detail* by Gerald Blaine and Lisa McCubbin.

Janet Auchincloss's letter to Eileen Slocum can be found in the National Archives.

"MEMORIES TO BE MADE" AND "'IT'S WE WHO MADE HIM'"

Interviews: Bess Abell; Senator George Smathers; Torbert Macdonald Jr., Laurie Macdonald; Julian Baldridge; Janet Auchincloss Interviews 1964.

Oral histories: Torbert Macdonald (JFK Library); Maud Shaw (JFK Library); Senator George Smathers (JFK Library); Janet Auchincloss (JFK Library).

I also referenced Janet Auchincloss Transcript 72/73 (in particular, "It's we who made him"); also, correspondence to the author from Joan Braden (1990).

One interesting fact is that the day after JFK's return to Washington with his friends from Miami—November 19, 1963—he would be the first president to ever "pardon" a turkey. Turkeys had been presented to U.S. presidents for years prior to JFK but for the purpose of Thanksgiving dinner. Lincoln was said to have unofficially spared one because his son liked the bird, but that didn't start a tradition. When Jack was presented a turkey in the Rose Garden on that November day, the bird wore a sign that read, "Good eating, Mr. President." However, Jack spared the turkey, stating "Let's keep him going." The *Washington Post* and *Los Angeles Times* called it a "pardon," thus the beginning of the tradition, though the word *pardon* wouldn't be used again until Ronald Reagan in 1987. George H. W. Bush formalized the event two years later.

PART XI: THE UNFINISHED LIFE

As well as my extensive research for my book *Jackie: Public, Private, Secret,* I relied on:

"BLOOD RED," "A DEEP LOSS," AND "ONE LAST TIME"

Interviews: Jamie Auchincloss; Julian Baldridge; Clint Hill (1998, 2000, 2010); John H. Davis (1999); and Joseph Gargan.

Oral histories: Joan Braden (JFK Library); Edward M. Kennedy (Edward M. Kennedy Institute).

Volumes: *The Death of a President* by William Manchester; *Camelot's Court* by Robert Dallek; *Robert Kennedy* by Evan Thomas; *An Unfinished Life* by Robert Dallek; *Lyndon Johnson: The Passage of Power* by Robert A. Caro; *A Day in the Life of President Kennedy* by Jim Bishop; *The Fitzgeralds and the Kennedys* by Doris Kearns Goodwin; *All Too Human* by Edward Klein; *Rose Kennedy and Her Family* by Barbara Gibson and Ted Schwartz; *Power at Play* by Betty Beale; *My Life with Jacqueline Kennedy* by Mary Barelli Gallagher; *Kennedy White House Years* by Carl Sferrazza Anthony; *A Hero for Our Time* by Ralph G. Martin; *A Question of Character* by Thomas C. Reeves; *In Search of History* by Theodore H. White; *White House Nanny* by Maud Shaw.

I also referenced Janet Auchincloss Transcript 72/73.

I referred to correspondence to me from Joan Braden (1990).

It's been reported in the past that Joan Kennedy was not able to attend JFK's funeral because she was too distraught. However, photographs recently released by the JFK Library do show her in attendance.

In 1964, as one of its 552 witnesses, Jacqueline Kennedy gave her memories of the assassination of President Kennedy in sworn testimony to the Warren Commission. Prior to that, she spoke with Theodore H. White of *Look* about the ordeal. Of course, she also told the story to many of her friends and family members.

Additionally: Clint Hill Interview with C-SPAN, May 2012.

"DID HE KNOW?"

Interview: Kathleen "Kerry" McCarthy.

"A BEAUTIFUL LIFE"

Interviews: Jamie Auchincloss; Hugh Auchincloss III; Janet Auchincloss Interviews 1964.

Oral histories: Joan Braden (JFK Library)

Volumes: *They've Killed the President* by Robert Sam Anson; *My Twelve Years with John F. Kennedy* by Evelyn Lincoln; *Not in Your Lifetime* by Anthony Summers; *The Kennedys* by Peter Collier and David Horowitz; *Times to Remember* by Rose Fitzgerald Kennedy; *Power at Play* by Betty Beale; *President Kennedy* by Richard Reeves; *Ethel* by David Lester; *The Other Mrs. Kennedy* by Jerry Oppenheimer; *Joan: The Reluctant Kennedy* by David Lester; *A White House Diary* by Lady Bird Johnson; *The Kennedy Women* by Laurence Leamer; *RFK* by C. David Heymann; *The Pleasure of His Company* by Paul Fay; *The Dark Side of Camelot* by Seymour Hersh; *The Assassination Tapes* by George O'Toole; *Rush to Judgment* by Mark Lane; *Counterplot* by Edward Jay Epstein; *The Imperial Presidency* by Arthur Schlesinger.

I also referenced Janet Auchincloss Transcript 72/73 (in particular, "It's a blur"); correspondence to me from Joan Braden, August 8, 1990 (in particular Jackie's quote, "I listened to what he had to say").

On September 7, 1995, I asked John Kennedy Jr. at a press function after his *George* magazine launch at New York's Federal Hall if he remembered saluting his father's casket on that fateful day. "To be honest, I don't know if I remember it happening," he told me, "or if I've seen so many pictures of it while growing that it only *feels* like a memory. My mother told me I had little gloves on that day which she said my Uncle Bobby made me take off because he thought they looked too sissified. I don't know if that's true, though." It turns out, this is true; RFK didn't like the way the gloves looked on his nephew who, incidentally, was celebrating his third birthday that day.

FURTHER ACKNOWLEDGMENTS

I would like to acknowledge other people and entities to whom I am especially grateful, including:

Lori Spencer (host of a valuable podcast series, which includes "Hidden History Revealed" and "Strange Bedfellows," both well worth listening to); Sue Vogelsinger (Radio interview/KFRY FM Community Radio, April 26, 2017, transcript; we also referred to her oral history at the JFK Library); Nancy Pelosi; Ruta Lee; Adora Rule; Harlan Boll; Denis Ferrara; Mark McIntire; Kartik Krishnaiyer; Fernand Amandi (political science professor and pollster at Miami University); Shannon Heupel; *Montgomery Advertiser*; Jean Peters Lewis; Ellen Mertins; Nancy Larson; Billie Gay Larson; Robin Wolfson; Valerie Allen; George Chakiris; Paula McBride Moskal; Claudine Albuquerque; Jeanette Watson-Sanger (author of the book *It's My Party*); Christina Goldstone; Madi Springer-Miller Kraus; Ryan Whisner; *Daily Jefferson County Union*; Jefferson County Historical Society; Gerald McGowan; Milo Jones; Chris Spangler; Molly Grogan; Mary Kutscke; Sonia Utterback; Chloe Reagan; Claire White; Paul D'amico; Mike DiVicino; Mike Leonetti; Hal Wingo; Harry Crosby; Snake Jagger; Terri Taylor; Bruce Fessier; *The Desert Sun*; Palm Springs Historical Society; Renee Brown; Negie Bogert; *Coachella Valley Weekly*; *Palm Springs Life Magazine*; Olga Reyes; Gracie De La Paz; Aftab Dada; Sylvia Schmitt; Betsy Duncan Hammes; Christina J. Goldstone; Ann Charles Firby; Joyce Griffin; Denice Lange; Patty Griffin Romans; St. Coletta of Wisconsin; Wisconsin Historical Society; Emily Nosske; University of Wisconsin; Frances Steele; *Palm Beach Daily*; the Florida Historical Podcast; Florida Historical Society; Historical Society of Palm Beach County; Holly Baker; Rose Guerrero; Michelle Gable; Peter Riva (the son of legendary actress Marlene Deitrich); Jonathan Tweed; Richard Finnerty; Celia Miles; Mona Miracle Booth; Jerome Pohlen; Connor Deeds; Cleveland History Center; Westlake Porter Public Library; Art Greenberg; Phil Levine; Cleveland Grays Armory; Martha Buck Bartlett; Cecil J. Williams; *Racine*

Journal Times; Denice Hale; Gianfranco Cappelluti; Massachusetts Historical Society.

Thanks also to the fine people at the Martha's Vineyard Museum (Linsey Lee, Bonnie Stacy, Heather Seger, and Bo Van Ryburn); *Martha's Vineyard Times*; *Montauk Sun* (Kenny Giustino); *Newport Daily News*; Newport Historical Society (Ingrid Peters); Mary Hopkins; Ossabaw Island Foundation; *Savannah Morning News*; *Martha's Vineyard Gazette* (Hillary Walcox); Thomasville County Historical Foundation; and the Georgia Research Center and the Sixth Floor Museum at Dealey Plaza (Stephen Fagin).

Thanks also to Vince Palamara, one of the world's leading experts on the Kennedy Secret Service detail, who has written several books about the subject and who assisted me in many ways for my books about the Kennedys. I urge you to visit his fascinating blog at http://vincepalamara.blogspot.com/.

My appreciation to Academy of Motion Picture Arts and Sciences; American Film Institute Library; Ancestry.com; AP Images; Associated Press Office (New York); Beverly Hills Library; Boston Herald Archives; Corbis Gamma Liaison; Corbis Getty Images; Globe Photos; Hedda Hopper Collection in the Margaret Herrick Library; Beverly Hills; Heritage Auctions, Hong Kong; League of Women Voters; Lincoln Center Library of the Performing Arts, Lincoln Center, New York; Los Angeles Public Library; *Los Angeles Times*; MPTV Images; Museum of Broadcasting, New York; MyRoots.com; Natchitoches Parish Tourist Commission; Natchitoches Tourism Bureau; *New York Daily News*; *New York Post*; *New York Times*; New York University Library; Newport Chamber of Commerce; Newport Country Club; *Newport Daily News*; Newport Garden Club; Newport Historical Society; Newport Mercury; Occidental College, Eagle Rock, California; *Philadelphia Daily News*; *Philadelphia Inquirer*; Philadelphia Public Library; Preservation Society of Newport County; Rex Features; *Shreveport Times*; Southampton Historical Museum; Southampton Press; St. Clare–Newport Senior Center; Time-Life Archives and Library, New York: Tour Natchitoches; University of California, Los Angeles.

PERSONAL ACKNOWLEDGMENTS

I want to thank my terrific editor, Charles Spicer, for all of his encouragement over the years. This is our fifth book together. Three previous books have been Kennedy related: *Jackie, Janet & Lee*; *The Kennedy Heirs*; and *Jackie: Public, Private, Secret*. Charles is such a talented editor and I appreciate him so much.

Thanks also to Charles's ever capable assistant, Hannah Pierdolla. My appreciation, as well, to Melissa Churchill, who did a wonderful job copyediting this manuscript.

I would also like to acknowledge my amazing literary agent, Dorie Simmonds of the Dorie Simmonds Agency Ltd. in London. Dorie has not only represented me for more than twenty-five years but is also a trusted friend.

Thank you to my television agent, Judy Coppage, of The Coppage Company, who read the first draft of *JFK: Public, Private, Secret* and gave me some much-needed encouragement. I'd also like to thank her assistant, Sydney Sterling.

I would like to thank my amazing attorney, Laurie Megery, of Myman Greenspan Fineman Fox Rosenberg & Light. I thank her and her team for such good and fair representation, and that includes her assistant Greg Maxey.

Special thanks also to Jo Ann McMahon and Felinda Adlawan of McMahon Accountancy Corporation.

I would also like to thank my close friend Jillian DeVaney, who read this book in manuscript stage, as she does all of my books, and offered invaluable insight.

My thanks to Jonathan Hahn, a brilliant writer and my personal publicist and best friend for almost twenty-five years. Thanks also to his wife, Lindsay Brie Mathers, for her love and support. She's also a very talented writer as well as motivational speaker.

Special thanks to my good friends Andy Steinlen, George Solomon, Richard Tyler Jordan, John Passantino, Linda DiStefano, Hazel Kragulac, Andy Skurow, Brad Scarton, Barbara Ormsby, Kac Young, Mark Mussari, Peter Dillard, Susan Batchelor, Donna McNeill, Keri Selig, and Winter Mead.

My friend Stephen Kronish, a true Kennedy scholar, wrote the excellent miniseries "The Kennedys," as well as the television adaptation of my book, "The Kennedys—After Camelot." Everything I know about writing for television, I learned from Stephen, and I thank him.

I wrote this book in memory of my good friend Andy Hirsch.

I have always been so blessed to have a family as supportive as mine. My thanks and love go out to Roslyn and Bill Barnett and Jessica and Zachary; Rocco and Rosemaria Taraborrelli and Rocco and Vincent; and Arnold Taraborrelli. A big smile, also, for Axel Taraborrelli.

I must also acknowledge those readers of mine who have followed my career over the years. I am indebted to each and every reader who has stuck by me. I am eternally grateful to anyone who takes the time to pick up one of my books and read it. Thank you so much.

All of my books are written with my late parents, Rocco and Rose Marie Taraborrelli, in mind at all times. I miss them.

J. Randy Taraborrelli
January 2025

INDEX

Johnson, Lyndon B.
   chosen as running mate, 259–260
   on JFK assassination, 483
   JFK's 1956 vice-presidential bid and,
     166
   presidential primary of 1960, 247, 248
   question of being on 1964 ticket, 469
   Vietnam and, 449, 466
   West Berlin visit, 324–325

Kaiser, Sid, 181
Kefauver, Estes, 165, 166, 200
Kennedy, Caroline (daughter), 212, 213,
     221, 236, 248, 331, 359, 371, 470
   birth, 150, 207–208
   christening, 210
   JFK on, 237
   JFK's funeral, 489
   JFK's reaction to birth of, 210
   JKF's relationship with, 375, 404, 417
   Secret Service nickname, 373
Kennedy, Edward (Ted, Teddy)
    (brother), 109, 168, 333
   on absent siblings, 221
   birth, 16
   Cuban Missile Crisis and, 395–396
   Fourth of July celebration (1952), 4
   graduation from Harvard, 163
   JFK's funeral, 489
   JFK's inaugural luncheon, 283
   JFK's presidential campaign and, 247
   Joe Jr.'s death and, 122, 124
   marriage to Joan Bennett, 435–436
   Mediterranean cruise, 162, 163, 173,
     175
   usher at JFK's wedding, 117
Kennedy, Ethel (sister-in-law), 78, 103,
     163, 186, 331, 392–394, 409
   Advise and Consent luncheon, 329
   Fourth of July celebration (1952), 4
   Hickory Hill sold to, 188
   Meyer, Mary, and, 401, 402
   Monroe, Marilyn, and, 359
   St. Patrick's Day celebration, 33,
     42–43

Kennedy, Jacqueline Bouvier (Jackie)
   (wife)
   birth and death of Patrick, 431–433
   birth of Caroline, 207–208
   birth of John Jr., 281
   on choice to stay in marriage, 192
   courtship with JFK, 2–7, 33–34, 42
     101–104, 47–48
   Cuban Missile Crisis and, 392–393
   Dancing Class ball with JFK, 47–48
   depression and anxiety, 139, 177–178,
     312, 314–315, 441, 444–445
   at Eisenhower inaugural ball, 85
   engagement to JFK, 105–106
   first meeting JFK, 33
   Fourth of July celebration (1952), 2–7,
     77–79
   injections by Dr. Jacobson, 312–313,
     314–316
   JFK's assassination, 481
   JFK's funeral, 489–490
   JFK's second proposal to, 475–476
   JFK tells her about Inga Arvad, 239
   Joe Sr.'s settlement to avoid divorce,
     187–190
   on living three lives, xviii
   miscarriage, 139
   Onassis, Aristotle, and, 445, 457
   parents and sister, 33
   personality traits, 3
   physical traits, 2–3
   poem about JFK, 144
   relationship with Joe, Sr., 79
   on Rose and Joe's relationship, 78
   on Rose as mother, 18–19
   on Rose's Catholic faith, 17–18
   Rose's first meeting, 5–7
   on Rose's physical traits, 6
   Secret Service nickname, 373
   sent to Parisian spa, 145
   separate vacations, 139–140, 141–142,
     161
   stillbirth of Arabella, 173–175
   tells JFK she wants a divorce, 186,
     187–188

ABOUT THE AUTHOR

Ashton Bingham

J. Randy Taraborrelli is the acclaimed author of numerous *New York Times* bestsellers about the Kennedys, including *Jackie, Ethel, Joan: Women of Camelot*, adapted as a miniseries by NBC, and *After Camelot: A Personal History of the Kennedy Family, 1968 to the Present*, adapted for television by Reelz. His other bestselling works include *The Kennedy Heirs* and *Jackie, Janet & Lee*. His most recent book, *Jackie: Public, Private, Secret*, debuted at number three on the *New York Times* bestseller list. Taraborrelli is currently adapting both *Jackie: Public, Private, Secret* and *JFK: Public, Private, Secret* for television.